Readings in Financial Planning

Huebner School Series *Gary K. Stone, Editor*

Group Health Insurance
Burton T. Beam, Jr.

Readings in Financial Planning
David M. Cordell (ed.)

Fundamentals of Financial Planning
David M. Cordell (ed.)

Readings in Income Taxation
James F. Ivers III (ed.)

McGill's Life Insurance
Edward E. Graves (ed.)

McGill's Legal Aspects of Life Insurance
Edward E. Graves and Burke A. Christensen (eds.)

Group Benefits: Basic Concepts and Alternatives
Burton T. Beam, Jr.

Planning for Retirement Needs
Kenn Beam Tacchino and David A. Littell

Readings in Wealth Accumulation Planning
The American College Faculty (eds.)

Fundamentals of Estate Planning
Constance J. Fontaine (ed.)

Estate Planning Applications
Ted Kurlowicz (ed.)

Planning for Business Owners and Professionals
Ted Kurlowicz, James F. Ivers III, and John J. McFadden

Financial Planning Applications
William J. Ruckstuhl

The Impact of the Political and Regulatory Process on Life Insurance
Jon S. Hanson

Financial Decision Making at Retirement
David A. Littell, Kenn Beam Tacchino, and David M. Cordell

The Practitioner's Guide to Advanced Pension Topics
David A. Littell and Kenn Beam Tacchino

Executive Compensation
John J. McFadden (ed.)

Huebner School Series

Readings in Financial Planning
Third Edition

David M. Cordell, Editor

The American College/*Bryn Mawr, Pennsylvania*

This publication is designed to provide accurate and authoritative information about the subject covered. While every precaution has been taken in the preparation of this material, the editor and The American College assume no liability for damages resulting from the use of the information contained in this publication. The American College is not engaged in rendering legal, accounting, or other professional advice. If legal or other expert advice is required, the services of an appropriate professional should be sought.

Library of Congress Catalog Card Number 97-77123
ISBN 1-57996-001-4

Printed in the United States of America

To the scores of teachers who helped me by sharing their expertise, enthusiasm, and time

Contents

Acknowledgments

Publication of this book required the collaborative efforts of the authors as well as many other individuals. I especially thank Susan Doherty, who typed the manuscript, and Renée Heron, who edited the manuscript, for their patience in enduring the endless stream of alterations I made in the long series of drafts. I also thank Jane R. Hassinger for helping to format the mathematical appendixes. Many other members of the faculty and staff of The American College contributed in countless ways, and I offer my appreciation to all of them.

David M. Cordell, PhD, CFA, CFP, CLU
Associate Professor of Finance
The American College

About the Editor

David M. Cordell, PhD, CFA, CFP, CLU, is associate professor of finance at The American College in Bryn Mawr, Pennsylvania. Cordell has written numerous articles in finance and investments for both academic and practitioner publications. He is author, editor, or contributing author of the following books: **Financial Decision Making at Retirement, The Financial Services Professional's Guide to The State of the Art, Financial Planning Applications, Tax Companion 1995, Solutions Handbook for Financial Planning,** and **Fundamentals of Financial Planning.** Cordell earned MBA and PhD degrees in finance from The University of Texas at Austin and holds three professional designations: Chartered Financial Analyst, Certified Financial Planner, and Chartered Life Underwriter.

Readings in Financial Planning

1

Meeting Client Needs through Financial Planning

Robert M. Crowe

Chapter Outline

Although providing financial planning advice and services to clients is a relatively new and still-emerging field of professional endeavor, very affluent individuals have had access to such help for many years. Moreover, some financial services professionals, such as accountants and life insurance agents, argue that they have been financial planners all their lives. Perhaps they are correct. However, it is generally recognized that financial planning services that cover a *spectrum* of client concerns have become available to most Americans in the middle- and upper-middle-income brackets only in about the past 25 to 30 years.

Financial services practitioners claiming to be financial planners first appeared in numbers in the late 1960s, a period of rising inflation and interest rates. The financial planning movement grew rapidly during the 1970s as the

1980s, inflation and interest rates were virtually out of control. Confronted with very high income tax rates along with these inflation and interest rates, American consumers clamored for help. The growth of the financial planning movement was explosive. Often, however, what practitioners labeled as financial planning service consisted mostly of selling "get rich quick" products and elaborate income tax dodges, usually accompanied by an abundance of "hype." A few practitioners, sometimes with near-messianic zeal, preached the message of *comprehensive* financial planning as the financial salvation of the American household.

By the mid-1980s, much of the turbulence in economic conditions began to settle down. In addition, when income tax reform eliminated the most extreme types of tax shelters from the marketplace, many so-called financial planners disappeared from the scene. Many advocates of the comprehensive approach to financial planning, at least when provided solely on a fee-for-service basis, came to realize that this type of financial planning is practical for only a small, affluent clientele.

In the 1990s the financial planning profession gained some stability and maturity. Now it is possible to describe more realistically what financial planning is and what client needs it can fulfill.

This chapter explains financial planning and describes it as a process. It discusses what financial planners actually do and summarizes the recommended content of a *comprehensive* financial plan. Further, the chapter reviews some of the key events in the historical development of financial planning as a profession during the past 30 years. Finally, the chapter discusses the basic conditions in the marketplace that provide opportunities for professional financial planners to serve clients, and it identifies some of the obstacles that planners must help clients overcome if financial goals are to be achieved.

WHAT IS FINANCIAL PLANNING?

One factor that has hampered the development of financial planning as a discipline and as a profession is the fact that there has been and continues to be very little agreement among practitioners as to what exactly financial planning is. Indeed, it sometimes seems that there are as many definitions of financial planning as there are people who call themselves financial planners. Complicating the issue is the fact that federal and state governmental regulators have their own definitions of what a financial planner is. (Chapter 2 discusses regulatory aspects of financial planning.) From a conceptual view, though, defining financial planning can concentrate on breadth of services provided: single purpose, multiple purpose, and comprehensive focus.

Single-Purpose View

Some practitioners take the position that the simple selling of a single financial product or service to a client in order to solve a single financial problem constitutes financial planning. According to this *single-purpose* or *specialist view,* all the following individuals would be examples of financial planners:

- a stockbroker who advises a customer to buy shares of common stock of a particular company
- a salesperson who sells to a client shares in a real estate limited partnership
- a preparer of income tax returns who suggests that a client establish a Keogh plan
- a banker who opens a trust account for the benefit of a customer's handicapped child
- a life insurance agent who sells key person life insurance to the owner of a small business
- a personal finance counselor who shows a client how to set up and live within a budget

Multiple-Purpose View

Other practitioners might argue that none or only some of the preceding persons are really financial planners. These practitioners would argue that real financial planning must embrace more than just solving a single financial problem of a client and must extend beyond the selling of a single financial product or service. Practitioners adhering to the *multiple-purpose view* might emphasize that there are three basic categories of client financial needs and financial products and services: insurance planning, tax planning, and investment planning. From their perspective, true financial planning should deal with at least a large part of one of these categories, and perhaps some aspects of a second category. They might even specify that true financial planning must always include at least some investment planning activity. According to the multiple-purpose view, the following individuals would probably qualify as financial planners:

- an insurance agent who sells all lines of life, health, property, and liability insurance
- a tax attorney who assists clients with their income, estate, and gift tax planning
- an investment adviser who is registered as such with the Securities and Exchange Commission

- a life insurance agent who also sells a family of mutual funds to meet both the protection and wealth accumulation needs of clients

Comprehensive View

Still other practitioners would say that financial planning means and is synonymous with comprehensive financial planning. According to this *comprehensive view,* financial planning must consider all aspects of the client's financial position, which includes all the client's financial needs and objectives, and must utilize several integrated and coordinated planning strategies for fulfilling those needs and objectives. The two key characteristics of comprehensive financial planning are

- that it encompasses all the personal and financial situations of clients to the extent that these can be uncovered, clarified, and addressed through information gathering and counseling
- that it integrates into its methodology all the techniques and expertise utilized in more narrowly focused approaches to client financial problem solving

Because of the wide range of expertise required to engage in comprehensive financial planning, effective performance commonly requires a team of specialists. The comprehensive planner's tasks are to coordinate the efforts of the team and to contribute expertise in his or her field of specialization.

In its purest form, comprehensive financial planning is a service provided by the planner on a fee-only basis. No part of the planner's compensation comes from the sale of financial products, thus helping to ensure complete objectivity in all aspects of the plan. Some team specialists also are compensated through fees, while others might receive commissions from the sale of products. In its less pure but often more practical form, comprehensive financial planning provides the planner with compensation consisting of some combination of fees for service and commissions from the sale of some of the financial products. Again, members of the team of specialists might receive fees or commissions.

Furthermore, in its purest form, comprehensive financial planning is performed for a client all at once. A single planning engagement by the planner and his or her team of specialists creates the one plan that addresses all the clients concerns and utilizes all the needed financial strategies. This plan is then updated with the client periodically and modified as appropriate. In its less pure form, comprehensive financial planning is performed incrementally during the course of several engagements with the client. For example, the planner in one year might prepare a plan to treat some of the client's tax concerns and insurance planning problems. In another year the planner might focus on the client's investment concerns and then dovetail the strategies for dealing with them with the previously developed tax and insurance strategies. In a third engagement the planner might address the remaining issues in the tax, insurance, and investment planning areas and coordinate all the recommended strategies and previously developed plans. Again, each incremental part, as well as the overall plan, is reviewed periodically and revised as appropriate.

FINANCIAL PLANNING AS A PROCESS

What, then, is financial planning? Can the financial services professional whose focus is on only a single type of financial problem and financial product for clients legitimately be called a financial planner? What if the professional's focus is broader than this but less than comprehensive? Is the comprehensive approach the only true form of financial planning? The debate goes on among financial services professionals even now. Moreover, this debate is not merely an exercise in semantics; it becomes intensely practical when questions are raised about such issues as who shall regulate financial planners, who shall set standards for the financial planning profession, what sort of education financial planners should have, or which financial services practitioners may hold themselves out to the public as financial planners.

Financial planning is a *process,* a methodology that is valid for both practitioners and self-planning individuals. There are six steps to the financial planning process: (1) establish financial goals, (2) gather relevant data, (3) analyze the data, (4) develop a plan for achieving goals, (5) implement the plan, and (6) monitor the plan. (Many professionals will reverse steps 1 and 2.)

Six Steps of Financial Planning
1. Establish financial goals.
2. Gather relevant data.
3. Analyze the data.
4. Develop a plan for achieving goals.
5. Implement the plan.
6. Monitor the plan.

Steps in Financial Planning

For practitioners this process for helping clients achieve their financial goals can be applied to the full range of client goals on a comprehensive basis. The process can also be applied on a more narrow basis to only a subset of those goals or even to only a single financial goal of a client. It is not the range of client concerns addressed that makes a practitioner a financial planner. Rather, it is the process that is used by the practitioner in addressing client concerns that makes a practitioner a financial planner. The following pages present a brief discussion of the six steps in the financial planning process.

Step 1: Establish Financial Goals

Few people begin a vacation without having a specific destination in mind. In contrast, millions of people make significant financial decisions without having a specific financial destination.

Goal setting is critical to creating a successful financial plan, but few people actually set clearly defined goals. By leading the client through the goal-setting exercise, the financial professional not only helps establish reasonable, achievable goals, but also sets the tone for the entire financial planning process.

Clients typically express concern about such topics as retirement income, education funding, premature death, disability, taxation, qualified plan distribution, and a myriad of others. Sometimes clients enumerate specific, prioritized goals, but they are more likely to present a vague list of worries that suggest anxiety and frustration rather than direction. The planner's responsibility is to help the client transform these feelings into goals.

Practitioners should query clients to learn what they are trying to accomplish. Usually the response is couched in general terms, such as "Well, we want to have a comfortable standard of living when we retire." At first glance this seems to be a reasonable goal, but a closer evaluation reveals that this goal is far too vague. When do they want to retire? What is meant by "comfortable"? Do they want to consider inflation? Do they want to retire on "interest only" or draw down their accumulated portfolio over their expected lives?

Skillful questioning may reveal a more precise goal, such as "We want to retire in 20 years with an after-tax income of $60,000 per year in current dollars, and we want the income to continue as long as we live without depleting the principle." Helping the client quantify goals is among the most valuable services a financial practitioner can provide.

Another important service of the practitioner is goal prioritization. Clients usually mention competing goals, such as saving for retirement and saving for education. Practitioners help clients rank these competing goals.

Step 2: Gather Relevant Data

Because there are many client concerns that a financial planner may need to address, the planner will have to gather considerable information from the client. Defining the client's current situation, determining what the client's desired future situation is and when it is to be achieved, and establishing what the client is willing and able to do in order to get there require information. This information must be accurate, complete, up-to-date, relevant to the client's goals, and well organized. Otherwise, financial plans based on the information will be deficient—perhaps erroneous, inappropriate, inconsistent with the client's other goals, or dangerous to the client's financial well-being.

After a client expresses goals, objectives, and concerns, the planner gathers all the information about the client that is relevant to the problem(s) to be solved and/or to the type of plan to be prepared. The more complex the client's situation and the more varied the number of his or her goals, the greater the information-gathering task.

Two broad types of information will need to be gathered: objective and subjective. A few examples of objective (factual) information that might be needed from the client include a list of securities holdings, inventory of assets and liabilities, a description of the present arrangement for distribution of the client's (and spouse's) assets at death, a list of annual income and expenditures, and a summary of present insurance coverages. Of at least equal importance is the subjective information about the client. The financial planner often will need to gather information about the hopes, fears, values, preferences, attitudes, and nonfinancial goals of the client (and spouse).

One piece of information worthy of special attention is client risk tolerance, which chapter 7 addresses in detail. Practitioners must determine the client's (and spouse's) attitude toward risk before making recommendations, preferably through use of a scientific, third-party evaluation. The American College's *Survey of Risk Tolerance*[1] provides the type of analysis that helps the practitioner suggest alternatives that are truly appropriate for the client. Such information offers the additional benefit of helping avoid (or at least defend) lawsuits from a dissatisfied client.

Before the financial planner begins the information-gathering process, he or she should *give* certain information to the client. First, the client should be made aware that he or she will have to invest time, perhaps a significant amount of time, in the information-gathering stage of financial planning. Even though part of the financial planner's responsibility is to avoid consuming the client's time unnecessarily, this commitment of time by the client is essential. The magnitude of the needed time commitment will depend on the scope and complexity of the client's needs and circumstances, but the proper development of even a narrowly focused and fairly uncomplicated plan requires information that only the client can furnish.

Second, the client should be made aware that he or she probably will have to provide the planner with some information that is highly confidential, perhaps even sensitive or painful, for the client to reveal. Again, the scope and complexity of the client's needs will influence this matter. The creation of even rather straightforward plans, however, may require clients to disclose such things as their income and spending patterns, their attitudes toward other family members, or their opinions as to the extent of their own financial responsibilities to others. Another prerequisite for the effective gathering of client information is a systematic approach to the task. Although there are many possible ways to systematize the gathering of information, one way that has been found useful by many financial planners is to use a structured fact finder form. Some fact finders are only a few pages long and ask for basic information, while others are thick booklets that seek very detailed data on each asset and amount. Most fact finders are designed for specific financial planning software to simplify data entry. For many client situations, a formal fact finder elicits considerably more information than needed. The sections that should be completed depend on the particular areas of concern to be addressed in each client's financial plan.

Obviously, information gathering is far more than asking the client a series of questions or filling out a form. Certainly that is required, but usually information gathering also requires examination and analysis of documents—such as wills, tax returns, and insurance policies—supplied by the client or the client's other financial advisers. It also requires advising, counseling, and listening during face-to-face meetings with the client and spouse. These skills are especially important because the planner needs to help the client and spouse identify and articulate clearly what they really want to accomplish and what risks they are willing to take in order to do so.

Step 3: Analyze the Data

Once the relevant information about the client has been gathered, organized, and checked for accuracy, consistency, and completeness, the financial planner's next task is to analyze the client's present financial condition. The objective here is to determine where the client is now *in relationship to the goals that were established by the client in step one.*

This analysis may reveal certain strengths in the client's present position relative to those goals. For example, the client may be living well within his or her means, and thus resources are available with which to meet some wealth accumulation goals within a reasonable time period. Maybe the client has a liberal set of health insurance coverages through his or her employer, thereby adequately covering the risks associated with serious disability. Perhaps the client's will has been reviewed recently by his or her attorney and brought up-to-date to reflect the client's desired estate plan.

More than likely, however, the financial planner's analysis of the client's present financial position will disclose a number of weaknesses or conditions that are hindering achievement of the client's goals. For example, the client may be paying unnecessarily high federal income taxes or using debt unwisely. The client's portfolio of investments may be inconsistent with his or her risk-taking tolerance. Maybe the client's business interest is not being used efficiently to achieve his or her personal insurance protection goals, or important loss-causing possibilities have been overlooked, such as the client's exposure to huge lawsuits arising out of the possible negligent use of an automobile by someone other than the client.

One conclusion from the planner's analysis may be that the client cannot attain the goals established in step one. For example, the client's resources and investment returns may preclude reaching a specified retirement income goal. In this case the practitioner helps the client to lower the goal or shows what changes the client must make to achieve the goal. Postponing retirement, saving more money, seeking higher returns, and deciding to deplete principal during retirement are four ways to help achieve the goal. Presented with alternatives, the client can restate the original goal by either lowering it or revising restrictive criteria to make it achievable.

Step 4: Develop a Plan for Achieving Goals

After the information about the client has been analyzed and, if necessary, the objectives to be achieved have been refined, the planner's next job is to devise a realistic plan for bringing the client from his or her present financial position to the attainment of those objectives. Since no two clients are alike, a well-drawn financial plan must be tailored to the individual, with all the planner's recommended strategies designed for each particular client's needs, abilities, and goals. The plan must be the *client's* plan, not the *planner's* plan.

It is unlikely that any individual planner can maintain an up-to-date familiarity with all the strategies that might be appropriate for his or her clients. Based on his or her education and professional specialization, the planner is likely to rely on a limited number of "tried and true" strategies for treating the most frequently encountered planning problems. When additional expertise is needed, the planner should always consult with an adviser who is a specialist in the field in question to help the planner design the client's overall plan.

Also there is usually more than one way for a client's financial goals to be achieved. When this is the case, the planner should present alternative strategies for the client to consider and should explain the advantages and disadvantages of each strategy. Strategies that will help achieve multiple objectives should be highlighted.

The financial plan that is developed should be specific. It should detail who is to do what, when, and with what resources.

Implicit in plan development is the importance of obtaining client approval. It follows that the plan must not only be reasonable, it must also be acceptable to the client. Usually interaction between practitioner and client continues during plan development, providing constant feedback to increase the likelihood that the client will approve the plan.

Normally, the report describing the plan should be in writing. Since the objective of the financial planning report is to communicate, its format should be such that the client can easily understand and evaluate what is being proposed. Some financial planners take pride in the length of their reports, although lengthy reports are often made up primarily of standardized or "boilerplate" passages. In general, the simpler the report, the easier it will be for the client to understand and adopt. Careful use of graphs, diagrams, and other visual aids in the report can also help in this regard.

After the plan has been presented and reviewed with the client, the moment of truth arrives. At this time the planner must ask the client to approve the plan (or some variation thereof). As part of this request, the planner must ask the client to allocate money for the plan's implementation. Keep in mind the warning of one college professor of financial planning who admitted that he never dared to use the “S word” in class—financial planning does involve *selling*. Even financial planners who are compensated entirely on a fee-for-service basis must *sell* the client on the need to work with the planner to develop and implement a plan.

Step 5: Implement the Plan

The mere giving of financial advice, no matter how solid the foundation on which it is based, does not constitute financial planning. A financial plan is useful to the client *only if it is put into action*. Therefore part of the planner’s responsibility is to see that plan implementation is carried out properly according to the schedule agreed upon with the client.

Financial plans that are of limited scope and limited complexity may be implemented for the client entirely by the planner. For other plans, however, additional specialized professional expertise will be needed. For example, such legal instruments as wills and trust documents may have to be drawn up, insurance policies may have to be purchased, or investment securities may have to be acquired. Part of the planner’s responsibility is to *motivate* and *assist* the client in completing each of the steps necessary for full plan implementation.

Step 6: Monitor the Plan

The relationship between the financial planner and the client should be an ongoing one. Therefore the sixth and final step in the financial planning process is to monitor the client’s plan. Normally the planner meets with the client at least once each year to review the plan, or more frequently if changing circumstances warrant it. The first part of this review process should involve measuring the performance of the implementation vehicles. Second, updates should be obtained concerning changes in the client’s personal and financial situation. Third, changes that have occurred in the economic, tax, or financial environment should be reviewed with the client.

If this periodic review of the plan indicates satisfactory performance in light of the client’s current objectives and circumstances, no action needs to be taken. However, if performance is not acceptable or if there is a significant change in the client’s personal or financial circumstances or objectives, the planner and client should revise the plan to fit the new environment. This revision process should follow the same six steps used to develop the original plan, though the time and effort needed will probably be less than in the original process.

Summary

The financial planning process described above is depicted schematically in figure 1-1. The blocks on the left represent the six steps in the process, while the blocks on the right indicate the main substantive activities that should occur in each step.

FIGURE 1-1
The Financial Planning Process

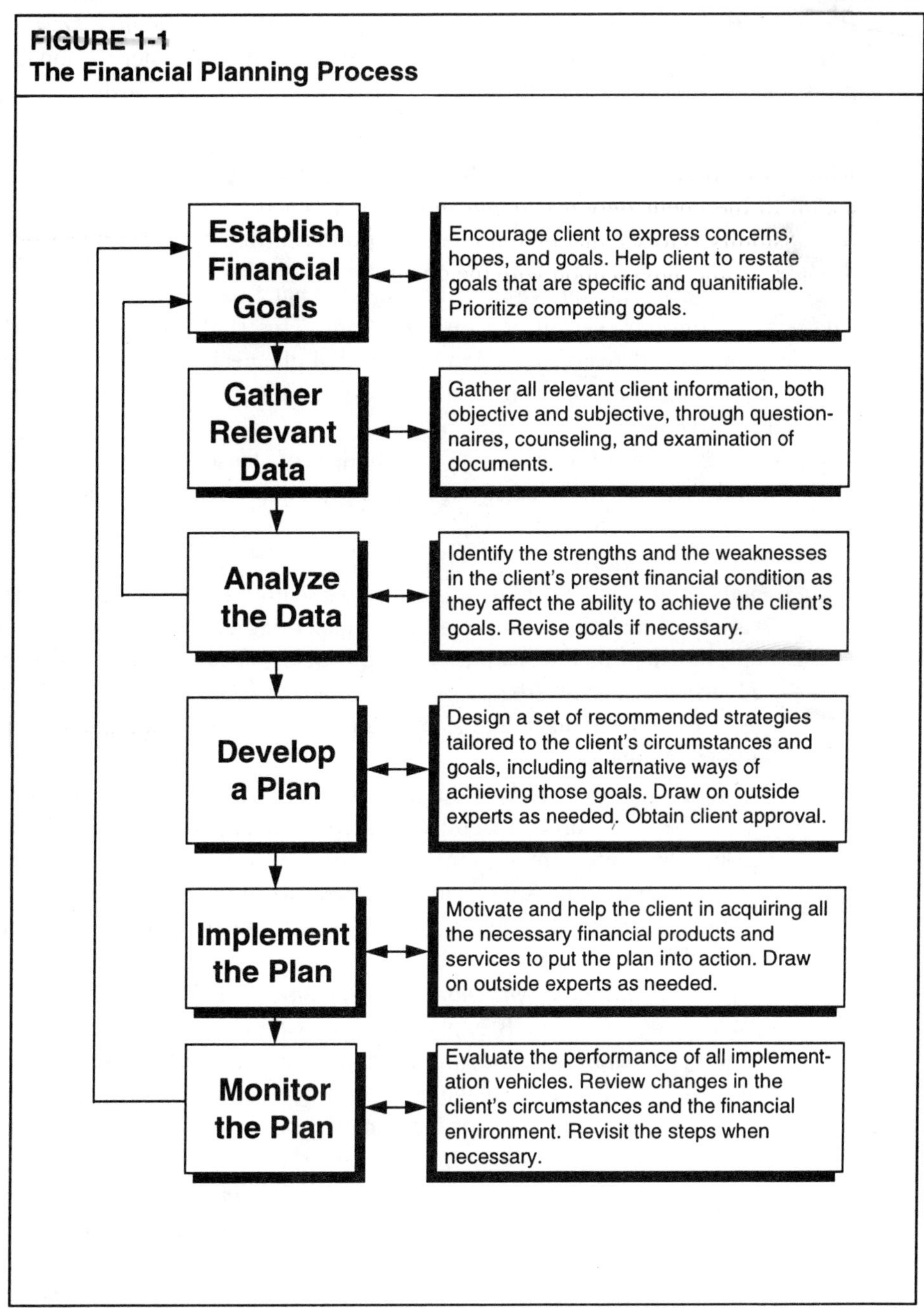

Establish Financial Goals
Encourage client to express concerns, hopes, and goals. Help client to restate goals that are specific and quanitifiable. Prioritize competing goals.
Gather Relevant Data
Gather all relevant client information, both objective and subjective, through question-naires, counseling, and examination of documents.
Analyze the Data
Identify the strengths and the weaknesses in the client's present financial condition as they affect the ability to achieve the client's goals. Revise goals if necessary.
Develop a Plan
Design a set of recommended strategies tailored to the client's circumstances and goals, including alternative ways of achieving those goals. Draw on outside experts as needed. Obtain client approval.
Implement the Plan
Motivate and help the client in acquiring all the necessary financial products and services to put the plan into action. Draw on outside experts as needed.
Monitor the Plan
Evaluate the performance of all implement-ation vehicles. Review changes in the client's circumstances and the financial environment. Revisit the steps when necessary.

Individuals who intend to take the Certified Financial Planner certification examination should review the steps in the financial planning process as listed in the first section of appendix G, *Job Knowledge Requirements of the Certified Financial Planner: Topics, Importance Values, and Target Cognitive Level.* The financial planning process in appendix G essentially combines steps 1 and 2 and inserts a new first step called "Establishing Client-Planner Relationships."

WHAT FINANCIAL PLANNERS ACTUALLY DO

In addition to the preceding description of the financial planning process, identifying the kinds of professional activities in which financial planners actually engage is another way to understand what financial planning is. One study sheds considerable light on this question.[2] This study surveyed a random sample of individuals who claimed to be financial planners, most of them holders of CFP, CLU, and/or ChFC professional designations, who had been active in the field for several years.

The study showed that the job activities of these practicing financial planners fall into six main categories. The principal specific activities within each category are described below.

- *marketing financial planning services*—Although these planners use a variety of techniques for obtaining and serving clients, they rely heavily on published media, such as writing articles and newsletters, as well as advertising. They frequently make personal presentations, such as lectures and seminars, and also obtain referrals from other professionals and from present clients.
- *evaluating client needs*—This category of activity centers on meeting with clients in order to collect information about them. The specific tasks considered most important to the survey respondents were interviewing and using questionnaires to explore the background, attitudes, financial resources, and obligations of clients that affect clients' financial goals and needs.
- *explaining financial planning concepts and clarifying client goals*—This set of tasks entails explaining issues and concepts related to such topics as estate plans, income taxes, insurance, investments, retirement-income plans, asset management, and budgeting. Also included is a discussion with the client of incompatibilities between the client's goals and the resources available for achieving them.
- *analyzing client circumstances and preparing financial plans*—Tasks in this category include an analysis of the client's financial records and documents, such as tax returns, insurance policies, and investment records. Other important tasks are the formulation of recommendations for meeting client goals in such areas as retirement, risk management, taxes, and investments.

- *implementing financial plans*—This task includes the preparation of the written document incorporating the recommended financial strategies and tactics, which are all tailored to meet the needs of the particular client. It also involves explaining the planner's fee structure, the fiduciary responsibilities of the planner to the client, and full and fair disclosure to the client of material facts and opinions about recommended products and services. (Of course, some of this explanation may also take place as part of the marketing activities of the financial planner.) The implementation activities also include selecting and offering alternative financial products to the client and may entail carrying out client requests to purchase or sell them.
- *monitoring financial plans*—A planner's activities in this category reflect the continuing nature of the desired relationship with clients. Planners review and evaluate changes in their clients' personal circumstances (births, deaths, divorces, and so on), changes in laws and economic conditions, and the performance of the plan that has been implemented. Changes in financial plans are recommended to clients as needed.

The reader will undoubtedly recognize the similarity between this set of activities in which financial planners say they actually engage and the six steps in the financial planning process discussed earlier in this chapter.

The International Association for Financial Planning (IAFP) provides information on the kinds of services most frequently provided by financial planners to clients. Retirement planning is the most frequently offered service, followed by estate planning, education planning, tax planning, and risk management. Other services offered by many financial planners included long-term-care planning and asset management.

CONTENT OF A COMPREHENSIVE FINANCIAL PLAN

As noted earlier, comprehensive financial planning is only one type of financial planning. In practice, it is the least frequently encountered type for most planners for several reasons. First, not many clients are willing to invest as much of their own time in the undertaking as comprehensive financial planning requires. Second, usually only affluent clients are willing and able to pay for all the time of the planner and his or her staff that is needed in developing a comprehensive financial plan. Third, not many clients can easily deal with the totality of their financial goals, capabilities, and difficulties all at one time. Instead, most prefer to concentrate on only one or a few related issues at a time. (As has been mentioned, however, even clients in the last group can have a comprehensive plan developed and implemented for them in incremental stages.)

FOCUS ON ETHICS
Beginning a Dialogue on Ethics

Each chapter contains an ethics dialogue box such as this one. Chapter 3 is devoted entirely to ethics and professionalism, but ethics is a topic that is woven into every part of a discussion on financial planning and the role of the financial planner. It is appropriate that the first box address a question that many planners have asked: "Is the highly ethical financial planner financially rewarded for being ethical? The answer is that she or he may be, but there is no guarantee. There are many examples to the contrary, just as there are vivid illustrations of the shady planner reaping significant financial gains. Disciplined ethical conduct, by itself, does not guarantee financial success.

Perhaps the question should be addressed from a different perspective. Do clients want to do business with someone who really understands financial planning but is of questionable morals? Do clients want to do business with someone whose integrity is unassailable but whose financial planning skills are marginal? The answer to both questions is no.

The skilled financial planner who is client centered and ethically well disciplined clearly has the attributes that clients desire and deserve. Again, ethical practice provides no guarantees of financial success. It is clear, however, that clients want to do business with financial planners that have earned their trust and are technically competent.

For those cases in which the planner is called upon to prepare a comprehensive financial plan for a client, whether entirely in one engagement or incrementally over a period of years, what should the plan contain? Clearly, comprehensive financial planning is such an ambitious and complex undertaking that it must cover numerous elements. The IAFP has developed and promulgated a set of guidelines in this regard. (The complete text of these guidelines for the content of a comprehensive financial plan appears as appendix 1A at the end of this chapter.)

A comprehensive financial plan should address all pertinent areas relating to the client, according to these guidelines. If the planner does not personally address each of the areas in the development of the plan (and in this author's experience, not many planners have the range and depth of expertise needed to do so alone), the planner should then serve as the coordinator for the development of the other areas of the plan.

According to the guidelines at least 13 pertinent areas should be addressed in a client's comprehensive financial plan. Although the order, depth, and style in which they are discussed in the plan document may vary, these 13 areas are as follows:

- First, a comprehensive plan should include personal data about the client and the client's family, such as names, addresses, dates of birth, social security numbers, phone numbers, and so on.
- Second, the plan should include the client's stated goals and objectives, indicating the priority of each one and the time frame for achieving each one.
- Third, the plan should identify problems in the client's present position, including such things as possible catastrophic medical costs, unplanned high costs of educating children, and unnecessarily high current tax burdens.
- Fourth, any assumptions used by the planner in preparing the recommended strategies, such as assumptions about future inflation rates and investment yields, should be explicitly spelled out in the plan document.
- Fifth, the plan should contain the client's balance sheet, showing his or her assets, liabilities, and net worth.
- Sixth, the plan should include a cash-flow management statement. This statement should identify all the client's sources and uses of cash and indicate his or her net cash flows.
- Seventh, a comprehensive financial plan should include a federal income tax statement and an analysis thereof.
- Eighth, the plan should analyze the client's financial exposure to losses of both a personal and business nature arising from mortality, morbidity, legal liability, and property damage. This section of the plan should also list and analyze the client's insurance coverages for such exposures.
- Ninth, the plan should provide a listing of the client's present investment portfolio, including an analysis of its liquidity, diversification, and risk characteristics.
- Tenth, the plan should analyze any future capital needs that the client will have for special purposes, such as retirement planning or children's education costs.
- Eleventh, a comprehensive plan should address the client's estate plan. There should be a review of the assets that will be included in the gross estate and an estimate of the estate tax burden that will be present.
- Twelfth, the plan should include a list of recommendations by the planner for dealing with the issues and problems identified earlier and for achieving the client's goals and objectives.
- Thirteenth, the plan should deal with implementation. It should contain a prioritized list of actions to be taken, including what is to be done, when, and by whom.

Elements of a Comprehensive Financial Plan*	
1.	Personal data
2.	Client goals and objectives
3.	Identification of issues and problems
4.	Assumptions
5.	Balance sheet/net worth
6.	Cash-flow management
7.	Income tax
8.	Risk management/insurance
9.	Investments
10.	Financial independence, retirement planning, education, and other special needs
11.	Estate planning
12.	Recommendations
13.	Implementation plan

*A comprehensive financial plan should contain at least these elements, though not necessarily in this order, according to guidelines developed by the IAFP.

THE EVOLUTION OF FINANCIAL PLANNING AS A PROFESSION

It was noted at the beginning of this chapter that financial planning is, in general, still a new and emerging profession. Its development as such has been facilitated by a number of organizations during the past 20 to 25 years.

Perhaps the earliest landmark event in the development of financial planning as a profession occurred in 1969 with the formation of the International Association of Financial Planners, later renamed the International Association for Financial Planning. The IAFP is a trade association that, among other things, promotes financial planning, conducts educational and training programs for members, sponsors market research about financial planning, and promotes ethical conduct among practitioners.

Several colleges and universities have played an important role in the development of the financial planning profession. In 1972 the College for Financial Planning, which is the educational institution that originally awarded the Certified Financial Planner (CFP) professional designation, was formed. (This function was later transferred to another organization, now called the Certified Financial Planner Board of Standards.) In 1973 holders of the CFP designation formed the Institute of Certified Financial Planners (ICFP), a membership organization to help build professionalism in the field.

A number of important developments occurred in the mid-1970s and thereafter at what was originally called The American College of Life Underwriters, further contributing to the financial planning movement. The name of the institution was changed to The American College to reflect a broadened educational mission within the financial services field. The College created a graduate-degree program, Master of Science in Financial Services, that originally included a full six-credit graduate course in financial counseling.

Discussions by the College's Board of Trustees with various constituencies of the institution led eventually to a broadened array of designation-level courses. This broadening in the curriculum culminated with the creation of a new professional designation in the early 1980s—Chartered Financial Consultant (ChFC). Meanwhile the College's sister organization, the American Society of Chartered Life Underwriters, also broadened its mission, membership, and programs, accepting the new categories of graduates of the College into the Society and changing its name to the American Society of CLU & ChFC.

Traditional colleges and universities also contributed to the emerging financial planning profession during the 1970s and 1980s, though on a much smaller scale than the College for Financial Planning and The American College, both of which serve a national student body. A number of schools developed curricula in financial planning at the undergraduate or master's level and began offering courses to help prepare people for the CFP and ChFC examinations. Now several states allow attainment of either the ChFC or CFP designations to satisfy the education requirement for registration as an investment adviser.

Two other forces that have spurred the growth and professionalization of financial planning have been the American Institute of CPAs (AICPA) and the Life Underwriter Training Council (LUTC). In 1987 the AICPA developed for its members an educational program leading to the designation that is now called Personal Financial Specialist. At about the same time the LUTC created a Financial Planning Skills course as part of its designation program for life insurance agents. This course teaches life insurance agents how to integrate noninsurance financial products with their regular portfolio of life insurance products.

OPPORTUNITIES AND CHALLENGES IN THE FINANCIAL PLANNING MARKETPLACE

A number of trends having important implications for financial planning practitioners have emerged in the United States in recent years. They all point to enormous opportunities for financial planners to render valuable service to clients.

One of the most important trends is that the population is growing older. The median age of Americans has risen from 27.5 to 32.5 in the past 20 years, meaning that a larger proportion of the population has moved into the period of highest earnings. Also, as people get older, they tend to devote a smaller share of their income to current consumption and a larger share to saving and investing.

One of the causes of the rising median age of Americans is that the members of the "baby boom" generation are no longer babies. The children born from the middle 1940s to the middle 1960s now range in age from the early 30s to the early 50s and constitute about 30 percent of the U.S. population. Another cause of the rising average age is that Americans are living longer. Approximately 12.6 percent of them are now age 65 or over as compared to 9.2 percent in 1960. This percentage will continue to rise during the latter half of the 1990s. Government statistics indicate that the average life expectancy for 65-year-old males is now over 15 years and for 65-year-old females is about 19.

The aging of the American population means that more and more consumers need retirement planning help during both their remaining years of active work and their retirement years. Also, an increasing proportion of the population needs assistance in planning for the cost of their children's college education.

A second important trend in the financial planning marketplace is that dual-income families are increasingly common. Mostly this is a result of more and more women reentering the labor force, even during the years when they have young children. Dual-income families typically have higher total incomes, pay higher income and social security taxes, and have less time to manage their finances. The opportunities for the financial planner to assist are obvious.

A third broad trend is the increasing volatility of financial conditions in the American economy. Three indicators of this volatility confronting and confusing American households in the past 35 years are the changes that have occurred in inflation rates, in the level of interest rates, and in common stock prices. For example, during the first half of the 1960s, annual increases in the consumer price index averaged only 1.3 percent; the prime interest rate charged by banks on short-term business loans averaged only about 4.68 percent, and the Standard & Poor's index of 500 common stock prices averaged around 72.0. Consider the dynamic patterns of these indicators since then, as shown in table 1-1.

Inflation and interest rates rose steadily in the late 1960s, and they were undoubtedly a motivating factor behind the growth in the number of financial planning practitioners. Inflation and interest rates then cooled but bounced up again sharply in the mid-1970s. After a 3-year respite, they rose very sharply in the late 1970s and into the 1980s. Throughout this entire period, stock prices rose only modestly.

Broad Trends Affecting Opportunities for Financial Planners

1. Rising median age
2. Increased impact of dual-income families
3. Volatility of financial conditions
4. Technological change

Inflation rates slowed again during the mid-1980s, as did the prime interest rate. Meanwhile the stock market rose dramatically but erratically. As the 1980s came to a close, inflation and interest rates were creeping up again and average common stock prices were gyrating sharply from day to day. Then in the early 1990s, inflation started cooling again, stock prices rose dramatically, and interest rates plummeted. The mid-1990s saw continued moderation of inflation, yet interest rates crept upward while the stock market set record highs.

TABLE 1-1
Consumer Price Index Changes (Urban Consumers), the Prime Rate, and the Standard & Poor's 500 Stock Index: 1965–1996

Year	Percentage Change in CPI	Average Prime Rate %	Average S & P 500 Index
1965	1.6%	4.54%	88.2
1970	5.7	7.91	83.2
1971	4.4	5.72	98.3
1972	3.2	5.25	109.2
1973	6.2	8.03	107.4
1974	11.0	10.81	82.8
1975	9.1	7.86	87.1
1976	5.8	6.84	102.0
1977	6.5	6.82	98.2
1978	7.6	9.06	96.0
1979	11.3	12.67	102.8
1980	13.5	15.27	118.7
1981	10.3	18.87	128.0
1982	6.2	14.86	119.7
1983	3.2	10.79	160.4
1984	4.3	12.04	180.5
1985	3.6	9.93	186.8
1986	1.9	8.33	236.3
1987	3.6	8.21	268.8
1988	4.1	9.32	265.9
1989	4.8	10.87	323.1
1990	5.4	10.01	335.01
1991	4.2	8.46	376.20
1992	3.0	6.25	415.75
1993	3.0	6.00	451.63
1994	2.7	7.15	460.42
1995	2.5	8.83	541.72
1996	3.3	8.27	670.49

Source: Statistical Abstract of the United States and *Federal Reserve Bulletin,* various issues.

In addition to the volatility of inflation rates, interest rates, and stock market prices, another destabilizing influence faced by American consumers has been the important changes in the U.S. income tax rules that affect all aspects of financial planning. Still another element of instability in the financial environment has been the failure rate among financial institutions, including some very large ones. In the 1980s and early 1990s failure rates among savings and loan associations, banks, and insurance companies were higher than they had been in many years.

Volatile economic conditions create greater demand for financial planning services. They also emphasize the need for financial planners to continuously monitor their clients' financial circumstances and to adjust the plans as circumstances dictate. These volatile financial conditions make it doubly important that planners thoroughly understand and abide by their clients' risk tolerances.

A fourth major trend in the financial planning market is the technological revolution that has occurred in the financial services industry. This revolution has made possible the creation of many new financial products and has made it easier to tailor these products to individual client needs. Also the technology has made possible improved analysis of the performance of these products by planners with the skills to do so.

CONSUMER NEEDS FOR FINANCIAL PLANNING

A basic and inescapable principle of economics is the law of scarcity: In every society, human wants are unlimited whereas the resources available to fill those wants are limited. The available resources must be somehow rationed among the wants. This rationing problem creates the need for financial planning even in affluent societies, such as the United States, and even among the most affluent members of such societies. To put it colloquially, there is just never enough money to go around.

What are the main financial concerns of American consumers? Are they able to handle those concerns on their own or do they need professional help? If they need professional help, with what type of problems do they need help? If they need professional help, do they recognize that they need help? In short, do U.S. consumers have a significant need and effective demand for professional financial planning services in the late 1990s?

The IAFP surveys American consumers periodically to identify their major financial concerns. In 1995 the survey found that 55 percent of American adults were at least somewhat concerned about running out of money during retirement,[3] and numerous subsequent studies have corroborated this finding.[4] College funding and long-term care for parents are two other major concerns of Americans. (Most financial planners think clients would be even more worried if they fully understood financial planning concepts.)

An important part of the 1996 IAFP survey[5] concentrated on parents of children under age 18. Ironically, 83 percent of these parents said that they have a financial plan, and three-quarters expressed confidence in their long-term financial well-being. Yet only 44 percent of them indicated that they were saving for their children's education. Less that 10 percent appeared to have all the elements that experts regard as vital to a financial plan, such as investments, insurance, budgeting, savings, and estate planning.

Table 1-2 shows results of the 1990 IAFP survey[6] that emphasized "squeezed families" defined as those of the baby boom generation who have children likely to need financial support and parents likely to need long-term care. Although data for the general population imply serious financial concerns, the data for squeezed boomers are even more ominous. Retirement, college funding, and long-term care are important to everyone, but especially to squeezed boomers.

Obstacles Confronting Consumers

The results of IAFP surveys and similar studies make it clear that many American households still have not gained control of their financial destinies. Certainly, there are many reasons why they have not developed financial plans that will enable them to do so. Three of the most important obstacles they face are the following:

TABLE 1-2
Who's Worried about What

	Total Public (n=1058)	Squeezed Boomer Families* (n=268)
Meeting mortgage payment is biggest economic concern	18%	24%
Long-term financial goal is comfortable retirement	30%	42%
Cost of parental long-term care will impact ability to save for children's education	53%	66%
Cost of college education will impact ability to help parent	50%	65%
Very or somewhat concerned about outliving retirement savings	52%	62%
Very or somewhat concerned about meeting financial responsibilities	46%	59%
Saving or planning to save more because of concerns	62%	75%

*People in the "baby boom" generation who have children likely to need financial help and parents likely to need long-term care

Source: International Association for Financial Planning, Atlanta, GA, *1990 Americans Cope with Their Finances.*

- *the natural human tendency to procrastinate*—Among the reasons for putting off the task of establishing a financial plan may be a lack of time due to a hectic lifestyle, the seeming enormity of the task of getting one's finances under control, and the belief that there is still plenty of time to prepare for achieving financial goals.

- *the very common tendency for Americans to live up to or beyond their current income*—The pressure in households to overspend for current consumption is enormous, and many families have no funds left with which to implement plans for the achievement of future goals.
- *the lack of financial knowledge among consumers*—Although in recent years there has undoubtedly been some growth in the financial sophistication of Americans, there is still widespread ignorance about how to formulate financial objectives and how to identify and properly evaluate all the strategies that might be used to achieve them. Compounding this problem was the continuous introduction during the financially turbulent 1970s and 1980s of "hot" new financial products, many of which disappeared not long after being introduced.

Financial Planner's Role

A basic inference that can be drawn from the results of consumer surveys is that Americans need help in managing their personal finances to achieve their financial goals. Moreover, many Americans seem to realize that they would benefit from professional help, and with better education, most others would reach the same conclusion. A major part of the financial planner's challenge is to help clients overcome obstacles by educating them and motivating them to gain control of their own finances.

NOTES

1. *Survey of Risk Tolerance,* The American College, P.O. Box 1400, Bryn Mawr, PA 19010. (610) 526-1490.
2. Larry Shurnik, "Job Analysis of the Professional Requirements of the Certified Financial Planner" (Denver: College for Financial Planning, 1987).
3. *1995 National Consumer Survey,* International Association for Financial Planning, Atlanta, GA. The telephone survey was conducted by The Wirthlin Group, which polled 500 people aged 21 and older with household incomes of at least $20,000.
4. David M. Cordell, "Personal Responsibility for Retirement Planning," *Journal of the American Society of CLU & ChFC,* November 1995, pp. 58-64.
5. *National Consumer Survey: Teaching Money Management Skills to Children.* International Association for Financial Planning, Atlanta, GA. The telephone survey was conducted by The Wirthlin Group, which polled 550 Americans who have children under age 18 living at home, who have annual household incomes of at least $30,000, and who play a major role in managing their household finances.
6. *1990 Americans Cope with Their Finances,* International Association for Financial Planning, Atlanta, GA. The telephone survey was conducted by the Gallup Organization. It polled 1,058 households representative of the United States as a whole and an additional sample of 600 households with incomes of $50,000 and up.

Appendix 1A

*Guidelines for a Comprehensive Financial Plan**

THE COMPREHENSIVE FINANCIAL PLAN

While most financial planning practitioners are highly trained in one or several of many disciplines, the consumer often seeks assurance that a planner will be able to provide a well-rounded, comprehensive plan that spans all aspects of his or her financial situation

The development of "Guidelines for a Comprehensive Financial Plan" by the International Association for Financial Planning has made it possible for the consumer to receive that assurance, by providing a benchmark against which to measure the thoroughness of a plan.

These guidelines, developed in 1987, were the first formal, written elements that should be included in a truly comprehensive financial plan.

OVERVIEW OF PLAN ELEMENTS

A comprehensive financial plan should contain an analysis of all pertinent factors relating to the client. While order and style of presentation may vary, the plan should include, but not necessarily be limited to, the following elements:

1. Personal data
2. Client goals and objectives
3. Identification of issues and problems
4. Assumptions
5. Balance sheet/net worth
6. Cash-flow management
7. Income tax
8. Risk management/insurance
9. Investments
10. Financial independence, retirement planning, education, and other
11. Estate planning
12. Recommendations
13. Implementation

* Reprinted with permission of the International Association for Financial Planning, Atlanta, GA 30328.

When developing a comprehensive financial plan, the planner is responsible for all of the elements of the plan, from data gathering through analysis and presentation to the client. Those elements of the plan that the planner does not personally perform remain the responsibility of the planner to coordinate.

When technical areas (such as legal and insurance services) are not personally performed by the planner, the financial plan or supplement should include supporting documentation that these areas have been or will be coordinated by the planner.

Analysis of each element of the plan should consist of a review of pertinent facts, a consideration of the advantages and/or disadvantages of the current situation, and a determination of what, if any, further action is required. The plan should include a summary statement providing the planner's comments on the analysis, and his or her recommendations, where appropriate, for each element of the plan.

GUIDELINES FOR A COMPREHENSIVE FINANCIAL PLAN

1. Personal Data

Should include relevant personal and family data for parties covered under the plan.

Comments:

- Should include, but not be limited to, name, address, social security number, birthdate and other relevant data.

2. Client's Goals and Objectives

A reiteration of the client's stated goals and objectives, indicating their priority and including a time frame where applicable.

Comments:

- The statement of goals and objectives will form the basic framework for the development of the financial plan.
- The client's goals and objectives should be expressed in as specific and precise language as possible. For example, a statement of a goal should read "Retire at age 62 in present home and maintain a current standard of living" rather than "A comfortable retirement."

3. Identification of Issues and Problems

A plan must address relevant issues and problems identified by the client, the planner and/or other advisers.

Comments:

- List personal and financial issues and problems that affect the client such as major illness, education costs, taxes, etc. While the client may be aware of many, if not all, of the issues, the planner may discover other areas that are or could develop into problems.
- These issues and problems, when combined with the client's goals and objectives, will complete the framework and direction for the financial plan. Since style and order are not the primary consideration, the analysis of recommendation section(s) of the plan may be more appropriate for identifying issues and problems.

4. Assumptions

Identify and state material assumptions used in the plan's preparation.

Comments:

- Assumptions should include, but not be limited to, inflation, investment growth rate, mortality, etc.

5. Balance Sheet/Net Worth

A presentation and analysis to include, but not be limited to, a schedule listing assets and liabilities with a calculation of net worth and itemized schedules of liabilities and assets to be included as appropriate.

Comments:

- In addition to the schedules, footnotes should be included as appropriate.

6. Cash-Flow Management

Statements and analysis to include, but not be limited to, a statement of the client's sources and uses of funds for the current year and for all relevant years, indicating net cash flow, as well as a separate income statement, where appropriate.

Comments:

- Sources—earned income, investment income, sale proceeds, gifts, etc.
- Uses—living expenses, debt service, acquisition of assets, taxes paid, etc.
- Net cash flow—both positive and negative.

7. Income Tax

An income tax statement and analysis to include, but not be limited to, the income taxes for the current year and for all relevant years covered in the plan.

Comments:

- Projections should show the nature of the income and deductions in sufficient detail to permit calculation of the tax liability. The analysis should identify the marginal tax rate for each year and any special situations such as alternative minimum tax, passive loss limitations, etc., that affect the client's tax liability.
- The financial plan should include footnotes to let the client know which taxes (i.e., state or city) have not been addressed.

8. Risk Management/Insurance

A. Analysis of a client's financial exposure relative to mortality, morbidity, liability and property, including business as appropriate.

Comments:

- Mortality—survivor income and capital needs analysis.
- Morbidity—impact of loss of health.
- Liability—legal exposure.
- Property—loss of value.
- Business—loss due to business involvement.

B. Listing and analysis of current policies and problems to include, but not be limited to, life, disability, medical, business, property/casualty and liability.

Comments:

- Analysis of existing coverage and/or risk exposure in relationship to the client's needs, goals and objectives.
- If any area of insurance is not within the competency range of the financial planner, the planner has the responsibility to coordinate with other

professionals and document such coordination in the financial plan. Documentation of the above areas can include the insurance professional's summary, if completed, or the professional's name and time frame when such review will be completed.

9. Investments

A listing of the current investment portfolio and an analysis or discussion of the liquidity, diversification and investment risk exposure of the portfolio. In addition, the suitability of the investments in relationship to the client's needs, goals and objectives should be addressed, to include, but not be limited to, risk tolerance, risk management of investments, suitability, liquidity, diversification and personal management efforts.

Comments:

- Risk tolerance—addresses the client's willingness to accept investment risk.
- Risk management—analysis of client's exposure relative to loss of invested capital.
- Suitability—appropriateness of the investment for the client.
- Liquidity—the availability of assets that can be converted into cash at acceptable costs.
- Diversification—appropriate mix of assets to meet the client's needs, goals and objectives.
- Personal management efforts—the degree to which the client wants to manage and is capable of managing his or her assets.

10. Financial Independence, Retirement Planning, Education, and Other Special Needs

An analysis of the capital needed at some future time to provide for financial independence, retirement, education, or other special needs. The analysis should include a projection of resources expected to be available to meet these needs at that time.

Comments:

- In achieving the above, inflation, growth of assets and company benefits should be considered where applicable.
- Special sections of the above topics may require a separate heading in the financial plan. For example, company benefits may require an analysis of types available, pre- and post-tax contributions needed, tax treatment of plans and investment of benefit plan assets.

11. Estate Planning

Identification of assets that can be included in the client's estate and an analysis of the control, disposition and taxation of those assets.

Comments:

- Control—authority to manage or direct the use of assets by means of title, trusteeship, power of attorney, etc.
- Disposition—transfer of ownership by will, trust, beneficiary designation or operation of the law.
- Taxation—taxation of the client's estate and the income tax and estate tax consequences to the beneficiaries.

12. Recommendations

Written recommendations that relate to goals and objectives as well as financial issues and problems.

Comments:

- Written recommendations should specifically address the client's goals and objectives and all issues and problems identified in the plan, as well as a determination of the actions necessary to compensate for any shortfalls. Recommendations should be clearly identified and stated. They should not be conveyed by implication or inference.

13. Implementation

A prioritized list of actions required to implement the recommendations, indicating responsible parties, action required and timing.

Comments:

- Implementation should include a schedule reflecting actions to be taken as well as priority, dates and responsible parties.

2

Regulation of Financial Planners

Jeffrey B. Kelvin and David M. Cordell

Chapter Outline

Financial planning is an emerging profession that continues to evolve. Because of the proliferation of financial planners that began in the late 1970s, regulation of financial planners has become an increasingly important topic to investors, consumer advocates, regulatory authorities, elected officials, and financial planners themselves. This chapter reviews federal legislation and regulatory actions that govern the activities of financial planners.

A good example of the rapidly changing regulatory environment is an important piece of legislation that Congress passed and the president signed in October 1996. As explained later in the chapter, the Investment Advisers Supervision Coordination Act of 1996 changed the regulatory environment significantly. As of July 1997, the Securities and Exchange Commission (SEC) no longer requires financial planners with less than $30 million of assets under management to register with the SEC as investment advisers. Exceptions to this exemption include advisers to investment companies and financial planners in states that have no investment adviser laws. In effect, regulation of "small" investment advisers becomes the exclusive purview of the states.

When reading about the development of the regulatory environment, keep in mind the size distinction that determines whether a financial planner needs to register as an investment adviser at the federal (SEC) level after July 1997. Although many practitioners will find that registration with the SEC is no longer necessary, most will find that state requirements for investment advisers are quite similar to federal requirements.

HOW FINANCIAL PLANNERS BECAME INVESTMENT ADVISERS

In the late 1970s and early 1980s when the proliferation of financial planners, plans, and products became evident, several committees in Congress grew concerned that, due to this growth in the industry, additional regulation would be necessary. There was talk in Washington at that time of new statutes and regulations to specifically cover the activities of financial planners so that consumers could be adequately protected. Much of this talk, of course, was precipitated by relatively isolated horror stories involving fraud and abuse.

The SEC became alarmed at the prospect of new legislation in this area since the agency felt that regulation of financial planners was its turf. When taking this attitude with Congress, the SEC was urged to develop a clear and concise position on the subject of what specific activities undertaken by financial services professionals would trigger the application of the existing federal securities laws. This was felt by the Congress to be an approach that could remove the need for new legislation.

SEC Release No. IA-770

The Securities and Exchange Commission took the position that the *Investment Advisers Act of 1940* was the statutory body of law that should control the area of regulation of financial planners. It is true that this legislation had been enacted 40 years earlier in a postdepression era during which a legislative framework to police and control the activities of discretionary money managers was the primary objective. However, the SEC in the early 1980s took the position that this same statute should be applied to the activities of financial planners. In August 1981, the Securities and Exchange Commission released its famous *Release No. IA-770.* This pronouncement set forth three separate tests which were to be applied to the activities of financial planners. In the event that all three tests were answered in the affirmative, the SEC took the position that the Investment Advisers Act of 1940 would apply to the planner's activities. If, however, any one of the three tests could not be answered in the affirmative, the Investment Advisers Act of 1940 would not apply to these professional activities. Let us review these three tests separately.

Advice or Analyses about Securities

The first test under IA-770 set forth the question of whether the financial services professional provides "advice or analyses" about a security. Since the term *security* is very broadly defined for federal securities law purposes, it can include a great many financial instruments in addition to the best-known securities, like common stocks or bonds. For example, the definition includes a certificate of deposit, commercial paper, a limited partnership, or even variable life insurance or variable annuity products. The official definition of the term *security* as set forth by Sec. 80b-2(a)(18) of the Investment Advisers Act of 1940 is as follows:

> Any note, stock, Treasury stock, bond, debenture, evidence of indebtedness, certificate of interest or participation in any profit-sharing agreement, collateral trust certificate, preorganization certificate or subscription, transferable share, investment contract, voting-trust certificate, certificate of deposit for a security, fractional undivided interest in oil, gas, or other mineral rights, or in general, any instrument or interest commonly known as a *security*, or any certificate of interest or participation in, temporary or interim certificate for, receipt for, or guarantee of, or warrant or right to subscribe to or purchase any of the foregoing.

It is clear, based on the breadth and scope of the definitions under this first test, that financial services professionals will invariably become involved with providing advice about securities.

The Business Standard

The second test as set forth by SEC Release IA-770 concerns whether the financial services professional is presented to the public as being "in the business" of providing advice about securities. This issue is answered by examining how the practitioner's services are communicated to the public. What is printed on the practitioner's business card or on the front door of the office? What does the telephone book advertisement say? How is the telephone answered? What is stated on the business card and letterhead? In short, does the practitioner raise any implication that he or she provides any advice about securities? All of these factors are pertinent in deciding whether the financial services professional is "in the business" of providing advice about securities.

The Compensation Test

The last test contained in the SEC release is perhaps the simplest one to apply, and yet the least understood. The issue concerns compensation received by the practitioner, and the test is met regardless of the source of payment. Therefore, although a practitioner who charges a fee to a client for the provision of investment advice will easily meet the third test of IA-770, one who charges no fee but does receive a commission on the sale of a securities product will also meet this test. Actually in the current environment it is practically impossible for a financial services professional to fail to meet this third test.

If all three of these tests are applicable to the specific activities of a financial services professional, the terms and provisions of the Investment Advisers Act of 1940 will apply.

SEC Release No. IA-1092 Reaffirms IA-770

SEC Release No. IA-770 was a landmark ruling from the SEC. As the financial planning profession continued to emerge in the mid to late 1980s, many individuals and groups called upon the Securities and Exchange Commission to comment once again on the three tests that had been set forth by IA-770 a few years earlier. It was felt by some that the original three-test approach might no longer be held applicable by the SEC. In October 1987, in response to multiple requests from various segments of the financial services community, the Securities and Exchange Commission issued *Release No. IA-1092*. This pronouncement is significant since it totally reaffirms the three-prong approach that had earlier been set forth by IA-770.

Therefore the original application by the Securities and Exchange Commission of the three-test approach still applies. As a practical matter, any financial services professional who by reason of his or her activities must answer all three tests in the affirmative will have activities subjected to the Investment Advisers Act of 1940 at the federal level.

In addition to total reaffirmation of the three-step test of IA-770, however, IA-1092 devoted renewed attention to the antifraud provisions of the Investment Advisers Act of 1940. These provisions are designed to protect consumers who use the services of investment advisers.

The 1987 release cites *SEC v. Capital Gains Research Bureau*, a Supreme Court case discussing the antifraud provisions. That case held that "an investment adviser is a fiduciary who owes his client an affirmative duty of utmost good faith, and full and fair disclosure of all material facts." As a general matter, the release states that an adviser must disclose to clients all material facts regarding potential conflicts of interest. In this way, the client can make an informed decision about entering into or continuing an advisory relationship with the adviser.

The release includes selected interpretive and no-action letters illustrating the scope of the duty to disclose material information in certain situations involving conflicts of interest. Additional disclosure might be required, depending upon the circumstances, if the investment adviser recommends that clients execute securities transactions through the broker/dealer with which the investment adviser is associated. In addition, the investment adviser is required to inform clients that they may execute recommended transactions through other brokers or dealers.

Release IA-1092 goes on to set forth specific examples of situations that require full disclosure on the investment adviser's filing statement with the SEC. Points raised by IA-1092 in the antifraud/full disclosure area include the following:

- An adviser who intends to implement, in whole or in part, the financial plan prepared for clients through the broker/dealer or insurance company with which the adviser is associated, must inform the clients that in implementing the plan the adviser will also act as agent for that firm.
- An investment adviser who is also a registered representative of a broker/dealer and who provides investment advisory services outside the scope of employment with the broker/dealer, must disclose to advisory clients that the advisory activities are independent of employment with the broker/dealer. Additional disclosure might be required, depending upon the circumstances, if an adviser recommends that a client execute securities transactions through the broker/dealer with which the adviser is associated. For example, an adviser is required to fully disclose the nature and extent of any personal interest in such a recommendation, including any compensation that would be received from the broker/dealer in connection with the transaction. In addition, an adviser is required to inform clients that they may execute recommended transactions with other broker/ dealers.
- A financial planner who recommends and uses only the financial products offered by the broker/dealer by which the financial planner is employed should disclose this practice and inform clients that the plan may be limited by such products.
- An investment adviser must not effect transactions in which he or she has a personal interest if this could result in the adviser's preferring his or her own interest to that of the advisory clients.
- An adviser who structures personal securities transactions and then trades on the market result caused by his or her recommendation to clients must disclose this practice.
- An investment adviser must disclose his or her personal securities transactions that are inconsistent with the advice given to clients.

- An investment adviser must disclose compensation received from the issuer of a security that the adviser recommends.

Exclusions and Exemptions From The Investment Advisers Act of 1940

It should be noted that despite the foregoing, there are six excluded areas of activities specifically set forth in Section 202(a) (11) of the Investment Advisers Act of 1940. These exclusions could have the effect of eliminating the need for the financial services professional to be subjected to the mandates of the statute. The six excluded areas are

- any bank or bank holding company as defined in the Bank Holding Company Act of 1956 that is not an investment company
- any lawyer, accountant, engineer, or teacher, if the performance of advisory services by any of these is solely incidental to the practice of his or her profession
- any broker, dealer, or registered representative thereof whose performance of advisory services is solely incidental to the conduct of his or her business as a broker or dealer and who receives no "special compensation" for his or her services
- the publisher of any newspaper, news magazine, or business or financial publication of general or regular circulation
- any person whose advice, analyses, or reports relate only to securities that are direct obligations of or obligations guaranteed as to principal or interest by the United States of America
- such other persons not within the intent of the law as the Securities and Exchange Commission may designate by rules and regulations or order

There are five other groups of individuals who, although they fall within the definition of investment adviser, are nevertheless exempt from registration under section 203(b) of the Investment Advisers Act of 1940:

- any investment adviser whose clients are all residents of the state within which the investment adviser maintains the principal office and place of business and who does not furnish advice or issue analyses or reports with respect to listed securities or securities admitted to unlisted trading privileges on any national securities exchange.
- any investment advisers whose only clients are insurance companies.
- any investment adviser who, during the course of the preceding 12 months, has had fewer than 15 clients and who neither present themselves to the general public as investment advisers nor act as investment advisers to any investment company registered under the Investment Company Act of 1940.

- any investment adviser that 1) is a charitable organization or is employed by a charitable organization and 2) provides advise, analyses, or reports only to charitable organizations, or to funds operated for charitable purposes, and
- any investment adviser that provides investment advice exclusively to church employee pension plans

In summary, the five groups of individuals discussed in the preceding paragraph are exempt from registration with the Securities and Exchange Commission even though they are considered investment advisers under the act. They must still comply with the act's antifraud provisions. On the other hand, an individual who falls into the first group of exception categories mentioned above will not be covered by the antifraud provisions and the Investment Advisers Act of 1940 does not apply to any of their activities.

INVESTMENT ADVISERS SUPERVISION COORDINATION ACT OF 1996[1]

After years of dispute about the direction of regulation of investment advisers, the Congress passed and the president signed the *Investment Advisers Supervision Coordination Act (Coordination Act),* which was part of the *National Securities Market Improvement Act of 1996.* The Coordination Act, which became effective in July 1997, gives authority to the SEC to deny adviser registration to felons within 10 years of conviction, and mandates a consumer hotline for inquiry concerning disciplinary actions and proceedings against registered investment advisers and associated persons.

However, the most important aspects of the Coordination Act and SEC Release No. IA-1633 (which specifies final rules relating to the Coordination Act) concern allocating the regulation of investment advisers between the SEC and state authorities based on the level of assets under an adviser's management. The result is that investment advisers, and thus financial planners, need to register with either the SEC or state authorities, but not with both.

State Versus SEC Registration

In general, the Investment Advisers Act of 1940, as revised by the Coordination Act, requires investment advisers, and thus financial planners, to register with the SEC if they are

- investment advisers defined under Section 202(a)(11);
- not excepted from the definition of investment adviser by Section 202(a)(11)
- not exempt from SEC registration under Section 203(b); and
- not prohibited from SEC registration by new Section 203A.

The first three items above were discussed earlier in this chapter. It is the fourth item that the Coordination Act added to the mix. Essentially, new Section 203A of the Advisers Act specifies four types of advisers that are *not* prohibited from SEC registration:

- advisers that have "assets under management" of $25 million or more;
- advisers to registered investment companies;
- advisers that are not "regulated or required to be regulated" as investment advisers in the state where they maintain their "principal office and place of business"; and
- advisers that are exempted from the prohibition by SEC rule or order.

Advisers With $25 Million of Assets Under Management

Advisers with less than $25 million of assets under management are regulated by state authorities, except, as described later, advisers in the four states that currently have no state securities regulation and certain other advisers. Advisers with more than $30 million in assets under management must register with the SEC. If assets under management are between $25 million and $30 million and they have no other basis for eligibility for SEC registration, they can elect either state or SEC registration. The purpose of this window is to protect advisers from going back and forth between state and SEC registration merely because of volatility in the securities market or changes in the client base.

Defining Assets Under Management. *Assets under management* is defined in Section 203A(a)(2) as the "securities portfolios with respect to which an investment adviser provides continuous and regular supervisory or management services." Thus, two determinations must be made before the value of an account can be counted toward meeting the $25 million threshold:

- Is the account a securities portfolio?
- Does the account receive continuous and regular supervisory or management services?

Under new SEC rules, securities portfolios include only those accounts of which at least 50% of the value consists of securities. Cash or cash equivalents may be treated as securities when making this calculation.

The question concerning continuous and regular supervisory or management services is more complicated. In general, accounts over which advisers have discretionary authority and for which they provide ongoing supervisory or management services are considered to receive continuous and regular supervisory or management services. An adviser will be deemed to provide continuous and regular supervisory or management services to a non-discretionary account if the adviser has an ongoing responsibility to select or make recommendations—based upon the needs of the client—as to specific securities or other investments the account may purchase or sell. If such recommendations are accepted by the client, the adviser is responsible for arranging or effecting the purchase or sale. Other factors that should be considered in deciding whether an account qualifies include

- Terms of the advisory contract. A provision in the contract that the adviser provides ongoing management services suggests that the adviser does provide continuous and regular supervisory or management services. Other provisions in the contract, or the actual management practices of the adviser, may rebut this suggestion.
- Form of compensation. A form of compensation based on the average value of assets under management over a specified period of time would suggest that the adviser provides continuous and regular supervisory or management services. On the other hand, a form of compensation based upon time the adviser spends with a client during a client visit would suggest otherwise.
- The management practice of the adviser. The extent to which the adviser actively manages assets or provides advice bears on whether the services are continuous and regular supervisory or management services. However, infrequent trades (such as those based on a "buy and hold" strategy, for example) should not be the sole basis for a determination that the services are not provided on a continuous and regular basis.

Calculation of Assets under Management. Once a determination is made that an account is a "securities portfolio" that receives "continuous and regular supervisory or management services," the value of the account may be included in "assets under management." If, however, the adviser provides continuous and regular supervisory or management services for only a portion of the account, only the portion of the account that receives such services should be included as assets under management. Current market value of the account should be determined using the same method as that used to determine the account value reported to clients or fees for investment advisory services.

Frequency of Determination. The continuing eligibility of an adviser to remain registered with the SEC must be determined once annually at the time the adviser updates its Form ADV, which is discussed later in this chapter. Thus, the registration status of an adviser whose assets under management falls below $25 million will not be affected unless the assets remained below $25 million after the end of the adviser's fiscal year. To allow an adviser facing potential cancellation of its SEC registration sufficient time to register under applicable state statutes, the SEC has adopted a "grace period" of 90 days after the date the adviser was required to file its updated Form ADV indicating that it would not be eligible for SEC registration.

Rule 203A-4 provides a *safe harbor* from the requirement to register with the SEC for state-registered advisers, if the advisers reasonably believe that they are not required to register with the SEC because they have less than $30 million of assets under management. No such similar safe harbor exists for an adviser that registered with the SEC under the mistaken belief that it had greater than $25 million in assets under management.

A state-registered adviser generally is required to register with the SEC "promptly" when the prohibitions of Section 203A no longer apply (for example, the adviser obtains $30 million of assets under management) unless the adviser is registered in a state that requires new Schedule I of Form ADV (or a substantially similar form or rule) to be filed and annually updated. Such an adviser may (but is not required to) postpone SEC registration until 90 days after the date the adviser is required to report $30 million or more of assets under management to its state securities authority.

Advisers to Registered Investment Companies

Any adviser that provides advisory services to a registered investment company pursuant to a contract (including a "sub-adviser") must register with the SEC regardless of the amount of assets under management. To qualify as an investment company adviser, the adviser must provide advisory services to an investment company that is registered under the Investment Company Act of 1940, and is operational, that is, has assets and shareholders other than organizing shareholders.

Advisers That Are Not Regulated or Required to be Regulated By a State

Two types of advisers are not "regulated or required to be regulated" by a state and thus must register with the SEC:

- advisers with their principal office in Colorado, Iowa, Ohio, or Wyoming (the four states that have not enacted investment adviser statutes); and
- advisers with their principal office in a foreign country.

The SEC's Rule 203A-3(c) defines *principal office and place of business* as the "executive office of the investment adviser from which the officers, partners, or managers of the investment adviser direct, control, and coordinate the activities of the investment adviser."

Advisers That Are Exempt From Prohibition on SEC Registration

Section 203A(c) authorizes the SEC to exempt advisers from the prohibition on registration if the prohibition would be "unfair, a burden on interstate commerce, or otherwise inconsistent with the purposes" of that section. The SEC used this authority to exempt, in Rule 203A-2, four categories of investment advisers from the prohibition from registering with the SEC (thereby effectively requiring them to register with the SEC):

- Nationally recognized statistical rating organizations, including ratings agencies, such as Moody's and Standard & Poors, that are registered as investment advisers.
- Pension consultants, including advisers of government plans and church plans, if the aggregate value of "assets of plans" receiving such services is at least $50 million. (Note that the exemption is available to advisers to employee benefit plans—not to plan participants.)
- Certain affiliates that directly or indirectly control, are controlled by, or are under common control with an investment adviser that is eligible to register (and is, in fact, registered) with the SEC. The exemption is available only if the principal office and place of business of the adviser is the same as that of the affiliated registered adviser. Control is defined as the power to direct or cause the direction of the management or policies of the adviser, whether through ownership of securities, by contract, or otherwise.
- Certain start-up investment advisers which have a reasonable expectation of eligibility to register with the SEC within 120 days.

Other Aspects of the Coordination Act

Section 203A(b) preempts the application of state laws requiring "registration, licensing, or qualification" to advisers registered with the SEC. In Release No. IA-1633, the SEC explained that Section 203A(b) "preempts not only a state's specific registration, licensing, or qualification requirements, but all regulatory requirements imposed by state law on SEC-registered advisers relating to their advisory activities or services, except those provisions that are specifically preserved" by the Coordination Act. The Coordination Act preserved three provisions of state investment adviser laws with respect to SEC-registered advisers:

- A state may enforce anti-fraud prohibitions, thus allowing a state to continue to investigate and bring enforcement actions with respect to fraud or deceit against an investment adviser or a person associated with an investment adviser.
- A state may require the filing of any documents filed with the SEC, solely for notice purposes, and a consent to service of process.
- A state may require the payment of filing, registration, or licensing fees. For three years after the enactment of the Coordination Act, if an adviser fails to pay the required fees, a state may require the registration of such adviser with the state.

Investment Adviser Representatives of SEC-Registered Advisers

The application of state law has been narrowed, but not eliminated, with respect to investment adviser representatives of SEC-registered advisers. Only representatives who deal directly with individual clients are subject to state registration requirements. In those cases, the representative will have to register only in the state(s) in which he or she has a place of business. If the representative is located only in states that do not register investment adviser representatives, then the representative is not subject to state registration requirements.

Supervised Persons. Section 203A(b) preempts state law with respect to *supervised persons* of SEC-registered advisers, except that a state may continue to license, register, or otherwise qualify any supervised person who is an investment adviser representative and has a place of business located within that state. New Section 202(a)(25) defines supervised person to mean a "partner, officer, director (or other person occupying a similar status or performing similar functions), or employee of an investment adviser, or other person who provides investment advice on behalf of the investment adviser and is subject to the supervision and control of the investment adviser."

Investment Adviser Representative. Rule 203A-3(a) defines *investment adviser representative* as a supervised person of an investment adviser if clients who are natural persons represent more than 10% of the clients of the supervised person. (Rule 203A-3(a)(1).) High net worth individuals (those that may enter into performance fee contracts under Rule 205-3) are excluded from treatment as natural persons. Supervised persons may rely on the definition of "client" in Rule 203(b)(3)-1 to identify clients, except that supervised persons need not count clients that are not United States residents. The rule contains exceptions for 1) supervised persons who provide advice to natural persons, but who do not, on a regular basis, solicit, meet with, or otherwise communicate with clients are excepted from the definition of "investment adviser representative," and (2) supervised persons who provide only impersonal investment advice. The SEC has defined *place of business* as an office at which the representative regularly provides investment advisory services, solicits, meets with, or otherwise communicates with clients, and any other location that is held out to the general public as a location at which the representative provides investment advisory services, solicits, meets with, or otherwise communicates with clients. (Rule 203A-3(b).)

Solicitor. A solicitor who is a partner, officer, director, or employee of a SEC-registered adviser is subject to state qualification requirements only if the solicitor falls within the definition of "investment adviser representative" under Rule 203A-3(a). A third-party solicitor for a SEC-registered adviser (that is, a solicitor who is not a partner, officer, director, or employee of the adviser) is not an investment adviser representative, and is subject to state qualification requirements to the extent state investment adviser statutes apply to solicitors. In some cases, a solicitor may solicit on behalf of both a state-registered adviser and a SEC-registered adviser. The SEC believes that the Coordination Act does not preempt states from subjecting such a solicitor to state qualification requirements.

What Federal Laws and Regulations Apply to State-Registered Advisers?

Although state-registered advisers are no longer subject to many provisions of the Investment Advisers Act or SEC rules, some provisions still apply.

- Section 206 continues to make it unlawful for any investment adviser to engage in fraudulent, deceptive, or manipulative practices.
- State-registered advisers continue to be subject to Section 204A's requirement to establish, maintain, and enforce written procedures reasonably designed to prevent the misuse of material nonpublic information (insider trading).
- State-registered advisers continue to be subject to Section 205, which contains prohibitions on advisory contracts that (1) contain certain performance fee arrangements, (2) permit an assignment of the advisory contract to be made without the consent of the client, and (3) fail to require an adviser that is a partnership to notify clients of a change in the membership of the partnership.
- State-registered advisers continue to be subject to Section 206(3), which makes it unlawful for any investment adviser acting as principal for its own account to knowingly sell any security to, or purchase any security from, a client, without disclosing to the client in writing before the completion of the transaction the capacity in which the adviser is acting and obtaining the client's consent. This limitation also applies if the adviser is acting as a broker for a person other than the client in effecting such a transaction.

Provisions of State Law Modified by the Coordination Act

State securities regulators may not enforce any law or regulation that would require an adviser to maintain books and records in addition to those required by the state in which the adviser has its principal place of business. Neither may state securities regulators enforce any law or regulation that would require an adviser to maintain a higher minimum net capital or to post any bond in addition to any that is required by the state in which the adviser has its principal place of business. These limitations apply only if the adviser is registered or licensed in the state in which it maintains its principal place of business, and is in compliance with the appropriate requirements of that state.

The Coordination Act also relieves advisers from some regulatory burden by establishing a *national de minimis standard* which states that investment advisers may not be required to register in any state unless the adviser has a place of business in the state, or, during the preceding 12-month period, has had more than five *clients* who are residents of the state. For purposes of counting clients for the national de minimis standard, the following will be deemed a single client: any natural person, and

- any minor child of the natural person;
- any relative, spouse, or relative of the spouse of the natural person who has the same principal residence;
- all accounts of which the natural person and/or the persons referred to above are the only primary beneficiaries; and
- all trusts of which the natural person and/or the persons referred to above are the only primary beneficiaries.

In general, this definition recognizes the family as an economic unit, and gives the adviser greater latitude in staying within the de minimis standard. The following will also be considered single clients:

- A corporation, general partnership, limited partnership, limited liability company, trust (other than a trust referred to above) or other legal organization that receives investment advice based on its investment objectives rather than the individual investment objectives of its shareholders, partners, limited partners, members, or beneficiaries; and
- Two or more legal organizations referred to above that have identical owners.

The Coordination Act did not affect the application of state law to investment adviser representatives of state-registered advisers. Thus, for example, a state may continue to require representatives of a state-registered adviser to register even if they do not have a place of business in the state, have less than six clients in the state, or do not meet the federal definition of investment adviser representative in Rule 203A-3(a).

Another change instituted by the Coordination Act relates to advisers to ERISA plans. ERISA permits employee benefit plan trustees to appoint certain entities as investment managers to manage plan assets, and that trustees delegating responsibilities to investment managers receive protection from liability with respect to investment decisions made by the investment managers. The Coordination Act amended Section 3(38)(B) of ERISA to include in the definition of *investment manager* investment advisers registered under the laws of any state, as well as federally-registered investment advisers and other types of entities. The definition of investment manager was amended to ensure that small investment advisers not registered with the SEC could serve as investment managers and would not be disadvantaged under ERISA. This amendment contains a sunset provision of two years from the date of enactment, which was October 11, 1996.

RESPONSIBILITIES OF INVESTMENT ADVISERS WHO MUST REGISTER WITH THE SEC

Each state that regulates investment advisers creates its own set of rules and responsibilities, but states will increasingly adopt standards similar to those required by the SEC. For those financial planners who are subject to SEC regulation, there are seven separate categories of responsibilities that need to be met: registration, record keeping, charging of fees, assignment of contracts, use of labels, delivery of brochures, and avoidance of fraudulent practices. These responsibilities are discussed in the following sections of this chapter.

Registration as a Registered Investment Adviser with the SEC

Financial services professionals who meet the IA-770 and IA-1092 tests and who are not exempt by The Coordination Act must comply with the mandates of the Investment Advisers Act of 1940. The chief requirement is that the practitioner become a *registered investment adviser (RIA)*. This is a burdensome administrative undertaking and is accomplished by completing what is known as *Form ADV*. A one-time filing fee (currently $150) must accompany the application. The form itself is complicated and will be rejected by the Securities and Exchange Commission's Office of Applications and Reports Services unless completed correctly in each and every regard. Form ADV itself is divided into two broad parts.

The first part of the form asks generalized questions, such as the name, location, and fiscal year of the applicant's business, the form of the business (that is, corporation, partnership, or sole proprietorship), the background of the applicant and any others associated with the applicant, and whether the applicant and the people associated with him or her have ever been convicted of crimes or are subject to certain injunctions. Part I also contains questions relative to the types of clients for which the applicant will provide discretionary or any other account management services.

The second part of the form requires more detailed and extensive information. This information includes the specific types of services offered by the applicant, a detailed explanation of the fee structure, the basic method of operation of the applicant's business, and even questions dealing with the kind of direct involvement the applicant has in securities transactions for clients. Part II also asks for the names of business associates of the applicant within the securities industry, additional information on the applicant, and, if certain additional conditions are met, a balance sheet.

If the Securities and Exchange Commission finds that the applicant has satisfactorily met the general standards upon which the registration is normally accepted, it must grant the RIA registration within 45 days of the filing date or, in the alternative, must begin proceedings to determine whether registration should be denied. As a practical matter, registration will be denied if these general standards have not been met or if the Securities and Exchange Commission determines that registration, if granted, would immediately be subject to suspension or revocation. This could be the result if, for example, the SEC discovers that the applicant has failed to disclose a prior securities law conviction. Note, though, that the SEC's acceptance of a registration says nothing about the applicant's competence.

Record-Keeping Responsibilities

Once the application of the registered investment adviser has been approved, the postregistration phase of compliance begins. One of the more significant elements of this postregistration phase is the record-keeping responsibility. It must be noted that there is a 16-step record-keeping requirement with which financial services professionals who are registered investment advisers must comply. Included as part of this is compliance with the *Insider Trading and Securities Fraud Enforcement Act of 1988.*

Specifically, *Sec. 204* of the Investment Advisers Act of 1940 provides the following:

> Every investment adviser who makes use of the mails or any means or any instrumentality of interstate commerce in connection with his, her, or its business as an investment adviser shall make and keep for prescribed periods such records, furnish such copies thereof, and make and disseminate such reports as the Securities and Exchange Commission, by rule, may prescribe as necessary or appropriate in the public interest or for the protection of investors. All records of such investors and advisers are subject at any time, or from time to time, to such reasonable periodic, special, or other examinations by representatives of the Securities and Exchange Commission as the Commission deems necessary or appropriate in the public interest or for the protection of investors.

The Securities and Exchange Commission has promulgated a detailed series of record-keeping requirements with which each and every registered investment adviser must comply. As mentioned above there are 16 separate things that must be done in order for the registered investment adviser to be totally in compliance in the postregistration phase. These 16 requirements are as follows:

- *Journal requirement:* Keep a journal in accordance with generally accepted accounting principles.
- *Ledger requirement:* Maintain a ledger in accordance with generally accepted accounting principles.

- *Securities purchased record:* Keep a complete record of all securities you have purchased or recommended.
- *Retention of canceled checks:* Save all your canceled checks and bank statements for a 5-year period.
- *Retention of paid and unpaid bills:* Assemble and save all documentation of paid and unpaid bills.
- *Retention of trial balances and financial statements:* Retain all trial balances and financial statements for a 5-year period.
- *Retention of written communication:* Keep records of all written communications you send to advisory clients and those sent to you by advisory clients.
- *Records of discretionary accounts:* Maintain a list of all accounts in which you have discretionary power.
- *Evidence of discretionary authority:* Retain all documents that grant you discretionary authority.
- *Retention of written agreements:* Save all written agreements executed between you and the advisory client.
- *Retention of communications recommending specific securities:* Keep a record of all advertisements, notices, or circulars, sent to 10 or more persons, that recommend specific securities to clients.
- *Record of securities transactions where RIA has direct or indirect ownership:* Maintain a separate record of all of your recommendations that have been made to an advisory client concerning specific securities in which you have direct or indirect beneficial ownership.
- *Record of securities transactions where RIA has direct or indirect ownership but is primarily engaged in business other than advisory services (for example, life insurance, tax planning, etc.):* Comply with the requirements of the previous item even if you are not primarily involved in investment advisory activities.
- *Brochure retention:* Keep copies of brochures given to clients. Keep signed receipts for the brochures from all advisory clients.
- *Retention of disclosure documents:* Retain copies of all disclosures signed by paid solicitors who refer business to you.
- *Insider-trading compliance:* Comply in every respect with the mandates of the Insider Trading and Securities Fraud Enforcement Act of 1988, as will be discussed below.

Because each and every practitioner who operates as a registered investment adviser will be subjected to an SEC examination, it is imperative that professional advisers totally comply with these record keeping mandates. There are both civil and criminal penalties available to the regulators as a method of enforcing these rules.

Discouraging Insider Trading: Written Policies and Procedures

Many observers consider insider trading to be a direct threat to the continued integrity of securities markets and, by extension, to the entire financial system.

Another mandate of the Insider Trading and Securities Fraud Enforcement Act of 1988 is that investment advisers must have written policies and procedures that reduce the likelihood of insider trading. An historical perspective will help explain how this requirement arose.

Legislative history shows that when the Securities Exchange Act of 1934 was being debated, insider trading was one of the major issues even back then. However, it was not until 1968 that there was finally a court decision which held that the use of inside information was a violation of federal securities laws (*SEC v. Texas Gulf Sulfur Company*). Since that case was handed down, Sec. 10(b) of the Securities Exchange Act of 1934 (particularly Sec. 10(b)-5) has provided a legal underpinning for the majority of the insider-trading cases brought by the Securities and Exchange Commission.

FOCUS ON ETHICS
Legal Compliance and Ethics

Financial services is a highly regulated industry and one that has been under attack by the regulatory agencies. The media coverage has been intensive, high profile, and negative. A major theme within the industry has been legal compliance. Some financial planners have felt the "straitjackets" of home-office demands that written sales materials and presentations be approved before they are used.

The demand for legal compliance needs to be applauded. While the services of financial planners are greatly needed by the public, the industry cannot expect to survive, let alone thrive, if it is losing the struggle of acting legally. This issue cannot be taken lightly.

Furthermore, financial planners are helping clients make their financial dreams become reality. The effective planner must understand a client's financial capability, obligations, and willingness to assume risk. In short, the planner must understand the client's financial aspirations in such depth that they can be converted into achievable goals. To succeed the financial planner must *earn* the trust and respect of the client. How is this done?

Being in legal compliance is merely the minimum boundary of acceptability. The effective financial planner will strive for a higher standard. It may be to live by The American College's Professional Pledge (see page 77), The Code of Ethics of the American Society of CLU & ChFC (page 81), or the Code of Ethics and Professional Responsibility of the CFP Board of Standards (page 85). On an introspective level, a worthy standard is a personal code of ethics that surpasses what others might impose on themselves.

Congress enacted the *Insider Trading Sanction Act of 1984* which, among other things, gave the SEC the authority to seek the imposition of civil penalties against insider-trading violations for as much as three times the profit gained (or loss avoided) as a result of the unlawful purchase or sale of securities. The government felt that such a provision would act as a deterrent. Of course, insider trading-problems increased, causing Congress to enact the Insider Trading and Securities Fraud Enforcement Act of 1988. Since registered investment advisers are viewed as being in a particularly vulnerable position within the insider-trading context, special provisions of the 1988 statute were enacted to deal specifically with the activities of registered investment advisers. Specifically, the 1988 insider-trading statute added Sec. 204A to the Investment Advisers Act of 1940, which provided the following:

> Every investment adviser subject to the Investment Advisers Act shall establish, maintain, and enforce written policies and procedures reasonably designed to prevent the misuse in violation of this act or the Securities Exchange Act of 1934, of material, nonpublic information by such investment adviser or any person associated with the investment adviser. The Securities and Exchange Commission as it deems shall adopt rules or regulations to require specific policies or procedures reasonably designed to prevent misuse in violation of this act or the Securities Exchange Act of 1934 of material, nonpublic information.

It should be noted that there are regulatory, civil, and even criminal penalties under Sec. 204A for failure to comply with this new statute section of the 1940 law. There is even a special bounty provision in Sec. 204A which grants authority to the SEC to award payments to persons who provide information concerning insider-trading violations. At the sole discretion of the SEC, the individual can receive up to 10 percent of the penalty imposed or settlement reached.

As a practical matter, insider-trading legislation imposes liabilities not only on broker/dealers and registered investment advisers but also on their employees for misuse by such employees of confidential information if the employer has failed to have effectively policed employee activities within the framework of insider trading. The insider-trading statute requires all employers to develop a compliance plan. Every registered investment adviser must have a plan in place.

It is possible to engage in insider trading in many different ways. Examples include conversations with officers of a company with whom the adviser regularly deals or just a normal conversation with clients (for example, "I'm taking my company private in a few months").

It is also possible for employees to receive inside information and act on it without the knowledge of the registered investment adviser. Therefore the RIA must have a plan. Also, when the RIA firm adopts policies, they must actually be adopted with a view that they will genuinely be enforced. If these policies are adopted pursuant to the statute but are never actually enforced, that can be worse than never having adopted a plan in the first place. An actual policy statement needs to be drafted and enforced. Management of the RIA must provide all employees with copies of the policy statement. This, in effect, is evidence of compliance.

To summarize, there are four basic types of requirements within the context of insider-trading compliance. These are

- development of written policies and procedures setting forth the legal prohibitions against insider trading, explaining key concepts underlying these prohibitions, and including any additional restrictions of the firm on insider trading and related activities
- communication of those policies and procedures to employees and supervisors throughout the firm who may learn material nonpublic information as a result of their positions at the firm
- implementation of those policies and procedures through assignment of specific responsibilities to supervisory personnel
- establishment of monitoring mechanisms to increase the likelihood that the firm will prevent, or at least detect, trading and tipping that is not in compliance with the policies and procedures

Fee Restrictions

The 1940 Advisers Act prohibited an investment adviser from basing fees on any share of the capital appreciation of all or any portion of the client's funds unless the advisory contract related to the investment of assets in excess of $1 million. In 1985, the SEC adopted Rule 205-3, which allows registered investment advisers to charge "performance fees" (also referred to as "incentive fees"), but only if the RIA is "managing $500,000 of a client's assets" or "reasonably believes" that the client has a net worth of at least $1 million.

Rule 205-3 requires that clients be advised by brochure that the performance-based fee arrangement "may create an incentive for the RIA to make investments that are riskier or more speculative than would be the case in nonperformance-based situations." The RIA must also give specific details about how the fee is to be calculated. In addition, the contract between the RIA and client must be based on an arm's-length relationship and the incentive fee must be based on at least one year's performance.

Assignability of Investment Advisory Agreements

Sec. 205 of the Investment Advisers Act prohibits an investment adviser from assigning or transferring an investment advisory contract unless the client expressly consents to such transfer. Congress, in enacting such a provision, wanted to make sure that an adviser would not be able to shift his or her existing responsibilities to some other practitioner or adviser without first obtaining the original client's full consent to the new relationship. Therefore if an existing registered investment adviser wants, for example, to retire, shut down operations, or move to some other location, such practitioner cannot assign the existing professional relationship to another without first obtaining the existing client's full consent to the assignment.

Prohibition of Labels

Sec. 208(c) of the Investment Advisers Act of 1940 provides that it shall be unlawful for any person registered as an investment adviser to represent that he or she is an "investment counsel" or to use the name "investment counsel" unless (1) his or her principal business consists of acting as an investment adviser and (2) a substantial part of that business consists of rendering investment supervisory services.

Although in the form of a no-action letter and not as an actual provision of the Investment Advisers Act of 1940, the SEC has also taken the position that a practitioner must not use the initials "RIA" after his or her name. The SEC was aware of a growing trend within the financial planning community of practitioners using the "RIA" initials after their names as some form of designation—such as CLU or ChFC. Specifically, the SEC stated that, since successful acquisition of professional designations such as CLU or ChFC requires the passing of rigorous course examinations, it would be misleading to use the initials "RIA" after a practitioner's name, in light of the fact that no courses or examinations are required (at least at the federal level) in order to obtain this status. However, in a somewhat surprising conclusion, the SEC announced that it would permit use of the complete phrase "registered investment adviser" after a financial planner's name.

Brochure Rule

In SEC Release No. IA-664, the Securities and Exchange Commission set forth Rule 204-3, which has become known as the brochure rule. Essentially any practitioner who is a registered investment adviser must deliver a written brochure to each and every client.

Since January 30, 1979, when the U.S. Securities and Exchange Commission promulgated SEC Release No. IA-664, all registered investment advisers have been required to deliver a written disclosure statement to each and every client. This concept requires every investment adviser to deliver a special disclosure statement not only to existing clients to whom investment advice has been given, but also to prospective clients. This disclosure must be delivered to clients or prospective clients either (1) within 48 hours of entering into an investment advisory agreement or (2) when the contract is entered into if the client can terminate such contract within 5 days.

Compliance with the brochure rule can be accomplished either by providing the client with a copy of part II of the Form ADV or, in the alternative, by preparing a separate narrative statement containing each and every piece of data that appears as part of part II of the Form ADV. The SEC seems to prefer the former approach.

There are 13 basic categories of data that the brochure must communicate to the financial planning client:

- types of clients
- source of information, method of analysis, and investment strategy
- business background and education
- other securities industry activities
- conditions for managing accounts
- review procedures
- advisory fee structure
- types of securities about which advice may be provided
- minimum educational standards imposed on associates/employees
- other business activities with which the planner may be involved
- interest in securities transactions
- brokerage discretion
- balance sheet in the event that the registered investment adviser maintains custody or possession of the client's funds or securities or requires prepayment of advisory fees 6 months or more in advance, and such fees are in excess of $500 per client

In summary, therefore, the brochure rule requires the registered investment adviser to deliver either part II of the Form ADV or the substitute brochure to the client or prospective client. It must also be noted, however, that if a continuing relationship exists between the registered investment adviser and the client, the RIA must offer to deliver an updated version of the brochure to the client at the end of each fiscal year. This portion of the brochure rule differs from the initial requirement in that, rather than the registered investment adviser being required to actually deliver the brochure disclosure statement to the client, it is satisfactory to merely offer to deliver such brochure in subsequent years.

The Antifraud Provisions

Sec. 206 of the Investment Advisers Act of 1940 has come to be known as the antifraud portion of the act. Specifically, it provides the following:

It shall be unlawful for any investment adviser, by use of the mails or any means or instrumentality of interstate commerce, directly or indirectly:

a. to employ any advice, scheme, or artifice to defraud any client or prospective client;
b. to engage in any transaction, practice, or course of business which operates as a fraud or deceit upon any client or prospective client;

c. to act as principal for his own account, knowingly to sell any security to or purchase any security from a client, or to act as broker for a person other than such client, knowingly to effect any sale or purchase of any security for the account of such client, without disclosing to such client in writing before the completion of such transaction the capacity in which he or she is acting and obtaining the consent of the client to such transaction. The prohibitions of this paragraph shall not apply to any transaction with a customer of a broker or dealer if such broker or dealer is not acting as an investment adviser in relation to such transaction.

d. to engage in any act, practice, or course of business which is fraudulent, deceptive, or manipulative. The Securities and Exchange Commission shall, for the purposes of this paragraph (d) by rules and regulations define and prescribe means reasonably designed to prevent such acts, practices, and courses of business as are fraudulent, deceptive, or manipulative.

These antifraud provisions of the Investment Advisers Act of 1940 have been interpreted to mean that the investment adviser becomes a *fiduciary* who owes the client "an affirmative duty of utmost good faith and full and fair disclosure of all the material facts." The antifraud provisions of the act also deal quite extensively with conflict of interest issues and, in general, hold the investment adviser to an exceedingly high standard of fiduciary responsibility.

The antifraud provisions of the act may even become operative in situations in which a securities transaction per se has not taken place. In essence, the SEC has decided that since Sec. 206 of the act does not refer to "dealings in securities" as most other general antifraud provisions in the federal securities law do, Sec. 206 is much broader and can be applied to transactions in which fraudulent conduct arose out of the investment advisory relationship between an investment adviser and his, her, or its clients, even if the conduct did not involve a securities transaction.

STATE REGULATION OF FINANCIAL PLANNERS

This chapter has been focused on the regulation of financial planners within the framework of the federal securities laws. It must be noted, however, that there are a whole separate series of regulatory responsibilities stemming from the various state securities laws and state securities commissions. At this time, 46 states require the registration of investment advisers. Some of the states single out the activities of financial planners as part of this requirement, while other jurisdictions merely lump the concept of financial planner and investment adviser together. It should be noted, however, that state registration sometimes involves a series of procedures that are even more difficult than those that exist at the federal level.

For example, many states require a minimum capitalization amount as a prerequisite to granting investment adviser registration approval. Some states require a bond and an audited financial statement to accompany the application as well. Almost every state requires that the participants in the registered investment advisory operation have certain NASD registration, such as the series 63 (uniform state securities test), series 22 (limited partnership/direct participation test), or series 65 (investment adviser) examination. In addition, the state securities commissions, unlike the SEC, will want to see all contracts, disclosure statements and documents, and literature used by the RIA/financial planner with the client. It is inadequate for the financial services professional to focus only on the federal regulatory implications of providing financial planning advice since the state component of the overall scheme is just as relevant.

CONCLUSION

Any argument that the financial planning industry is unregulated must be dismissed as unfounded. This chapter has focused on the various systems used to regulate financial planning professionals. There is obviously a highly comprehensive system of regulation involving a variety of legal and regulatory mandates at both the federal and state level. The financial services professional must become familiar with these responsibilities and must grow accustomed to complying with these mandates on a continuing basis.

NOTES

1 This section was adapted from *The Great Divide: Amendments to the Investment Advisers Act and Related Commission-Rulemaking* which was written by Robert E. Plaze and Catherine M. Saadeh of the SEC's Division of Investment Management in September 1997 and posted on the internet at http://www.sec.gov/rules/extra/grtdiv.htm.The authors did not participate in this adaptation and are not responsible for any misinterpretation of the original document.

3

Ethics and Professionalism

Robbin Derry, Ken Cooper, and Ronald F. Duska

Chapter Outline

An important consideration in the financial planning environment is ethics and professionalism. While clearly a separate topic from meeting client needs and legal and regulatory concepts, ethics and professionalism are closely related to both. First, a significant obligation of a professional is service to others, which is of paramount concern in ethics. Financial professionals, as agents who are required to consider their clients' best interests, are necessarily involved in an ethical dimension. Second, since law is primarily a codification of ethical principles, the understanding of the relationship of legal compliance to ethics is crucial. Hence an analysis of what ethics is and how it relates to the law and client needs is an important enterprise for the financial adviser.

The financial services field has been plagued by ethical lapses. Charges of improper conduct appear all too frequently. In the life insurance industry, opinion polls document that the majority of consumers trust their own agents, but there is widespread distrust of agents in general. The Insurance Information Institute recently completed a biannual consumer survey giving the life insurance industry its lowest favorability rating in a 26-year span.[1]

This decline in public confidence is related to the many charges and millions of dollars in fines and other penalties that have been assessed. These transgressions are frequently amplified by media coverage.

How can this be happening to the financial services industry? Ethical standards represent the basis for client trust, an essential ingredient in successful financial planning. The American College Code of Ethics brochure includes the following statement:

> Throughout the life span of The American College education and ethics have been inextricably combined. Dr. Solomon S. Huebner, the pioneering educator who founded the College, seldom spoke of education without also speaking of ethics. To him a professional relationship between agent and client had to be based on sound ethical principles.[2]

Whether motivated by the desire to avoid the current ethical problems or the attractiveness of the industry's cultural heritage, the financial planner will benefit by developing an understanding of ethics and professionalism. This chapter will explore

- the role of ethics
- the codification of standards of conduct
- the quality of professionalism
- the practice of ethical decision making
- ethical issues in financial services

THE ROLE OF ETHICS

There was a time when the search for a practical way to describe applied ethics seemed analogous to the familiar story of the three blind men's attempt to describe an elephant. There are still many views on what the "ethics elephant" looks like.

Most of our conscious encounters with ethics occur when we observe ethical violations: a public official is caught accepting a bribe; physicians are accused of performing unnecessary surgery; the media stages an event or betrays a trust to grab a headline; and a salesperson misleads a client to ensure the completion of a sale. This tabloid approach, while unfortunately real, only provides a negative glimpse of ethics. Ethics can and should be viewed as a positive influence.

In its most abstract form, ethics is just one of several branches of philosophy. It is that part concerned with moral behavior, that is, the product of moral standards and moral judgment. As Socrates said, "We are discussing no small matter, but how we ought to live."[3]

Deciding "how we ought to live" is the foundation of ethics. If we approach it conscientiously, the results will appear in daily conduct. Each person takes his or her morality to work each day. Regardless of how clear personal standards may be, on the job we soon discover that colleagues, competitors, and clients are governed by what appears to be a different vision of "how we ought to live." Sometimes the vision is considerably different. Regardless, ethics needs to be understood as a powerful element in the financial planning environment.

Ethics is the glue that holds our entire economic and free enterprise system together. Without ethical behavior business deals would collapse, working conditions would be intolerable, and trust would be nonexistent. In business activities people act based on the trust that their associates will behave ethically. When an employee is assigned a task, the supervisor trusts that the employee will not misuse the information, the time, or the resources that accompany the task. A life insurance agent and a client make a verbal agreement to meet again after the agent has had a chance to analyze the client's needs. The agent trusts that the client will come to the meeting and listen to the needs analysis, while the client trusts that the agent will keep personal information confidential. When a manager offers a bonus for high performance, subordinates trust that the reward will indeed be forthcoming upon achievement of such performance. All day people act in ways that demonstrate a trust in the fundamental assumptions of fair treatment, honest communication, accurate representation of intentions, and the avoidance of deception.

Certainly there are unethical people that we have learned not to trust. There are many situations in which it is wise to be cautious. But in situations where there is little trust, it is more difficult to make agreements or to conduct business. Business diminishes and disintegrates without trust. The behavior of untrustworthy individuals and organizations is too unpredictable to risk involvement. When a person lies (deceives, cheats, or steals), it is difficult to restore trust in that individual. If a business develops a reputation for fraud and deception, it is extremely challenging for that business to overcome that reputation. With the erosion of confidence, customers, suppliers, stockholders, and even potential employees will take their resources elsewhere.

Ethics is not public relations. It is not about creating a good image, nor is it a luxury that a company may indulge in after it meets the critical bottom line. Ethics is about how people conduct business, every hour of every day. It is about prompt response to client complaints and honest feedback to subordinates, peers, and superiors. Ethical behavior is being honest with ourselves and others. It involves the quality of the work to which individuals put their names. It is giving clients all the information they need to make decisions that are in their best interest.

The concept of ethics represents a set of fundamental assumptions that underlie nearly all relationships and transactions within society. These are assumptions about the way we treat people: what our rights and the rights of others are, where our individual rights end and the rights of others begin, how individual and community property ought to be treated, and what constitutes fair and equitable treatment of all people.

Discussing ethical conflicts is one important way that people can express their moral values to those with whom they live and work. If trust in ethical behavior facilitates and underlies all economic transactions, then people must be sure to build ethical behavior into their business decisions and operations. Only if they integrate an awareness of ethics into their daily work lives will they create a working environment that is founded on strong ethical principles.

What about competitive business practices? Isn't business fundamentally about trying to gain the advantage over competitors? Does ethical behavior put a manager at a competitive disadvantage?

A manager, an insurance agent, a financial planner, or an investment adviser can be ethical, competitive, and tough about goals all at the same time. Business is not just about competition. It is also about cooperation. It is about meeting the needs of customers. It is about making deals that work for the good of as many people as possible. If a business focused entirely on competing with rivals and neglected its customers, the business would quickly fail.

Honest competition is healthy, contributing to a stronger economy, higher quality service, and a better selection of consumer products. However, competition is not the fundamental purpose of business, and some aspects of competition are destructive.

Ethical behavior implies doing what is right, and that is sufficient justification. Two pragmatic reasons also justify ethical behavior in business. The first reason is that ethical expectations and trust serve to hold business, the economy, and society together. To the extent that people act unethically, these systems fail. The outcome may be that our own business systems falter as a result of distrust, deception, or a lack of consumer confidence. Adherence to ethical business practices adds a cornerstone to the foundation of any business organization.

The second reason to be ethical in business practices is that individual actions create the work environment in which people spend most of their waking hours. People are constantly creating their own living and working context by how they treat others, by statements they make, by attitudes they hold, and by the practices they condone. Ethical behavior profoundly improves their quality of life.

THE CODIFICATION OF STANDARDS OF CONDUCT

Each person is the major contributor in shaping his or her environment. A person's initiatives or reactions to ethical challenges determine the character of all his or her relationships. If people lie, cheat, and steal, they are then living in a lying, cheating, and stealing environment. An ethical environment is the only possible one in which society can progress economically, physically, morally, and spiritually. This is the ethical responsibility: to actively create a context in which everyone can survive. The fulfillment of this responsibility requires people to assess the ethical implications of all actions, the long-term costs, and the alternatives as well as to listen to others who are affected.

The practical result of this process is the development of frames of reference that citizens use to make decisions. Societal units such as nations develop laws that represent a framework based on what the governing unit considers to be minimal standards of conduct. Penalties are established, often severe, to discourage people from violating laws. Frequently industries and/or specific business organizations develop standards of conduct known as codes of ethical conduct, statements of values, rules of conduct, etc. Since people always aspire to standards more demanding than the law, these standards become the benchmark against which the organization's ethical conduct is measured. It follows that we, as individuals, often have our own codes of ethical conduct. One of the early studies on business ethics done by Raymond Baumhart found that the number one influence on a business executive's ethical decision making was a personal code of behavior.[4]

Law and ethics are both standards of conduct that govern a nation, the morality of an organization, and the moral actions of individuals. Those desiring to be a part have more or less voluntarily accepted the standards.

There are other ways to examine the relationship between law and ethics. Figure 3-1 shows that law and ethics overlap, but each has its own domain as well. The dotted lines at the intersection of law and ethics represent their mutable boundaries. Laws are largely ethical standards that society has codified in order to insist on and enforce certain behaviors. Ethical issues that are deemed sufficiently important may become laws; laws considered to be excessive or intrusive may be either ignored or struck down in court proceedings.

FIGURE 3-1
Relationship between Law and Ethics

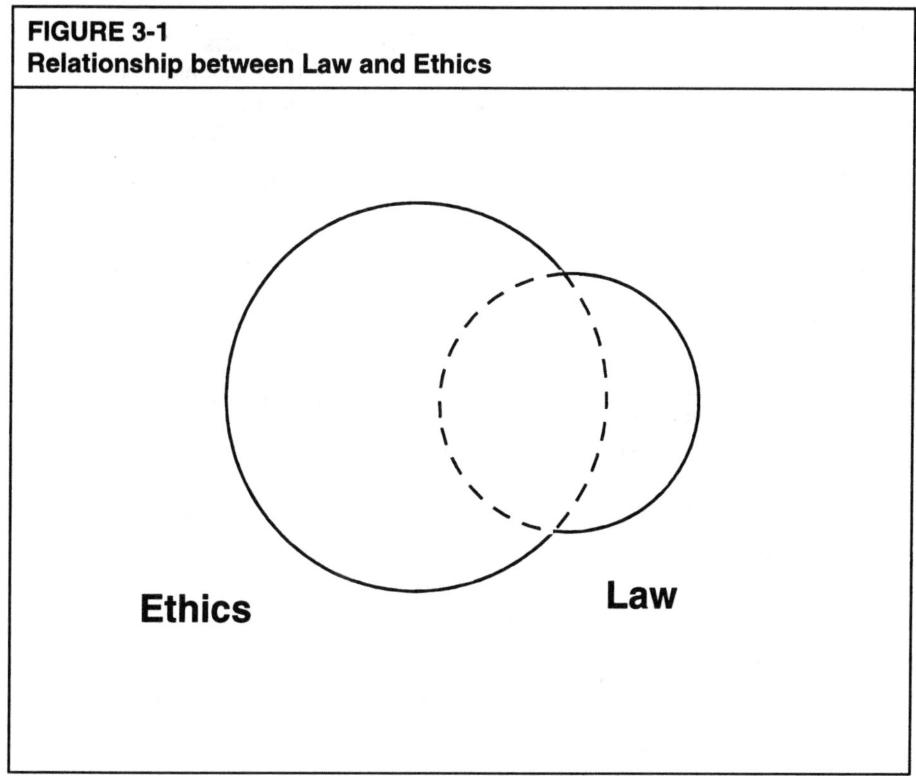

The specific areas of business law and business ethics overlap in similar ways, as shown in figure 3-2. In the area at the intersection of business law and business ethics are such issues as fulfilling contractual agreements, nondiscriminatory treatment of different racial groups in hiring and promotion decisions, and meeting minimal quality-control standards in manufacturing processes.

Within the realm of business ethics (outside the realm of business law) are such issues as the acceptable level of toxic waste to emit or dump into the environment when one knows that the legal standards are inadequate or nonexistent. Other examples are low-level but constant verbal abuse in the workplace, manipulative sales practices, and intimidation of subordinates.

In the purely legal realm are trade regulations, product specifications, and contractual relationships with suppliers, customers, the community, shareholders, and investors. Many "purely legal" rules quickly become ethical issues if they are violated, intentionally misinterpreted, or ignored. In fact, laws represent codified ethical standards. They are the minimum moral requirements that we have agreed to demand for society as a whole.

FIGURE 3-2
Relationship between Business Law and Business Ethics

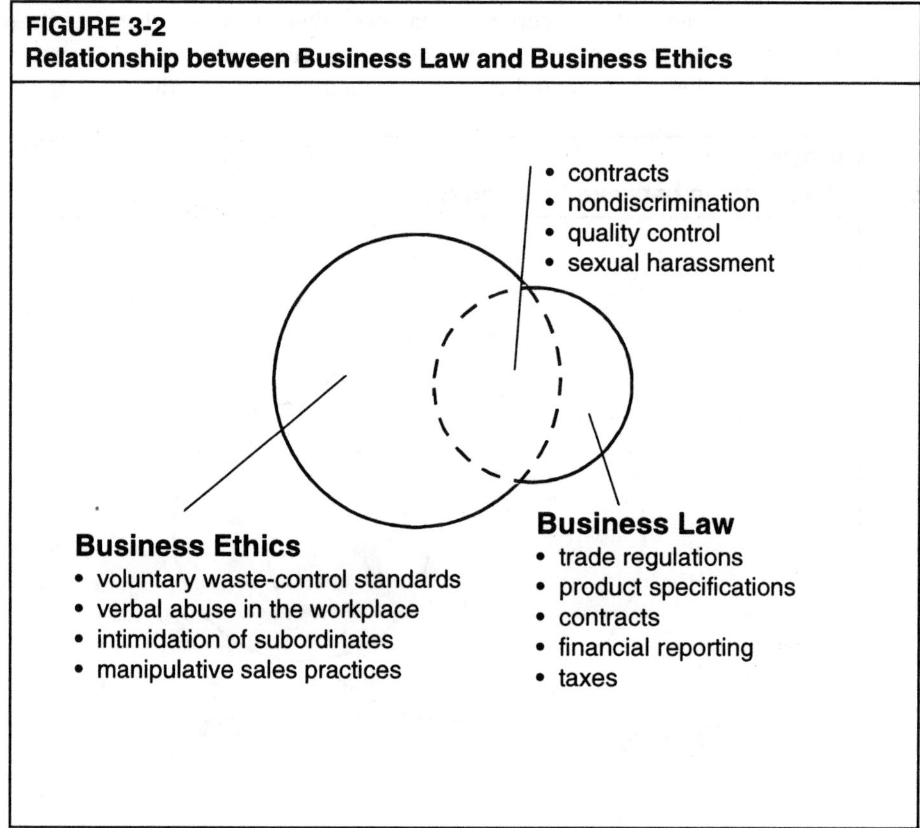

Both diagrams help to focus on a common misunderstanding. The term *compliance* is often used as if it were synonymous with *ethics*. Compliance means obedience to the law. A "compliance" emphasis may even undermine ethics, because it is targeted at meeting legal requirements rather than addressing the causes of ethical misconduct.

Lynn Sharp Paine states that "legal compliance is unlikely to unleash moral imagination or commitment. The law does not generally seek to inspire human excellence or distinction. Those managers who define ethics as legal compliance are implicitly endorsing a code of moral mediocrity for their organizations."[5]

"You can't legislate morality" is a popular saying. But morality, or the definition of right and wrong behavior, is precisely the focus of the American legal system. Laws regarding stealing, killing, invading another's privacy, defrauding, and misrepresenting intentions all reflect ethical rules. If these are violated, a penalty is imposed on the violator. So society *does*, in fact, *legislate* the most important aspects of morality.

It is true, however, that society cannot legislate *all* morality. Laws cannot be made to cover every situation that arises. Laws cannot mandate decent treatment and concern for other human beings, although that is certainly an ethical issue. If an attempt were made to define and mandate all moral behavior, it would be impossible to enforce. Furthermore, citizens in democratic countries generally prefer fewer laws and greater personal freedom. With a significant increase in laws governing individual behavior, courts and prisons would be even more crowded. People want a certain amount of personal independence to resolve their ethical dilemmas, but they also need to adhere to some common moral standards, since their decisions about such dilemmas inevitably affect others. Similarly, of course, their ethical decisions affect us, and we expect them to adhere to a shared morality as well.

The law is relatively clear-cut. Lawyers, police officers, and court officials are all employed to provide guidance on how to follow the law. Although lawyers don't always agree and the body of law is always evolving, there is a concrete and accessible legal system.

Ethical rules, however, are not as clear-cut. An ethical problem is not as easily defined as a legal problem. A situation that raises ethical conflicts for Susan may not raise any such conflicts for John. This is because they each have a different sense of responsibility associated with particular moral values. For example, honesty to Susan may mean that she should give her true opinion when colleagues ask her what she thinks. Honesty to John may mean that he is always at work on time and never takes sick days unless he is completely incapable of coming into the office. If Susan doesn't share John's interpretation of honesty, she will feel no ethical dilemma at all about taking a sick day to go for a hike in the woods. And John may feel that it is perfectly acceptable, even moral, to politely lie about a colleague's poor performance. They both would agree that honesty is an important ethical standard, but they would disagree on the situations that raise conflicts over that value.

As this example shows, ethical behavior is not as readily defined as legal behavior. There is no concrete body of ethical standards that serves as recourse in ethical dilemmas. However, there are commonly accepted standards regarding the basic norms governing the moral life. These include such rules as

- Don't kill.
- Don't cause pain.
- Don't disable.
- Fulfill obligations.
- Don't cheat.
- Don't deceive.

Some of these are laws, while others are not. They are all commonly held expectations about life in our society, reflecting our values of individual rights and obligations to others. These values and the resulting moral rules extend into the realm of business, since business operates within the larger realm of society as a whole.

Financial Services Codes of Ethics

To ensure as much freedom to its citizens as possible, nations establish laws as a minimum standard, the "moral mediocrity" that Paine addressed earlier. Many aspire to much higher standards. Within the financial services industry, codes of ethics have been developed by most organizations. These are the equivalent to a binding organizational moral law.

The American College, the American Society of CLU & ChFC, and the Certified Financial Planner Board of Standards have all developed strong, binding codes of ethics. Each of these codes, which appear in appendixes 3A, 3B, and 3C, emphasizes the importance of understanding the client's needs and acting to fulfill those needs.

The American College Code of Ethics

The American College Code of Ethics, which is reproduced in appendix 3A, was adopted in June 1984. Although only actions that occur after October 1, 1984, are subject to the code, the standards established by the code apply to students in the CLU and ChFC programs who matriculated on July 1, 1982, or later. All earlier CLU and ChFC matriculants were invited to subscribe to the code and to accept its mandates voluntarily. The jurisdiction of the College does not extend to pre-1982 matriculants who have not consented to be bound by the code.

The Code of The American College consists of two parts: a professional pledge and eight canons. The pledge reads:

> In all my professional relationships, I pledge myself to the following rule of ethical conduct: I shall, in light of all conditions surrounding those I serve, which I shall make every conscientious effort to ascertain

and understand, render that service which, in the same circumstances, I would apply to myself.

These are the eight canons:

I. Conduct yourself at all times with honor and dignity.
II. Avoid practices that would bring dishonor upon your profession or The American College.
III. Publicize your achievement in ways that enhance the integrity of your profession.
IV. Continue your studies throughout your working life so as to maintain a high level of professional competence.
V. Do your utmost to attain a distinguished record of professional service.
VI. Support the established institutions and organizations concerned with the integrity of your profession.
VII. Participate in building your profession by encouraging and providing appropriate assistance to qualified persons pursuing professional studies.
VIII. Comply with all laws and regulations, particularly as they relate to professional and business activities.

The sanctions that may be imposed by The American College for violation of its code of ethics include temporary or permanent suspension of the right to use the CLU designation, the ChFC designation, or both. The college may also relay its decision to other parties, such as government agencies and relevant institutions or organizations.

The American Society of CLU & ChFC Code of Ethics

The code of the American Society of CLU & ChFC is similar in spirit but differs in style and content. The Society's code, which is reproduced in appendix 3B, is made up of two imperatives, each having four guiding statements and numerous interpretations. The first imperative is: "To competently advise and serve the client." Competent advice and service should be "in the client's best interest," which should take precedence in any conflict of the agent's and client's interests. Society members must also respect the client's confidentiality and render continuing advice and service. To best serve the client *competently,* the member must maintain and improve his or her professional abilities through continuing education.

The second imperative is: "To enhance the public regard for professional designations and allied professional degrees held by members." Enhancement of public regard entails that the member be law-abiding and maintain his or her integrity and professionalism, encourage others to continue their education, and not detract from other professionals.

The members of the American Society are expected to be professional standard-bearers. It is in this context that the second imperative is particularly relevant. This imperative is more than a concern for the image of the American Society and the field as a whole. It also reinforces the importance of acting in ways that will be seen to be entirely ethical even when exposed to the bright light of public scrutiny. Often unethical actions are taken when it is thought that no one will know. Under this imperative, actions or decisions that a financial services professional would not want to defend in public are completely unacceptable. In addition, the Guides elaborate behaviors that the American Society feels are consistent with its goals and standards.

The Certified Financial Planner Board of Standards Code of Ethics

A third code is the Code of Ethics and Professional Responsibility adopted by the Certified Financial Planner Board of Standards, which is reproduced in appendix 3C. It consists of two parts: principles and rules. The principles are statements expressing the ethical and professional ideals expected of CFP designees. The rules provide practical guidelines derived from the principles. The principles mention character traits the CFP should possess: integrity, objectivity, competence, fairness, confidentiality, professionalism, and diligence. What the seven principles require is that the CFP designee offer services with integrity and honesty, treating all interested parties fairly and not misrepresenting products. The service should be competent and diligent, that is, prompt and thorough. Adherents make decisions with objectivity, which requires putting the client's needs to the forefront, and in a professional manner, always respecting the client's confidentiality. Each of these seven principles is supplemented by detailed rules that tell how they are to be applied.

Practical Application

What do these codes mean in terms of daily professional practice? The American College pledge says, "I shall . . . render that service which . . . I would apply to myself." The Society's code calls for putting the client's interest before one's own. The CFP code calls for the practitioner to act "in the interest of the client." Though not identical, all mandate something like the Golden Rule, "Do unto others as you would have them do unto you."

To offer a client the same thorough attention to detail that a financial planner would apply to an investment for himself or herself is no small requirement. Think about the kind of service a planner would give to himself or herself and to close relatives or friends. The planner would make absolutely certain to understand all the apparent and hidden costs. The planner would want to know how much it would cost now and whether the cost over the life of the product would be fixed or variable. The planner would want to clearly understand the potential risks of the investment or policy. So much for the inappropriate derivative sales, churning of investment accounts, or needless life insurance policy replacements we have witnessed lately.

If a product is interest-sensitive, is the planner (or the client) able to regularly monitor its financial stability? What are the costs of withdrawal? Does the planner understand the potential benefits of the product in the short term as well as in the long term? Does he or she know exactly how to maximize those benefits or what actions to take to reduce the potential harms? The planner would not go into an investment or policy purchase without making use of as much knowledge about the product as he or she was able to responsibly acquire.

One of the benefits of being in the financial services business is having access to information and knowledge that the general public doesn't have. Some clients have a particularly strong interest in knowing all the professional details, but some clients simply aren't interested in details. But the agent relationship requires that the practitioner make that knowledge available to help the client make better-informed investment decisions.

The American College's professional pledge says that the financial services professional will render that service to clients that he or she would expect. It is the professional's responsibility to present the information in a way that clients can understand and use in their decision making.

Of course, a financial planner cannot force someone to listen. Nonetheless, it is definitely the planner's obligation to provide the client with the needed information and to present this information in a manner that the client can understand. And the professional should help the client understand why he or she needs the information about the product and what its financial effect will be in the short and long term.

Focus on the Client

The pledge also stipulates that the financial services professional will take into account the conditions surrounding the client and that the professional "shall make every conscientious effort to ascertain and understand" such conditions. This means one cannot simply "sell off" products and be a salesman. There must be what is known as "consultative" or "client-focused" planning or selling. Such an approach requires the practitioner to gather as much information as possible from the client about needs, goals, interest, and assets in order to put together an investment or insurance package that will best meet the client's needs.

The sale of products is essentially client-driven. Practitioners must approach clients with a willingness to listen carefully. Clients can best provide the information regarding their own needs and goals. Clients may also think that they know which product best fits those goals, but practitioners should keep the client focused on articulating needs and goals so they can find the best product or service to match those goals.

Consultative planning or selling is a sound approach to building good relationships with clients and selling life insurance and other financial products. It is also an ethical requirement because of the nature of the client-planner relationship. Most practitioners have the dual role of agent for a financial services company and agent for the client. As the agent of the company, they must accurately represent the company's products or services to the client. Most financial services professionals who deal primarily with the products of one company feel that their obligation to the company is to look to those products first to meet their client's needs and go outside their home company for products only if an appropriate policy or investment is not available with that company.

This traditional approach serves several purposes. First, the planner is able to gain in-depth knowledge of the products of one or two companies, which would be nearly impossible if a person tried to cover all the products on the market. This knowledge enables the planner to serve the client better. Second, it saves the financial planner extensive research time to be able to work from a body of familiar products. Of course, in some instances this could be detrimental to a client who needs more extensive research to find just the right product. It is important that the planner honestly inform the client of the planner's primary relationship with a particular company. The client should understand that these products are the ones that the planner will research and present in most cases. It is deceptive and clearly unethical to fail to disclose that primary relationship.

The financial planner is also an agent for the client. The client trusts the agent with confidential information. Courts have increasingly found that the common law understanding of the word agent is "agent of the client." Courts have held that when a financial services professional induces reliance on his or her expertise, that person incurs liability for decisions made on the basis of the expertise. When a financial planner says in effect to a client, "I am your agent," the planner does indeed take on the responsibilities and liabilities of an agent of the client.

Many educators, speakers, and managers stress the importance of selling a financial service or product solely on the basis of client need. Selling on any other basis, such as the needs and interests of the salesperson, the sales manager, or the company, makes no sense in the long term. The salesperson may be persuasive enough to make fast sales in order to meet a bonus deadline, or the company may be promoting a particular product with higher commission rates. But unless the product really meets the needs of the client over the long term, that client will not keep up the payments, which ends up being costly for the company. Clients who feel that they were sold products that did not meet their needs are not likely to be repeat customers. A client will not refer friends and relatives to a salesperson if the client doesn't believe in the salesperson's ability to listen carefully and respond. So while the short-term sales may look good, the long-term financial position of the salesperson, the selling agency, and the selling company are hurt by any sales that do not meet client needs. The same arguments, of course, support continuing attention to the changing needs of clients over time.

In summary, it is both ethically required and financially wise for the financial planner to thoroughly understand the client's needs and act to fulfill those needs as much as possible. The codes of ethics of The American College, the American Society of CLU & ChFC, and The Certified Financial Planner Board of Standards reinforce this standard.

To take actions that would enhance public regard for the profession (which is even more demanding than enhancing public regard for oneself) is to act in ways that are commonly regarded as highly professional. As shown in the next section, professionalism requires competence and reliability. These characteristics are integral to upholding the ethical expectations of The American College, the American Society of CLU & ChFC, and the CFP Board.

THE QUALITY OF PROFESSIONALISM

The adjective *professional* is loosely attached to many careers and is used in significantly different ways. An example would be the professional athlete who is highly skilled, but the determining factor is that he or she gets paid. Amateur athletes, regardless of how talented, are not professional because they are not compensated.

Today there is much discussion about the professional politician. This is a person who has chosen politics as a career. Frequently the term is used in a derisive way to describe a politician who is more interested in manipulating the system for personal gain than developing public policy.

There are a few occupations that are widely viewed as professions. Included on most lists are doctors, lawyers, and clergy. Similar status is often given to pharmacists, engineers, and architects. Still others could be added to the list.

What do people mean when they say, "She is a real professional" or "His behavior was completely unprofessional"? What is commonly understood as professional conduct?

In the first example the positive connotation includes such characteristics as job proficiency, reliability, dedication, thoroughness, dependability, a commitment to providing good service, and an awareness that one's quality of performance affects the reputations of others.

In contrast, the term *unprofessional* suggests shoddy or careless performance; a lack of concern for customers or clients; disregard for the reputation of a larger group of people; and a narrow, selfish concern for one's own well-being.

Burke A. Christensen, JD, CLU, former general counsel and vice president of the American Society of CLU & ChFC, suggests that "a professional is a

Characteristics Defining a Professional

- Specialized knowledge not generally understood by the public
- Threshold entrance requirement
- Sense of altruism
- Code of ethics

person engaged in a field that requires (1) specialized knowledge not generally understood by the public, (2) a threshold entrance requirement, (3) a sense of altruism, and (4) a code of ethics."[6]

Of these requirements, numbers one and four are immediately evident in the financial services field. Certainly financial consultants and insurance agents have a specialized knowledge not generally understood. Holders of CLU, ChFC, and CFP designations and members of the American Society also adhere to professional codes of ethics.

The CLU, ChFC, and CFP designations represent a kind of threshold entrance requirement, even though there are many successful people working in the field who have not earned them. In addition to a professional designation or degree, however, thorough and continuing education in the fundamentals of the financial services profession is an important aspect of meeting clients' needs. This field is increasingly competitive and complex. Federal and state regulations are constantly evolving. Understanding these changes is essential to providing sound advice to clients. The truly professional financial adviser must in some way meet both an entrance requirement of foundational education and a requirement of continuous professional education.

Requirement number three, a sense of altruism, is the characteristic that facilitates adherence to the codes of ethics. Altruism is defined as an unselfish regard for the welfare of others.

The requirement of altruistic behavior may contradict many assumptions about business and competition. But altruism is only one characteristic of a professional, not the only characteristic. A professional is not required to entirely give away services or resources without self-regard. The professional is required to adhere to ethical standards unselfishly, to take others' needs and views into account. The welfare of others is as important as the professional's own. Altruism does not supplant the professional's own welfare, but it does balance it.

Altruism does not allow one to focus exclusively on one's own success and well-being. Altruism does facilitate the achievement of the characteristics commonly expected of a professional: competence, reliability, and high ethical standards. While altruism is an unselfish concern for others, it is clearly not without its benefits to the altruist. Demonstration of concern for others often wins great trust and reliance. However, it is the worst kind of hypocrisy to feign altruism in order to create the image of trustworthiness and reliability. The image of altruism is quite different from deeply felt altruism, and the false image will inevitably be uncovered to reveal the underlying motivations. Such deception is not worth the personal and professional cost.

The important questions facing professionals are twofold. What environment do we want to create? What environment do we want to work in? This is quite different from the question, how do we want to be perceived? The former questions are about daily choices and our expectations of others. The latter question is about image.

Insurance and financial services professionals are understandably concerned about their image in American society. But working merely to improve the image is the wrong approach. The critical issue is what these professionals are doing, not what people think they are doing. Professional respect and credibility for this field will follow professional behavior. Adherence to the highest ethical standards as elaborated here will contribute significantly toward the achievement of professional behavior and subsequently to professional respect.

THE PRACTICE OF ETHICAL DECISION MAKING

Making ethical decisions is easy when the facts are clear and the choices are evident. However, the situation is often clouded by ambiguity, incomplete information, multiple points of view, and conflicting responsibilities. In such situations—which managers experience all the time—ethical decisions depend on both the decision-making process itself and on the experience, intelligence, and integrity of the decision maker.[7]

The development of sound moral judgment requires education and practice. Moral education begins in childhood and extends throughout life. The quality of that education varies with many environmental factors. The examples from which people learn to pattern their lives range from tenderness to brutality, from consideration to greed, from fairness to bigotry. How people are affected and how those around them respond teach enduring lessons.

Accordingly the practice of ethical decision making is influenced by environmental pressures and expectations. In work organizations, these are aspects of the prevailing "organizational culture." Loyalty, for example, may be more highly valued than candor. Short-term sales performance may be more readily rewarded than superior quality service over the long term. Such rewards teach individuals what is acceptable behavior within that system. These messages may influence the moral reasoning process that is used in ethical dilemmas.

This section addresses how to make ethical decisions and how organizations can better integrate ethical decision making into daily operations. The improvement of ethical practice in the workplace must take place on both the individual and the organizational levels. Individuals are ultimately the decision makers, but they are influenced by organizational goals and pressures. Individuals often make decisions within the context of particular organizational roles that they would not make in their personal lives. Therefore it is critical to examine the organizational factors in ethical dilemmas. It is also important that individuals have a reliable method of making ethical decisions. Both the organizational and individual contributions to ethical practice will be addressed here.

Individual Decision Making

Most ethical decisions are made spontaneously by drawing on a usually reliable intuitive sense of what is right. It usually directly or indirectly reflects the values of the prevailing religion and the national culture. As decisions become more challenging due to significance or complexity, solutions are developed through thoughtful reflection. Decisions are made by examining a particular issue in light of the decision maker's personal values. Normally a frame of reference is developed and consistently employed. Examples include the following guidelines:

- Would your decision satisfy the Golden Rule?
- Would you want your decision to appear on the evening news?
- Is the decision consistent with the teaching of the (religious) faith?

Other frameworks are more elaborate but manageable. Members of Rotary International are encouraged to adopt this four-step frame of reference:

- Is it the TRUTH?
- Is it FAIR to all concerned?
- Will it build GOODWILL and BETTER FRIENDSHIPS?
- Will it be BENEFICIAL to all concerned?

Dr. Norman Vincent Peale and Ken Blanchard have developed a three-step ethics check:

1. Is it legal?
2. Is it balanced?
3. How will it make me feel about myself?[8]

Finally, Laura Nash has developed an elaborate framework for examining the ethics of a business decision, as shown in table 3-1.[9]

When confronted with a difficult ethical dilemma, it is beneficial to have a frame of reference that leads to systematic analysis. The selected method will vary in complexity and underlying values. Each person must find the approach that, when applied, leads to acceptable and dependable decisions.

Ethical Decision Making in Organizations

Organizations, it is sometimes argued, are only paper entities; they do not make policies or shape lives and careers. It is always individuals, not organizations, who make decisions and take actions.

However, when individuals take on jobs and roles in an organization, their decisions and actions are influenced by ethical codes and organizational goals. That is appropriate to a large extent. When a person is paid to do a particular job in order to meet the company's stated goals, it is reasonable to expect him or her to perform in accordance with the objectives of the position.

TABLE 3-1
Twelve Questions for Examining the Ethics of a Business Decision

1. Have you defined the problem accurately?
2. How would you define the problem if you stood on the other side of the fence?
3. How did this situation occur in the first place?
4. To whom and to what do you give your loyalty as a person and as a member of the corporation?
5. What is your intention in making this decision?
6. How does this intention compare with the probable results?
7. Whom could your decision or action injure?
8. Can you discuss the problem with the affected parties before you make your decision?
9. Are you confident that your position will be as valid over a long period of time as it seems now?
10. Could you disclose without qualm your decision or action to your boss, your CEO, the board of directors, your family, society as a whole?
11. What is the symbolic potential of your action if understood? If misunderstood?
12. Under what conditions would you allow exceptions to your stand?

Because of the influence of the organization's expectations on individual action, it is worthwhile to carefully consider the role of the organization in the ethical decision making that occurs daily. There are three critical steps to follow in analyzing and improving the level of ethical decisions within a work organization: (1) communicate clear ethical goals and standards, (2) create positive reinforcement and rewards for ethical behavior, and (3) recognize and remove barriers to good ethical decisions.

Steps Toward Ethical Decision Making in Organizations

- Communicate clear ethical goals and standards
- Create positive reinforcement and rewards for ethical behavior
- Recognize and remove barriers to good ethical decisions

Communicate Clear Ethical Goals and Standards

The first step is to communicate ethical standards. They must be practical, specific, and clear. Many corporate mission statements and ethical codes include a commitment to "the highest standards of business ethics." But what does that really mean in practice? In order to fulfill goals set forth in a mission statement, detailed operating strategies need to be established throughout all levels of the company. Broad ethical principles must be defined in more specific terms for each work environment.

There are many issues in our daily work lives that need the spotlight of ethical analysis. Here are some examples of ethical actions that might be taken in specific work situations:

- Solicit and hear constructive criticism from subordinates.
- Respond to customer complaints within 24 hours.
- Be alert to and eliminate destructive stereotypes.
- Give credit for ideas where credit is due.
- Create opportunities for growth for subordinates.
- Develop products and systems that are need-driven.

These might seem to be remarkably small issues, but it is the small daily events that affect the work environment and therefore determine how much work actually gets done daily. When a company is committed to ethical actions and standards on a daily basis, there is no question about how the company is to respond in a time of crisis. Everyone knows what the standards are because the expectations for ethical behavior have been clearly communicated by words and repeated actions.

Communicate Clear, Positive Reinforcements and Rewards for Ethical Behavior

Once specific ethical standards have been articulated, how can they be implemented? The second step is to create reinforcement and rewards for the desired behavior. A frequent concern about rewards for ethical behavior is the difficulty in measuring such behavior. However, if clear standards and expectations have been set in advance, it is not difficult to assess whether these have been achieved consistently.

A discussion of ethical issues and potential ethical conflicts in an organization's meetings will encourage individuals to raise their concerns and to share their reasoning. This step alone accomplishes small miracles in the workplace. Moral stress results in high turnover rates, while the freedom to discuss ethical issues is a major contribution to alleviating moral stress. This forum also provides the leader of the meeting with the opportunity to articulate ethical standards.

Good ethical decisions and consistent actions can be rewarded with greater access to resources and opportunities. Recognition and appreciation in either a public or private setting increase employees' awareness of the value of ethical behavior to the company.

There are numerous ways to communicate that ethical thinking is critical to the success of the organization. But if clear ethical policies are not established and adherence to them is not rewarded, no one inside or outside the company will recognize the importance of the ethical standards in daily operations.

FOCUS ON ETHICS
Professionalism Begins with Ethics

Writing with the financial services industry in mind, Dr. Ronald C. Horn, CPCU, CLU, Williams Professor of Insurance Studies at Baylor University, developed a list of seven characteristics that he considered necessary for a particular occupation to be considered a profession.[10] First on Horn's list was a commitment to high ethical standards. The complete list follows:

- a commitment to high ethical standards
- a prevailing attitude of altruism
- mandatory educational preparation and training
- mandatory continuing education
- a formal association or society
- independence
- public recognition as a profession

Compare this list with Christensen's four characteristics of a professional listed on page 65. Both lists emphasize that ethical standards are a critical component of a professional.

Recognize and Remove Barriers to Good Ethical Decisions

The third step is to observe and revise all organizational practices and systems that are inhibiting good ethical decision making. Consider such practices as wide-spread inability to talk about ethics in the workplace, a culture that values toughness over the ability to recognize and reason through moral problems, reprimands within departments for raising problems that need to be addressed, closed doors instead of open doors.

In many organizations the reward system, including the compensation system, contributes to unethical behavior because it creates pressure to shortcut ethical considerations for success. In this case, it is important to evaluate the barriers to changing those aspects of the reward system that contribute to unethical actions. Why has the system been perpetuated? Who has vested interests in the system as it exists? Have there been any attempts to change it in the past? If there are obvious ethical "costs," what are the offsetting "benefits" to continuing the system as it is?

Barriers to ethical actions may take the form of peer pressure, as is often the case in, for example, the perpetuation of discrimination. Or the barriers may exist because there are financial or other benefits accruing to managers in powerful decision-making positions, who therefore protect their interests in the current system.

Another useful aspect to consider when assessing the barriers is to ask who gets rewarded. What are the characteristics of those who are promoted in this organization? What have they done to earn promotions? What are their selling techniques? Are they straightforward and honest or manipulative and deceptive? What are the reputations of the successful people?

When one looks around and asks why individuals are not acting up to their highest moral ideals in an organization, there are often many apparent explanations. If these "justifications" for unethical actions are not addressed, the strong ethical standards articulated in the corporate mission statement or code of conduct will never be implemented.

ETHICAL ISSUES IN FINANCIAL SERVICES

It is often suggested that almost any issue potentially has ethical dimensions. Every industry has practices that warrant scrutiny from an ethical perspective. Recent events have made some of the financial services transgressions abundantly clear. Legal actions and the media interpretations of them have been significant factors in the public's diminished confidence in the financial services industry. A frequently heard explanation is that industry ethical problems can be traced to a small group of individuals who have acted improperly. So the argument continues that the overwhelming majority of industry personnel have high ethical standards. If we could just get rid of those bad apples or could identify them before they were hired, the problem would go away.

No one will argue with the bad apple theory. There *are* a few individuals in the industry who are responsible for many of the high-visibility ethical problems. The solution is not as simple as it may appear, however.

Prosecutors and regulatory agencies have made it clear that simply to punish or dismiss a few people won't solve the problem. Who hired them? Who trained them? Who provided the sales scripts and brochures? Who provided the illustration framework and recommended the variables to be inserted? Indeed, everyone must assume responsibility to restore ethical respectability.

Many regulators and consumer advocates assert that restoring ethical health to the financial services industry requires actions that span the boundaries of any single organization. They point out that this is a highly competitive industry where the successful are well compensated. This structure, left unregulated, will always have more than its share of ethical problems. The issue, this argument continues, is not one of a few bad apples or a few bad companies. It is a systemic problem that must be tightly regulated at the state or perhaps even at the federal level. If it isn't, the industry is doomed, or at the least, alternative distribution systems with different compensation scales will replace the existing one.

How can we be certain who is right? Odds are that no one argument is the complete truth, but there are two crucial things to remember. The first is the importance of providing each client with the needed financial protection. The second is that this high-quality service should be provided as efficiently as possible. The client deserves both. Today's ethical issues should be viewed for what they are—signals of imperfection and the impetus for improvement.

There have been several surveys undertaken to determine what the industry's major ethical issues are. The results vary little from one survey to the next. Count on each to include the misuse of illustrations leading to deceptive sales documents and presentations, investment churning, life insurance policy replacements, and disclosure. In addition, there are issues that cut across industry lines, such as discrimination and stereotyping.

Inappropriate Illustrations

The use of nonguaranteed and noncurrent rates as illustrations in selling interest-sensitive life insurance and other products can conflict with The American College's, the American Society's, and the CFP Board's codes of ethics as well as with standards of professionalism. Sometimes the illustrations are unrealistic. Is the nonguarantee disclosure statement adequate? Often it is not, because of the usual problems with small print. Is the client really clear about the security of the investment and its historic earnings record? Only the most honest and realistic illustrations meet the requirements of the codes of ethics and the standards of professional competence and reliability. It is often impossible to argue that the client is being given all necessary information.

If further evidence is needed to demonstrate the unethical foundation of improper illustrations, consider the long-term effects on the companies who mislead clients as to the potential return on their investments. The number and cost of problems facing companies that have consistently oversold clients is staggering.

This issue leads in nearly all the industry's ethical issues surveys. The American Society of CLU and ChFC has been a leader in helping industry personnel effectively and ethically use illustrations. An example is the life insurance illustration questionnaire (IQ), which is reproduced in appendix 3D. IQ helps agents to recognize and evaluate ethical aspects of illustrations by addressing questions from five categories: general, mortality, interest or crediting rates, expenses, and persistency. Because of the popularity of variable life insurance and the great potential for illustration abuse with that product, the American Society developed the variable life insurance illustration questionnaire (VIQ), which is reproduced in appendix 3E. VIQ addresses the same factors as IQ except that investment performance replaces interest or crediting rates. While no single approach will provide an instant solution to the illustration abuses, IQ and VIQ are welcome attempts to deal directly with an ethical problem.

Churning

Churning is the process of generating brokerage commissions through unnecessary securities transactions. Churning is associated with discretionary accounts, in which the broker can make transactions without consulting the client. The act of advising a client to make unnecessary transactions is also churning.

Selling a stock and then purchasing another stock with very similar characteristics is an example of churning. The transaction transfers wealth from the client to the broker in the form of commissions without improving the client's portfolio. Further, such transactions may create undesirable tax consequences.

The first and most important question is, Is it in the client's interest? Does this activity fulfill the requirements of professionalism: demonstrating reliability and competence and responding to a client's needs? It often fits none of these. If competent, the financial adviser or sales representative would not be changing advice every few weeks or months.

The temporary success of financial advisers who churn their clients' accounts is based on deception. The adviser induces trust in his or her ability to achieve the client's objectives. Only when this trust is given is the adviser able to persuade the client that constant sales and acquisitions are in the client's interest. In reality these actions only benefit the adviser or broker. The entire practice may be unethical for several reasons: wrongfully inducing trust, breaching that fiduciary trust, and often harming the client financially. Harming the client has long-term detrimental effects on the company and the industry as well.

Replacement and Twisting

Replacement is the process of terminating a life insurance policy and buying another. Although there are cases that are beneficial to clients, replacement in this context refers to situations in which the salesperson generates commissions by actions that work to the client's detriment. For example, the salesperson may suggest cashing in a whole life policy and replacing it with a term policy. In the short run, it may appear that the client can buy more coverage for less money while freeing up some cash. In the long run, the cost of insurance may prove to be much higher.

Since states are the primary insurance regulators, legal definitions of replacement vary considerably. Insurance agents and financial planners must abide by the laws in the appropriate jurisdiction. Still, from an ethics standpoint, the obvious question emerges: Is the new policy clearly in the client's interest? If the replacement is not absolutely in the client's best interest—and usually it isn't—the proposed action is not ethical. Use this line of reasoning. Would you be prepared to see this action become widely available and practiced by all persons? What could an organization do to create reinforcements for new sales and eliminate rewards for replacement selling?

Twisting is a form of replacement in which the agent induces the policyowner to drop an existing policy from another company through misrepresentation or incomplete information. Twisting is illegal in all states.

The American Society of CLU & ChFC has developed an extremely helpful document called *Replacement Questionnaire (RQ)—A Policy Replacement Evaluation Form,* which is reproduced in appendix 3F. Using RQ helps advisers and insurance agents recognize important issues and evaluate whether replacement is truly in the client's best interest.

Inadequate Disclosure

What information does the client need in order to make a good decision about a product or service being recommended? If the financial planner, agent, or adviser has a greater financial interest in one product than another but does not disclose that to a client, is the client misled that an unbiased presentation of each product is being given? What is the client's interest? What is truly in the professional's interest? Reliability and honesty contribute to trust. Does the client always want to know or need to know? Probably not, but the client should know by the professional's behavior that he or she can ask for and receive any information that is relevant to a decision. It is part of maintaining trust.

Discrimination and Stereotyping

In all workplaces, it is important to be alert to one's own biases and stereotypes. Are we open to hiring, training, and supporting people of different ethnic and religious backgrounds? Do we assume that some people will be more successful than others? Do we provide men and women with similar opportunities and resources? Are we aware of the effects of sexist language? Are we alert to our own assumptions about different groups of people?

The demographics of the workforce will change dramatically over the decade of the 1990s. It is projected that by the year 2000, the large majority of the entering workforce will consist of groups that are now minorities or treated as minorities: women, blacks, Hispanics, and Asians. These groups will bring different backgrounds and cultural training to many relatively homogeneous environments. These groups are still virtually invisible at the higher levels of the corporate world, giving evidence of continuing discrimination.

As has been seen from the codes of ethics, the demands of professionalism, and the method of impartial legislation, ethical judgments require the financial services professional to take into account the perspective of others, whether they are the needs and interests of the client or those of all affected persons. The professional who learns to do this should increasingly outgrow discriminatory assumptions and practices. Discrimination and stereotyping are based on ignorance, fear, and inappropriately narrow views of others different from ourselves. These practices are extremely destructive to society.

Our most significant ethical responsibility is to create an environment in which we can all survive. To achieve this, we must take actions that increase trust, meet the needs of those who have put their trust in us, and build organizational systems that encourage reliable, trustworthy, and competent behavior.

Other Issues

These five issues should not be considered a comprehensive listing of the ethical issues facing the financial services industry today. Others have suggested that any such listing should include rebating, commission design, keeping oneself informed, disclosure of all conflicts of interest, competition bashing, concealing product limitations, incompetence, and misrepresentation of one's ability to provide a service.

The ethical challenge is great. The industry demands respect, trust, integrity, and honesty. Reaching for higher ethical standards is in everyone's best interests. Likewise, it is the responsibility of every financial services employee.

NOTES

1. Michael Quint, "Images of Life Insurance Takes a Hit in a Consumer Survey," *New York Times,* September 28, 1994, p. D5.
2. *The American College Code of Ethics,* a brochure published by The American College.
3. James A. Rachels, *The Elements of Moral Philosophy* (New York: McGraw-Hill, 1986), p. 1.
4. Raymond Baumhart, "How Ethical Are Businessmen?" *Harvard Business Review,* July-August 1961, p. 7.
5. Lynn Sharp Paine, "Managing for Organizational Integrity," *Harvard Business Review,* March-April 1994, p. 111.
6. Burke A. Christensen, *Journal of the American Society of CLU & ChFC,* January 1990, p. 21.
7. Kenneth Andrews, "Ethics in Practice," *Harvard Business Review,* September-October 1989, p. 100.
8. Kenneth Blanchard and Norman Vincent Peale, *The Power of Ethical Management* (New York: Morrow, 1988), p. 27.
9. Laura Nash, "Ethics Without The Sermon," *Harvard Business Review,* November-December 1981, p. 81.
10. Ronald C. Horn, *On Professions, Professionals, and Professional Ethics* (Malvern, PA: American Institute for Property and Liability Underwriters, Inc., 1978), p. 40.

Appendix 3A

The American College Code of Ethics

Throughout the life span of The American College, education and ethics have been inextricably combined. Dr. Solomon S. Huebner, the pioneering educator who founded the College, seldom spoke of education without also speaking of ethics. To him a professional relationship between agent and client had to be based on sound ethical principles.

At the College courses and designations have changed over the years, but the ethical emphasis has remained constant and all new students enter a designation program aware that it involves more than just education.

Until recently that has been enough.

Now a new climate surrounds financial services. Institutional lines and prerogatives have become blurred. The role of those who serve the financial needs of the public has changed. Competition has increased. New products and services abound.

In this climate the College feels an imperative to be more forceful in the application of long-standing ethical principles. What was once a matter of persuasion is now a matter of requirement.

RATIONALE FOR THE CODE OF ETHICS

The College's major programs are of two distinct types. Some lead to degrees that are based solely on educational achievement and have no postgraduation ethical requirements. Those that lead to designations, however, have not only educational and experience prerequisites but also ethical requirements that continue beyond graduation and require the maintenance of ongoing standards of conduct. The display of a designation is a continuing representation that the holder will act competently and ethically in all professional relationships.

Before conferring a designation, the College has historically examined the experience as well as the educational and ethical qualifications of candidates for its designations. Unless an individual acted fraudulently to obtain a designation, no postgraduation action to remove a designation was ever taken. However, since the adoption in June 1984 of the College's Code of Ethics, the board of trustees has acted to assure postconferment fidelity to the ethical standards that accompany Huebner School designations.

THE PROFESSIONAL PLEDGE AND THE CANONS

The Code consists of two parts: the Professional Pledge and eight Canons.

The Pledge to which all Huebner School designees subscribe is: "In all my professional relationships, I pledge myself to the following rule of ethical conduct: I shall, in light of all conditions surrounding those I serve, which I shall make every conscientious effort to ascertain and understand, render that service which, in the same circumstances, I would apply to myself."

The eight Canons are:

I. Conduct yourself at all times with honor and dignity.

II. Avoid practices that would bring dishonor upon your profession or The American College.

III. Publicize your achievement in ways that enhance the integrity of your profession.

IV. Continue your studies throughout your working life so as to maintain a high level of professional competence.

V. Do your utmost to attain a distinguished record of professional service.

VI. Support the established institutions and organizations concerned with the integrity of your profession.

VII. Participate in building your profession by encouraging and providing appropriate assistance to qualified persons pursuing professional studies.

VIII. Comply with all laws and regulations, particularly as they relate to professional and business activities.

ADMINISTRATION

The certification officer of the College is empowered by the board of trustees to implement the Code by investigating complaints and reports of violations, which may originate with state commissioners of insurance, other public and judicial bodies, individuals, and established institutions or organizations. In certain instances the College itself may initiate action based on an apparent violation.

Violations that may cause the certification officer to begin an investigation include conviction of a misdemeanor or felony, suspension or revocation of a license, or suspension or revocation of membership in an established institution or organization.

Although only actions that occur after October 1, 1984 are subject to the Code, the standards established by the Code apply to students in the CLU and ChFC programs who matriculated on July 1, 1982 or later. All earlier CLU and ChFC matriculants were invited to subscribe to the Code and to accept its mandates voluntarily. Jurisdiction does not extend to pre-1982 matriculants who have not consented to be bound by the Code. The Code of Ethics also applies to students in the RHU and REBC programs who matriculated on January 1, 1996 or later.

PROCEDURES

I. Initiation of Action

The College, acting through the certification officer, investigates all alleged violations of its Code that are reported by state or federal authorities, individuals, and/or established financial services institutions or organizations.

II. The Certification Officer

A. The certification officer of the College makes a preliminary appraisal to determine whether
   1. the complaint involves a violation of the Code
   2. there is sufficient evidence for presentation to the certification committee

B. The certification officer determines the facts of the complaint by
   1. reviewing the charges with the complainant(s)
   2. relaying the complaint to the person charged and permitting him or her to respond
   3. examining all the facts that appear relevant to the complaint

C. After completing the above steps the certification officer
   1. determines whether to discontinue action or to present the case to the certification committee
   2. transmits the determination in writing to all parties involved in the complaint
   3. reviews the earlier steps if new information comes to light
   4. prepares the file and presents the complaint to the certification committee if the case so warrants

III. The Certification Committee

A. Membership. The certification committee is composed of a chairperson who must be a trustee of the College and three to five members, including one senior administrative officer of the College. (Note: The College's legal counsel may serve in an advisory role.)

B. Duties
   1. The certification committee reviews the case and requests any additional information that it considers necessary.
   2. After reviewing the case, the certification committee may either dismiss the complaint or decide that the Code has been violated and impose an appropriate sanction.
   3. The decision is conveyed in writing to all parties involved in the complaint.

C. Action. The certification committee decides to impose a sanction only by unanimous vote.

IV. Sanctions

A. The certification committee may order suspension or revocation of the right to use the CLU designation, the ChFC designation, the RHU designation, the REBC designation, or a combination of designations. The suspension or revocation notice is sent by registered mail.

B. If no appeal is received, a copy of the suspension or revocation notice is sent to the complainant(s) and made a part of the College's permanent records.

C. The College reserves the right to transmit the decision to other parties.

V. Appeals

A. A suspension or revocation may be appealed by notifying the certification committee chairperson in writing within 30 days of receiving the suspension or revocation notice.

B. When an appeal is received, the chairperson of the certification committee notifies the chairman of the board of trustees, who appoints a hearing committee composed of no fewer than three members who may be trustees but not College staff members. The members may have no prior connection with the case or with any company with which the appellant has been associated.

C. The certification officer or a member of the certification committee who voted the sanction presents the case and may answer questions but may not participate in the deliberations.

D. The appellant may present his or her position, call witnesses, and point to the alleged errors in the decision.

E. If the appellant is represented by counsel, the hearing committee must also be so represented. Counsel to the committee may be present to clarify issues even if the appellant is not represented.

F. A recorder who is not a member of the hearing committee keeps minutes of the proceedings.

G. The hearing committee sets the rules for conduct of the hearing.

H. A majority vote based on information provided during the hearing is required and is final and binding on the College and the appellant.

I. The decision and statement of reasons for the decision is sent by the hearing committee chairperson to the College. The certification officer notifies the appellant and the complainant(s) of the committee's decision by registered mail within 15 days of the hearing.

J. The College reserves the right to convey the decision to other parties.

Appendix 3B

The American Society of CLU & ChFC Code of Ethics

Men and women who have chosen to enter into membership in the American Society voluntarily bind themselves to the Code of Ethics of their professional organization.

The purpose of the Code is to give further force to the Pledge taken by all holders of the CLU and ChFC designations and to provide a series of standards by which those involved in providing insurance and financial planning and economic security may conduct themselves in a professional manner. The Code is founded upon the two ethical imperatives of competent advice and service to the client and enhancement of the public regard for the CLU and ChFC designations.

Competent advice and service to the client is at the very essence of any professional calling. Enhancement of the public regard for professional designations gives voice to the concept that in accepting Society membership, an obligation is also accepted to all other holders of similar and allied professional designations and degrees.

In its design, the Code presents the two ethical Imperatives, supported by Guides which give specificity to the Imperatives and interpretive comment which is intended to aid in a uniform understanding of the Guides.

A violation of the Code would expose a member to sanctions which range from reprimand to revocation of membership in the American Society. A member is in violation of the Code when a final judgment is made that the member has breached an ethical imperative through failure to adhere to one or more of the Guides.

For ease of drafting and reading, the masculine gender and singular number have been used. When appropriate, masculine is to be read as feminine and singular as plural. The word "client" is used under the First Imperative since standards concerning advice and service have greatest applicability to the relationship of client to professional insurance and financial services practitioner.

FIRST IMPERATIVE:

To competently advise and serve the client . . .

Guide 1.1:

A member shall provide advice and service which are in the client's best interest.

Interpretive Comment.

A. A member possessing a specific body of knowledge which is not possessed by the general public has an obligation to use that knowledge for the benefit of the client and to avoid taking advantage of that knowledge to the detriment of the client.

B. In a conflict of interest situation the interest of the client must be paramount.

C. The member must make a conscientious effort to ascertain and to understand all relevant circumstances surrounding the client.

D. A member is to accord due courtesy and consideration to those engaged in related professions who are also serving the client.

E. A member is to give due regard to any agent-principal relationship which may exist between the member and such companies as he may represent.

Guide 1.2:

A member shall respect the confidential relationship existing between client and member.

Interpretive Comment.

A. Competent advice and service may necessitate the client sharing personal and confidential information with the member. Such information is to be held in confidence by the member unless released from the obligation by the client.

Guide 1.3:

A member shall continue his education throughout his professional life.

Interpretive Comment.

A. To advise and serve competently, a member must continue to maintain and to improve his professional abilities.

B. Continuing Education includes both the member adding to his knowledge of the practice of his profession; and, the member keeping abreast of changing economic and legislative conditions which may affect the financial plans of the insuring public.

C. A member may continue his education through formal or informal programs of study or through other professional experiences.

Guide 1.4:
A member shall render continuing advice and service.
Interpretive Comment.

A. Advice and service, to be competent, must be ongoing as the client's circumstances change and as these changes are made known to the member.
B. A client with whom a member has an active professional relationship is to be informed of economic and legislative changes which relate to the client-member relationship.

SECOND IMPERATIVE:
To enhance the public regard for professional designations and allied professional degrees held by members . . .

Guide 2.1:
A member shall obey all laws governing his business or professional activities.
Interpretive Comment.

A. Business activities are non-personal activities carried on outside the life insurance community; professional activities are non-personal activities carried on within the life insurance community.
B. A member has a legal obligation to obey all laws applicable to his business and professional activities. The placement of this Guide within the Code raises this obligation to the level of an ethical obligation.

Guide 2.2
A member shall avoid activities which detract from the integrity and professionalism of the Chartered Life Underwriter designation, the Chartered Financial Consultant designation, or any other allied professional degree or designation held by members.
Interpretive Comment.

A. Personal, business, and professional activities are encompassed within the scope of this Guide.
B. Activities which could present a violation of this Guide might include:
   (1) A member's failure to obey a law unrelated to the member's business or professional activities.
   (2) A member impairing the reputation of another practitioner.
   (3) A member unfairly competing with another practitioner.
   (4) Actions which result in the member discrediting his own reputation.
   (5) A member discrediting life underwriting as a profession, the institution of life insurance or the American Society of CLU & ChFC.
   (6) A member advertising the Chartered Life Underwriter or Chartered Financial Consultant designation or membership in the American

Society in an undignified manner, or in a manner prohibited by the Bylaws of the American Society.

Guide 2.3:
A member shall encourage others to attain the Chartered Life Underwriter and/or the Chartered Financial Consultant designations.
Interpretive Comment.

A. Enhancement of the public regard for the CLU and ChFC designations depends upon a continuing increase in the number of holders of the designations who are available to advise and serve the public.
B. Encouraging others who might be qualified to enter into a practice is one hallmark of a professional.

Guide 2.4:
A member shall avoid using the Chartered Life Underwriter or Chartered Financial Consultant designation in a false or misleading manner.
Interpretive Comment.

A. The CLU and ChFC designations are granted by the American College to specified individuals. Acts which directly or indirectly extend the member's personal designation to others would present a violation of this Guide.
B. Chartered Life Underwriter (CLU) or Chartered Financial Consultant (ChFC) may not be used in a name of a business in a manner which would reasonably lead others to conclude that someone other than the named member held the designation. Example:
   (1) John Jones, CLU & Associates is permissible.
   (2) John Jones & Associates, Chartered Financial Consultants is not permissible.

Appendix 3C

Certified Financial Planner Code of Ethics and Professional Responsibility*

CONTENTS **Page**

CODE OF ETHICS AND PROFESSIONAL RESPONSIBILITY

PREAMBLE AND APPLICABILITY

The *Code of Ethics and Professional Responsibility* (Code) has been adopted by the Certified Financial Planner Board of Standards, Inc. (CFP Board) to provide principles and rules to all persons whom it has recognized and certified to use the CFP certification mark and the marks CFP and Certified Financial Planner (collectively "the marks"). The CFP Board determines who is recognized and certified to use the marks. Implicit in the acceptance of this authorization is an obligation not only to comply with the mandates and requirements of all applicable laws and regulations but also to take responsibility to act in an ethical and professionally responsible manner in all professional services and activities.

For purposes of this Code, a person recognized and certified by the CFP Board to use the marks is called a CFP designee or Certified Financial Planner designee. This Code applies to CFP designees actively involved in the practice of personal financial planning, in other areas of financial services, in industry, in related professions, in government, in education, or in any other professional activity in which the marks are used in the performance of their professional responsibilities. This Code also applies to candidates for the CFP designation who are registered as such with the CFP Board. For purposes of this Code, the term CFP designee shall be deemed to include candidates.

COMPOSITION AND SCOPE

The Code consists of two parts: **Part I—Principles** and **Part II—Rules.** The Principles are statements expressing in general terms the ethical and professional ideals expected of CFP designees and which they should strive to display in their professional activities. As such the Principles are aspirational in character but are intended to provide a source of guidance for a CFP designee. The comments following each Principle further explain the meaning of the Principle. The Rules provide practical guidelines derived from the tenets embodied in the Principles. As such, the Rules set forth the standards of ethical and professionally responsible conduct expected to be followed in particular situations. This Code does not undertake to define standards of professional conduct of CFP designees for purposes of civil liability.

Due to the nature of a CFP designee's particular field of endeavor, certain Rules may not be applicable to that CFP designee's activities. For example, a CFP designee who is engaged solely in the sale of securities as a registered representative is not subject to the written disclosure requirements of Rule 402 (applicable to CFP designees engaged in personal financial planning) although he or she may have disclosure responsibilities under Rule 401. A CFP designee is obligated to determine what responsibilities the CFP designee has in each professional relationship including, for example, duties that arise in particular circumstances from a position of trust or confidence that a CFP designee may have. The CFP designee is obligated to meet those responsibilities.

The Code is structured so that the presentation of the Rules parallels the presentation of the Principles. For example, the Rules which relate to Principle 1—Integrity, are numbered in the 100 to 199 series while those Rules relating to Principle 2—Objectivity, are numbered in the 200 to 299 series.

COMPLIANCE

The CFP Board of Governors requires adherence to this Code by all those it recognizes and certifies to use the marks. Compliance with the Code, individually and by the profession as a whole, depends on each CFP designee's knowledge of and voluntary compliance with the Principles and applicable Rules, on the influence of fellow professionals and public opinion, and on disciplinary proceedings, when necessary, involving CFP designees who fail to comply with the applicable provisions of the Code.

TERMINOLOGY IN THIS CODE

Client denotes a person, persons, or entity for whom professional services are rendered. Where the services of the practitioner are provided to an entity (corporation, trust, partnership, estate, etc.), the client is the entity, acting through its legally authorized representative.

Commission denotes the compensation received by an agent or broker when the same is calculated as a percentage on the amount of his or her sales or purchase transactions.

Conflict(s) of interest denotes circumstances, relationships or other facts about the CFP designee's own financial, business, property and/or personal interests which will or reasonably may impair the CFP designee's rendering of disinterested advice, recommendations or services.

Fee-only denotes a method of compensation in which compensation is received solely from a client with neither the personal financial planning practitioner nor any related party receiving compensation which is contingent upon the purchase or sale of any financial product. A *related party* for this purpose shall mean an individual or entity from whom any direct or indirect economic benefit is derived by the personal financial planning practitioner as a result of implementing a recommendation made by the personal financial planning practitioner.

Personal financial planning or **financial planning** denotes the process of determining whether and how an individual can meet life goals through the proper management of financial resources.

Personal financial planning process or **financial planning process** denotes the process which typically includes, but is not limited to, the six elements of data gathering, goal setting, identification of financial issues, preparation of alternatives and recommendations, implementation of client decisions from among the alternatives, and periodic review and revision of the plan.

Personal financial planning subject areas or **financial planning subject areas** denotes the basic subject fields covered in the financial planning process which typically include, but are not limited to, financial statement preparation and analysis (including cash flow analysis/planning and budgeting), investment planning (including portfolio design, i.e., asset allocation, and portfolio management), income tax planning, education planning, risk management, retirement planning, and estate planning.

Personal financial planning professional or **financial planning professional** denotes a person who is capable and qualified to offer objective, integrated, and comprehensive financial advice to or for the benefit of individuals to help them achieve their financial objectives. A financial planning professional must have the ability to provide financial planning services to clients, using the financial planning process covering the basic financial planning subjects.

Personal financial planning practitioner or **financial planning practitioner** denotes a person who is capable and qualified to offer objective, integrated, and comprehensive financial advice to or for the benefit of clients to help them achieve their fianncial objectives and who engage in financial planning using the financial planning process in working with clients.

PART I—PRINCIPLES

Introduction

These Principles of the Code express the profession's recognition of its responsibilities to the public, to clients, to colleagues, and to employers. They apply to all CFP designees and provide guidance to them in the performance of their professional services.

Principle 1 — Integrity

A CFP designee shall offer and provide professional services with integrity.

As discussed on Composition and Scope, CFP designees may be placed by clients in positions of trust and confidence. The ultimate source of such public trust is the CFP designee's personal integrity. In deciding what is right and just, a CFP designee should rely on his or her integrity as the appropriate touchstone. Integrity demands honesty and candor which must not be subordinated to personal gain and advantage. Within the characteristic of integrity, allowance can be made for innocent error and legitimate difference of opinion; but integrity cannot co-exist with deceit or subordination of one's principles. Integrity requires a CFP designee to observe not only the letter but also the spirit of this Code.

Principle 2 — Objectivity

A CFP designee shall be objective in providing professional services to clients.

Objectivity requires intellectual honesty and impartiality. It is an essential quality for any professional. Regardless of the particular service rendered or the capacity in which a CFP designee functions, a CFP designee should protect the integrity of his or her work, maintain objectivity, and avoid subordination of his or her judgment that would be in violation of this Code.

Principle 3 — Competence

A CFP designee shall provide services to clients competently and maintain the necessary knowledge and skill to continue to do so in those areas in which the designee is engaged.

One is competent only when he or she has attained and maintained an adequate level of knowledge and skill, and applies that knowledge effectively in providing services to clients. Competence also includes the wisdom to recognize the limitations of that knowledge and when consultation or client referral is appropriate. A CFP designee, by virtue of having earned the CFP designation, is deemed to be qualified to practice financial planning. However, in addition to assimilating the common body of knowledge required and acquiring the necessary experience for designation, a CFP designee shall make a continuing commitment to learning and professional improvement.

Principle 4 — Fairness

A CFP designee shall perform professional services in a manner that is fair and reasonable to clients, principals, partners, and employers and shall disclose conflict(s) of interest in providing such services.

Fairness requires impartiality, intellectual honesty, and disclosure of conflict(s) of interest It involves a subordination of one's own feelings, prejudices, and desires so as to achieve a proper balance of conflicting interests. Fairness is treating others in the same fashion that you would want to be treated and is an essential trait of any professional.

Principle 5 — Confidentiality

A CFP designee shall not disclose any confidential client information without the specific consent of the client unless in response to proper legal process, to defend against charges of wrongdoing by the CFP designee or in connection with a civil dispute between the CFP designee and client.

A client, by seeking the services of a CFP designee, may be interested in creating a relationship of personal trust and confidence with the CFP designee. This type of relationship can only be built upon the understanding that information supplied to the CFP designee or other information will be confidential. In order to provide the contemplated services effectively and to protect the client's privacy, the CFP designee shall safeguard the confidentiality of such information.

Principle 6 — Professionalism

A CFP designee's conduct in all matters shall reflect credit upon the profession.

Because of the importance of the professional services rendered by CFP designees, there are attendant responsibilities to behave with dignity and courtesy to all those who use those services, fellow professionals, and those in related professions. A CFP designee also has an obligation to cooperate with fellow CFP designees to enhance and maintain the profession's public image and to work jointly with other CFP designees to improve the quality of services. It is only through the combined efforts of all CFP designees in cooperation with other professionals that this vision can be realized.

Principle 7 — Diligence

A CFP designee shall act diligently in providing professional services.

Diligence is the provision of services in a reasonably prompt and thorough manner. Diligence also includes proper planning for and supervision of the rendering of professional services.

PART II — RULES

Introduction

As stated in **Part I — Principles,** the Principles apply to all CFP designees. However, due to the nature of a CFP designee's particular field of endeavor, certain Rules may not be applicable to that CFP designee's activities. The universe of activities performed by CFP designees is indeed diverse and a particular CFP designee may be performing all, some or none of the typical services provided by financial planning professionals. As a result, in considering the Rules in Part II, a CFP designee must first recognize what specific services he or she is rendering and then determine whether or not a specific Rule is applicable to those services. To assist the CFP designee in making these determinations, this Code includes a series of definitions of terminology used throughout the Code. Based upon these definitions, a CFP designee should be able to determine which services he or she provides and, therefore, which Rules are applicable to those services.

Rules That Relate to the Principle of Integrity

Rule 101

A CFP designee shall not solicit clients through false or misleading communications or advertisements:

(a) *Misleading Advertising:* A CFP designee shall not make a false or misleading communication about the size, scope or areas of competence of the CFP designee's practice or of any organization with which the CFP designee is associated; and

(b) *Promotional Activities:* In promotional activities, a CFP designee shall not make materially false or misleading communications to the public or create unjustified expectations regarding matters relating to financial planning or the professional activities and competence of the CFP designee. The term "promotional activities" includes, but is not limited to, speeches, interviews, books and/or printed publications, seminars, radio and television shows, and video cassettes; and

(c) *Representation of Authority:* A CFP designee shall not give the impression that a CFP designee is representing the views of the CFP Board or any other group unless the CFP designee has been authorized to do so. Personal opinions shall be clearly identified as such.

Rule 102

In the course of professional activities, a CFP designee shall not engage in conduct involving dishonesty, fraud, deceit or misrepresentation, or knowingly make a false or misleading statement to a client, employer, employee, professional colleague, governmental or other regulatory body or official, or any other person or entity.

Rule 103

A CFP designee has the following responsibilities regarding funds and/or other property of clients:

(a) In exercising custody of or discretionary authority over client funds or other property, a CFP designee shall act only in accordance with the authority set forth in the governing legal instrument (e.g., special power of attorney, trust, letters testamentary, etc.); and
(b) A CFP designee shall identify and keep complete records of all funds or other property of a client in the custody of or under the discretionary authority of the CFP designee; and
(c) Upon receiving funds or other property of a client, a CFP designee shall promptly or as otherwise permitted by law or provided by agreement with the client, deliver to the client or third party any funds or other property which the client or third party is entitled to receive and, upon request by the client, render a full accounting regarding such funds or other property; and
(d) A CFP designee shall not commingle client funds or other property with a CFP designee's personal funds and/or other property or the funds and/or other property of a CFP designee's firm. Commingling one or more clients' funds or other property together is permitted, subject to compliance with applicable legal requirements and provided accurate records are maintained for each client's funds or other property; and
(e) A CFP designee who takes custody of all or any part of a client's assets for investment purposes, shall do so with the care required of a fiduciary.

Rules That Relate to the Principle of Objectivity

Rule 201

A CFP designee shall exercise reasonable and prudent professional judgment in providing professional services.

Rule 202

A financial planning practitioner shall act in the interest of the client.

Rules That Relate to the Principle of Competence

Rule 301

A CFP designee shall keep informed of developments in the field of financial planning and participate in continuing education throughout the CFP designee's professional career in order to improve professional competence in all areas in which the CFP designee is engaged. As a distinct part of this requirement, a CFP designee shall satisfy all minimum continuing education requirements established for CFP designees by the CFP Board.

Rule 302

A CFP designee shall offer advice only in those areas in which the CFP designee has competence. In areas where the CFP designee is not professionally competent, the CFP designee shall seek the counsel of qualified individuals and/or refer clients to such parties.

Rules That Relate to the Principle of Fairness

Rule 401

In rendering professional services, a CFP designee shall disclose to the client:

(a) Material information relevant to the professional relationship, including but not limited to conflict(s) of interest; changes in the CFP designee's business affiliation, address, telephone number, credentials, qualifications, licenses, compensation structure, and any agency relationships, and the scope of the CFP designee's authority in that capacity.
(b) The information required by all laws applicable to the relationship in a manner complying with such laws.

Rule 402

A financial planning practitioner shall make timely written disclosure of all material information relative to the professional relationship. In all circumstances such disclosure shall include conflict(s) of interest and sources of compensation. Written disclosures that include the following information are considered to be in compliance with this Rule:

(a) A statement of the basic philosophy of the CFP designee (or firm) in working with clients. The disclosure shall include the philosophy, theory and/or principles of financial planning which will be utilized by the CFP designee; and
(b) Resumes of principals and employees of a firm who are expected to provide financial planning services to the client and a description of those services. Such disclosures shall include educational background, professional/employment history, professional designations and licenses held, and areas of competence and specialization; and
(c) A statement of compensation, which in reasonable detail discloses the source(s) and any contingencies or other aspects material to the fee and/or commission arrangement. Any estimates made shall be clearly identified as such and shall be based on reasonable assumptions. Referral fees, if any, shall be fully disclosed; and
(d) A statement indicating whether the CFP designee's compensation arrangements are fee-only, commission-only, or fee and commission. A CFP designee shall not hold out as a fee-only financial planning practitioner if the CFP designee receives commissions or other forms of economic benefit from related parties; and
(e) A statement describing material agency or employment relationships a CFP designee (or firm) has with third parties and the fees or commissions resulting from such relationships; and
(f) A statement identifying conflict(s) of interest.

Rule 403

A CFP designee providing financial planning shall disclose in writing, prior to establishing a client relationship, relationships which reasonably may compromise the CFP designee's objectivity or independence.

Rule 404

Should conflict(s) of interest develop after a professional relationship has been commenced, but before the services contemplated by that relationship have been completed, a CFP designee shall promptly disclose the conflict(s) of interest to the client or other necessary persons.

Rule 405

In addition to the disclosure by financial planning practitioners regarding sources of compensation required under Rule 402, such disclosure shall be made annually thereafter for ongoing clients. The annual disclosure requirement may be satisfied by offering to provide clients with the current copy of SEC form ADV, Part II or the disclosure called for by Rule 402.

Rule 406

A CFP designee's compensation shall be fair and reasonable.

Rule 407

Prior to establishing a client relationship, and consistent with the confidentiality requirements of Rule 501, a CFP designee may provide references which may include recommendations from present and/or former clients.

Rule 408

When acting as an agent for a principal, a CFP designee shall ensure that the scope of his or her authority is clearly defined and properly documented.

Rule 409

Whether a CFP designee is employed by a financial planning firm, an investment institution, or serves as an agent for such an organization, or is self-employed, all CFP designees shall adhere to the same standards of disclosure and service.

Rule 410

A CFP designee who is an employee shall perform professional services with dedication to the lawful objectives of the employer and in accordance with this Code.

Rule 411

A CFP designee shall:

(a) Advise the CFP designee's employer of outside affiliations which reasonably may compromise service to an employer, and

(b) Provide timely notice to the employer and clients, unless precluded by contractual obligation, in the event of change of employment or CFP Board licensing status.

Rule 412

A CFP designee doing business as a partner or principal of a financial services firm owes to the CFP designee's partners or co-owners a responsibility to act in good faith. This includes, but is not limited to, disclosure of relevant and material financial information while in business together.

Rule 413

A CFP designee shall join a financial planning firm as a partner or principal only on the basis of mutual disclosure of relevant and material information regarding credentials, competence, experience, licensing and/or legal status, and financial stability of the parties involved.

Rule 414

A CFP designee who is a partner or co-owner of a financial services firm who elects to withdraw from the firm shall do so in compliance with any applicable agreement, and shall deal with his or her business interest in a fair and equitable manner.

Rule 415

A CFP designee shall inform his or her employer, partners or co-owners of compensation or other benefit arrangements in connection with his or her services to clients which are in addition to compensation from the employer, partners or co-owners for such services.

Rule 416

If a CFP designee enters into a business transaction with a client, the transaction shall be on terms which are fair and reasonable to the client and the CFP designee shall disclose the risks of the transaction, conflict(s) of interest of the CFP designee, and other relevant information, if any, necessary to make the transaction fair to the client.

Rules That Relate to the Principle of Confidentiality

Rule 501

A CFP designee shall not reveal—or use for his or her own benefit—without the client's consent, any personally identifiable information relating to the client relationship or the affairs of the client, except and to the extent disclosure or use is reasonably necessary:

(a) To establish an advisory or brokerage account, to effect a transaction for the client, or as otherwise impliedly authorized in order to carry out the client engagement; or
(b) To comply with legal requirements or legal process; or
(c) To defend the CFP designee against charges of wrongdoing; or
(d) In connection with a civil dispute between the CFP designee and the client.

For purposes of this rule, the proscribed use of client information is improper whether or not it actually causes harm to the client.

Rule 502

A CFP designee shall maintain the same standards of confidentiality to employers as to clients.

Rule 503

A CFP designee doing business as a partner or principal of a financial services firm owes to the CFP designee's partners or co-owners a responsibility to act in good faith. This includes, but it not limited to, adherence to reasonable expectations of confidentiality both while in business together and thereafter.

Rules That Relate to the Principle of Professionalism

Rule 601

A CFP designee shall use the marks in compliance with the rules and regulations of the CFP Board, as established and amended from time to time.

Rule 602

A CFP designee shall show respect for other financial planning professionals, and related occupational groups, by engaging in fair and honorable competitive practices. Collegiality among CFP designees shall not, however, impede enforcement of this Code.

Rule 603

A CFP designee who has knowledge, which is not required to be kept confidential under this Code, that another CFP designee has committed a violation of this Code which raises substantial questions as to the designee's honesty, trustworthiness or fitness as a CFP designee in other respects, shall promptly inform the CFP Board. This rule does not require disclosure of information or reporting based on knowledge gained as a consultant or expert witness in anticipation of or related to litigation or other dispute resolution mechanisms. For purposes of this rule, knowledge means no substantial doubt.

Rule 604

A CFP designee who has knowledge, which is not required under this Code to be kept confidential, and which raises a substantial question of unprofessional, fraudulent or illegal conduct by a CFP designee or other financial professional, shall promptly inform the appropriate regulatory and/or professional disciplinary body. This rule does not require disclosure or reporting of information gained as a consultant or expert witness in anticipation of or related to litigation or other dispute resolution mechanisms. For purposes of this Rule, knowledge means no substantial doubt.

Rule 605

A CFP designee who has reason to suspect illegal conduct within the CFP designee's organization shall make timely disclosure of the available evidence to the CFP designee's immediate supervisor and/or partners or co-owners. If the CFP designee is convinced that illegal conduct exists within the CFP designee's organization, and appropriate measures are not taken to remedy the situation, the CFP designee shall, where appropriate, alert the appropriate regulatory authorities including the CFP Board in a timely manner.

Rule 606

In all professional activities, a CFP designee shall perform services in accordance with:

(a) Applicable laws, rules, and regulations of governmental agencies and other applicable authorities; and
(b) Applicable rules, regulations, and other established policies of the CFP Board.

Rule 607

A CFP designee shall not engage in any conduct which reflects adversely on his or her integrity or fitness as a CFP designee, upon the marks, or upon the profession.

Rule 608

The Investment Advisers Act of 1940 requires registration of investment advisers with the U.S. Securities and Exchange Commission and similar state statutes may require registration with state securities agencies. CFP designees shall disclose to clients their firm's status as registered investment advisers. Under present standards of acceptable business conduct, it is proper to use registered investment adviser if the CFP designee is registered individually. If the CFP designee is registered through his or her firm, then the CFP designee is not a registered investment adviser but a person associated with an investment adviser. The firm is the registered investment adviser. Moreover, RIA or R.I.A. following a CFP designee's name in advertising, letterhead stationery, and business cards may be misleading and is not permitted either by this Code or by SEC regulations.

Rule 609

A CFP designee shall not practice any other profession or offer to provide such services unless the CFP designee is qualified to practice in those fields and is licensed as required by state law.

Rule 610

A CFP designee shall return the client's original records in a timely manner after their return has been requested by a client.

Rule 611

A CFP designee shall not bring or threaten to bring a disciplinary proceeding under this Code, or report or threaten to report information to the CFP Board pursuant to Rules 603 and/or 604, or make or threaten to make use of this Code for no substantial purpose other than to harass, maliciously injure, embarrass and/or unfairly burden another CFP designee.

Rule 612

A CFP designee shall comply with all applicable post-certification requirements established by the CFP Board including, but not limited to, payment of the annual CFP designee fee as well as signing and returning the Licensee's Statement annually in connection with the license renewal process.

Rules That Relate to the Principle of Diligence

Rule 701

A CFP designee shall provide services diligently.

Rule 702

A financial planning practitioner shall enter into an engagement only after securing sufficient information to satisfy the CFP designee that:

(a) The relationship is warranted by the individual's needs and objectives; and
(b) The CFP designee has the ability to either provide requisite competent services or to involve other professionals who can provide such services.

Rule 703

A financial planning practitioner shall make and/or implement only recommendations which are suitable for the client.

Rule 704

Consistent with the nature and scope of the engagement, a CFP designee shall make a reasonable investigation regarding the financial products recommended to clients. Such an investigation may be made by the CFP designee or by others provided the CFP designee acts reasonably in relying upon such investigation.

Rule 705

A CFP designee shall properly supervise subordinates with regard to their delivery of financial planning services, and shall not accept or condone conduct in violation of this Code.

Questions and Answers: Life Insurance Illustration Questionnaire (IQ)

What is the IQ?

Developed by the American Society of CLU & ChFC, the Life Insurance Illustration Questionnaire (IQ) is a set of 27 informational questions for response by insurance companies. The IQ is intended to help educate insurance agents on the methodology used by companies to generate life insurance proposals, better known as "sales illustrations." The current version of the IQ is dated 4/96 and includes several new questions as well as language introduced by new illustration regulations. The new format will indicate the policy(ies) covered by the company's response, as well as the date the IQ response was last prepared.

Why was the IQ developed?

The IQ was developed to assist insurance agents obtain the information they need to better understand and evaluate how the non-guaranteed and fluctuating risk elements of a life insurance policy can affect future performance. In today's rapidly changing world, it is critical for agents to understand and be able to explain to their clients how changes in interest rates, investment gains, mortality, persistency and expenses can affect the future performance of a life insurance policy. It is much easier to assist the client in forming appropriate long-term expectations regarding policy performance with a knowledge of these non-guaranteed assumptions.

Isn't a sales illustration based on the policy itself?

Yes. Individual states require that policy illustrations be based on current assumptions. This means that illustrations include more than just the underlying guaranteed policy values. They also include projections of non-guaranteed benefits and values which assume that current assumptions will continue into the future. Thus, an illustration is merely an insurance company's estimate of how an insurance policy might perform over time if a given set of assumptions as to interest rates earned on premium deposits, mortality experience and expense costs were to occur exactly as projected. Since the potential for future performance to exactly match all current assumptions is low, it is safe to say that the sales illustration will never accurately portray the policy's actual performance.

Where do illustrations come from?

There are a variety of sources for illustrations. They may be prepared by the insurance company in response to an agent's request. These usually contain a disclaimer noting the "figures presented are only illustrations and are not promises or guarantees." Still others are prepared using software created by independent vendors who have incorporated the issuing company's information into their system. Illustrations are also prepared on the insurance agent's computer, in which case it may have no direct relationship to the insurance company.

Regardless of how the illustration is prepared, it is still only an estimate of future performance, which in turn is based on static assumptions which are mathematically projected as many as 50 years into the future. Obviously, then, an illustration cannot be any more accurate than the assumptions on which it is based.

Do illustrations have any benefit?

Yes. Even though the numbers cannot predict actual policy performance, they do serve a vital function. Illustrations can be useful in developing the best combination of policy specifications to achieve the insurance buyer's objective. For any given "what if?" considerations on behalf of a client, an illustration can show varying projections of future cash values and death benefits, the possible use and magnitude of projected dividends, and the potential number of premiums that might have to be paid by the policy owner before policy values themselves might support required premiums.

Specifically, the insurance buyer can learn more about how the policy works by examining benefits under alternative illustrations that project a non-participating policy's potential for higher and lower interest rates and higher and lower mortality expenses (or higher and lower dividend scales in the case of a participating policy). Though not exact and not guaranteed, these projections are of benefit to the insurance buyer because they demonstrate that policy values *will* fluctuate and vary from that which was originally illustrated at the time of purchase. Illustrations also show how various policy features can be used to come up with a range of potential benefits and costs. However, it is important to bear in mind that while illustrations may help in the decision making process, they simply do not contain sufficient information for the purpose of choosing *which* of two or more policies under consideration should be purchased.

How is the "IQ" useful to clients?

The IQ enables agents to learn more about the internal assumptions which ultimately control policy (versus illustration) performance. After an in-depth examination of the inner workings of a life insurance policy, the life insurance professional will have a much better understanding and greater knowledge of what goes into an "illustration."

This understanding of where the figures come from and what they actually represent will enable agents to better communicate the risks as well as the benefits of a life insurance contract to their clients. Agents can provide clients with details on the guaranteed and non-guaranteed elements inherent in the policy. This information will help avoid disappointment in years to come.

Was the "IQ" designed to disclose pricing information?

No. The IQ does not seek non-public, proprietary pricing information about an insurance company or its products. Furthermore, it does not seek numerical responses of any kind about any aspect of an insurance company's practices. In fact, much of the information sought by the IQ is already answerable from information made public by the insurance companies in their responses to various state regulatory filings (e.g., Schedule M). The IQ is designed to reorganize this otherwise public information for disclosure and presentation to agents. Perhaps the IQ's greatest benefit is that it opens up a significant line of inquiry, education, and dialogue between the life insurance professional and her or his insurance company.

The IQ is intended to facilitate better communications between insurance companies and insurance agents. It was not designed to be used directly with the client at the point of sale. Knowledge obtained through a careful reading of an IQ response does not enable the agent to produce a more accurate illustration.

In order to reinforce the educational value of the IQ and to confirm the important relationship between companies and their agents, the Society does not accumulate company responses for reproduction or dissemination.

Can illustrations be misleading?

When life insurance sales illustrations appear to promise future financial performance levels that are unrealistically higher than those guaranteed by the underlying insurance policy contract itself, clients can be misled if they are not aware of the assumption basis of the illustration and the risks attendant with "too good to be true" illustration values.

Can misleading illustrations be avoided?

Misleading illustrations can be avoided when insurance professionals explain that ultimate policy performance is not influenced by a "sales illustration." but by actual experience as it materializes over many years.

Company as well as policy performance is based on the following non-guaranteed risk elements:

- Mortality experience
- Investment performance
- Policy lapse rates
- Expenses

These four factors are available for comparison through such insurance industry resources as *Best's Life Reports* and *Standard & Poor's Insurance Rating Service.* They are often available at public libraries or from insurance companies.

Word of caution: A company's past experience may not be an accurate guide as to what will happen in the future and focusing on results from just one or a select number of years could suggest an outcome different from ultimate performance.

How does the "IQ" help agents get information?

Rather than searching through many sources for difficult to obtain information, the IQ allows agents to review responses from companies that have completed the IQ Questionnaire. The IQ covers such topics as the company's method of crediting earnings on investments to policies. Also, it includes questions on whether the company assumes any changes in mortality experience, and if so, what are the changes. In addition, it reviews the methods used in assessing expenses (including but not limited to investment expenses, taxes and administration.

Since the answers will often contain complicated actuarial information, the American Society has developed an educational component for agents as part of the IQ Program. Video tapes and local tutorials are available to Society members as well as members of the financial services industry and allied professionals who can benefit from learning more about how to interpret the Illustration Questionnaire. Local Society Chapters are typically the best source of IQ educational material.

How does pending state regulation of illustrations affect the IQ?

Illustration regulations will be passed by many states in 1996 with an anticipated effective date of January 1, 1997. These regulations will compel life insurance companies to illustrate policies under a set of guidelines and rules that are significantly more controlled than for policies issued before the effective date of the regulations. Among the most significant changes is a requirement that carriers annually certify that post-regulation policies continue to meet stringent supportability tests.

The role of the IQ is to educate the agent about the assumptions which underlie the illustration of non-guaranteed elements in the policies they sell. While it would seem that a "regulated and certified" policy illustration would provide renewed confidence and accurate illustrated values, certification depends on the improbability that assumptions can accurately be forecast into an uncertain future. Agents will need to remind their clients of this reality, and the IQ continues to be an ideal educational forum for that purpose.

How many companies have responded to the IQ?

As of June , 1996, the American Society is aware of 99 companies that have published their responses to the IQ. As agents and their clients have become aware of and seek answers to the IQ, more companies are providing responses.

Will the American Society publish IQ responses?

No, the American Society's purpose is to assure the continuing education and professionalism of its members. The Society will not collect, publish nor distribute responses from companies that have answered the IQ, although a listing is available of the companies known to the Society to have published an IQ response. For those interested in a particular company's response to the IQ questionnaire, contact the company directly. If the company is not listed in the area phone directory, contact the local public library and ask for *Best's Life Reports. Best's* includes a listing of the major insurance company's headquarters with their address and phone number.

Introduction to the Life Insurance Illustration Questionnaire (IQ)

The Life Insurance Illustration Questionnaire (IQ) is an educational tool; its use by companies or agents is entirely voluntary.

The purpose of the IQ is to help the reader understand the different non-guaranteed performance assumptions which insurance companies use to design and create sales illustrations. The IQ may be particularly useful to agents, their clients (under the agent's guidance) and the clients' other advisors.

It has been developed for non-SEC regulated products. The reader should understand that sales illustrations are useful in developing the best combination of policy specifications to achieve the buyer's objective. However, illustrations have little value in predicting actual performance or in comparing products and companies.

Most life insurance products sold today have adjustable pricing. This can be accomplished either as a traditional "participating" product or as a product with "non-guaranteed pricing elements" such as changeable interest crediting rates, mortality charges, expense charges, etc. All adjustable pricing products incorporate some guarantees. However, the sales illustrations are usually designed to present potential benefits and costs under a set of non-guaranteed assumptions more optimistic than the guarantees. The insurance company generally limits its responsibility to the guarantees. So the risks associated with the possible inability of a product to achieve the higher illustrated benefits, or lower illustrated costs, than those generated by the guarantees are borne by the policyholder. A study of the responses to the IQ should help the reader better understand those risks.

Life Insurance Illustration Questionnaire

Information about this response:

Contact Person: ______________________________ Date Completed: ________________

Policy(ies) Covered: ____

Are there any more IQs that cover other policies of this Company?

☐ No ☐ Yes _____ (how many)

Do the illustration(s) covered by this IQ response comply with the NAIC Life Insurance Illustrations Model Regulation?

☐ No ☐ Yes

In the following responses, "scale" means the scale of dividends or other non-guaranteed elements used in the illustrations.

Revised 4/96

I. General

1. With respect to participating policies, does the company employ the contribution principle*? If not how do practices differ?
   *The contribution principle calls for the aggregate divisible surplus to be distributed in the same proportion as the policies are considered to have contributed to the divisible surplus.

2. With respect to non-participating policies:

   a) Describe the non-guaranteed elements.

   b) What is the company's policy and discretion with respect to the determination and redetermination of non-guaranteed pricing elements?

3. Do any of the experience factor(s) underlying the scales of dividends or other non-guaranteed elements used in the illustration differ from actual recent historical experience? If so, describe.

4. Is there a substantial probability that the current illustrative values will change if actual recent historical experience continues unchanged?

5. Is it company policy to treat new and existing policyholders of the same class the same or consistently with respect to the underlying factors used in pricing? Please elaborate.

6. With respect to joint and survivor policies, describe all the effects of the first death on the policy and any riders (e.g., change in cash values, mortality charges, premiums).

II. Mortality

1. Do the mortality rates underlying the scale used in the illustration differ from actual recent historical company experience? If so, describe. Define actual recent historical experience (e.g., company experience for the last 5 years).

2. Does the illustration assume mortality improvements in the future? If so, describe.

3. Do the mortality or cost of insurance charges used in the illustration include some expense charge? If so, describe.

4. Do the underlying mortality rates vary by product (e.g., whole life, universal life, survivorship life), policy size or by any other feature (e.g., term riders)? If so, specify. (Provide general description of differences - not the actual rates used).

5. Indicate the approximate duration, if any, when all underlying mortality rates vary only by attained age (i.e., when does select become ultimate?).

III. Interest or Crediting Rates

1. The interest rate used in the dividend scale or credited in the illustration is (does):

   a) ❑ a Portfolio rate (Describe) ❑ an Investment Generation ("New Money") rate (Describe) ❑ Other (Describe)

   b) ❑ a Gross rate ❑ a Net rate, which is net of
   - ❑ investment expenses
   - ❑ income taxes
   - ❑ profit or expense charges
   - ❑ other ____________

   c) Include ❑ Realized ❑ Unrealized ❑ No Capital Gains.

   If capital gains are included, describe the general method (e.g., smoothed over ____ years).

2. Do the interest rate(s) reflect the earnings on all invested assets? A portion of the assets? New investments over certain number of years? (If so, specify number of years.) An index? (If so, briefly describe.)

3. At any policy duration, do the company investment earnings rates required to support the scale used in the illustration exceed the company's actual recent historical earnings rate on the investment segment backing that block of policies?

4. Does the interest rate used in the underlying scale reflected in the illustration vary between new and existing policies? Describe.

5. Except for any impact of using an investment generation approach, do the interest rates used in the scale reflected in the illustration vary by policy duration? Describe.

6. Do the illustrated interest rates vary by product, class or otherwise? Describe.

7. How does individual policy loan activity affect the illustrated interest rates? Describe.

IV. Expenses

1. Do the expense factors used in the scale reflected in the illustration represent actual recent historical company experience? If so, what is the experience period? If not, describe the basis under which the experience factors are determined.

2. Are the expense factors based on a ❑ fully allocated ❑ marginal or ❑ generally recognized approach, as defined in the NAIC Model Regulations?

3. Are the expense charges used in the underlying scale reflected in the illustration adequate to cover the expenses incurred in sales and administration? If not, how are remaining expenses covered (e.g., charges against interest rate, increased mortality charges)?

4. How are investment expenses and all taxes assessed?

5. Are expense factors used in the scale reflected in the illustration different for new and existing policies? If so, describe.

6. Do the expense factors underlying the scale reflected in the illustration vary by product, class or otherwise? If so, describe.

7. Do the expense charges used in the dividend scale or charged in the illustration vary by duration after the initial expenses are amortized? If so, describe.

V. Persistency

1. If the actual persistency is better than that assumed, would that negatively affect illustrated values?

2. Persistency bonuses are generally amounts illustrated as being paid or credited to all policyholders who pay premiums for a specified number of years. Does the illustration involve such a bonus?

   a. If so, is it ❑ non-guaranteed or ❑ guaranteed?

   b. Is there any limitation on company discretion in deciding whether to pay or credit the bonus?

   c. What conditions must be met to pay or credit the bonus?

   d. What is its form (e.g. cash amount, additional interest credit, refund of mortality and/or loading charges)?

   e. Does the company set aside any reserve or other liability earmarked for future bonuses?

This IQ was developed as an educational resource for insurance professionals by the American Society of CLU & ChFC, 270 S. Bryn Mawr Avenue, Bryn Mawr, Pa. 19010

Revised 4/96

American Society of CLU & ChFC®

Questions and Answers: Variable Life Insurance Illustration Questionnaire (VIQ)

1. What is the IQ/VIQ?

Developed by the American Society of CLU & ChFC and introduced to the life insurance industry Spring 1993, the Life Insurance Illustration Questionnaire (IQ) is a set of 27 informational questions for response by insurance companies. The IQ is intended to help educate insurance agents on the methodology used by companies to generate life insurance proposals, better known as "sales illustrations." There are two versions of this educational product: the IQ is appropriate to participating and non-participating "general account" products. The current version of the IQ is dated 4/96 and includes several new questions as well as language introduced by new illustration regulations. The new format will indicate the policy(ies) covered by the company's response, as well as the date the IQ response was last prepared.

The VIQ is appropriate to variable life insurance products. The VIQ is dated 9/96 and is similar in format to the IQ but for its focus on variable life insurance products.

2. Why was the VIQ developed?

The VIQ was developed to assist insurance agents obtain the information they need to better understand and evaluate how the non-guaranteed and fluctuating risk elements of a variable life insurance policy can affect future performance. In today's rapidly changing world, it is critical for agents to understand and be able to explain to their clients how changes in investment returns, mortality, persistency and expenses can affect the future performance of a variable life insurance policy. It is much easier to assist the client in forming appropriate long-term expectations regarding policy performance with a knowledge of these non-guaranteed assumptions.

3. Isn't a sales illustration based on the policy itself?

Yes. Individual states (regulating insurance companies) and the Securities & Exchange Commission (SEC)/ National Association of Securities Dealers (NASD) require that variable policy illustrations be based on current assumptions. This means that illustrations include projections of non-guaranteed benefits and values which assume that current assumptions of both expense and investment gain will continue into the future. Thus, an illustration is merely an insurance company's estimate of how an insurance policy might perform over time if a given set of assumptions as to investment gains earned on premium deposits, mortality experience and expense costs were to occur exactly as projected. Since there is little chance that future performance will exactly match all current assumptions, it is safe to say that the sales illustration will never accurately portray the policy's actual performance.

4. Where do illustrations come from?

There are a variety of sources for illustrations. They may be prepared by the insurance company in response to an agent's request. These will contain a disclaimer generally noting that "figures presented are only illustrations and are not promises or guarantees." Still others are prepared using software created by independent vendors who have incorporated the issuing company's information into their system. Illustrations are also prepared on the insurance agent's computer, in which case it may have no direct relationship to the insurance company.

Regardless of how the illustration is prepared, it is still only an estimate of future performance, which in turn is based on static assumptions which are mathematically projected as many as 50 years into the future. Obviously, then, an illustration cannot be any more accurate than the assumptions on which it is based.

5. Do illustrations have any benefit?

Yes. Even though the numbers cannot predict actual policy performance, they do serve a vital function. Illustrations can be useful in developing the best combination of policy specifications to achieve the insurance buyer's objective. For any given "what if?" considerations on behalf of a client, an illustration can show varying projections of future cash values and death benefits and/or the need for a given amount of premium payments. Thus, the insurance buyer can learn more about how the policy works by examining benefits under alternative illustrations that project a variable policy's potential for higher and lower investment gains and higher and lower mortality expenses. Though not exact and not guaranteed, these projections are of benefit to the insurance buyer because they demonstrate that policy values will fluctuate and vary from that which was originally illustrated at the time of purchase. Illustrations also show how various policy features can be used to come up with a range of potential benefits and costs. However, it is important to bear in mind that while illustrations may help in the decision making process, they simply do not contain sufficient information for the purpose of choosing which of two or more policies under consideration should be purchased.

6. How is the "VIQ" useful to clients?

The VIQ enables agents to learn more about the internal assumptions which ultimately control policy (versus illustration) performance. After an in-depth examination of the inner workings of a variable life insurance policy, the life insurance professional will have a much better understanding and greater knowledge of what goes into an "illustration."

This understanding of where the figures come from and what they actually represent will enable agents to better communicate the risks as well as the benefits of a variable life insurance contract to their clients. Agents can provide clients with details on the guaranteed and non-guaranteed elements inherent in the policy. This information will help avoid disappointment in years to come.

7. Was the "VIQ" designed to disclose pricing information?

No. Neither the IQ nor the VIQ seeks non-public, proprietary pricing information about an insurance company or its products. Furthermore, it does not seek numerical responses of any kind about any aspect of an insurance company's practices. In fact, much of the information sought by the VIQ can be obtained from the policy's Prospectus which is required to be delivered to the policy buyer. The VIQ is designed to reorganize this information for disclosure and presentation to agents. Perhaps the VIQ's greatest benefit is that it opens up a significant line of inquiry, education, and dialogue between the life insurance professional and her or his insurance company.

The VIQ's focus is to facilitate better communications between insurance companies and insurance agents. It was not designed to be used directly with the client at the point of sale (although agents may certainly choose to do so with the express permission of his or her Broker/Dealer). Knowledge obtained through a careful reading of an VIQ response does not enable the agent to produce a more accurate illustration.

In order to reinforce the educational value of the VIQ and to confirm the important relationship between companies and their agents, the Society does not accumulate company responses for reproduction or dissemination.

8. Can illustrations be misleading?

When life insurance sales illustrations appear to promise future financial performance levels that appear unrealistically high, clients can be misled if they are not aware of the investment and pricing assumption basis of the illustration and the risks attendant with "too good to be true" illustration values.

9. Can misleading illustrations be avoided?

Misleading illustrations can be avoided when insurance professionals explain that ultimate policy performance is not influenced by a "sales illustration" but by actual experience as it materializes over many years.

Company as well as policy performance is based on the following non-guaranteed risk elements:

- Mortality experience
- Investment performance
- Policy lapse rates
- Expenses

These four factors are available for comparison through such insurance industry resources as Best's Life Reports and Standard & Poor's Insurance Rating Service. Historical investment returns of the underlying sub-accounts can be obtained from services such as Morningstar and Lipper Analytic Services. These publications are often available at public libraries or from insurance and stock brokerage companies.

A word of caution: A company's past experience may not be an accurate guide as to what will happen in the future and focusing on results from just one or a select number of years could suggest an outcome different from ultimate performance.

10. How does the "VIQ" help agents get information?

In addition to a reading of the variable policy's Prospectus, the VIQ allows agents to review responses from companies that have completed the VIQ Questionnaire. The VIQ covers such topics as whether the company assumes any changes in mortality experience, and if so, what are the changes. In addition, it reviews the methods used in assessing expenses (including but not limited to mortality and expense charges, taxes and administration).

Since the answers will often contain complicated actuarial information, the American Society has developed general education for agents as part of the IQ program. Video tapes and local tutorials are available to Society members as well as members of the financial services industry and allied professionals who can benefit from learning more about how to interpret an insurance company's response in an IQ/VIQ. Local Society Chapters are typically the best source of IQ/VIQ educational material.

11. How does pending state regulation of illustrations affect the VIQ?

Illustration regulations will be passed by many states in 1996 with an anticipated effective date of January 1, 1997. These regulations will compel life insurance companies to illustrate policies under a set of guidelines and rules that are significantly more controlled than for policies issued before the effective date of the regulations. Among the most significant changes is a requirement that carriers annually certify post-regulation policies that they continue to meet stringent supportability tests. While variable life insurance policies are excluded from the regulations, discussions are being held between the NAIC and SEC/NASD to extend traditional policy illustration regulations to include variable life insurance illustrations.

The role of the VIQ is to educate the agent about the assumptions which underlie the illustration of non-guaranteed elements in the policies they sell. While it would seem that (when variable illustrations are covered by state regulations) "regulated and certified" policy illustration would provide renewed confidence and accurate illustrated values, certification depends on the improbability that assumptions can accurately be forecast into an uncertain future. Agents will need to remind their clients of this reality, and the VIQ continues to be an ideal educational forum for that purpose.

12. How many companies have responded to the IQ/VIQ?

As of September, 1996, the American Society is aware of 99 companies that have published their responses to the IQ. Companies who sell variable life insurance products will be receiving during Fall 1996 the VIQ format for voluntary completion and communication to their agents. As agents and their clients become aware of and seek answers to the IQ/VIQ, more companies are providing responses.

13. Will the American Society publish IQ/VIQ responses?

No, the American Society's purpose is to assure the continuing education and professionalism of its members. The Society will not collect, publish nor distribute responses from companies that have answered the IQ/VIQ, although a listing is available of the companies known to the Society to have published an IQ/VIQ response. For those interested in a particular company's response to the IQ/VIQ questionnaire, contact the company directly. If the company is not listed in the area phone directory, contact the local public library and ask for Best's Life Reports. Best's includes a listing of the major insurance company's headquarters with their address and phone number.

Introduction to the Variable Life Insurance Illustration Questionnaire (VIQ)

The Variable Life Insurance Illustration Questionnaire (VIQ) is an educational tool; its use by companies or agents is entirely voluntary.

The purpose of the VIQ is to help the reader understand the different non-guaranteed performance assumptions which insurance companies use to design and create variable sales illustrations. The VIQ may be particularly useful to agents, their clients (under the agent's guidance) and the clients' other advisors.

The reader should understand that variable sales illustrations and actual historical performance may be useful in selecting a policy and the investment mix most appropriate to the purchaser's investment risk tolerance. However, illustrations do not predict actual future performance nor can they be used as the primary basis of comparing products and/or companies.

In general, life insurance products sold today typically have adjustable pricing. This can be accomplished either as a traditional "participating" product or as a product with "non-guaranteed pricing elements" such as changeable interest crediting rates, mortality charges, expense charges, etc.

For variable life insurance ***products***, the investment risk is generally transferred to the policyowner; mortality and expense charges are typically subject to the carrier's actual ongoing experience.

Sales ***illustrations*** are usually designed to present potential benefits and costs under a prescribed set of investment assumptions in conjunction with projections of non-guaranteed mortality, expense and persistency factors.

The risks associated with the possible inability of a product to achieve the illustrated benefits and/or illustrated costs are borne by the policyholder. The insurance company generally limits its responsibility to the guarantees contained in the policy. Both the death benefit and cash value in a variable life insurance policy generally vary with future investment performance of the funds selected by the policyowner.

A study of the responses to the VIQ should help the reader better understand the risks assumed by the policyowner.

Variable Life Insurance Illustration Questionnaire

Information about this response:

Company: ____________________

Date Completed: ____________________

Contact Person: ____________________

Policy(ies) Covered: ____________________

Are there any more VIQs that cover other policies of this Company?

No ☐ Yes ☐ Describe:

Notes:

1) Variable life insurance policies do not - as of 9/15/96 - fall within the scope of the NAIC Insurance Illustration Model Regulations. At such time that Illustration Regulations apply to Variable Life Illustrations, this VIQ will be modified as necessary.

2) In the following responses, "scale" means the scale of dividends or other non-guaranteed elements used in the illustrations.

I. General

1. With respect to participating policies, does the company employ the contribution principle* ? If not how do practices differ?
   *The contribution principle calls for the aggregate divisible surplus to be distributed in the same proportion as the policies are considered to have contributed to the divisible surplus.

2. With respect to policies with non-guaranteed pricing elements other than dividends:

   a) Describe the non-guaranteed elements.

   b) What is the company's policy and discretion with respect to the determination and redetermination of non-guaranteed pricing elements?

3. Do any of the experience factor(s) underlying the scales of dividends or other non-guaranteed elements used in the illustration differ from actual recent historical experience? If so, describe.

4. Except for investment performance, is there a substantial probability that the current illustrative values will change if actual recent historical experience continues unchanged?

5. Is it company policy to treat new and existing policyholders of the same class the same or consistently with respect to the underlying factors used in pricing? Please elaborate.

6. If this VIQ response includes policies issued on a joint and survivor basis, describe all the effects of the first death on the policy and any riders (e.g., change in cash values, mortality charges, premiums).

II. Mortality

1. Do the mortality rates underlying the scale used in the illustration differ from actual recent historical company experience? If so, describe. Define actual recent historical experience (e.g., company experience for the last 5 years).

2. Does the illustration assume mortality improvements in the future? If so, describe.

3. Do the mortality or cost of insurance charges used in the illustration include some expense charge? If so, describe.

4. Indicate the approximate duration, if any, when all underlying mortality rates vary only by attained age (i.e., when does select become ultimate?).

5. Do the underlying mortality assumptions for the illustration differ from those for otherwise corresponding non-variable policies and, if so, how?

III. Investment Performance

1. Does the policyowner assume all of the investment risk?

   ❑ Yes ❑ No

   Please explain.

2. Is the original or initial death benefit guaranteed regardless of investment performance?

   ❑ Yes for ____ years or to age ____ ❑ No

   If yes, under what conditions is the guarantee effective (e.g., premiums at a specified yearly and/or cumulative level, or more, must be paid prior to the end of the guarantee period)?

IV. Expenses

1. Do the expense factors used in the scale reflected in the illustration represent actual recent historical company experience? If so, what is the experience period? If not, describe the basis under which the experience factors are determined.

2. Are the expense factors based on a ❑ fully allocated ❑ marginal or ❑ generally recognized approach, as defined in the NAIC Model Regulations?

3. Are the expense charges used in the underlying scale reflected in the illustration adequate to cover the expenses incurred in sales and administration? If not, how are remaining expenses covered (e.g., charges against separate accounts, increased mortality charges)?

4. How are investment expenses and all taxes assessed? Are the fund expenses in the illustration based on an average of all funds, or on specific funds?

5. Are expense factors used in the scale reflected in the illustration different for new and existing policies? If so, describe.

6. Do the expense factors underlying the scale reflected in the illustration vary by product, class or otherwise? If so, describe.

7. Do the expense charges used in the dividend scale or charged in the illustration vary by duration after the initial expenses are amortized? If so, describe.

8. Do the underlying expense assumptions for the illustration differ from those for otherwise corresponding non-variable policies and, if so, how?

V. Persistency

1. If the actual persistency is better than that assumed, would that negatively affect illustrated values?

2. Persistency bonuses are generally amounts illustrated as being paid or credited to all policyholders who pay premiums for a specified number of years. Does the illustration involve such a bonus?

   a. If so, is it ❑ non-guaranteed or ❑ guaranteed?

   b. Is there any limitation on company discretion in deciding whether to pay or credit the bonus?

   c. What conditions must be met to pay or credit the bonus?

   d. What is its form (e.g., cash amount, additional investment credit, refund of mortality and/or loading charges)?

   e. Does the company set aside any reserve or other liability earmarked for future bonuses? Describe.

3. Do the underlying persistency assumptions for the illustration differ from those for otherwise corresponding non-variable policies and, if so, how?

This VIQ was developed as an educational resource for insurance professionals by the American Society of CLU & ChFC, 270 S. Bryn Mawr Avenue, Bryn Mawr, Pa. 19010

American Society of CLU & ChFC's Replacement Questionnaire (RQ)

Questions and Answers

1. What is the Replacement Questionnaire (RQ)?

The RQ is a series of questions intended to uncover important information that must be thoughtfully considered by an agent before making any recommendations to a client about policy replacement. Replacement is the discontinuance or exchange of one policy to purchase another.

The RQ provides the agent with a consistent and responsible method for evaluating regulatory, legal and tax issues associated with replacements.

2. Why was the RQ developed?

The American Society developed the RQ to help CLUs and ChFCs meet their professional obligation to their clients when exploring a policy replacement. The RQ serves as both an educational tool as well as a method for an agent to identify and clarify relevant issues as to whether an existing life insurance policy should or should not be replaced.

3. How does the RQ benefit consumers?

Because life insurance policies are complex agreements, analyzing possible replacements is even more complex for consumers. CLUs and ChFCs are reminded that **replacement is generally not in the consumer's best interest,** and the RQ gives the agent the opportunity to review some of the important issues surrounding policy replacement. If a consumer replaces an existing policy through an agent who has used the RQ, the consumer will be better assured of having made an informed decision.

4. Why or when, if ever, should a consumer consider policy replacement?

The American Society lists in the introduction to the RQ some of the reasons why most replacements are not in the policyholder's best interest. There may be, however, situations where a client's or an issuing company's circumstances have changed so that a replacement may be in the client's best interest. The RQ assists the responsible agent in determining whether or not a particular set of facts warrants a recommendation to replace a policy.

5. What questions should a consumer ask when considering a replacement?

The consumer should ask the agent to detail, in writing, the advantages and disadvantages of a replacement. Some additional questions are:

a. If I replace my current policy, how soon within the *new* policy will I have access to the same amount of cash value that I currently have in my *existing* policy?

b. What is the difference in *guaranteed* values between the two policies?

c. Can the payment of a death claim be challenged if I die within two years of buying the new policy?

d. If interest rates continue to go down, how will the proposed policy perform? How would my existing policy perform?

6. Is the RQ applicable to all types of life insurance policies?

Yes, although it may be used somewhat differently with different products, the RQ will develop useful information.

Policies which are regulated by the SEC/ NASD are referred to as "variable" life insurance products, and the rules for client communication are strictly regulated. Agents are required to have any client communications about variable products approved in advance by their broker-dealer.

7. Are there state laws on replacement and how do they protect the consumer?

Many states have regulations requiring varying levels of disclosure when a replacement policy is being considered. These rules differ state by state and are usually just a notification to the policyowner and to the existing company that a replacement is being contemplated. The RQ does not replace any state requirements. It is strictly a supplemental document to clarify the issues involved in a replacement.

8. Are there features from the existing policy that may be lost if it is replaced?

In most cases, there will be a loss of one or more important features. Some of the most common include:

a. Any policy that has been *in force* more than two years is deemed incontestable for possible misstatements at the time the policy was purchased; a new policy would typically require a *new* two-year period during which the death claim can be contested for possible misstatements.

b. The old policy may have a low, fixed loan rate while the new policy may have a variable loan rate.

c. There may be "nonforfeiture values" and guarantees contained in the old policy that are more favorable than in the new policy. For example, some policies sold in the mid-1980s had an interest guarantee as high as 6.5%; today's policies may guarantee only 4 to 4.5%.

d. The original policy may have been purchased before tax law changes; the more favorable rules were generally "grandfathered," especially if those changes were adverse to new policies.

e. The new policy may not be underwritten on as favorable a basis as the original policy.

There may be other features that may be lost, and consumers need the help of a professional agent who uses the RQ to identify them all.

9. Are there any tax consequences when considering a replacement?

There may be. Anytime a life insurance policy is surrendered, a calculation must be made in order to determine if there is a gain in the policy for income tax purposes. Also, there may be a loss of other income tax benefits, e.g., deductibility of interest payments and "grandfathered" benefits.

10. How is the Society's RQ related to the Society's Insurance Questionnaire (IQ)?

The RQ and the IQ serve two different educational purposes. The RQ helps agents evaluate many of the critical issues pertaining to a policy replacement. The IQ assists agents in understanding the assumptions which underlie the nonguaranteed elements found in policy illustrations. The RQ includes a section on IQ disclosures which are used for evaluating the assumptions underlying the two policies under review.

Replacement Questionnaire (RQ)

A Policy Replacement Evaluation Form

To CLUs/ChFCs:

Replacing an existing life insurance policy with a new one generally is not in the policyholder's best interest. New sales loads and other expenses, the new company's right to challenge a death claim during the suicide and contestibility periods, changes in age or health and the loss of important grandfathered rights are some of the obvious reasons that **most replacements cannot be justified.** On the other hand, there may be circumstances where a replacement is in your client's best interest. The ethical agent will provide his or her client with the impartial information needed to make an informed decision, including reasons the client should not replace the current policy and/or how to modify the existing policy to accomplish their goals. The need for additional coverage is not, by itself, a justification for replacement.

This Form is designed to assist you in evaluating some of the facts and circumstances that a policyholder should take into consideration when addressing the possibility of replacing a life insurance policy. It can be used for both internal and external replacements. **The definition of "replacement" is much broader than the cancellation of one policy and the issuance of another.** The legal meaning of the word "replacement" is determined by state law and varies substantially by state. You should be familiar with your own state's definition of the word. However, for purposes of simplifying the definition, we may think of "replacement" in general terms as an action which eliminates the original policy or diminishes its benefits or values. Examples of this are policy loans, taking reduced paid-up insurance or withdrawing dividends. Since no form can cover every possible situation, you may need additional material to enable your client to make a truly informed decision.

Please note that "illustrated" results in this Form are always nonguaranteed. Also, keep in mind that different companies use different assumptions in preparing illustrations and that illustrations alone should never be used to compare policies. However, current in-force illustrations for the existing policy and current illustrations for the proposed policy must be provided to the client, showing the effects of applicable surrender charges. In situations where the current policy will be changed, but not terminated, comparisons should include in-force ledgers of the policy before and after the change, if available. Reduced scale illustrations (or illustrations with lower yield assumptions) should be provided on both existing and proposed policies to demonstrate volatility in the performance of nonguaranteed policy elements under different circumstances. The reduced scale illustrations should be consistent with those required by the NAIC model illustration regulations, when effective.

This Form is intended for evaluation purposes. It is not a substitute for state replacement requirements. This Form is not designed for direct use with clients. Further, if either the existing or proposed policy is variable life insurance, use of this Form with the client must be approved by your broker-dealer.

Replacement Questionnaire (RQ)

A Policy Replacement Evaluation Form

A. 1. What does the policyholder want to achieve that the existing policy cannot provide?

____

____

____

2. Has the current carrier been contacted to see if the policy can be modified to meet the policyholder's objectives?

____

B. 1. Recognizing that the replacement of an existing policy generally results in the reduction of cash surrender value as a result of new acquisition costs, what is the cash surrender value of:

a. The original policy **immediately** before replacement ______________________
b. The original policy **immediately** after the replacement ______________________
c. The proposed policy **immediately** after the replacement ______________________

These cash surrender values should be obtained directly from the insurance carrier's policyowner service department and not from an illustration, since illustrations typically reflect end of year values.

2. Illustrations should **never** be the sole criteria for evaluating a replacement. Additionally, Illustrated Cash Values and Illustrated Death Benefits are **never** reliable predictions of future results. If these non-guaranteed values and benefits are the basis for considering a replacement, the agent should attempt to know and understand the underlying assumptions in both the inforce illustration for the current policy, as well as the sales illustration for the proposed policy. In addition to reviewing illustrations, the agent should attempt to obtain an Illustration Questionnaire (IQ), which may be available directly from the companies or may be requested through the client. The agent and the client should be aware that there may be differences in the assumptions used by each company which may render a comparison based upon such illustrations invalid.

How many years from now before the proposed policy's cash surrender values and death benefits exceed those benefits in the current policy?

a. Guaranteed Cash Surrender Values ______ years and subsequent.
b. Guaranteed Death Benefits ______ years and subsequent.
c. Illustrated Cash Surrender Values ______ years and subsequent.
d. Illustrated Death Benefits ______ years and subsequent.

3. If the proposed policy is a variable life policy, what gross yield rate is being assumed? ____%

   What is your justification for that rate? ________________________________

C. 1. Describe the differences in the plans of insurance. ________________________________

   ____

2. Describe any term riders or term elements (above the base policy). Include the ratio of the initial term amount to the total death benefit and any term rate guarantees which may or may not be included.

   Current policy: ________________________________

   Proposed policy: ________________________________

3. Other than term riders, what riders do the policies include?

   Current policy: ________________________________

   Proposed policy: ________________________________

4. How long is the initial death benefit **guaranteed** to be in force at the **illustrated** premium?

   Current policy: ______ years. Proposed policy: ______ years.

5. What premium is necessary to **guarantee** coverage at initial/current levels for life?

   Current policy: $__________. Proposed policy: $__________.

D. 1. Is there a potential taxable gain if the current policy is replaced?

   ❑ YES ❑ NO If yes, how is it to be managed?

   ____

2. If there is a taxable gain, **and if there is a loan,** how is the loan to be managed?

   ❑ The new policy will assume the existing loan.

   ❑ The loan will be repaid.

   ❑ The policyowner will recognize taxable income.

E. Is an IRC Sec. 1035 exchange planned to preserve basis? ❑ YES ❑ NO

F. If a replacement is under consideration because a more favorable rate classification is available, has a reduction or removal of the rating on the existing policy been requested? If so, what was the result. If not, explain why such a request has not been made.

   ____

G. Does the proposed policy qualify as life insurance under IRC Section 7702?

   ❑ YES ❑ NO

H. What is the issue date of the current policy? ______________________

The following "grandfathered" features will be lost if the policy is replaced. (See Appendix for explanation of items 3-9.)

1. The current policy is incontestable by the insurance company. ❑ YES ❑ NO
2. The period has expired during which the insurance company can deny policy benefits in the event of the insured's suicide. ❑ YES ❑ NO

The current *life insurance policy* was issued on or before:	YES	NO	The current *annuity policy* was issued before:	YES	NO	The current *second to die policy* was issued before:	YES	NO
3. 8/06/63	❑	❑	6. 10/21/79	❑	❑	9. 9/14/89	❑	❑
4. 6/20/86	❑	❑	7. 8/14/82	❑	❑			
5. 6/20/88	❑	❑	8. 2/28/86	❑	❑			

I. If the current policy is term, is a conversion to permanent insurance available? ❑ YES ❑ NO
If so, other than the suicide and incontestable provisions would a conversion to permanent insurance be more advantageous?
❑ YES ❑ NO Explanation: ____

____

J. Financial Strength Ratings. Much has been made of ratings in the last few years; financial strength is important, but it is not the sole determining factor in selecting a life insurance company. A drop in ratings alone generally is not a sufficient reason to replace a policy. It is also important to know that there can be differences of opinion among rating agencies and that small differences in ratings generally are not significant. Furthermore, financial strength ratings are not necessarily indicative of policy performance. If reviewed with the client, a detailed explanation of the ratings must be provided in accordance with state regulations.

	Current Company Rating (Rank)*	Proposed Company Rating (Rank)	Date & Source of Answer
A. M. Best (15 ranks)	__________	__________	________________
Duff & Phelps (18 ranks)	__________	__________	________________
Moody's (19 ranks)	__________	__________	________________
S & P Claims Paying Ability** (18 ranks)	__________	__________	________________

* For example, an AA rating from S & P is the third highest **rank** out of 18 possible ratings.
** S & P offers two rating services. Claims Paying Ability is on a par with the other services listed here; S & P's Qualified Solvency Rating is a much differently oriented rating and is inappropriate for use in this context.

K. Policy loans:	Current Policy	Proposed Policy
1. Gross rate	__________	__________
2. Fixed or Variable?	__________	__________
3. Permanent policies: Direct Recognition?	__________	__________
4. Universal life, etc. a. Current spread?	__________	__________
b. Is spread guaranteed?	❑ YES ❑ NO	❑ YES ❑ NO

L. Additional remarks:

____

____

____

____

Appendix
Grandfathered Features Explanation
(See question H.)

3. The current policy was purchased on or before 8/6/63, so IRC Section 264(a)(3) which limits deductions for interest indebtedness does not apply. If the current policy has met the "four out of seven" test of IRC Section 264(c)(1), interest on indebtedness is deductible to the extent otherwise allowed by law. Personal interest deductions are generally denied for tax years beginning after 1990, irrespective of when the policy was purchased. IRC Sec. 163(h)(1).

4. The current policy was purchased on or before June 20, 1986. Certain policies purchased for business purposes after this date have a $50,000 ceiling on the aggregate amount of indebtedness for which an interest deduction is allowed. IRC Sec. 264(a)(4).

5. Policy was issued on or before 6/20/88 and is not subject to Modified Endowment Contract rules. IRC Sec. 7702A. Substantial increases in the death benefits of grandfathered contracts after 10/20/88 may cause the imposition of the MEC rules. H.R. Conf. Rep. No. 1104, 100th Cong., 2d Sess. (TAMRA '88) reprinted in 1988-3 CB 595 - 596.

6. Variable annuity contracts purchased before 10/21/79 are eligible for a step-up in basis if the owner dies before the annuity starting date. IRC Sec. 72; Rev. Rul. 79-335, 1979-2 CB 292.

7. An annuity issued prior to 8/14/82 is subject to more favorable (basis out first) cost recovery rules for withdrawals. IRC Sec. 72(e). Such policies are not subject to the 10% penalty on withdrawals made prior to age 59 1/2. IRC Sec. 72(q)(2).

8. To the extent contributions are made after 2/28/86 to a deferred annuity held by a non-natural person (such as a business entity), the contract will not be entitled to tax treatment as an annuity. IRC Sec. 72(u).

9. A survivorship life policy issued prior to 9/14/89 is not subject to the 7-pay MEC test if there is a reduction in benefits. IRC Sec. 7702A(c)(6).

This Appendix is provided for educational purposes only. You should seek competent legal counsel before applying this to any specific situation.

4

Effective Communication in Financial Counseling[1]

Lewis B. Morgan

Chapter Outline

INTRODUCTION

Many people take communication for granted. After all, it is an activity that most of us have engaged in since our childhood years, so why not take it for granted? The sad truth, however, is that many of us are ineffective communicators simply because we make that very assumption.

Communication is far too important a skill, especially in the field of counseling, to treat lightly. It is the single most critical skill that a counselor brings to a counseling session.

The purpose of this chapter is to examine the communication process as it typically exists in a counselor-client relationship. Our goal is to enable financial planners to become exceptionally effective communicators in their dealings with clients. Perhaps you already consider yourself to be effective in the area of communication; however, there are probably aspects of the communication process in which you can improve. This chapter will attempt to bring these aspects into sharper focus and provide you with techniques for becoming the very best communicator/counselor that you have the potential of being.

The chapter begins with a delineation of the various types of structured communication: interviewing, counseling, and advising. From there it proceeds to some of the essentials inherent in financial counseling: structuring the counseling relationship; establishing rapport; and dealing with resistance. Next it looks at some of the characteristics of effective counseling: unconditional positive regard, empathy, genuineness, and self-awareness.

The second part of the chapter focuses on basic communication principles and skills such as nonverbal communication, using the skills of attending to a client, listening and then responding to a client, and asking effective questions.

THREE TYPES OF STRUCTURED COMMUNICATION

Laypeople often use the terms interviewing, counseling, and advising interchangeably; yet each term has characteristics that are uniquely its own and that differentiate it from the other two. Let us look at each of these three terms and see how they are alike and how they are different.

Three Types of Structured Communication

- Interviewing
- Counseling
- Advising

Interviewing

One of the most common forms of structured communication is interviewing. Interviewing can be defined as a process of communication, most often between two people, with a predetermined and specific purpose, usually involving the asking and answering of questions designed to gather meaningful information. For example, a television sports announcer might interview a coach at halftime to get information about what mistakes his team made in the first half, what he plans to do differently in the second half, and how he hopes to win. Or an interview might take place in a personnel office where a job applicant is interviewed for a position with the firm. The interviewer will want to know the following: What assets will the applicant bring to the job? What is her employment history? Where does she see herself fitting into the firm? What salary does she expect? In both instances cited, there is a specific purpose to the interview in that relevant information is being sought through a question-and-answer dialogue.

Stewart and Cash, in their book, *Interviewing: Principles and Practices,* refer to two basic types of interviews: the directive and nondirective interview.[2] In the directive interview, the interviewer directs and controls both the pace and the content to be covered. It is a much more formalized and structured style of interaction. Often the interviewer even completes a questionnaire form as the interviewee answers pointed questions—for example, What is your age? Where do you live? Where was your last job? What is the highest level of education completed? The advantages of the directive interview are that it can be brief and that it provides measurable data. Its disadvantages are that it is often inflexible and does not allow the interviewee to choose topics for discussion.

The nondirective interview, on the other hand, allows both the interviewer and the interviewee a wider range of subject areas to be discussed, and the interviewee usually controls the pacing and purpose of the interview. Thus the advantages of the nondirective interview include greater flexibility, more in-depth responses, and the potential of a closer relationship between interviewer and interviewee. Its disadvantages are that it consumes more time and often generates data that are difficult to measure objectively.

All interviews, whether directive or nondirective, share common characteristics. Interviews typically take place in a formal and structured setting. Questions are the primary source of communication used by the interviewer. The subject matter discussed is specific to the overall purpose of the interview, and digressions from the subject are usually not encouraged. Finally, the interview is usually a relatively short-term relationship between interviewer and interviewee.

Counseling

The second term, counseling, is often confused with interviewing, even though they are not synonymous. Counseling implies help giving, often of a psychotherapeutic nature, and the help-giving aspect is more than implied in counseling; it is built in and an integral part of the process. Simply stated, a counselor's job is to provide assistance to clients as they explore their present situations, begin to understand where they are in relation to where they would like to be, and then act to get from where they are to where they want to be. Even though this may sound like a simple process, it is not. It usually is a long-term process, typified by struggles, setbacks, and, eventually, insights leading to an ultimate change in behavior as clients strive to live more fulfilling lives.

While financial counseling takes place over a period of time, the interview is usually a one-time interaction. As such, an interpersonal relationship develops between counselor and client, something that usually does not occur in an interview. When we discussed interviewing, we stated that the question was the primary stock-in-trade of the interviewer. While questions are also utilized in counseling, they are not the primary response modality. In certain counseling settings such as mental hospitals and mental health clinics, an intake interview constitutes the first step in the therapeutic process. In this intake interview, many personal questions are asked, either in a written or oral format, but once the intake procedure is concluded, the communication assumes a different form. While questions may still be asked periodically, they are not the predominant form of counselor response. A counselor may paraphrase what the client has said, reflect a feeling, share feedback or perceptions, clarify, summarize, interpret, provide information, and confront. In short, counseling is not as stylized as interviewing because the format is less formal and less structured. Much more of the humanness of both the counselor and the client comes into focus, all with the purpose of providing help to the client.

Advising

Still a third type of structured communication is advising, which is often confused with counseling. In fact, many people who are unfamiliar with counseling think that what they will receive is advice. Perhaps one reason for this misconception stems from the journalistic proliferation of advice such as is offered in newspaper columns by "Dear Abby" and her sister, Ann Landers. This is not to say that advice is never offered by counselors, because it is; but most counselors believe that the very best kind of advice is self-advice, rather than expert advice.

Several situations might require such advice. A college student planning a program of studies is typically assigned an academic adviser in his or her major field of study. The adviser's role is, simply, to advise the student about program sequence, course prerequisites, specific course content, graduation requirements, and possible career opportunities in the major area. In short, the adviser is the expert and, as such, provides excellent advice. A tax adviser might provide advice on tax shelters, investments, tax deferral, and so on. In both instances, advisers know much more about their field of expertise than do their clients, and their clients use this knowledge in order to reach decisions.

In financial counseling, there are bound to be occasions when counselors give advice. After all, financial counselors are the experts and thus their advice has proven value. The danger in offering advice too soon in the counseling relationship is that the client's ability to make decisions is discounted in favor of the expert's opinion. Perhaps the best way to give advice, if advice is given at all, is to hear clients out first in order to understand their situation more completely and to assess their goals, and then to explain what alternatives or options are available.

Advice giving remains a controversial issue in counseling literature. Its critics maintain that advice fosters dependency and robs clients of the right to make decisions for themselves. It is important for each counselor to question his or her haste in offering ready answers to somewhat complex situations. Is there some inner need like dominance or control being satisfied? Is the advice giver willing to assume the responsibility for another person's life? Is the advice giver projecting his or her own needs, problems, or values into the advice?

So while it is true that many people come to a financial counselor ostensibly looking for advice or the right answer, it is also true that many people choose not to take the advice when it is offered, or if they do take the counselor's advice and later discover that it was unsound, they rightfully blame the counselor.

There is a place for tentative suggestions that leave the final decision about courses of action entirely up to the client. In this manner, clients are free to make decisions that are right for them and thus assume the responsibility for their own lives. Advisers who do this are functioning in a wholly professional and ethical manner.

ESSENTIALS IN FINANCIAL COUNSELING

In the preceding section we differentiated the three types of planned, purposeful communication: interviewing, counseling, and advising. Each one of these types of communication can be found in the financial counseling relationship. For instance, interviewing in the form of data collection for a fact finder might well constitute the early stages of the communications process. After the data are collected, the second phase would probably consist largely of counseling—listening closely to the client and trying to understand the client's inner world of needs, desires, fears, attitudes, values, and goals. The third and final stage of communication in financial counseling would undoubtedly include giving expert advice, or at least carefully exploring possible alternatives for achieving the client's objectives. Let us look at the dynamics of communication and how it works in actual practice.

Structure

In any kind of planned and purposeful communication setting, the first element that needs to be attended to is structuring. Structuring serves to determine both the format and the subject matter of the interaction that is to follow. The counselor's task is to make the purpose of the session clear to the client at the outset. This would include the inevitable introductions, an explanation of the process involved, a discussion of forms that are used and the amount of time that will be required, a discussion of the confidential nature of the relationship, and some prediction of what kinds of outcomes the client might reasonably expect. This structuring need not be lengthy and cumbersome; in fact, it is far better to structure in a clear, straightforward, and succinct fashion. Consider the following example of structuring:

Counselor: "In order for me to be able to provide the best possible service for you, we'll probably need to see each other on three or four separate occasions, although I want you to know that I'm available to you as often as you need me. Today I thought we'd start by getting some information about your financial situation. To do this, I'll use the fact finder pages, which will remain confidential between the two of us. As we go about our business together, I suspect that we'll be able to come up with a financial plan that will be sensible and help you meet your goals. Do you have any questions?"

The counselor's approach in the foregoing example is friendly and promises cooperation. The client is made to feel important, that he or she is the focal point of the counseling situation. The statement offers hope that the results of client counseling will meet the needs and goals of the client.

In the early stages of counseling, the client may be apprehensive or uncertain about how to begin. A good guide to follow is to begin where the client is. If the client is, in fact, anxious at the outset, some time should be spent discussing the mere difficulty of getting started. Talking about this will invariably alleviate most of the client's anxieties. It is important to keep in mind that whenever feelings emerge, it is best to focus upon those feelings rather than ignore them. If, for example, a client, in the middle of a session, appears distressed over some aspect of his or her situation (for example, an impending divorce), some time must be given to discussing these feelings. Until the feelings are addressed and expressed, a further discussion of content is unproductive and meaningless.

Rapport

Rapport is best established through the personhood of the financial counselor. Attributes that go a long way toward a rapprochement between counselor and client would include a friendly and interested concern; an unhurried, leisurely pace; an accepting, nonjudgmental attitude; attentive, active listening; and an egalitarian relationship. In such a climate, clients are free to be themselves, since they don't have to be afraid that what they say will be evaluated in a negative way by the counselor. Furthermore, they begin to realize that the ultimate responsibility for planning, setting goals, and taking action rests with them and not the counselor.

Perhaps the most important attribute of personhood in establishing rapport is the financial counselor's acceptance of the client and the client's awareness of this acceptance. This attitude stems from a sincere desire on the part of the counselor to respect the uniqueness of each client and a genuine wish to be of help. And it might be well to add that accepting others is easier said than done, especially with people who are markedly different from us in terms of their values, attitudes, socioeconomic status, and so on. Despite this difficulty, it is absolutely imperative that counselors accept their clients, because unless a client feels accepted by his counselor, the relationship will never really become a partnership of equals.

Recognizing Resistance

Resistance often occurs in even the best of counseling relationships. It can be expressed as either overt or covert hostility toward the counselor. Open hostility is the easiest type to recognize and, in most cases, to handle. We all know what angry people look and sound like: their faces become flushed; their jaws tighten; they clench their fists; their voices rise; their language becomes more expressively angry. The only effective thing to do at this point is to reflect this anger, as in saying, "I can sense your anger. You don't like what I've just said, do you?" This allows clients to vent whatever pent-up feelings of anger they have, and the anger slowly begins to dissipate and then the behavior can become more rational.

Covert hostility is more difficult to recognize and can be more difficult to deal with, since clients themselves may not even be aware of their anger. Some indications of covert hostility are missed appointments; being late for appointments; being sarcastic or cynical; being overly genteel or polite; not getting down to business. Whatever the evidence of covert hostility is, the best approach is *not* to interpret the behavior for the client as latent hostility or passive-aggressiveness but simply to focus on the behavior itself and let the client analyze or interpret it. For instance, the counselor might say, "I've noticed that whenever we talk about your spouse's handling of the family budget, you become sarcastic. What do you think might be going on?" Again, this helps the client to focus on the feedback received and allows angry feelings to be vented. Resistance must be addressed as directly as possible if any good is to come of the counseling relationship.

Other types of resistance behaviors that counselors might encounter during counseling relationships would include withdrawal or passivity; dwelling in fantasy or nonreality; ambivalence or vacillation; and the use of inappropriate humor, to name a few. As mentioned, the counselor should not analyze or interpret a client's resistance behavior since analysis tends only to raise the client's defensiveness. Instead the counselor should be aware of what is occurring, note whether it is a recurrent pattern, and at an appropriate point share such observations in a nonjudgmental manner with the client.

Common Areas of Resistance

Client resistance is almost a given in a financial counseling relationship, probably because clients, when they enter into a counseling relationship, yield a certain amount of their privacy and personal power over the situation to the counselor. Resistance is a way of defending oneself, or restoring some of the balance of power to oneself. Certain discussion areas, because of their sensitive nature, seem to be particularly vulnerable to client resistance.

One such sensitive subject area is death and dying. Because of its uncertainty, death is extremely anxiety-producing to some people. Dr. Elizabeth Kubler-Ross, an eminent authority on death and dying, postulates that there are five stages that a person facing death passes through: denial, anger, bargaining, depression, and acceptance. The first four of these stages are all different forms of resistance that the person uses for self-protection. Financial counselors, when discussing future plans with older people, need to be particularly sensitive to the feelings of their clients. Counselors must listen and observe very closely what clients communicate when discussing death and dying. Counselors must be empathetic to feelings and communicate accurately what is heard and observed. A genuine concern for the feelings and attitudes of clients must be manifested. Counselors must also be aware of their own feelings about death, so that they do not interfere with what clients are feeling and attempting to communicate.

Counselors can help to restore some control over the future by involving clients fully in decision making and planning for contingencies. This allows clients to feel useful, worthwhile, and somewhat in control of their situation.

Another area where resistance may be encountered involves marital tensions, such as separation/divorce, parent-child disputes, sex, the empty-nest syndrome, and midlife crises. While financial counselors are not expected to be highly qualified marriage or family counselors, they should be astute enough to recognize when a married couple is resisting because of an underlying, unexpressed marital problem. And once it is recognized, counselors should be willing and able to focus with the couple on the problem area. Otherwise, if the problem is ignored, whatever decisions are reached will be less valid than those that would be reached after a full airing of the problem. Besides providing a possibly welcome catharsis for the couple, focusing on the problem can enable them to muster their forces in order to arrive at a mutually satisfactory solution. In counseling couples who are in disagreement on a crucial subject, the counselor needs to listen closely to what both partners have to say. It is far too common, unfortunately, to let the more dominant partner do most of the speaking and deciding. Since the outcome of the decision affects both partners, both should be involved in the discussion. To do any less almost guarantees an unsatisfactory conclusion.

Another sensitive area involves the executive who has failed to attain the degree of success he had dreamed of in his profession. His dreams shattered and unfulfilled, he may resort to cynicism, biting sarcasm, or empty humor in an attempt to endure it. Rather than laugh along with him, the effective counselor *reflects* the underlying feeling to let the client know that he or she understands his disappointment. A simple statement like, "I suppose it's a bitter pill to swallow when you've worked so hard to see your personal hopes go unfulfilled," allows your client to feel understood and appreciated. More often than not, the client will begin to discuss more openly how he feels. And once people are able to express their feelings, they are well on the way to addressing their problems in an effective manner.

Resistance behaviors, in any case, are a certain tip-off that the client is having difficulty subscribing to the counselor's line of reasoning. It does no good for the counselor to proceed with business as usual, ignoring the obvious resistance; nothing can be accomplished as long as the resistance continues. The resistance must be dealt with openly and objectively if there is any chance that it will be diminished, allowing the participants to get on with the business at hand.

PROFILE OF THE EFFECTIVE COUNSELOR

The main thing a counselor brings to the counseling hour is himself or herself. Financial counselors, first and foremost, must be themselves in their relation to and interaction with their clients. Each counselor is a human being, complete with strengths and frailties. But each counselor is also a professionally trained individual, a person who, ideally, enjoys listening to and trying to understand other people and to accept them as they are. The effective counselor is also sincere and genuine in attempting to help others learn how to help themselves. This attitude generates interesting, challenging, and highly gratifying work; and it is—more than anything else—hard work when done professionally.

Carl Rogers, in his classic book, *Client-Centered Therapy,* postulated that there are three conditions necessary to bring about constructive client change: (1) unconditional positive regard, (2) accurate empathy, and (3) genuineness.[3] Most counseling theorists agree that if an effective counselor-client relationship is to exist, the counselor must value the client as a unique individual (unconditional positive regard), must be able to perceive and understand what the client is experiencing (accurate empathy), and must be open and spontaneous (genuine).

A constructive counselor-client relationship serves not only to increase the opportunity for clients to attain the goals that are important to them, but also serves as a model of a good interpersonal relationship. Some questions that all counselors ought to ask themselves from time to time are the following:

- Knowing yourself, do you think it will be possible for you to value your clients, especially those who think, feel, and act differently from you?
- How easy or difficult will it be for you to view the world from another's perspective without imposing your own standards, beliefs, and attitudes on that person? Will your own values, ideas, and feelings hinder your understanding of another person?
- How open do you care, or dare, to be with a client? Will you be able to just be yourself, or will you role-play how you think a professional counselor should be?

These are important questions to consider before engaging yourself in the dynamics of a counseling relationship. Far too many financial counselors assume that they have the right kind of personality to counsel others without ever scrutinizing themselves in the same way.

Let us examine the three core conditions to which Rogers refers, and a fourth condition, self-awareness.

Four Characteristics of the Effective Counselor

1. Unconditional positive regard
2. Accurate empathy
3. Genuineness
4. Self-awareness

Unconditional Positive Regard

This quality is often misconstrued as agreement or disagreement with the client. Rather, it is an attitude of valuing the client, or being able to express appreciation of the client as a unique and worthwhile person. Liking and respecting another person have a circular effect. When you value clients, your sense of liking will be communicated to them; this by itself will enhance their feelings for themselves and add to their appreciation of themselves as worthwhile human beings.

Accurate Empathy

Accurate empathy means that your sense of the client's world fits the client's self-image. This gives clients the feeling that you are in touch with them. When clients say something like, "Yes, that's it," or "That's exactly right," it indicates that your response was right on target, and that they feel you are closely following and understanding them.

Learning to understand is not an easy process. It involves the capacity to lay aside your own set of experiences in favor of those of your clients—as seen through their eyes, not yours. It involves skillful listening so you can hear not only the obvious, but also the subtleties of which even the client may be unaware.

Developing accurate empathy also means identifying and resolving your own needs so they do not interfere with your understanding of the feelings and concerns of your client. The counselor who identifies too strongly with the client's state, however, impedes rather than facilitates the counseling objective.

Genuineness

Genuineness means, simply, that the counselor is a "real" person, that is, there is no facade, no role-playing of what a professional counselor is considered to be. Professional counselors are wholly aware of themselves and their feelings, thoughts, values, and attitudes. More importantly, counselors who are genuine are not afraid to express themselves openly and honestly at all times. Financial counselors do not have to become something different for each client with whom they have a relationship. They are role-free; they are themselves at all times.

A counselor who is genuine communicates in a spontaneous and expressive manner and does not conceal anything, is open and willing to listen to whatever the client is willing to discuss, and is consistent. He or she does not think or feel one thing but say another.

One author suggests that effective counselors can

- express directly to others whatever they are experiencing
- communicate without distorting their messages
- listen to others without distorting their messages
- be spontaneous instead of planned or programmed
- respond openly in a specific and concrete manner
- be willing to manifest their own vulnerabilities and frailties
- learn how to be psychologically close to others
- commit themselves to others

A tall order? Perhaps. And yet, for a financial counseling relationship to be effective, it is mandatory that counselors allow themselves to be genuine with their clients. Otherwise, the relationship deteriorates into a charade of two human beings playing prescribed roles with each other, and this defeats the purpose.

Self-Awareness

There is general consensus among counselor-educators that counselors need to be highly aware of themselves and particularly aware of their own attitudes and values. Counselors who are aware of their own value systems have a better chance of avoiding the imposition of their values onto their clients. This quality is of vital importance since we want to help our clients make decisions that stem from their own value systems, rather than from ours. The more we know about ourselves, the better we can understand, interpret, evaluate, and control our behavior and the less likely we are to attribute aspects of ourselves to the client, a rather common defense mechanism known as projection. Before we can be aware of others, it is essential that we be solidly grounded in self-awareness.

Barbara Okun, in her book, *Effective Helping,* suggests that counselors should continually try to determine their own needs, feelings, and values by answering the following questions:[4]

- Am I aware when I find myself feeling uncomfortable with a client or with a particular subject area?
- Am I aware of my avoidance strategies?
- Can I really be honest with the client?
- Do I always feel the need to be in control of situations?
- Do I often feel as if I must be omnipotent in that I must do something to make the client "get better" so that I can be successful?
- Am I so problem-oriented that I'm always looking for the negative, for a problem, and never responding to the positive, to the good?
- Am I able to be as open with clients as I want them to be with me?

The adage "Know thyself" should apply to financial counselors and other helping professionals even more than it does to the population at large. A very large part of our responsibility as counselors is to know ourselves as thoroughly as possible, so that we are then able to provide the very best kind of objective, informed counseling to our clients. A counselor who has "blind spots" about himself or herself will surely be less effective in a helping situation than a counselor who is comfortably self-aware. This is not to say that the counselor is a problem-free, completely self-actualized individual; rather, it means that the counselor is a human being, with a multitude of strengths and even some weaknesses, but the weaknesses are known by the counselor and do not interfere with the dynamics of counseling another person.

Orientation to Values

As human beings, we have value systems that are the result of years of living on this planet. Many of our values are inculcated in us by our parents, by schooling, by religion, by our peers, and by society. However they come to us, they are as much a part of us as our physical and psychological characteristics. This is not to say that they are a permanent, static part of our being, because our values can, and do, change. A vivid example of this type of change came during the 1960s and early 1970s when a whole society's value system was rocked to the core by momentous events such as the assassinations of the Kennedys and Martin Luther King, Jr., the civil rights movement, the war in Vietnam, the women's rights movement, and the Kent State killings. This truly was a time when an entire nation's value system was challenged, and as a result, certain of our long-cherished values were thrust into a state of flux and some ultimately changed. And what happened to the nation was repeated many times over with many individuals in our midst. People who at first accepted the Vietnam War as a rightful intervention by a powerful nation into the affairs of a far-off country slowly changed their feelings about not only that war, but armed conflict in general. And virtually the same thing happened on other controversial issues such as abortion, human rights, euthanasia, and drugs.

The point is that values, while deeply internalized, are not immutable. Counselors need to remind themselves of this fact as they work with clients who are confused and afraid in approaching important decisions. While it is true that we are in many ways a reflection of our past history, we are—or can be—much more than that. There is no need to be shackled to our past. We can, if we choose, overcome our past and live new lives, based upon who we are now and what we believe in and hold to be valuable to us both now and in the future. This is a liberating concept and, as such, frees individuals to think, feel, and behave in ways that are compatible with their present being, rather than dooming them to repeat the past and live in ways that are no longer meaningful.

The financial counselor's role in this situation is to act as a catalyst rather than as a maintainer of the status quo. The implied danger, of course, is that counselors might try to force change in their clients' values and attitudes where none is desired or sought after, or that counselors might subtly or not so subtly try to impose their values on clients. Both of these dangers must be consciously guarded against. What counselors must do is listen carefully to clients as they sift through the various value choices faced, so when clients must finally make the choice, it can be done freely, without encumbrances from the past. Clients must actually be opened up to the freedom of making choices that are relevant and meaningful to their very existence. Good counselors have a knack for being able to do this.

Differences in Values

Each of us has within us a hierarchy of values that makes order of our lives. An older executive facing retirement might, for example, rank security above risk taking when deciding how to invest money. On the other hand, a younger financial counselor might rank risk taking above security in the hierarchy of values. What happens, then, when the risk-taking counselor sits down to counsel the security-minded preretirement executive? If the counselor is sensitive and understanding, he or she will listen to the older person, and try to get a sense of what is important to the client, what the client is willing and unwilling to do. The effective financial counselor does not try to sell the client a product that the counselor believes is right but that the client believes is wrong, unsafe, or risky.

Counseling is caring, and caring means that the counselor cares enough—has enough faith in the client's worth as a unique human being—to permit that client to make value choices that fit his or her value system. The financial counselor can and should provide information that will help the client make the choice, but the choice ultimately belongs with the client, not the counselor. Only in this way are we counselors.

In addition to the differences in values, which often are reflective of the differences in age between counselor and client, we should also consider several other "isms"—sexism and racism—and how they impinge upon the counselor-client relationship. Let us look first at sex differences. Sexist counseling occurs when the counselor uses his or her own sex ideology as a framework for counseling. In the field of financial counseling this might take place when a male counselor discourages a female client from doing something that has traditionally been thought to be in the man's world, such as returning to work while there is an infant at home to be cared for. This kind of subtle advice giving, besides reflecting the obvious sex-role bias of the counselor, is not in keeping with what is happening in many households today. Further, it is intrusive in that the responsibility for making that decision is clearly the client's and not the counselor's. It is critical that counselors learn to recognize their own biases and sex-role stereotypes and not inflict them upon people whom they are trying to help.

In the case of married couples, financial counselors typically counsel both husband and wife. It is important to understand what both partners have to say. It is far too common to defer to the male of the household, the perceived "breadwinner," without taking into consideration what the female spouse has to contribute. When both husband and wife are in complete agreement, no problem exists. But when they disagree—and this is often communicated through nonverbal signals like a sigh, a frown, or an angry glance—it is important to make a point of bringing the subject up for a full discussion. It is far better to spend whatever time it takes to bring both partners to a mutually acceptable decision than to proceed with one person's plan of action, knowing that it doesn't satisfy the other person.

Racism, despite notable progress in the civil rights movement over the past two decades, is still with us in many forms. Counselors engage in racism when they limit the choices of their clients based solely on their clients' race, or when they make faulty assumptions about their clients because of racist stereotyping.

The issue of whether white counselors can be effective in a relationship with African Americans or Hispanics has been the subject of much research, though no conclusive findings exist. An effective counselor should be able to work with people of all races, since all people seem to have the same basic psychological needs and problems. Counselors need to be conscious of their own biases regarding race and to guard against allowing their biases to adversely affect the quality of the counseling relationship. The counseling strategies employed should not differ with regard to the race of the client, any more than they should not differ depending on the sex, age, or religion of the client.

BASIC COMMUNICATION PRINCIPLES

In the previous section we discussed the attributes of an effective counselor. In this section we will explore communication as a process and attempt to relate fundamental principles of communication to effective financial counseling. An effective counselor is also an effective communicator.

Communication is often thought of as one person sending a message through both verbal and nonverbal channels to another person or persons with the intention of evoking a response. A speaker asks, "How are you?" and the listener (or receiver of the communication) answers, "Just fine—except for my back."

Effective communication takes place when the receiver interprets the sender's message in precisely the same fashion in which the sender intended it. Difficulties in communication arise when the receiver misunderstands and/or misinterprets the sender's message. Since any individual's intentions are private and rarely clearly stated, the receiver of the message has the difficult job of decoding the message without knowing for a fact what the sender's intentions are.

In addition, communication failures can also be attributed to the wide variety of stimuli with which individuals are bombarded during the course of a conversation. People try to communicate while watching television or listening to the radio, or they attempt to conduct two conversations simultaneously. But all noise is not auditory; some is emotional in nature. For example, labor-management negotiations are often fraught with suspicion and mistrust. Prejudices and biases, then, are emotionally built-in stimuli that interfere with objective listening and effective communication.

Related to this communication failure is the sad but simple truth that individuals listen in order to evaluate and render judgment about the speaker, which, in turn, makes the speaker guarded and defensive about what he or she is attempting to communicate. Perhaps the best example of this type of ineffective communication is a city council meeting, where one side advocates the raising of taxes, while the other side interrupts, casts aspersions, and generally fights for all it is worth against the tax hike. Whenever there are two people, or two groups, each with a strong vested interest in an emotional issue, the likelihood of there being clear communication is virtually nil.

Communication, even in the best of circumstances, should not be taken for granted. Let us look now at some basic principles of communication theory.

- Communication is learned through experience, but experience itself does not necessarily make one an effective communicator. As children, we learn how to communicate by imitating our models—parents, brothers, sisters, neighbors, playmates, babysitters. Unfortunately, not all of our models are effective communicators; thus, we acquire poor habits of communication early, and those habits, like all habits, are difficult to break. A child reared in a home where everyone talks at the same time and no one listens carries this model upon leaving the home.
- The meaning of words is illusory; words do not mean—people do. Words are merely symbols. Consider, for example, a simple word like rock. The teenager immediately thinks of loud music; the geologist thinks of a hard object created millions of years ago; the burglar thinks of a diamond ring; the old lady thinks of her favorite chair, and so on. The point is that a word can have almost as many meanings as there are people who use it.
- Language is learned; thus, in a sense, we are programmed, and the meaning of words stays within us for future reference. This programming is extremely helpful since, once we learn a word, it

usually remains ours for a lifetime. However, this programming can also serve as an impediment to open communication with others, in that we often refer back to our original conceptions of words without thinking how others might interpret them. For example, the word girl, once used to refer to any female, is now clearly inappropriate in referring to an adult woman in this age of women's rights.

- No two people are programmed alike; therefore no symbol can always be interpreted the same way. Individuals differ in the nature and degree of their understanding. We perceive things differently, from our own frame of reference, so meanings differ.
- It is impossible for any individual to encode or process all parts of a message. Besides the fact that words are often inadequate in describing accurately what we are feeling or thinking, there is also the problem of distortion, that is, an individual's altering the event to suit his or her own purposes. But even if we have the precise word and communicate it without distortion, we still are faced with the problem of the receiver's receiving it in the same way in which it was intended.
- Some experts claim that the single greatest problem with communication is the assumption of it. Too many people assume that their messages are automatically understood. We also sometimes assume that our perceptions are more right than the perceptions of someone else. Where human communication is concerned, no assumptions can or should be made.
- We can never not communicate. Anything we say or do can be interpreted in a meaningful way as a message. Even during periods of silence, communication takes place. Nonverbal behavior (which will be discussed in some detail shortly) such as eye contact, facial expressions, gestures, body posture, voice inflections, hesitations, and the like, all speak volumes. In fact, most sociological research claims that approximately two-thirds of the total message is communicated via nonverbal channels, especially where human emotions are concerned.
- Listening is communication, too. Unfortunately, not everyone is a good listener; yet, that should not be too surprising, since listening as a communication skill is rarely, if ever, taught formally. To speak precisely and to listen carefully present a real challenge to all of us. The way in which we listen and respond to another person is crucial for building a fulfilling relationship. When we listen carefully, with understanding and without evaluation, and when we respond relevantly, we implicitly communicate to the speaker, "I care about what you are saying, and I'd like to understand it."
- The most effective communication occurs when the receiver of a message gives understanding responses, sometimes called paraphrases. A client might say, "I don't know. . . . I doubt that we can afford to send both of our kids to college." A financial counselor using an

understanding response would respond to the above statement with, "So you're just not sure you have the resources for a college education right now." While it might be tempting to try to convince the clients at this juncture that there is a way to finance their children's college education, the understanding response communicates a desire to understand the clients without evaluating these statements as right or wrong. It also helps the counselor to see the expressed ideas and feelings of clients from their point of view.

- Personalizing messages enhances the communication process and the counseling relationship. The hallmark of personal statements is the use of the personal pronouns, I, me, and my. Using generalized pronouns such as everyone, anyone, or somebody to refer to your own ideas only tends to confuse clients and, hence, results in ambiguity and faulty understanding. Personal statements like, "I can appreciate your concern over not having adequate resources," reveals your own feelings to clients and increases the personal quality of the relationship.

ELEMENTS OF NONVERBAL BEHAVIORS

As mentioned above, clients communicate many feelings and attitudes to counselors through nonverbal behaviors, including (but not limited to) fear, anxiety, sincerity, confusion, anger, aggression, happiness, hostility, interest, boredom, and concern. The two main sources of nonverbal behaviors are the *body* and the *voice*. From these two sources come seven types of nonverbal signs of meaning: *body position, body movement, gestures, facial expressions, eye contact, voice tone*, and *voice pitch*. Each of these types of nonlinguistic signs conveys a wealth of information to the observant financial counselor. It should be noted that the counselor's first impressions of the meaning or significance of any body language must be checked out against other clues given by the client.

Elements of Nonverbal Behaviors

- The body
  –Positions
  –Movements
  –Gestures
  –Facial expressions
  –Eye contact
- The voice
  –Tone
  –Pitch

The Body

When learning to improve one's ability to observe the nonverbal behaviors of clients, it is important to notice the various ways by which the body actually communicates, either in agreement or in variance with what is actually said. In particular, the counselor should notice and learn to interpret the communications that are transmitted by the client's body positions and movements.

Positions

Overall body posture is the first thing the observant counselor notices. Clients who sit erect and comfortably are usually relaxed. If they lean slightly forward, it is usually a sign of interest and involvement in the counseling session. If they slouch, or seem to draw away from the counselor, they may have no interest or trust in the counselor—or they may be bored. Good client posture may indicate self-assurance and positive self-esteem. Poor posture may signal a lack of self-assurance or low self-esteem.

The counselor should also notice the position of the client's arms and legs. When the legs are uncrossed and the arms are positioned comfortably at the sides, the client is usually relaxed and open. Tightly crossed arms and legs, on the other hand, may indicate distrust or unreceptiveness. The facial position of the client should also be noticed. Most people's faces are expressive of a wide range of ever-changing feelings. The client whose face appears frozen in one position may be signaling fear, anxiety, or anger, or some other prepossessing feeling that could become a block or obstacle to open communication with the counselor.

Movements

The client who frequently changes body positions may be indicating physical or emotional discomfort, or a lack of interest. The counselor should take note of such movements and try to relate them to information gleaned later.

There is reason to believe that body language may be more honest or pure than verbal communication. In certain positive, straightforward human experiences we know that it is. The impulsive hug or kiss of greeting for people we care for is the most obvious example. But people also communicate through the body when they don't want to communicate, or when they are hiding or contradicting themselves. For example, a client may say, "No, I'm not nervous about investing in a tax shelter," while biting his nails, pulling at his hair, or fidgeting distractedly. People often say what they think they may be expected to say in a given situation or context, not realizing what they may actually be communicating through body language.

Gestures

Hand and arm gestures are usually used to illustrate or accent verbal statements. Hands clasped so tightly that the knuckles are whitened and taut certainly signify something, perhaps fear or anxiety. While jerky hand and arm gestures may indicate anxiety, smooth and flowing gestures usually mean that the client is relaxed and interested in the counseling session. Frequent crossing and uncrossing of the legs, or bouncing a leg that is crossed, may indicate nervousness, boredom, or lack of interest.

Facial Expressions

The financial counselor can learn much from a client's facial expressions. Look for frowns, smiles, or nervous habits, such as biting the lips. Look especially to see if the client's facial expressions change as topics change, and note whether the expression is appropriate or incongruent. For example, if the client talks about anger, does she appear angry? If she facially expresses disgust about her husband's spendthrift ways, do her intentions in her last will and testament reflect that feeling by providing for her children through a trust, rather than leaving everything outright to her husband?

Eye Contact

Eye contact, or the lack of it, in the counseling session can indicate the client's feeling. If the client's eyes are downcast and rarely meet the gaze of the counselor, the client could be shy, anxious, or fearful (though not necessarily toward the counselor). On the other hand, if the client stares or glares constantly at the counselor, anger or hostility could be indicated. If the client's eyes rove all around the room, looking at the walls and ceiling while the counselor is filling out the data-gathering form, there could be a serious lack of interest in the relevance of data gathering. A client who is open and interested in the counseling session will usually meet the gaze of the counselor. This eye contact of the client usually indicates interest in the session and a positive and concerned attitude toward counseling. Needless to say, reciprocity from the counselor is likely to be perceived by the client in the same way.

The Voice

Nonverbal voice clues can be observed in the tone and pitch of the client's voice. Tone and pitch are qualities of the voice that may indicate the speaker's feelings, quite apart from what is actually said. They should be observed closely.

The Tone

Tone is loudness or softness. The client who talks very loudly or shouts may be indicating anger or hostility. The client who talks very softly may be exhibiting fear or shyness.

The Pitch

Pitch is the quality of a voice that indicates how high or low the voice is on a musical scale. A high-pitched voice may indicate anxiety, fear, or anger. A low-pitched voice may indicate either comfort or control of strong emotions.

Obviously, some people's voices are naturally louder than others. The natural pitch of different voices also varies greatly. The point is not to type these differences but to observe and determine which vocal qualities are natural to a particular client so as to recognize variations. If these vocal qualities do vary during counseling sessions in relation to personal and financial details, they can be important clues to the strong emotions that often affect a client's motivations, needs, and objectives. The counseling sessions themselves are often an inducement to clients to open up and give vent to feelings about their financial condition. Thus voice tone and pitch are important factors for counselors to observe and consider in relation to all other clues that characterize the client and reveal the individual's self-image.

Interpreting the Meaning of Nonverbal Behaviors

It is important for financial counselors to note that in all the descriptions above of nonverbal behaviors, of body language, we have stated that a behavior may or usually does indicate one or more feelings. Nonverbal behaviors are clues that must be clearly observed and compared with what the client says in order to determine whether they are appropriate or compatible with their actions. For example, if a client blurts out, "I am furious with the broker who sold me that bunch of junk bonds last year!" and strikes the desk, the gesture is compatible with the verbal message—it agrees with what the client says. If the client makes the same statement and sits calmly smiling, however, there is incompatible behavior—the body language does not jibe with the verbal message. When the financial counselor observes incompatible behavior of this sort in a client, it should be mentioned to the client in order to clarify which element of the communication is correct.

Nonverbal behaviors are clues or indicators. While they signify something, their meanings can be clouded by incompatibility, distortion, or vagueness. Premature assumptions about what they really mean would be as unprofessional as failing to notice them altogether. For example, a client's palsied hands might be due to one or more of the following causes: nervousness, fear, Parkinson's disease, too much coffee, chemical poisoning, or alcoholism. The client who always talks loudly may be either angry or hard of hearing, or merely an overbearing individual. The client who shows no interest in counseling may be worn out with worrying whether his recent commodities futures trading is going to wipe him out with margin calls, or whether he should buy term or whole life for estate liquidity, or whether he will have an estate. He may be on tranquilizers over worry about a son and heir who himself abuses drugs. For any number of reasons the client may need psychological counseling or therapy before he can undertake financial counseling. In short, not all the problems that clients may bring to financial counseling sessions are financial in origin or nature. When present, these nonfinancial problems will distort client messages and add to the difficulties of clarifying them.

Observant counselors need to be astute enough to discern from among all the verbal and nonverbal clues and be aware that in most client cases there will be a mixture of compatible and incompatible evidence. Counselors thus understand who clients are, where they are, where they want to go; and can then suggest the optimal ways to help each one get there. *Do not assume that you know what a given behavior means.* Check it out and clarify your perception with each client.

And do not forget that as a counselor *you* communicate in both verbal and nonverbal ways, too, just as the client does, and that your communications behaviors very much affect the client. This is particularly true of nonverbal messages. Therefore any of the communications and psychological considerations in this chapter that you may agree are important with respect to the client are also important for you. As a financial counseling professional you will want to remove from your own behaviors those elements that present obstacles and barriers to successful communication with the client and with other professionals with whom you deal. The client is then more likely to accept your role in the counseling situation and, ultimately, the plan you develop for meeting his or her financial needs and objectives. Similarly, other professionals whose expertise you will often need to call upon in developing and implementing a plan will respect your role as a financial counselor and planner.

ATTENDING AND LISTENING SKILLS

Paying attention to clients is the first necessary component in good communication. No matter how expert your other communication skills are, if you are inattentive to your clients' verbal and nonverbal behaviors, you are apt to lose them at the very outset. How often have you been in the company of another person who shies away from looking at you, who glances nervously at his wristwatch, who interrupts you, and who, literally and figuratively, turns his back to you? Surely, if you have had this kind of experience, you can recall how uncomfortable and ill at ease you were with this inattentive behavior.

If a counselor's goal is to understand clients, the counselor must first pay close attention to or focus on their verbal and nonverbal messages. Poor attending and poor listening lead to poor understanding.

FOCUS ON ETHICS
How Ethical Behavior Improves Communication

What happens when words are insufficient? Many clients misunderstand the specifics of the plan being recommended by a financial counselor. This becomes compounded when complex financial instruments are recommended to implement the plan. It is much like drivers and automobiles. Most drivers really need transportation, and cars solve this problem. That doesn't mean that they understand how their cars work.

A financial planner once stated that there are two essential rules to effectively dealing with a client. The first is to earn his/her trust because trust helps break down communications barriers. Different counselors may accomplish this in different ways, but it is necessary for the client to feel free to ask the challenging questions and continue to probe until a satisfactory level of understanding is achieved. There may be limits to what the client can understand and then earned trust is essential.

The second rule is similar. Once established, the maintenance of earned trust remains a critical factor in the counselor-client relationship. The fact that clients do not fully understand does not necessarily imply that they should not act. Indeed, if they understood every aspect of financial planning, they would not need a planner. Clients often make decisions based solely on their trust in their financial adviser.

There is no better way to earn and maintain trust than to develop an unassailable reputation for ethical and professional behavior. A valuable side benefit is improved communication.

Physical Attending

Gerard Egan, a renowned counselor-educator, categorizes attending behavior into (l) physical attending, or using your body to communicate and (2) psychological attending, or listening actively. He uses the acronym, SOLER, as a reminder of the five basic attributes associated with physical attending. Let us look at these five attributes.

- S: Face the other person *squarely*.

When there is face-to-face, direct contact, the communication process is enhanced. You communicate nonverbally to the other person, "I'm here with you; I'm tuned-in and ready to face the issues with you head-on." Turning your body away lessens your involvement with the other person.

- O: Adopt an *open* posture.

There is something to be said about receiving a person with open arms. Crossed arms and crossed legs can inadvertently communicate a holding-off of the other person. An open posture—open arms and uncrossed legs and an open smile—communicates receptiveness to the other person and, hence, increases good communication and decreases defensiveness.

- L: *Lean* toward the other person.

This is another physical signal of interest, involvement, caring. Two people who care about each other, when involved in conversation, almost always can be seen leaning toward each other. On the other hand, two people who are observed leaning away from one another, or sitting rigidly straight in their chairs, seem to be either bored or disinterested, or extremely cautious and defensive about getting involved with each other.

- E: Maintain good *eye* contact.

Good eye contact consists of looking at another individual when you are in conversation. Poor eye contact consists of rarely looking at the other person, or looking away when he or she looks at you or staring constantly with a blank expression on your face. The eye contact should be natural and spontaneous. Since you are interested in your client, you will want to use your eyes as a vehicle of communication.

- R: Be *relaxed* while attending.

It is possible to be both intense while focusing on the client and relaxed at the same time. A nervous, fidgety, or rigid counselor communicates these feelings to the client. A counselor who sits in a casual fashion, who speaks naturally and spontaneously, and who uses natural gestures has the advantage of being free to focus intently upon the client and his or her communication, as well as helping to facilitate naturalness and spontaneity in the client.

SOLER: The Acronym for Physical Attending

S: Face the other person *squarely.*
O: Adopt an *open* posture.
L: *Lean* toward the other person.
E: Maintain good *eye* contact.
R: Be *relaxed* while attending.

As has been mentioned previously, it is impossible not to communicate, so as a counselor you might as well use your body—gestures, posture, eyes—to communicate whatever message you wish to communicate. Otherwise, the body may communicate something you do not wish to communicate. In other words, try to make your body work for you in behalf of your counseling relationship.

Active Listening

So far, attending has been described as a physical activity; active listening brings in the psychological activity involved in attending. Many of us take listening for granted, but there is a distinct difference between simply hearing and actively listening. Hearing means the receiving of auditory signals. A person says, "I have a bad headache," and we hear that message and respond, "That's too bad," or "Here, have a couple of aspirin." An active listener, on the other hand, might respond, "You look as though it's really getting you down." In short, the active listener responds not only to the verbal message received through the auditory channel, but also to the unspoken, or nonverbal message, communicated by the sender's body, facial expression, or tone of voice.

Active listening, then, means putting the nonverbal behavior, the voice, and words together—all the cues sent out by the other person—to get the essence of the communication being sent. An active listener is an understanding listener, one who attempts to see the world from the other's frame of reference. If you can state in your own words what the other person has said, and that person accepts your statement as an accurate reflection of what he or she has said, then it is safe to say that you have listened actively and understood with accuracy.

But it must be stated that active listening is not merely parroting another's words—a computer can be (and has been) programmed to do that. Active listening means involving yourself in the inner world of another person while, at the same time, maintaining your own identity and being able to respond with meaningfulness to the messages of that other person.

Responding during Active Listening

As indicated above, active listening is hard work and requires intense focusing and concentration. Years of not listening have made most of us poor listeners. We are distracted easily; we tend to evaluate and judge what is being said while it is being said, so that we are framing our own responses to the speaker's statement before the speaker is finished talking and, thus, we miss the message.

There are several simple ways of responding to people so that they feel accepted and understood. Let us look at some of these response modalities.

Perhaps the simplest response modality is what Allen Ivey refers to as "minimal encouragers to talk," or "continuing responses." Nonverbally, if you want someone to continue talking, you might smile or nod your head to communicate agreement and/or understanding. Equally as effective in communicating your understanding is a minimal encourager like "uh-huh," "mmmm," "then?" "and . . . ?" These relatively unobtrusive responses encourage the speaker to continue talking. They communicate to the speaker, "Go on, I'm with you."

Another type of response that enhances communication is the *restatement-of-content* response. The rationale for restatement is to let speakers hear what they have said on the assumption that this may encourage them to go on speaking, examining, and looking deeper. Restatement communicates to the client, "I am listening to you very carefully, so much so that I can repeat what you have said." The most effective restatements are those that are phrased in your own words, a paraphrase of what the speaker has stated. To do this effectively, we must temporarily suspend our own frame of reference and attempt to view the world from the other person's perspective. Suppose the client says to you, "I'm really in a financial bind, what with taxes, inflation, fuel bills; I don't know how we make it from one month to the next." An accurate restatement might be expressed, "So things are tough for you financially. It seems like you can't make ends meet." The client, hearing this understanding response, is encouraged to delve more deeply into the situation, feeling that the counselor has, indeed, heard the message on the same wavelength upon which it was transmitted. The bond between client and counselor is, thus, strengthened, and greater opportunities for creative problem solving are opened up.

Just as we manifest understanding for our clients by responding to the content of the message, so may we also show our understanding of the client's experience by responding to the feelings expressed. Sometimes feelings are expressed directly, and at other times they are only implied or stated indirectly. In order to respond to a person's feelings, we must observe the behavioral cues like tone of voice, body posture, gestures, and facial expression, as well as listen to the speaker's words. Consider this client statement, "Within the next few months, we need to buy a new refrigerator and another car. [Sighs] I just don't know where the money is going to come from." A *reflection-of-feeling* response might go, "You sound pretty hopeless about your financial state. It sure is hard to break even, let alone get ahead, these days." Again, by responding in an empathic way to the client's statement, you communicate a deep understanding of the person's experience; in addition, you progress one step further by addressing the nonverbalized feelings. We illustrate to the client that we understand so well what he or she is stating that we can paraphrase both words and feelings. It is helpful to both the client and the counselor to struggle to capture in words the uniqueness of the client's experience. The most effective types of understanding responses capsulize both the feeling and the content of the client's message. The basic format for this type of response is "You feel __________ [feeling] because __________ [content]."

This response enables clients to get in closer touch with the feelings that are an outgrowth of their situations. And that, in turn, facilitates the working through of the problem, because the counselor involves clients in exploring themselves in the problem. Because you have accurately understood and responded to them, clients will go on to share other personal experiences that bear upon the presented problem.

A word might be added here about the difficulties that some people have in dealing with feelings, either their own or the feelings of others. Problems often arise in interpersonal relationships because one or more of the involved persons choose to repress, distort, or disguise their feelings rather than admit that feelings are present and then discuss them openly. This is particularly true of so-called negative feelings like anger, sadness, anxiety, frustration, discomfort, and confusion. In actuality, no feelings are negative since they all are part of being human. In any case, counselors who wish to communicate effectively need to address their own feelings as well as those of their clients. The mutual expression of feelings is an integral part of building a close, trusting, caring relationship.

Two other types of understanding responses need to be mentioned. Each is related to the restatement-of-content and the reflection-of-feeling responses; yet, there is a subtle shade of difference. First is the *clarifying response* that tends to amplify the speaker's statement. The clarifying response does not add anything new to what the speaker has said; it simply expands what has already been stated. The counselor attempts to restate or clarify for the client what the client has had some difficulty in expressing clearly. It is akin to a translation of the client's words into language that is more familiar and understandable to both client and counselor. Suppose a client says, "I'm not sure. Nothing makes sense anymore. Things get more confusing the more I think about them. It's a real puzzle to me." A counselor, by way of clarification, might say, "I can sense your bewilderment. Let me see if I can help out. From what you've said previously, I get the impression that you want to get your mortgage straightened out before you increase your monthly savings. Is that it?" If the financial counselor has, indeed, been following the flow of the client's experience, this statement will help to clarify the client's confusion over the situation. To the extent that the counselor's response is on target, the puzzle becomes suddenly clear and more readily solved.

Another side to the clarifying response concerns the counselor's need to have things clarified. When the counselor is puzzled, then it is certainly legitimate to ask for clarification as, "I'm sorry. I don't follow what you're saying. Can you make that more clear for me?"

Clarified responses are helpful because they:

- facilitate client self-understanding
- attend especially to the client's feelings
- communicate the counselor's understanding
- move the client toward a clearer definition of the problem

The other type of understanding response is *summarization.* Summaries are especially helpful toward the end of an interview, since they focus and capsulize a series of scattered ideas to present a clear perspective. The summary has the effect of reassuring clients that you have been tuned in to their many messages. For the counselor, it serves as a check on the accuracy with which the various messages have been received.

It is often better to have the client do the summarizing. In this way, the client maintains the responsibility for bringing the messages together into a meaningful conclusion. As in clarifying, themes and emotional overtones should be summarized, and the key ideas should be synthesized into broad statements reflecting basic meanings. An example of an effective summary might be: "So today you described your overall financial situation as bleak, although you think you might be able to increase your savings if you could refinance your mortgage. I know you're rightly concerned about that." If the financial counselor has accurately summarized the essence of the interview, the client then has a better handle on the intricacies of the situation, and a resolution is closer at hand.

What we have covered thus far are the basics of nonverbal behaviors, the skills of attending and active listening, and the five basic types of responses associated with active listening: "minimal encouragers to talk," restatement of content, reflection of feeling, clarification, and summarization.

Five Types of Responses Associated with Active Listening

1. "Minimal encouragers to talk"
2. Restatement of content
3. Reflection of feeling
4. Clarification
5. Summarization

The element common to all five of these response modalities is that the counselor follows, or tracks, the client's lead. This response communicates a high level of understanding and enables the client not only to experience what it feels like to be understood, but also to progress further toward an ultimate resolution of the situation. Now we will explore other types of responses in which the counselor, to a certain extent, takes the lead and deviates somewhat from the client's preceding responses.

COUNSELOR LEADING RESPONSES

When the financial counselor decides to make a leading response, it is the counselor's frame of reference that comes into focus. Up to this point, the counselor's responses have followed from the client's statements, but here the emphasis shifts. An obvious danger of this shift is that the counselor may move in a direction in which the client is not yet ready or willing to move. Despite this danger, if the counselor has followed the client closely so far, and if a good relationship has been established, then this different kind of response should not threaten the client, as long as it is interposed carefully and tentatively.

The first of the leading responses is known simply as explanation. Explanation is a relatively neutral description of the way things are. It deals in logical, practical, factual information. It is often offered at the client's request, although there are instances when the counselor will offer an explanation without its being requested. A client may be confused by some terminology that the counselor has used and ask, for example, "Exactly what is an annuity?" The counselor's explanation should be simple, concise, and comprehensible. Long-winded explanations tend to become vague and hard to follow. The counselor should also guard against explaining things in a condescending, patronizing, or pedantic tone. The best explanations are those that are exchanged between equal partners (not superior-subordinates) in a relationship.

Another type of leading response is the interpretive response. Interpretations can be particularly risky when the counselor goes too deep too soon, or when the interpretation is off base. Interpretations often come across as sounding overly clinical, diagnostic, and authoritarian. Despite these drawbacks, interpretations can be extremely effective responses because they often cut to the heart of the matter. When the interpretation makes sense to the client, it definitely accelerates the interview. We should keep in mind that the goal of all interpretive efforts is self-interpretation by the client in order to increase the client's ability to act effectively. The following is an example of a facilitative interpretation:

Client: "I'm not sure whether I want to retire early. I like to keep busy, and I don't know what I'd do with all that free time."

Counselor: "So the prospect of an early retirement is a bit frightening. Maybe you're afraid that you'd just waste your time away?"

Notice that the financial counselor's interpretation did not stray too far from what the client had said. The counselor used the words "frightening" and "afraid," but probably did so on the basis of some fear or trepidation detected in the client's voice. Further, the counselor responded tentatively, using qualifiers like "a bit" and "maybe," and converted the second statement into a question by a raised voice at the end of the sentence. This enables the client to assimilate the counselor's response without feeling as though it has been offered as a fiat from above. The client, thus, is free to accept, modify, or deny the counselor's interpretation, and this is very important. If the counselor's interpretation is inaccurate, it is far better to discover that early than to proceed indefinitely along the wrong path.

A third type of leading response frequently employed by counselors is reassurance, or encouragement. A reassuring response is designed with the intention of making the client feel better, to bolster his or her spirits, and to offer support in a time of need. It communicates clearly to the client that "I am here by your side, ready to aid you in any way that I can." As a means of helping, however, the reassuring response tends to be merely a temporary measure. It is akin to offering a tissue to someone who is crying; the crying may stop temporarily, but the underlying causes have been left untouched. For this reason the counselor must be careful not to use reassurance indiscriminately. The understanding (reflection-of-feeling) response discussed in the previous section on active listening is far more effective when emotions surface. The understanding response communicates accurate empathy; the reassuring response offers only sympathy, and very few people like to feel pitied. Contrast the effect of these two different kinds of responses on our hypothetical client:

Client: "I get so furious whenever my broker ignores me! It's almost as though I don't exist!"

Counselor: (using reassuring response): "Well, don't feel so bad. It doesn't do much good to get so worked up. Try not to worry about it, and you'll feel better."

Counselor: (using reflection of feeling): "I can feel the rage as you speak. You feel like a nonperson around your broker, that you are not getting adequate service for the money you are paying, and that infuriates you."

The first counselor response patches a Band-Aid on a deep wound and is therefore ineffectual. The second response reflects the deeply felt anger and, in so doing, helps the client work through the anger. Reassurance, while not a harmful response, promises pie in the sky and delivers nothing.

The final type of leading response is called advice, or suggestion. Many people actively seek the advice of others, possibly hoping that the advice giver will make the difficult decision for them, or solve their problems for them. And, as chance or human nature would have it, there is certainly no dearth of people in this world willing to dole out free advice. In a financial counseling relationship, however, the best kind of advice is self-advice. Counselors who have been responding in an understanding fashion are already well on their way toward helping clients discover, in their own way and in their own time, what advice is best for them. There are times within a counseling relationship when proffering advice is acceptable, but these times are few. When advice is given, it should be offered tentatively, in the form of a suggestion, or several suggestions, about which the client has the final decision. Otherwise, the counselor not only leads, but takes over the ultimate responsibility for the client's financial plan, and each person has the right to formulate his or her own plan. Advice giving robs the client of this right.

Counselor Leading Responses

- Explanation
- Interpretive
- Reassurance/encouragement
- Advice/suggestion

In the next section, we will look at still another type of counselor response—perhaps the most commonly used response—the question. Questions come in many varieties, some much more effective in communication than others.

THE QUESTION

The question is surely one of the most timeworn response modes used by financial counselors. Many counselors see their main role as an interviewer or an interrogator. The question seems appropriate only when it is an honest attempt to gather information that the counselor requires and to which the client has access. Unfortunately, the question is not always used in this fashion. Moreover, the question-answer dialogue sets up a pattern of communication that is difficult for the participants to break: the client waits for the inevitable question; the question comes, followed by the answer (and not much more), and then comes the wait for the next question. Questioning almost always casts the counselor in the role of authority figure and the client in the role of a somewhat passive subordinate, certainly not the type of interpersonal relationship conducive to effective counseling.

Despite the disadvantages of the question mentioned above, there are times when only a well-phrased question will suffice, particularly when we are seeking data from the client. Even here, though, there is a qualitative difference among the various types of questions that might be asked. Several categories of questions will be discussed in the following section.

Open-ended versus Close-ended Questions

Ideally, questions posed by the counselor should be open-ended and should call for more than just a yes or no response on the part of the client; otherwise, they tend to stifle interaction. The open-ended question allows the client to select a response from his or her full repertory. The close-ended question limits the client to a specific, narrow response, often either a yes or a no. The open-ended question solicits the client's opinions, thoughts, ideas, values, and feelings. The close-ended question typically solicits singular facts or one-word replies.

Contrast the differences in the following sets of questions. The first question in each set is close-ended; the second question in each set is open-ended.

1. a. Are you ready to start an investment program?
   b. How do you feel about starting an investment program?
2. a. Have you given any thought to retirement?
   b. What thoughts do you have about retirement?
3. a. Are you afraid to start saving something now?
   b. Why have you decided to wait to start saving?

As can be readily seen from the above examples, the open-ended questions ask for more complete, comprehensive information. In a way, they force the client to formulate thoughts, ideas, and feelings into fully rounded responses. On the other hand, the close-ended questions solicit only a one-word or short-answer response, requiring little thought and offering virtually no feedback.

Leading Questions

Other types of close-ended questions that are not only ineffective but also manipulative are those termed leading questions. These questions usually begin with, "Don't you think . . . ," or "Do you really feel . . . ." More often than not they lead the client toward a conclusion that the counselor (not the client) has already formulated, so that there is the element of dishonesty in even asking the question. It is far more effective, and honest, for the counselor to rephrase the leading question into a declarative statement in the form of sharing a perception or opinion with the client. Consider the following leading questions:

> "Don't you think you should start an investment program now?"
> "Do you really feel that $100 a month is enough?"
> "Are you sure you've considered all possibilities?"

With just a bit of reflection, we can see that the counselor is actually saying:

> "I think you ought to start an investment program now."
> "I don't feel that $100 a month will be enough."
> "I'm sure there are other possibilities you haven't considered."

The latter statements are much more honest and to the point than the questions from which they stem. Generally speaking, declarative statements communicate far more clearly than the manipulative leading questions. A good rule of thumb to follow in everyday intercourse is to make as many statements as possible and save the questions for honest information seeking.

The Either/Or or True/False Question

Another kind of relatively ineffective question is of the either/or or true/false variety. While this question is not quite as close-ended as the leading question, it is only slightly less closed, since it limits the client to only two options. For example:

> "Do you plan to stay in this house or move to an apartment?"
> "Are you more apt to take a risk or play it safe?"

Clients might prefer both options, or neither, or a third or fourth option; but here they are forced to choose from what we have offered them. The world is not simply black or white; there are various shades of gray; yet, when we phrase questions so that clients are forced to choose from one of two options, we are restricting the clients' responses. We can improve on the preceding examples by asking:

> "What are your plans after retirement regarding housing?"
> "How do you usually make your decisions?"

Again, we see that by opening up the question we allow clients to respond freely from their own frame of reference, and not from ours. And this is what good interviewing is all about.

Why Questions

Even though why questions can be classified as open-ended questions and, thus, theoretically sound, such is not the case. On the surface, questions beginning with why appear to be legitimate enough, signifying the inquiry into causal relationships, as in, "Why are you planning to retire at age 62?" Unfortunately, why questions carry with them a connotation of implied disapproval by the questioner, thus forcing the person being asked the question to justify or defend his or her thoughts, ideas, or actions. Even when that is not the meaning the questioner intends, that is generally how the why question is received. The why question tends to question the client's motivation (or lack of motivation) and, thus, creates a certain defensiveness.

Perhaps the chief reason that why questions are received so poorly dates back to the manner in which parents put children on the spot: "Why didn't you pick up your room?" "Why don't you have your shoes on?" "Why can't you be more careful?" And, of course, this line of inquiry is later picked up by teachers with students: "Why don't you have your homework?" "Why didn't you study for this test?" In short, as children we learned that when an adult asked us a question beginning with why, it meant, "Change your behavior; think as I think; behave the way adults do." And we carry that lesson with us throughout life, usually responding to why questions in a defensive, negative manner.

So unless there is a valid reason for asking a why question and when no other type of question will suffice, it is generally better to avoid why questions.

Question Bombardment

Still another kind of faulty questioning technique occurs when we ask double, triple, or even quadruple questions without waiting for a response. This is frequently referred to as question bombardment. As absurd as this may sound, it occurs far too frequently in interviews to escape comment. For example: "What type of investment program appeals to you most—stock, municipal bonds? Or would you rather look into annuities? When do you think you'd be ready to begin?" The first question in the series is open-ended in nature and can stand by itself quite well; yet the interviewer isn't content to let well enough alone, but instead tacks on other, more restricting close-ended questions. The result is that the client is caught in a hailstorm of questions all at one time and, more often than not, gets the opportunity to respond to only one of the several questions asked. If more than one question needs to be asked, it is better to form separate questions, waiting for a full response to each question before going on to the next one. The other issue to be addressed, though, is whether so many questions need to be asked in the first place.

Categories of Questions

- Open-ended questions
- Close-ended questions
- Leading questions
- Either/or and true/false questions
- Why questions
- Question bombardment

Concluding Remarks

Questioning is a major component in the repertory of most interviewers. Yet that need not be so. If we wish to become better communicators, one thing that we can do is to convert some of our questions (especially close-ended, leading, either/or, and why questions) into statements. With a statement, we assume responsibility for what we say. With a question, we shift the responsibility to the other person, which may sometimes be necessary. Far too often, however, we simply shirk our own responsibility for, and involvement in, the interaction when we revert to questioning. As stated previously, counseling is not the same as interviewing. If we hope to do counseling, we need to do far more than simply ask one question after another.

NOTES

1. Portions of this chapter dealing with elements of nonverbal behaviors have been excerpted from a two-part article entitled "Practical Communications Skills and Techniques in Financial Counseling," by Dale S. Johnson, PhD, CFP, published in *The Financial Planner,* 11, no. 6 (June 1982): pp. 98-105, and 11, no. 7 (July 1982): pp. 62-71. They are reprinted by arrangement with the editor of that journal.
2. Charles J. Stewart and William B. Cash, *Interviewing Principles and Practices,* 7th ed. (Dubuque, IA: Brown & Benchmark, 1993).
3. Carl R. Rogers, Library of Congress #51-9139. 1951.
4. Barbara F. Okun, *Effective Helping: Interviewing & Counseling Techniques,* 4th ed. (Pacific Grove, CA: Brooks-Cole Publishing Co., Division of Wadsworth, Inc., 1992).

5

Time Value of Money: Basic Concepts and Applications

Robert M. Crowe

Chapter Outline

THE BASICS OF TIME VALUE

Why is it that when individuals take out a loan they must repay more money than they borrowed? Why is it that a supplier of materials you use in your business offers you a discount from the full amount of the invoice if you pay within 30 days? Why does the savings and loan association credit depositors' savings accounts with interest? Why is it when you deposit a perfectly good check in your checking account the bank may deny you access to the money for a few days? Why is it inadequate for an investor to evaluate a proposed investment project on the basis of its payback period, that is, the number of years it will take for the total cash inflows from the project to equal the initial cash outlay? Why does the winner of a lottery prize of $1 million after taxes, payable in $100,000 annual installments over 10 years, actually receive less than $1 million of value?

The answer to all of these and dozens of similar questions centers on the time value of money (TVM). These questions arise in all fields of business and personal financial planning, real estate, marketing, investments, accounting, insurance, banking, and many other fields.

Some erroneously believe that a dollar is a dollar is a dollar. The fact is that dollars to be paid or received in different time periods have different values. Ask yourself these questions: When would you rather receive your federal income tax refund check—as soon as you file your return or 3 months later? When would you rather collect the rent from the tenants in your apartment building—at the beginning of each month or at the end?

Opportunity Cost

Solely on the basis of intuition, most people probably would conclude, quite properly, that they would prefer to receive money sooner rather than later. Why? Because the sooner they receive money the sooner they can use it, either by spending or investing it, for their own benefit. If they wait for the money, they opportunity to engage in the best alternative activity (spending or investing the money now) with the same resource (the specified sum of money).

Conversely, most people would intuitively conclude that if they must pay out a specified sum of money, they would prefer to pay it later rather than sooner. Why? Because the longer they can delay the payment, the longer they can use the money, either spend it or invest it, for their own benefit. If they pay the money early, they incur an opportunity cost.

The Role of Interest

Since a given sum of money due in different time periods does not have the same value, a tool is needed in order to make the different values comparable. That tool is *interest.* Interest can be viewed as a way of quantifying the opportunity cost incurred by one who waits to receive money or one who gives up the opportunity to delay paying it.

For example, if you deposit $1,000 in a savings account and leave it there for one year, you expect to have more than $1,000 in the account at the end of that time. You expect your account to earn interest. By postponing the use of your money and allowing the bank to use it, you incur an opportunity cost. The bank gives you interest as compensation for your cost.

To reverse the situation, assume a loan you took out at your bank matures in one year, at which time you are obligated to pay $10,000. If you repay the loan today, one year early, you should be required to pay less than the full $10,000. If you forgo the opportunity to delay the repayment, you should be compensated in return by having the amount payable reduced.

The specific interest rate used to quantify opportunity cost is made up of two components: a risk-free rate and a risk premium. At a minimum, the opportunity cost of letting someone use your money is the rate of return you could have earned by investing it in a perfectly safe instrument. A reasonable measure of this minimum opportunity cost is the rate of interest available on 3-month U.S. Treasury bills. These bills are always available and, for all practical purposes, risk-free. At the time of this writing, 3-month T-bills were yielding between 5 and 5.25 percent on an annual basis.

In addition, most situations in which you allow someone else to use your money entail some risk of loss for you. For example, the market value of your investment instrument may decline. The purchasing power of your principal sum may be eroded by inflation. The person or organization using your funds may default on scheduled interest and principal payments. Tax laws may be changed to lower the after-tax return on your investment. These and other types of risk associated with letting someone else use your funds should be reflected in a risk premium, or in an add-on to the risk-free opportunity cost of money. Theoretically, the higher the degree of risk, the greater the risk premium and, therefore, the higher the interest rate you should require.

Simple Interest versus Compound Interest

There are two ways of computing interest. *Simple interest* is computed by applying an interest rate to only an original principal sum. *Compound interest* is computed by applying an interest rate to the total of an original principal sum and interest credited to it in earlier time periods.

To illustrate the difference, assume $100 is deposited in an account that earns 6 percent simple interest per year. At the end of each year the account will be credited with $6.00 of interest. At the end of 5 years there will be $130 in the account (if no withdrawals have been made), as shown in table 5-1.

TABLE 5-1
Accumulation of $100 in 5 years at 6% Simple and Compound Interest per Year

	Simple Interest			Compound Interest		
Year	Principal Sum	Interest	Ending Balance	Principal Sum	Interest	Ending Balance
1	$100.00	$6.00	$106.00	$100.00	$6.00	$106.00
2	$100.00	$6.00	$112.00	$106.00	$6.36	$112.36
3	$100.00	$6.00	$118.00	$112.36	$6.74	$119.10
4	$100.00	$6.00	$124.00	$119.10	$7.15	$126.25
5	$100.00	$6.00	$130.00	$126.25	$7.58	$133.83

If instead the account earns 6 percent compound interest per year it will grow to a larger amount, again as shown in table 5-1. The extra $3.83 in the account when it is credited with compound interest is interest earned on previous interest earnings.

Notice the difference in the annual amount by which the account grows when compound rather than simple interest is credited. The balance grows by a constant amount, $6.00 per year, when simple interest is credited. In the case of compound interest, however, the account balance grows by an increasing amount each year. The rate of growth, however, remains the same, 6 percent in this illustration.

Most of the day-to-day situations calling for a recognition or calculation of the time value of money involve compound interest, rather than simple interest. Hence this and the following chapter will deal only with compound interest.

Compounding versus Discounting

The process by which money today, a *present value,* grows over time to a larger amount, a *future value,* is called *compounding.* The process by which money due in the future, a *future value,* is reduced over time to a smaller amount today, a *present value,* is called *discounting.*

Figure 5-1 shows the difference between present and future value, with compound interest as the link between the two. Compounding may be viewed as a movement up the curve, while discounting may be viewed as a movement down the curve. Note also that the link between present and future value in figure 5-1 is shown as a curve, rather than as a straight line, to reflect the application of compound interest rather than simple interest. When compound interest is used, the future value rises each year by an increasing amount of money (or the present value declines by a decreasing amount of money).

FIGURE 5-1
Compound Interest as the Link between Present Value and Future Value

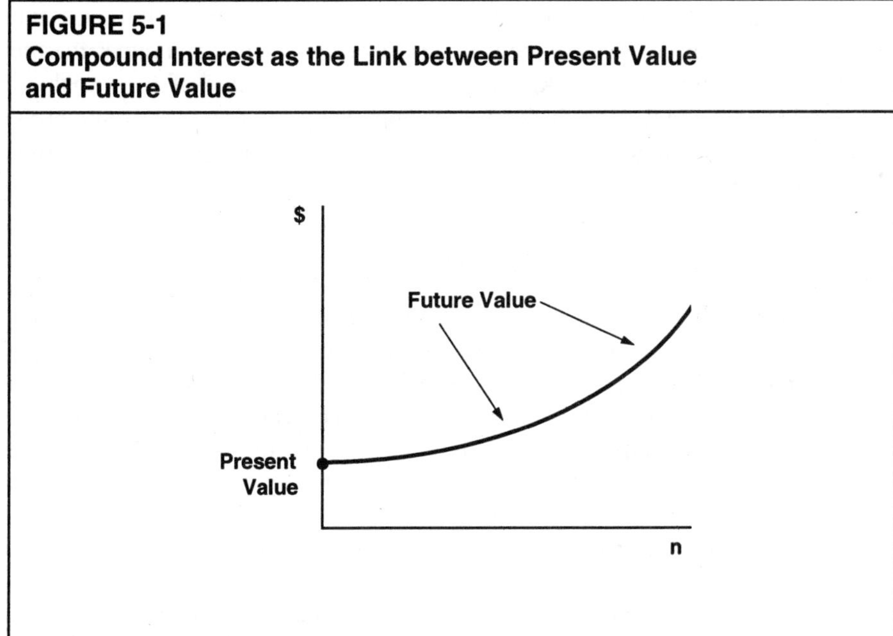

This figure depicts compound interest as the link between the two values. Dollar amounts are reflected by the vertical axis, and the number of periods during which compounding or discounting occurs is reflected on the horizontal axis. As one moves up the curve (compounding), the future value grows by increasing amounts. As one moves down the curve (discounting), the present value declines by decreasing amounts.

Two major factors influence the shape of the curve in figure 5-1. These are (1) the number of periods over which compounding or discounting occurs, and (2) the interest rate used in the compounding or discounting process. All other things being equal, the greater the number of periods, the greater the length of the curve. Consequently, as the number of periods is increased, the difference between the present value and the future value also increases. Similarly, all other things being equal, the greater the interest rate, the steeper the slope of the curve. Thus as the interest rate is increased, the difference between the present value and the future value also increases.

These relationships among the number of periods (n), the interest rate (i), the future value of money (FV), and the present value of money (PV) may be summarized as follows: in compounding, FV moves in the same direction as n and i (it increases as they increase); in discounting, PV moves in the opposite direction from n and i (it decreases as they increase).

Note that there are four key variables in the most basic problems involving the time value of money. They are the number of periods, the interest rate, the present value, and the future value. In the most basic problems, you will be given three of the variables and be called upon to solve for the fourth. In more complex time-value problems the four variables are the number of periods, the interest rate, the amount of each payment in a series of payments, and either the present value or the future value. Again, you will be given three of the variables and asked to compute the fourth. And some apparently complex time-value problems are simply combinations of two or more of these basic four-variable problems that are linked together.[1]

The Power of Compound Interest

Of course your concern with compound interest is not so much with the shape of a curve as with the effect that compound interest has on time value. That effect is extremely powerful, especially when a high interest rate or a long period of time is involved. For example, in the year 1980 the consumer price index, a fairly good measure of the rate of inflation, rose by 13.5 percent over the preceding year. If that rate of inflation had continued throughout the decade of the 1980s and into the latter half of the 1990s, the same bag of groceries that cost $100 in 1980 would have cost about $355 in 1990! By 1997 it would have cost $861!!

One more example will help to emphasize the point. Peter Minuit is said to have purchased the island of Manhattan in the year 1626 for about $24 worth of beads. If instead of buying Manhattan at the beginning of 1626 he had put the $24 into a bank account paying 6 percent compound interest per year and left the money there continuously, at the end of 1997, 372 years later, he would have had a bank account of over $62 billion, if income taxes are ignored. You are invited to judge for yourself whether Peter made a wise purchase.

But to carry the illustration a step further, notice in table 5-2 how slowly Peter Minuit's account would have grown in the first 300 years. His money was on the flat part of the curve in figure 5-1. By 1925 he wouldn't even have become a billionaire. He really would have become fabulously wealthy only in the past 70 years, during which time his wealth would have grown by over $60 billion. In 1997 alone it would have increased by about $3.5 billion! (Again, an important point to remember is that the *rate* of growth of his wealth was constant throughout the period, 6 percent per year. It is the *amount* of growth that accelerates under compound interest.)

TABLE 5-2
Accumulation of $24 in 372 Years at 6% Compound Interest per Year

Year	Ending Balance
1626	$25
1675	$442
1725	$8,143
1775	$150,000
1825	$2,763,000
1875	$50,895,000
1925	$937,500,000
1975	$17,268,877,000
1997	$62,229,044,000

Effect of Income Taxes

One factor that must be considered in the analysis of several types of time-value-of-money problems is the impact of income taxes—federal, state, and local. For example, the rate of return nominally realized on most investments should be adjusted downward to an after-tax basis. Similarly, the nominal size of a payment or interest rate on a loan should be adjusted downward by the borrower if the payments are deductible for income tax purposes. We have not explicitly factored tax considerations into the problems discussed in this chapter and the next but have, instead, implicitly assumed that all values in the problems discussed are after-tax values.

Frequency of Compounding or Discounting

As you will see in the next chapter of this book, there is another factor, in addition to the interest rate and the number of years, that affects the size of the present and future values of money. That factor is the frequency with which the interest rate is applied in the compounding or discounting process.

Throughout this and most of the next chapter, it will be assumed that the interest rate is applied once per year, which is called annual compounding or discounting. You should recognize, however, that in many cases interest rates are applied several times within a year—for example, semiannually (twice a year), monthly (12 times a year), or daily (usually computed in commercial transactions by applying the interest rate 360 times per year).

All other things being equal, the greater the frequency with which compounding or discounting occurs, the greater is the effect on the growth of a future value or the decline of a present value. For example, a $1,000 principal sum that is credited with 8 percent compound interest will grow to a future value of $1,166.40 in 2 years if compounding occurs annually. If compounding occurs semiannually, on the other hand, it will grow to $1,169.86; and if compounding occurs monthly, it will grow to $1,172.89. Conversely, the present value of $1,000 due 2 years from now is $857.34 if an 8 percent annual interest rate is applied once per year. If the discounting is applied semiannually, however, the present value is only $854.80.

The explanation of why the frequency of compounding or discounting produces these results and of how to compute present and future values based on various frequencies will be deferred to the next chapter. Meanwhile, you should assume in the text and problems for each chapter that compounding and discounting occur only once per year.

Measuring the Number of Periods

Before moving on you should keep in mind one other factor regarding the compounding or discounting process—the importance of being accurate in measuring the number of periods during which the compounding or discounting occurs. That, in turn, depends on whether the process begins and ends at the beginning or the end of the periods in question.

If that sounds a bit confusing, refer back to the example of Peter Minuit in table 5-2. In that illustration, year number one was 1626, and the account balance for that year was $25. That result occurred because it was assumed that $24 was deposited on January 1, 1626, the *beginning* of year one, and the account balance was computed on December 31, 1626, the *end* of year one. As a consequence, year one produced approximately $1.00 of interest.

On the other hand, what if Peter had deposited the initial $24 at the *end* of year one? Obviously, the ending account balance for that year would have been $24, and no interest would have been earned in that year.

The effect of this change in the assumption about when the initial deposit was made, whether at the start or the end of the first year, carries over into all remaining years. In table 5-2 the ending balance for 1997, some $62.2 billion, was the result of compounding for 372 years, that is, from January 1, 1626, to December 31, 1997. If Peter had begun his investment just 12 months later, at the end of 1626, compounding would have occurred for only 371 years by December 31, 1997, and his account balance would have grown to only about $58.7 billion. In other words, the 12-month delay would have cost him over $3.5 billion of interest earnings. What a difference a year makes!

In order to be sure you are counting n, the number of periods, accurately in solving time value of money problems, it is helpful to draw time lines, such as those in figure 5-2, and to mark the timing of known dollar values in the problem with vertical arrows along the time line and the timing of unknown dollar values with question marks. The reason for drawing certain arrows below the line and others above it will be explained shortly. For the present you need only to recognize how the *timing* of each sum of money in a problem, both the known and unknown sums, is depicted on a time line. The upper time line, for example, depicts a case where you are to calculate the future value as of the beginning of the sixth period (which is the same as the end of the fifth period) of a deposit made at the beginning of the first period. The lower time line depicts a situation in which you are to compute the present value as of today (the start of period one) of a series of payments that will occur at the end of each of the next four periods. Time lines can be constructed for all types of time-value-of-money problems, as will be shown frequently throughout this chapter and the next one.

FIGURE 5-2
Time Lines as a Help in Counting Number of Periods of Compounding or Discounting

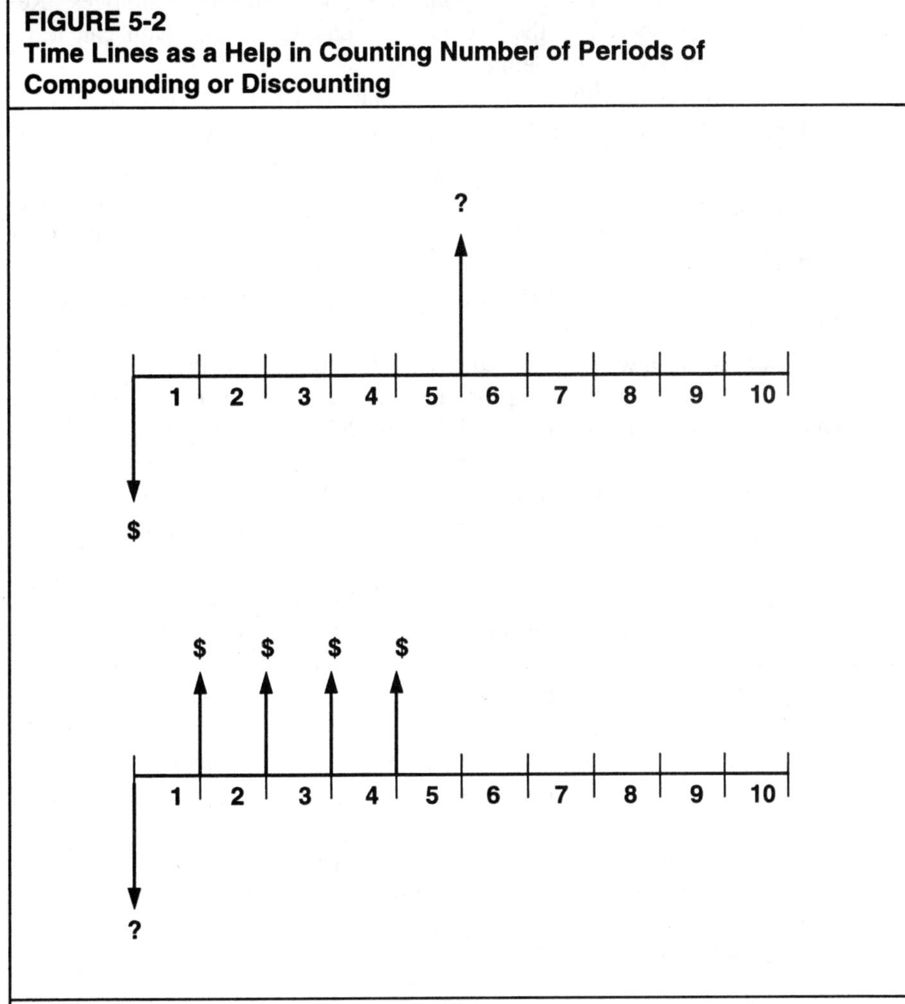

The top time line reflects a problem in which a present value is deposited at the start of period one and you are asked to solve for the future value at the start of period six, or the end of period five. The lower time line depicts a problem in which a sum of money is to be paid at the end of each of the next four periods and you are asked to solve for their present value as of the start of period one.

Plan of the Time-Value Discussion

The balance of this chapter utilizes and builds upon the elementary concepts presented thus far. Emphasis is placed upon explaining *how to solve* various types of basic problems involving the time value of money. The same emphasis is present in the following chapter, where somewhat more advanced and complex time-value-of-money problems are explained. Practical illustrations are used constantly to demonstrate principles and solution techniques. Review problems are presented at the end of each chapter so that you can test your mastery of each type of problem explained.

Although this and the following chapter deal with the interactions among numbers—dollars, interest rates, and time periods—you do not need a sophisticated knowledge of mathematics in order to perform any of the calculations. An ability to add, subtract, multiply, and divide, as well as an ability to raise a number to a power, will be helpful. Even these are not totally essential, however, if you have access to a calculator. (The procedure for raising a number to a power by means of a calculator is described in appendixes C, D, and E at the end of this book.)

These two chapters contain an explanation of several tools and can be used to solve time-value-of-money problems. At the low-tech end of the spectrum, explanations are provided for solving them by directly applying mathematical formulas to the data. A rung higher up the technological ladder is the use of tables of time-value factors of various types. Still higher on the ladder, two of the most popular electronic calculators with time-value capabilities are also explained.

The explanation of the various types of time-value problems treated in these chapters proceeds in a logical progression from the least complicated to more advanced types. The rest of this chapter deals with the future value and present value of single sums of money, as well as the future value and present value of level streams of money payments, called annuities. Chapter 6 then takes up the future value and present value of nonlevel streams of money payments. These topics are then applied to investment decisions through an explanation of discounted cash flow analysis. Then the assumption that compounding, discounting, and payments occur only once per year is dropped, and an explanation is provided on how to deal with any of the preceding types of problems where compounding, discounting, or payment frequency is greater than annual.

Now, to begin.

FUTURE VALUE OF A SINGLE SUM

The most frequently encountered and easiest to understand application of the time-value-of-money concept involves the future value of a single sum. As explained earlier, determination of a future value of a sum of money entails a process of compounding, or increasing, the present value at some interest rate for some period of time. The most common example is the growth of a sum placed in an interest-bearing savings account. Recall, for example, that in table 5-1 a \$100 deposit made today (present value) will grow to \$133.83 (future value) at the end of 5 years at 6 percent compound interest.

Basic Time-Value Formula

The basic formula for computing the future value of a single sum of money, from which all other time-value formulas are derived, is the following:

$$\text{FVSS} = \text{PVSS} \times (1 + i)^n$$

where

FVSS = the future value of a single sum
PVSS = the present value of a single sum
i = the compound annual interest rate, expressed as a decimal
n = the number of years during which compounding occurs

In other words, add the interest rate (expressed as a decimal) to one, and raise this sum to a power equal to the number of years during which the compounding occurs. Then multiply this by the present value of the single sum or deposit in question to compute the future value of that single sum.

For example, assume that \$5,000 is placed on deposit today in an account that will earn 9 percent compound annual interest. To what amount will this sum of money grow by the end of year 7? The problem is depicted on a time line in figure 5-3.

It is important, both conceptually and mathematically, to recognize that in every time-value-of-money problem there is an implicit tradeoff over time of a sacrifice for a gain, a cost for a benefit. For example, you may be willing to loan money to a friend today (a cost or cash outflow in the present) in order to be repaid a larger amount later (a benefit or larger cash inflow in the future). Throughout the time-value-of-money discussions in this book, the nature of this tradeoff will be pointed out over and over. For purposes of consistency among the time lines used to depict various types of problems to be discussed, present values will be depicted below the line, as will periodic cash outflows. Future values and periodic cash inflows will be shown as above-the-line factors.

To return to the problem at hand, then, the \$5,000 that is placed on deposit today represents a present value. The amount to which it will grow at 9 percent compound annual interest by the end of the seventh year is the future value. The basic time-value formula can be used to compute the solution as follows:

$$\begin{aligned} FVSS &= PVSS \times (1 + i)^n \\ &= \$5{,}000 \times 1.09^7 \\ &= \$5{,}000 \times 1.828039 \\ &= \$9{,}140.20 \end{aligned}$$

FIGURE 5-3
Time Line Depiction of FVSS Problem

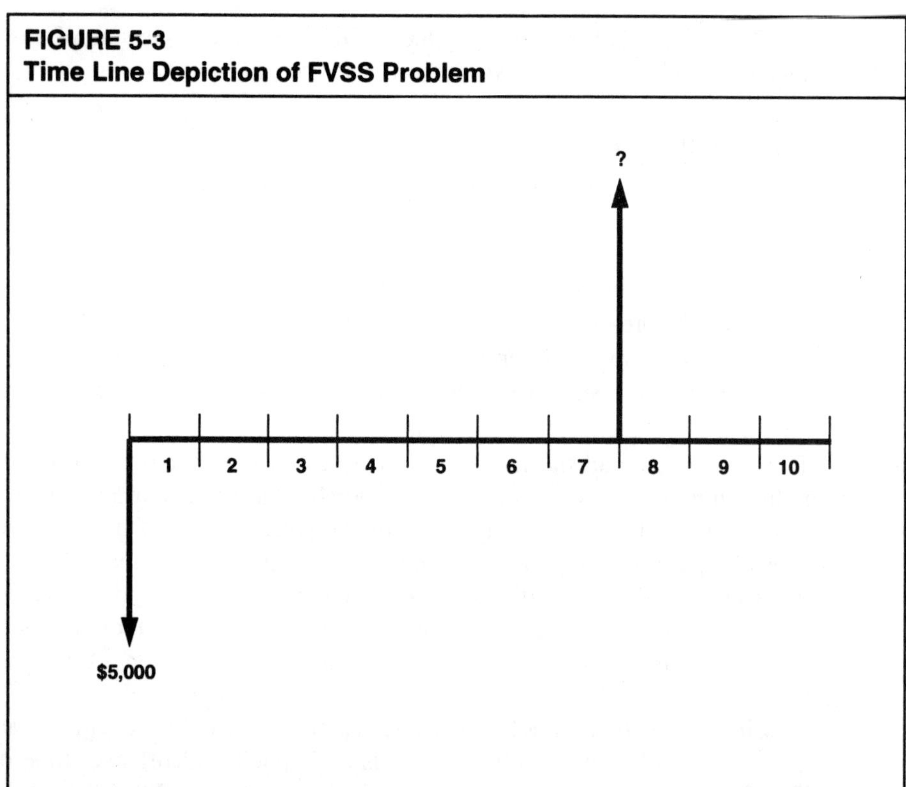

This time line depicts a problem in which a known single sum, $5,000, is deposited today, at the start of year one, and you are to calculate its future value as of the end of year seven. The time line also illustrates the basic tradeoff present in all time-value-of-money problems. Here the tradeoff is a cash outflow today (the deposit, shown below the time line) for a larger cash inflow later (the account balance at the end of the seventh year, shown above the time line).

To reiterate a point made earlier in this chapter, note what would happen to FVSS if i were more than 9 percent or if n were more than 7 years. In either case the quantity $(1 + i)^n$ would be larger than 1.828039, so that when multiplied by $5,000 the FVSS would be larger than $9,140.20. That is, future value increases as the interest rate or the number of years increases, and it falls as either of them is lowered.

FVSS Table

The process of raising (1 + i) to the nth power can be time consuming and tedious, as well as filled with possibilities for making arithmetic errors. To simplify the task, a table has been constructed showing the value of $(1 + i)^n$ for various rates of interest and numbers of periods. (See table B.1 in appendix B.) Excerpts from the table are presented below. All that needs to be done is to select the correct factor from the table and multiply it by the present value of the sum in question to compute its future value.

For example, look down the 9 percent column to the row for seven periods and find the factor 1.8280, virtually the same amount that was computed in the preceding example when the quantity 1.09 was raised to the seventh power.[2] What that computation and the table have disclosed is that if the present value of a single sum is one, its future value at 9 percent or seven periods is 1.8280. Since the present value of the single sum in the illustration is not one but $5,000, the factor for one must be multiplied by $5,000 to produce the future value of that sum of money, namely, $9,140.20.

Take another look at table 5-3. Note as you move from left to right across a particular row in the table, to higher and higher interest rates, the FVSS factor increases. Also, as you move from top to bottom down a particular column in the table, to higher and higher numbers of periods, the FVSS factor increases. Once again, FVSS rises as either i or n rises, and vice versa.

TABLE 5-3
Future Value of a Single Sum Factors

n/i	7%	8%	9%	10%	11%
1	1.0700	1.0800	1.0900	1.1000	1.1100
2	1.1449	1.1664	1.1881	1.2100	1.2321
3	1.2250	1.2597	1.2950	1.3310	1.3676
4	1.3108	1.3605	1.4116	1.4641	1.5181
5	1.4026	1.4693	1.5386	1.6105	1.6851
6	1.5007	1.5869	1.6771	1.7716	1.8704
7	1.6058	1.7138	1.8280	1.9487	2.0762
8	1.7182	1.8509	1.9926	2.1436	2.3045
9	1.8385	1.9990	2.1719	2.3579	2.5580
10	1.9672	2.1589	2.3674	2.5937	2.8394
11	2.1049	2.3316	2.5804	2.8531	3.1518
12	2.2522	2.5182	2.8127	3.1384	3.4985
13	2.4098	2.7196	3.0658	3.4523	3.8833
14	2.5785	2.9372	3.3417	3.7975	4.3104
15	2.7590	3.1722	3.6425	4.1772	4.7846

Computing FVSS with a Financial Calculator

A powerful tool for solving time-value-of-money problems is the financial calculator. This type of calculator greatly speeds the task of solving these problems, especially the more complex ones described later. Three of the most popular electronic calculators with finance functions currently on the market are the HP-12C Programmable Financial Calculator, the HP-17B II Financial (Business) Calculator, both produced by Hewlett-Packard Company, and the BA-II Plus calculator produced by Texas Instruments Incorporated. In this book an explanation will be furnished showing how to solve on these three calculators each type of time-value-of-money problem as it is encountered.[3] The individual keystrokes in each sequence of calculator keystrokes shown are separated by commas. If at some point in a sequence you key in an incorrect number, you can correct the mistake by immediately pressing the CLX key on the HP-12C, the left arrow or CLR key on the HP-17B II calculator, or the right arrow or CE/C key on the BA-II Plus.

Using the HP-12C

To use the HP-12C calculator to solve problems involving future value of a single sum, turn the machine on by pressing the ON key in the lower left corner of the keyboard. Next, depress the yellow f key[4] and the CLX key, which has REG printed above it. This serves to clear any data that may have been stored earlier in the financial and several other "registers" (memory units) of the machine. If you wish to clear only the financial registers, press the yellow f key and the x $\lessgtr$ y key, which has FIN printed above it, instead. (It is a good idea to get into the habit of clearing the memory of the calculator each time you use it.) Next, depress the yellow f key and the number 2. This will cause the machine to display dollar values carried to two decimal places, which is the level of precision to be used for dollar values throughout most of this chapter and the following one. (As will be explained later, other values, such as those for n and i, will sometimes be entered or displayed with other numbers of decimal places.)

By the way, what you have just done affects only the number of decimal places *displayed*. In most calculations it does not have any impact on the precision with which the machine performs the actual calculations.

The next steps are to enter the three known values in the FVSS problem, namely, PVSS, n, and i. These may be entered in any order. The language of the HP-12C, however, includes an important convention that reflects the cost-benefit tradeoff in all time-value problems referred to earlier. This convention, called the cash flow sign convention, requires that at least one (and usually only one) value entered into the calculator in a time-value problem be entered as a negative number. This is accomplished through use of the CHS (change sign) key in the top row of the keyboard. If this is not done, the cash flow sign convention usually causes solutions to problems to be displayed as negative numbers. For purposes of consistency, present values will be entered or displayed as negative numbers. Also, as will be explained later, the amount of a payment that constitutes a cash outflow in a series of payments in some types of problems will be entered or displayed as a negative number on the HP-12C.

Now take a moment to review the keys in the left-hand portion of the top row of the keyboard. These keys (n, i, PV, PMT, FV), as well as the yellow and blue functions they activate and the CHS key, will be used in solving various types of time-value-of-money problems.

To return to the example given earlier, assume you wish to know the amount to which a single sum of $5,000 will grow in 7 years at 9 percent compound interest. Since i is 9, press the 9 key, then the i key. Since n is 7, depress 7, then n. And since the sum of money today is $5,000, press 5000, CHS (since it is the present value), and PV. Finally, press FV and the answer, $9,140.20, should appear on the display.[5]

If you wish to change one of the data items in the problem, you may do so without reentering all the information. For example, if you wish to recalculate the same problem with a 12 percent interest rate, simply press 12, i, and FV. The new amount, $11,053.41, should appear on the display.

Using the HP-17B II

If you are using the HP-17B II to solve TVM problems, you should first take care of a number of housekeeping chores. Turn the machine on by pressing the CLR key in the lower left corner of the keyboard. Turn it off by pressing the colored shift key[6] just above it and then the CLR key again. (Note that OFF is printed in color above the CLR key.) Now adjust the contrast level on the display screen to one that is comfortable for you. Do this by holding down the CLR key and pressing the + key or the – key several times. Next, select the Algebraic system of entry logic by pressing shift and MODES on the DSP key. Now press the menu key, the key labeled ^, that is directly below ALG on the screen. Then press the EXIT key in the upper right portion of the keyboard. Do not change this setting—ever!

Next, set the number of decimal places to be displayed on the screen. We will use two decimal places for most dollar values in this book, so press DSP, the menu (^) key under FIX, then 2, and the INPUT key in the upper left portion of the keyboard. (In some cases, such as when dealing with large dollar amounts, we will display figures with no decimal places. In other cases, such as when calculating an interest rate, we may use four decimal places.

By the way, the setting for the number of decimal places applies only to what appears on the display. It does not normally affect the precision with which the machine performs actual calculations.

Of *extreme* importance as a housekeeping chore, you should set the HP-17B II for one payment period per year and one compounding period per year. In chapter 6 we will take up problems in which more than one payment or compounding period occurs in a year, but for now we will keep life simple. Press shift, MAIN on the EXIT key, the FIN menu key, the TVM menu key, the OTHER menu key, 1, the P/YR menu key, shift, MAIN, and CLR. Do not change this setting—ever!

One more important housekeeping chore that should be performed before every time-value problem is taken up is to clear the calculator of any data left in it from a previous problem. To do this, press shift, MAIN, the FIN menu key, shift, CLEAR DATA on the INPUT key, shift, and MAIN. Get into this habit every time you turn the calculator on and every time you wish to solve a new problem. Otherwise, you may produce incorrect results for the problem.

Now that all of the housekeeping has been taken care of, you will not need to do it again (except to clear the machine). The various settings will remain in the machine continuously, unless and until you specifically change them. So let's proceed to compute the future value of a single sum. Turn the machine on and press shift and MAIN. On the display screen you will see the calculator's main memory system. We will use only the finance menu system, so press the FIN menu key. The next level of the menu shows TVM, ICNV, CFLO, BOND, and DEPRC. In this chapter we will use only the TVM functions, so press the TVM menu key.

The next steps are to enter the three known values in the FVSS problem into the calculator. In doing so, it is important to remember the cost-benefit tradeoff present in all TVM problems as was explained earlier. Entering a number as a negative is accomplished through the use of the +/– key, which is located next to the INPUT key. For purposes of consistency, *present values* will be entered or displayed as negative numbers. Also, as will be explained later, the amount of a payment that constitutes a cash *outflow* in a series of payments in some types of problems will be entered or displayed as a negative number.

Now take a moment to review the TVM menu. The display shows one payment per year, which we entered earlier, and either END MODE or BEGIN MODE. We can ignore these modes for now, as they will not affect the calculations to be performed in this chapter. The display also shows the labels N, I%YR, PV, PMT, FV, and OTHER. The menu keys for these labels will be used to solve many types of TVM problems.

To return to the example given earlier, assume that you wish to know the amount to which a single sum of $5,000 will grow in seven years at 9 percent compound interest. Since the number of periods is 7, depress 7, then the N menu key. Since the interest rate is 9, press the 9 key, then the I%YR menu key. And since the sum of money today is $5,000, press 5000, the +/– key (since it is a present value), and the PV menu key. Finally, press the FV menu key and the answer, $9,140.20, will appear on the display.[7]

If you wish to change one or two of the data items in the problem, you may do so without reentering all the information. For example, if you wish to recalculate the same problem with a 12 percent interest, simply press, 12, the I%YR menu key, and the FV menu key. The new answer, $11,053.41, will appear on the display.

Using the BA-II Plus

In order to solve time-value-of-money problems using the BA-II Plus calculator, turn the machine on and clear the display screen by pressing the ON/OFF key in the upper right-hand corner of the keyboard. Next, clear the calculator of any previous information contained in the calculator's memory units. This is accomplished by pressing the gray key labeled 2nd in the upper left-hand corner[8] and the number 0 key, which has MEM printed above it. Then press 2nd and the FV key, which has CLR TVM printed above it. Then to complete the task, press 2nd again, followed by CE/C key with CLR Work printed above it. (It is a good idea to get into the habit of clearing the memory of the calculator each time you use it.) Next press 2nd, the decimal point key with Format printed above it, the number 2 key (for the number of decimal places desired), and finally the ENTER key. This will cause the machine to round numbers to two decimal places, which is the level of precision we will use for dollar values. (As will be explained later, other values, such as those for n and i, will sometimes be entered or displayed with other numbers of decimal places.)

By the way, what you have just done affects only the number of decimal places *displayed.* In most calculations it does not have any impact on the precision with which the machine performs the actual calculations.

The BA-II Plus uses two modes for solving the problems we will be discussing: the standard-calculator mode (which is used for routine arithmetic and for most basic time-value-of-money problems) and the prompted-work sheet mode (which is used to solve some advanced problems we will discuss later). For now, put the machine in the standard-calculator mode by pressing 2nd followed by the CPT key that has QUIT printed above it.

Take a moment to review the keys in the third row from the top of the keyboard. These keys (N, I/Y, PV, PMT, and FV), along with the 2nd key and the CPT (compute) and ENTER keys in the top row, will be used in solving various types of time-value-of-money problems.

The language of the BA-II Plus includes an important convention that reflects the cost-benefit tradeoff inherent in all time-value problems as described earlier. This convention requires that at least one (and usually only one) value entered into the calculator in a time-value problem be entered as a negative number. This is accomplished through the use of the +/– key in the bottom row of the keyboard. For consistency, present values will be entered or displayed as negative numbers. As will be explained later, the amount of a payment that constitutes a cash outflow in a series of payments in some types of problems will also be entered as a negative number on the BA-II Plus.

To return to the example given earlier, assume you wish to know the amount to which a single sum of $5,000 will grow in 7 years at 9 percent compound interest. These three known values should be entered into the calculator. They may be entered in order. Since the interest rate per year is 9 percent, press 9 and I/Y. Then enter the number of years involved by pressing 7 and N. Next is the sum of money today. Press 5,000, +/– (to change it to a negative value because it is a present value), and PV. The BA-II Plus is shipped with internal settings that assume 12 payment periods per year and 12 compounding periods per year. The following entries will convert the settings to one payment period and one compounding period per year: 2nd, P/Y, 1, 2nd, SET, ENTER, ↓, 1, 2nd, SET, ENTER, CE/C, ENTER. Finally, press CPT and FV and the answer, $9,140.20, should appear on the display.[9]

If you wish to change one of the data items in the problem, you may do so without reentering all the information. For example, if you wish to recalculate the same problem with a 5-year compounding period, simply press 5, N, CPT, and FV. The new amount, $7,693.12, should appear on the display.

Rule of 72

Occasionally you may find it necessary to obtain a precise measurement of the effect of interest in the compounding process and that a rough estimate of the future value of a single sum will suffice. In such cases a simple device called the "rule of 72" may be useful.

The rule of 72 is a quick method of estimating how long it will take for a sum to double in value at various compound interest rates. In this method the number 72 is divided by the applicable interest rate expressed as a whole number. The quotient is the number of periods in question.[10]

For example, at a compound annual interest rate of 9 percent, a $100 principal sum will double in value and reach $200 in approximately (72 ÷ 9 =) 8 years. It will double again and reach $400 in approximately another 8 years and double still again, reaching $800, at the end of approximately 8 more years. At a compound annual interest rate of 6 percent, on the other hand, the growth of the principal sum will be slower, since it will take about (72 ÷ 6 =) 12 years for each doubling to occur.

Remember that the rule of 72 produces only approximations, and that for most purposes you will want to be more precise. Moreover, the amount of imprecision produced by using the rule of 72 increases as the interest rate and the principal sum are increased. (As a partial corrective measure, some prefer to divide the interest rate into the number 78 for interest rates of 20 percent or more.) More precise methods for computing the effects of compounding than the rules of 72 or 78 will be used in the balance of this chapter and the following one.

Computing n or i

In some types of problems involving future value of a single sum, FVSS and PVSS are known, as well as either i or n. The task in such cases is to use the three known values to compute the fourth.

For example, assume that you plan to deposit $1,200 in a savings account and withdraw the money when the account balance reaches $1,500. How long will you have to wait if the annual compound interest rate on the account is 7.5 percent?

The reader who is mathematically talented can solve this problem through the basic time-value formula by substituting the known values in it as shown below, and then solving for n.[11]

$$1500 = 1200 \times 1.075^n$$

Alternatively, if you happen to have an FVSS table with a column of factors for an interest rate of 7.5 percent, read down the column to find the factor closest to 1.25, which is 1500 ÷ 1200. Then read across to the years column to determine the approximate n. (From table B.1 in appendix B, you can find that the approximate n is 3 years.)

It should be obvious that neither the formula nor the table provides a quick and precise method for dealing with the problem of computing n. An electronic calculator with finance functions, however, can compute n as readily as it computes FVSS.

On the HP-12C, for example, after clearing the machine as described, enter the three known values in any order and solve for the fourth. Press 7.5, i, 1500, FV, 1200, CHS (in accordance with the machine's cash flow sign convention), PV, and n. The answer, 4.00 years, should appear on the display.

Actually this is an incomplete answer because of a design limitation of the HP-12C in dealing with this type of problem. If the answer is not an integer, or whole number, the HP-12C usually rounds the answer up to the next higher integer. This in effect means that the final year contained in the displayed value for n is actually only a partial year. (The HP-12C rounds down to the next lower integer if the portion of n to the right of the decimal point is less than .005, resulting in a slight understatement of the actual n.) If you wish a more precise value for n on the HP-12C, the best approach is to use the formula in note 11 at the end of this chapter, together with the log function of the calculator.

The HP-17B II and the BA-II Plus provide a more precise answer to the problem of computing n than does the HP-12C. If you are using the HP-17B II, set the calculator to display, say, four decimal places. Then go to the TVM menu system and clear its memory. Then use the menu keys to enter 7.5 as I%YR, 1200 as a negative PV, and 1500 as FV. Press the N menu key and the answer, 3.0855 years, will be displayed.

If, instead, you are using the BA-II Plus, after clearing the machine's display and memory and setting it to, for example, four decimal places as described earlier, press 7.5, I/Y, 1500, FV, 1200, +/–, PV, CPT, and N. The answer, 3.0855 years, appears on the display.

Instead of solving for n in a time-value problem, in many cases the task will be to solve for i. For example, what compound annual interest rate must you earn on your money if you have $6,000 to invest today and wish to have $10,000 in 5 years? Solving this type of problem is complex mathematically. Hence an explanation involving the use of a formula is not attempted here.

Use of the FVSS table to compute an interest rate is more feasible, at least for simple problems. The approach in the present example is to look across the row for the number of periods in the problem, five, until you find the FVSS factor closest to 1.6667, which is the FVSS, $10,000, divided by the PVSS, $6,000. In table B.1 in appendix B the factors 1.6474 and 1.6851 appear in the 5-year row. Look at the interest rates at the top of these columns and you can properly conclude that the interest rate in this problem is somewhere between 10.5 percent and 11.0 percent. Perhaps that is a sufficiently close approximation for some purposes. Alternatively, you could use a process of interpolation to get closer to the exact answer. Much greater convenience and precision in solving for i, however, is possible with a financial calculator.

On the HP-12C, for example, set the number of decimal places to four and enter the three known values in any order: 10000, FV, 5, n, 6000, CHS, PV, i. After a few seconds the answer should appear as 10.7566 percent. On the HP-17B II, with the calculator displaying four decimal places, clear the TVM memory and use the menu keys to enter 5, N, 6000, +/–, PV, 10000, FV, and I%YR. The answer will appear as 10.7566%. Or on the BA-II Plus, after you make sure the memory is clear, set the number of decimal places to four and press 5, N, 6000, +/–, PV, 10000, FV, CPT, I/Y to produce the answer, 10.7566 percent. (As with the HP-12C, any order in which you choose to enter the three known variables on the other two calculators is acceptable.)

PRESENT VALUE OF A SINGLE SUM

The preceding pages dealt with the question of compounding, of computing how a known single sum of money accumulates over time to an unknown future value. Now the question will be reversed. Given the future value of a single sum of money, what is it worth today? What is its present, or discounted, value?

For example, assume that in 4 years it will be necessary to spend $125,000 to replace an asset that is wearing out. How much money should be on hand today in an account earning 10 percent compound interest in order to reach that goal? Or assume that you are scheduled to receive a $75,000 lump-sum distribution from a trust 5 years from now. For how much would you sell that right today (if you are permitted to do so) if interest rates are 7 percent? (See figure 5-4.)

Using the Time-Value Formula

You learned earlier that FVSS can be found through the formula

$$\text{FVSS} = \text{PVSS} \times (1 + i)^n$$

Students of elementary algebra will recognize that this formula can be rearranged to

$$PVSS = FVSS \times \left[\frac{1}{(1 + i)^n}\right] = \frac{FVSS}{(1 + i)^n}$$

That is, FVSS multiplied by the mathematical reciprocal of $(1 + i)^n$, which is the same as dividing FVSS by $(1 + i)^n$, produces the PVSS. Discounting is thus the reverse of compounding. When compounding you should multiply the known sum by $(1 + i)^n$, whereas in discounting you should multiply it by the reciprocal of that quantity (or divide it by that quantity).

FIGURE 5-4
Time Line Representation of PVSS Problems

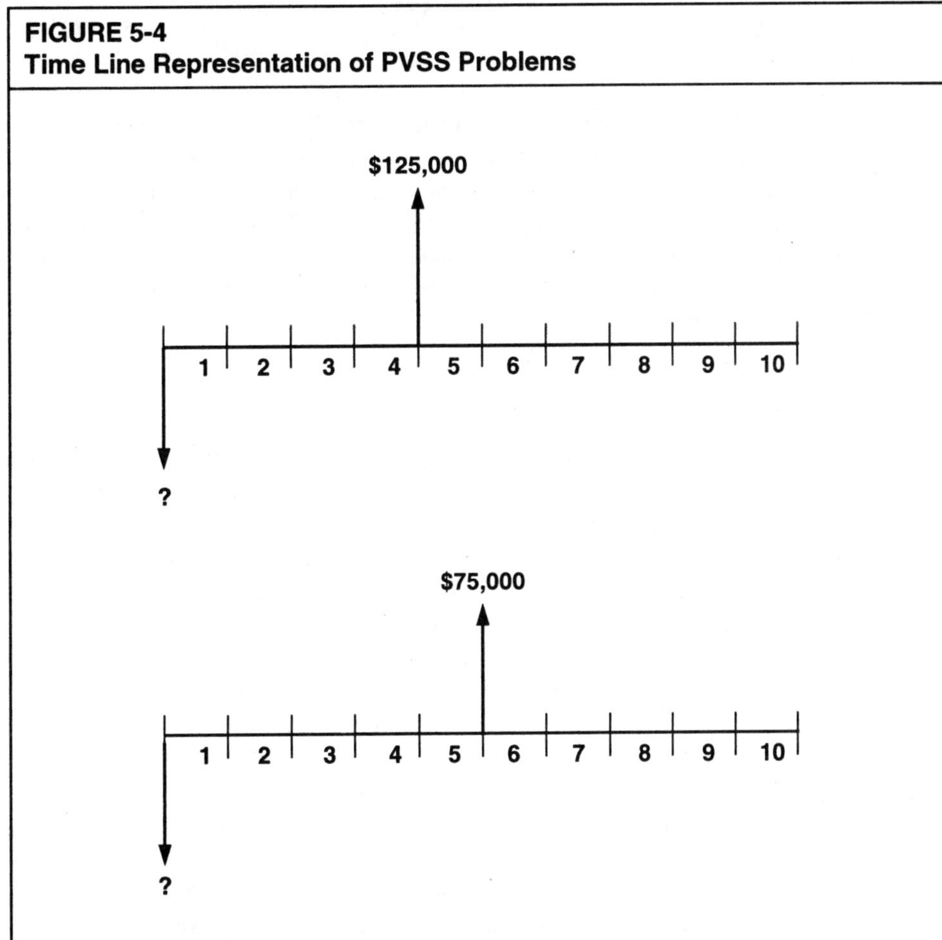

The time line on the top represents a problem in which you are asked to determine the present value of a $125,000 single sum due 4 years hence. In the time line on the bottom the problem is to compute the PVSS when FVSS is $75,000 due in 5 years.

In the top of figure 5-4, then, you need to have $125,000 in 4 years for replacement of the wearing-out asset. If you can earn 10 percent compound interest, you should set aside today a total of a little over $85,000. That is,

$$\text{PVSS} = \$125{,}000 \times \left[\frac{1}{1.10^4}\right] = \frac{\$125{,}000}{1.10^4} = \frac{\$125{,}000}{1.4641} = \$85{,}376.68$$

This amount, accumulating at 10 percent compound annual interest, will grow to the necessary $125,000 when it is needed in 4 years.

And the present value of that $75,000 trust fund distribution due to be received in 5 years, if the interest rate is 7 percent, is a little more than $53,000.

$$\text{PVSS} = \$75{,}000 \times \left[\frac{1}{1.07^5}\right] = \frac{\$75{,}000}{1.07^5} = \frac{\$75{,}000}{1.4026} = \$53{,}472.12$$

Note the effect of a change in i or n on PVSS. If either of these is increased, the denominator of the formula increases and, when it is divided into FVSS, the resulting PVSS declines. For example, the present value of the $75,000 trust fund distribution due in 5 years is only $46,569.39 if the interest rate used in discounting is 10 percent; it is still smaller, $34,987.87, if it is due in 8 years and the interest rate is 10 percent. A decrease in either i or n, on the other hand, causes PVSS to rise.

Using the PVSS Table

The calculation of present values by means of the formula is as tedious, time consuming, and susceptible to errors as is the calculation of future values. To simplify the process of computing PVSS, a table has been constructed showing the value of $1 \div (1 + i)^n$ for various rates of interest and numbers of years. (See table B.2 in appendix B.) Excerpts from that table are presented below.

This table, it should be remembered, is a direct by-product of table 5-3, which showed FVSS factors. All that was done to produce table 5-4 was to divide each factor in table 5-3 into one; that is, each PVSS factor is the reciprocal of the FVSS factor for the same n and i.

To compute the present value of a single sum, select the appropriate factor from the PVSS table and multiply it by the future value of the sum in question. For example, to the present value of $125,000 needed in 4 years and discounted at a 10 percent interest rate, look down the 10% column to the row for four periods. The factor, .6830, is multiplied by $125,000 to produce the answer, $85,375. And the present value of $75,000 to be received in 5 years and discounted at 7 percent is $53,475 ($75,000 x .7130).

Once again, review table 5-4 to see the effect of changes in n and i on PVSS. As you move down any interest-rate column to higher levels of n, the PVSS factor, and hence PVSS, declines. And as you move across the row for any number periods to higher levels of i, the PVSS factor, and hence PVSS, declines.

TABLE 5-4
Present Value of a Single Sum Factors

n/i	7%	8%	9%	10%	11%
1	0.9346	0.9259	0.9174	0.9091	0.9009
2	0.8734	0.8573	0.8417	0.8264	0.8116
3	0.8163	0.7938	0.7722	0.7513	0.7312
4	0.7629	0.7350	0.7084	0.6830	0.6587
5	0.7130	0.6806	0.6499	0.6209	0.5935
6	0.6663	0.6302	0.5963	0.5645	0.5346
7	0.6227	0.5835	0.5470	0.5132	0.4817
8	0.5820	0.5403	0.5019	0.4665	0.4339
9	0.5439	0.5002	0.4604	0.4241	0.3909
10	0.5083	0.4632	0.4224	0.3855	0.3522
11	0.4751	0.4289	0.3875	0.3505	0.3173
12	0.4440	0.3971	0.3555	0.3186	0.2858
13	0.4150	0.3677	0.3262	0.2897	0.2575
14	0.3878	0.3405	0.2992	0.2633	0.2320
15	0.3624	0.3152	0.2745	0.2394	0.2090

Computing PVSS with a Financial Calculator

Using the HP-12C to Compute PVSS

The task of computing the present value of a future sum of money is greatly simplified by the HP-12C financial calculator. As explained earlier, clear the machine and set it to display two decimal places. The next step is to enter the three known values into the machine in any order. Then press the PV button to solve for the present value of the single sum in question.

For example, assume that you own a zero coupon bond that will mature in 13 years, at which time it will pay you $1,000. Meanwhile, it will pay you nothing. What would you sell the bond for today if you believe you could invest the proceeds elsewhere and earn 9 percent compound interest?

Enter 9, i, 13, n, 1000, FV. The calculator is now programmed to compute the present value of the $1,000 due to be received in the future. Depress the PV key and the answer, $326.18, should be displayed. (Remember that the HP-12C's cash flow sign convention referred to earlier shows the answer as a negative number if all the data are entered as positive numbers.) That is, if you were to invest $326.18 at 9 percent compound interest, you would have $1,000 at the end of 13 years. (You may wish to verify this by computing the FVSS of $326.18 as explained earlier in this chapter.)

Using the HP-17B II to Compute PVSS

If you wish to use the HP-17B II to compute the present value of a single sum, set the calculator to display two decimal places. Clear the TVM menu system's memory. Then enter the three known variables in the problem by pressing the appropriate menu keys. Lastly, press the PV menu key to produce the answer.

For example, assume that you own a zero-coupon bond that will mature in 15 years for $1,000. Meanwhile, it will pay you nothing. What would you sell the bond for today if you believe you could invest the proceeds elsewhere and earn 8 1/2 percent compound interest?

Enter 15 as the N, 8.5 as the I%YR, and 1000 as the FV. Press the PV menu key to find the answer, and $294.14 will be displayed. (Remember that present values are displayed as negative numbers because the three known variables were all entered as positive numbers.) That is, if you were to invest $294.14 at 8.5 percent compound interest, you would have $1,000 at the end of 15 years. (You may wish to verify this by computing the FVSS of $294.14 as explained earlier in this chapter.)

Using the BA-II Plus Calculator to Compute PVSS

If you wish to use the BA-II Plus calculator to compute the present value of a single sum, clear the memory and set the machine to display two decimal places, as was explained earlier. Then enter the three known values into the calculator in any order. Finally, press the CPT and PV keys to compute the present value of the single sum in question.

For example, assume that you own a zero coupon bond that will mature in 6 years, at which time it will pay you $1,000. Meanwhile, it will pay you nothing. What would you sell the bond for today if you believe you could invest the proceeds elsewhere and earn 11 percent compound interest?

Enter 1000, FV, 11, I/Y, 6, N. The calculator is now programmed to compute the present value of the $1,000 due to be received in the future. Depress the CPT and PV keys and the answer, $534.64, should be displayed. (Remember that the BA-II Plus shows the answer as a negative number if all the data are entered as positive numbers.) That is, if you were to invest $534.64 at 11 percent compound interest for the next 6 years, you would have $1,000 at the end of that time. (You may wish to verify this by computing the FVSS of $534.64 as explained earlier in this chapter.)

Rule of 72

Earlier in this chapter, the rule of 72 was presented as a quick method for estimating how long it takes a sum of money to double in value. It can also be used to estimate how long it takes a sum of money to halve in value. For example, if an average annual inflation rate of 8 percent should be experienced over an extended period, a person's $50,000 salary would fall in purchasing power to $25,000 in approximately (72 ÷ 8 =) 9 years (if the salary remains at $50,000).

Computing n or i

As is true of future-value problems, it is sometimes useful to be able to compute either n or i, given the other and given FVSS and PVSS. For example, assume that you owe $5,000 to be paid in a lump sum in 2 years. The lender offers to accept $4,750 today in satisfaction of the loan. Should you accept the offer? The answer depends at least partly on the rate of return (interest) the lender is effectively offering you.

This can be determined by using table B.2 in appendix B. First divide the present value, $4,750, by the future value, $5,000. The answer is .9500. Then look across the row for two periods and find the PVSS factor closest to .9500. That factor is .9518, which is in the 2.5% column. Hence the lender is offering you about 2.5 percent per year to pay the loan early. That hardly sounds like a bargain!

Alternatively, you can use a financial calculator. Set your HP-12C to display four decimal places. Then enter 5000, FV, 4750, CHS (again, present values should be entered as negative numbers), PV, 2, n. Then press the i key to produce the answer, 2.5978 percent. Or set your HP-17B II to display four decimal places. Then press 2, the N menu key, 4750, +/– (because it is a present value), the PV menu key, 5000, the FV menu key, and the I%YR menu key. The answer is 2.5978 percent, the rate of return you would realize by paying off the loan today. Or set your BA-II Plus to display four decimal places. Then press 2, N, 4750, +/– (again, present values should be entered as negative numbers), PV, 5000, FV. Then depress the CPT and I/Y keys. The lender has offered you a compound annual rate of return on your money of 2.5978 percent.

To reverse this illustration, if you insist on obtaining an 8 percent compound annual rate of return on your money, when would you be willing to pay the lender $4,750 to discharge your $5,000 debt? If you wish to use table B.2 to find the number of periods, look down the 8% column to find the factor nearest to .9500. The closest the table comes is to .9259 in the row for one period. This means you would not be willing to pay off the loan more than one year early.

As was explained earlier, the HP-12C provides only an approximate answer to this type of problem. Press 4750, CHS, PV, 5000, FV, 8, i, n to produce the answer, one year. The HP-17B II and the BA-II Plus are more precise. Set the HP-17B II to display four decimal places. As always, clear the TVM menu. Then enter 8 as the I%YR, 4750 as the negative PV, and 5000 as the FV. Press the N menu key to produce the answer, 0.6665 years. Or set the BA-II Plus to display four decimal places, press 8, I/Y, 4750, +/–, PV, 5000, and FV. Now press CPT and N to compute the answer, 0.6665. That is, if you repay the $5,000 loan about

8 months early (two thirds of one year) for $4,750, your compound annual rate of return will be 8 percent.

FUTURE VALUE OF AN ANNUITY OR ANNUITY DUE

Earlier in this chapter we explained how to compute the future value of a *single* sum placed on deposit or paid into an account credited with compound interest. Now we will build upon and expand that case to deal with the calculation of the future value of a *series* of deposits or payments. For example, if $300 is deposited, or paid, into an account each year and is credited with 11 percent compound annual interest, how much will be in the account at the end of 6 years?

This type of problem will be referred to as a future value of an annuity (FVA) or a future value of an annuity due (FVAD) problem. An *annuity* is a series of payments of equal amounts made at the end of each of a number of periods. An *annuity due* is a series of payments of equal amounts made at the beginning of each of a number of periods.[12]

There are many personal and business situations where sums of money are invested periodically. Some corporations, for example, make available payroll deduction plans whereby employees may save for a desired objective by having a stipulated amount withheld from each paycheck and invested in U.S. government savings bonds. Many individuals deposit a pre-established amount each week or month in Christmas Club or Vacation Club accounts at banks or credit unions. Many wage earners and self-employed individuals deposit funds each year in Individual Retirement Accounts (IRAs) or Keogh plans at banks, thrift institutions, brokerage firms, insurance companies, or mutual funds. Tax-advantaged employee benefit programs such as 401(k) and tax-deferred annuity plans are vehicles for employees to make periodic deposits, often matched by employer contributions, to save for retirement. Corporate sinking fund contributions to accumulate money for the purchase of fixed assets are another example of the annuity principle.

Assumptions

To simplify the solution of FVA and FVAD problems, it will be assumed for now that the deposits or payments are made annually. This assumption will be modified in the next chapter. Also it will be assumed that the deposits all earn the same rate of compound interest, though obviously each earns it for a different length of time.

In that connection, it is particularly important in annuity problems to be accurate in measuring the length of time during which each deposit earns compound interest. One possible assumption is that the deposits are made at the beginning of each year (an annuity due); the other is that they are made at the end of each year (an annuity). The difference between the two future values, all other things being equal, can be quite large.

For example, assume five annual payments of $1,000 each earn 7 percent compound interest. At the end of the fifth year the future value of these periodic payments will be $6,153.29 if they are made at the beginning of each year versus only $5,750.74 if they are made at the end. The $402.55 difference between the two future values, FVAD and FVA, is due to the fact that each deposit earns one more year of interest under the first assumption than under the second. That is, when deposits are made at the start of each year the first deposit earns interest for 5 years rather than 4, the second for 4 years rather than 3, etc., and the last deposit earns interest for one year rather than none. (See figure 5-5.)

FIGURE 5-5
Time Line Representation of FVAD and FVA Problems

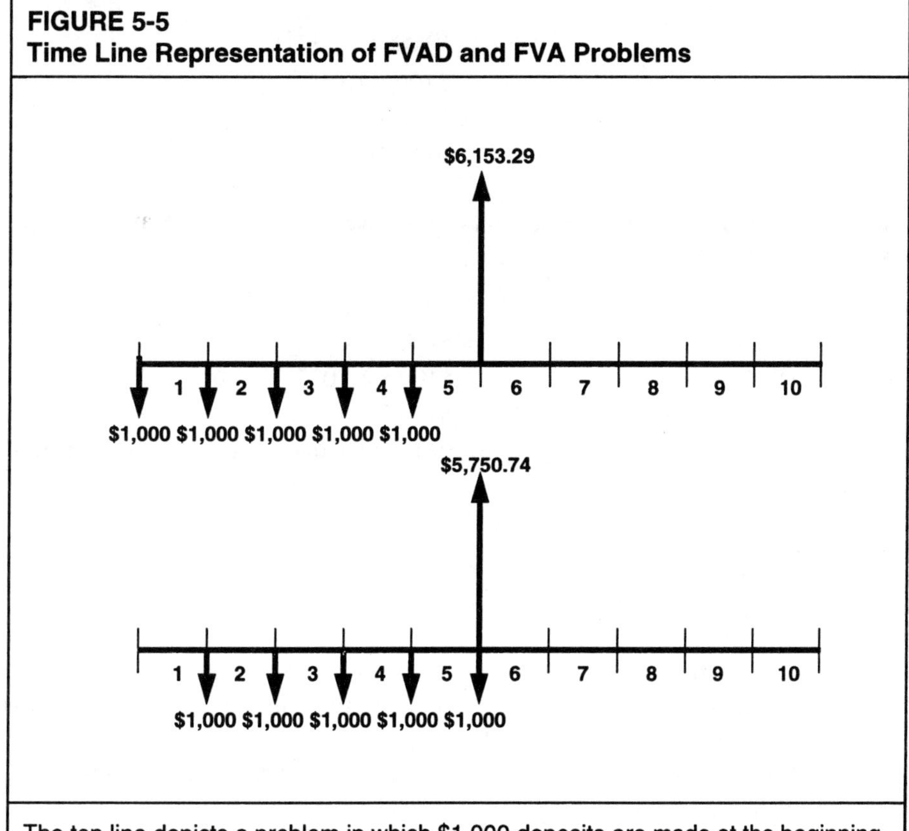

The top line depicts a problem in which $1,000 deposits are made at the beginning of each of 5 years (an annuity due), and the problem is to determine the future value as of the end of the fifth year. In the lower time line the problem is the same in all respects except that all deposits are made at the end of each of the 5 years (an annuity).

Using a Time-Value Formula

Problems calling for calculation of the future value of an annuity or annuity due can be viewed as collections of FVSS problems. Each annuity payment or deposit is a single sum that earns compound interest for a different number of years. Hence the FVA or FVAD is really the sum of a series of FVSS calculations.

To illustrate, assume that $100 is deposited at the end of each of 4 years and earns 5 percent compound annual interest. What is the total future value of these deposits at the end of the fourth year? The first deposit earns interest for 3 years (that is, from the end of year one till the end of year four). Hence its future value is

$$\begin{aligned} \text{FVSS} &= \text{PVSS} \times (1 + i)^n \\ &= \$100 \times 1.05^3 \\ &= \$100 \times 1.1576 \\ &= \$115.76 \end{aligned}$$

The future value of the second deposit, which earns interest for 2 years, is

$$\begin{aligned} \text{FVSS} &= \text{PVSS} \times (1 + i)^n \\ &= \$100 \times 1.05^2 \\ &= \$100 \times 1.1025 \\ &= \$110.25 \end{aligned}$$

The future value of the third deposit, which earns interest for one year, is

$$\begin{aligned} \text{FVSS} &= \text{PVSS} \times (1 + i)^n \\ &= \$100 \times 1.05^1 \\ &= \$105.00 \end{aligned}$$

And the future value of the fourth deposit is $100, the same as its present value, because it earns no interest. Thus the FVA in this illustration is $431.01 ($115.76 + $110.25 + $105.00 + $100).

If, on the other hand, the deposits had been made at the beginning of each year, their future values would have been as follows:

1st	$\$100 \times 1.05^4$	=	$121.55
2nd	$\$100 \times 1.05^3$	=	115.76
3rd	$\$100 \times 1.05^2$	=	110.25
4th	$\$100 \times 1.05^1$	=	105.00
	FVAD	=	$452.56

As an alternative to the foregoing approach of summing the future value of each of the separate deposits, the same result can be achieved in one step by using a somewhat more complex formula for cases where the deposits are made at the end of each year.

$$FVA = \text{annual deposit x} \left[\frac{(1 + i)^n - 1}{i}\right]$$

In the previous illustration,

$$FVA = \$100 \text{ x} \left[\frac{1.05^4 - 1}{.05}\right]$$

$$= \$100 \text{ x} \left[\frac{.2155}{.05}\right]$$

$$= \$431.01$$

For cases in which the deposits are made at the beginning of each year, the same formula may be used, but with one important modification. To reflect the fact that each deposit will be credited with one extra year of interest, it is necessary to multiply the result of the preceding formula by (1 + i). That is, if deposits are made at the beginning of each year, the formula becomes

$$FVAD = \text{annual deposit x} \left[\frac{(1 + i)^n - 1}{i}\right] \text{x} (1 + i)$$

$$= \$100 \text{ x} \left[\frac{1.05^4 - 1}{.05}\right] \text{x} (1 + i)$$

$$= \$100 \text{ x} \left[\frac{.2155}{.05}\right] \text{x } 1.05$$

$$= \$431.01 \text{ x } 1.05$$

$$= \$452.56$$

A simple way to keep the FVAD calculation in mind is to calculate FVA through the end-of-year formula above. If the problem is a beginning-of-year case, multiply the result by (1 + i) to produce the FVAD.

Using a Table to Compute FVA and FVAD

Those who are somewhat less mathematically inclined may prefer to avoid memorizing and applying the formulas contained in the preceding section. They will, undoubtedly, be heartened to learn that most of the work has already been done for them, and that the results of computing the quantity

$$\frac{(1 + i)^n - 1}{i}$$

for various rates of interest and numbers of periods appear in a table. (See table B.3 in appendix B.) Excerpts from that table appear below. To compute the FVA (the future value of a series of periodic payments made at the end of each year) simply multiply the appropriate factor in this table by the amount of one of the payments. To compute FVAD, multiply the result of the foregoing calculation by (1 + i).

TABLE 5-5
Future Value of an Annuity Factors

n/i	7%	8%	9%	10%	11%
1	1.0000	1.0000	1.0000	1.0000	1.0000
2	2.0700	2.0800	2.0900	2.1000	2.1100
3	3.2149	3.2464	3.2781	3.3100	3.3421
4	4.4399	4.5061	4.5731	4.6410	4.7097
5	5.7507	5.8666	5.9847	6.1051	6.2278
6	7.1533	7.3359	7.5233	7.7156	7.9129
7	8.6540	8.9228	9.2004	9.4872	9.7833
8	10.2598	10.6366	11.0285	11.4359	11.8594
9	11.9730	12.4876	13.0210	13.5795	14.1640
10	13.8164	14.4866	15.1929	15.9374	16.7220
11	15.7836	16.6455	17.5603	18.5312	19.5614
12	17.8885	18.9771	20.1407	21.3843	22.7132
13	20.1406	21.4953	22.9534	24.5227	26.2116
14	22.5505	24.2149	26.0192	27.9750	30.0949
15	25.1290	27.1521	29.3609	31.7725	34.4054

For example, assume that an individual deposits $2,000 at the end of each year for 13 years in an IRA account earning 11 percent compound interest per year. How much will be in the account at the end of the thirteenth year? In table 5-5 or B.3, locate the FVA factor in the 11% column, row 13. The future value of these periodic deposits will be $52,423.20 ($2,000 x 26.2116). If, on the other hand, the 13 deposits are made at the beginning of each year, the FVAD will be 11 percent higher, because each deposit will earn one extra year's interest. Hence the FVAD is $58,189.75 ($2,000 x 26.2116 x 1.11).

Using a Financial Calculator to Compute FVA and FVAD

As with the types of time-value problems discussed earlier in this chapter, an electronic calculator with finance functions is a very useful tool for solving FVA and FVAD problems. Among the advantages of the calculator over formulas or tables are its great speed, its reduced likelihood of error, and the great range of values for n and i that it can handle.

Solving FVA or FVAD on the HP-12C

To use the HP-12C, clear the memory units and set the calculator to display two decimal places. In annuity and annuity due problems you will be using a new key on the top row of the keyboard, PMT (payment), to reflect the fact that a series of deposits is involved, rather than a single sum. Also when solving a problem involving a series of payments or deposits you must always remember to instruct the calculator as to whether the payments or deposits will be made at the end of each period (FVA) or at the beginning (FVAD). This will be accomplished through use of the blue g key and the blue END or blue BEG function in the top row of the keyboard.

To illustrate, assume that a young couple deposits $5,000 today and at the start of each of the next 4 years in a savings account to accumulate a down payment for a house. If the account is credited with 8 percent compound interest per year, how much of a down payment will the couple have 5 years from now? (See the time line depiction of this type of problem in figure 5-6.)

Depress the following keys to reflect the known information: 5000, CHS (because, as was noted earlier, deposits that represent cash outflows are treated as negative numbers according to the cash flow sign convention), PMT, 8, i, 5, n, blue g, BEG (because the deposits are made at the start of each of the 5 years), FV. The answer, the FVAD, $31,679.65, should appear on the display. If the deposits had been made at the end of each of the 5 years, the keystrokes would be identical except for the substitution of END for BEG after blue g. The answer under this new assumption, the FVA, would be $29,333.00. You can produce this new solution simply by pressing blue g, END, and FV, rather than reentering all the information in the problem.

Solving FVA or FVAD on the HP-17B II

If your calculator is the HP-17B II, set it to display two decimal places and clear the TVM menu system's memory. In annuity and annuity due problems, you will be using a new menu key, the one for PMT, which is located between the PV and FV menu keys, to reflect the fact that a series of deposits or payments is involved, rather than a single sum. Also, when solving an annuity-type problem, you must *always* remember to instruct the calculator as to whether the payments or deposits will be made at the end of each period (FVA) or at the beginning (FVAD). This is accomplished by going to the TVM menu, pressing the OTHER menu key, and pressing the menu key for BEG or END, as appropriate. For now set the calculator for BEG.

FIGURE 5-6
Time Line Representation of FVAD Problem

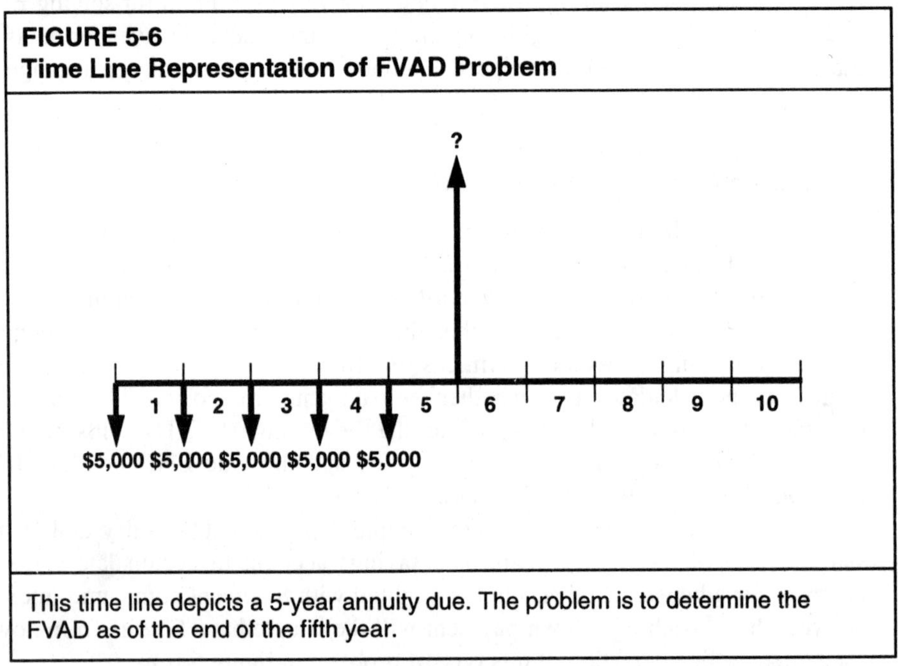

This time line depicts a 5-year annuity due. The problem is to determine the FVAD as of the end of the fifth year.

To illustrate, assume that Jack and Jill deposit $5,000 today and again at the start of each of the next four years in their credit union savings account to accumulate funds for the purchase of a piece of land. If the account is credited with 8 percent compound interest per year, how much will be in the account five years from now? (See the time line depiction of this problem in figure 5-6).

Press the following keys to reflect the known information: 5000, +/– (because, as noted earlier, deposits that represent cash outflows are treated as negative numbers), the PMT menu key, 8, the I%YR menu key, 5, and the N menu key. Now press the FV menu key and the answer, the FVAD, $31,679.65, appears on the screen. If the deposits had been made at the end of each year, rather than at the beginning, the answer, the FVA, would be 8 percent lower. You can produce the new solution without reentering all the data. Simply press the OTHER menu key, the END menu key, the EXIT key, and the FV menu key. The FVA is $29,333.00.

Solving FVA or FVAD on the BA-II Plus

If you wish to use the BA-II Plus, clear the memory units and set the calculator to display two decimal places. In annuity and annuity due problems you will be using a new key in the third row of the calculator keyboard, PMT (payment), to reflect the fact that a series of deposits is involved, rather than a single sum. Also when solving a problem involving a series of payments or deposits you must always remember to instruct the calculator as to whether the payments or deposits will be made at the end of each period (FVA) or at the beginning (FVAD). This will be accomplished through the use of the 2nd key and the BGN function printed above the PMT key.

To set the calculator to reflect when the payments occur in each period, press 2nd and BGN. The display should show either BGN or END. If the current setting is the one you want, press 2nd and QUIT. If the current setting is not the one you want, press 2nd, SET (which is printed above the ENTER key in the top row of the keyboard), 2nd, and QUIT.

To illustrate, assume that a married couple deposits $5,000 today and at the start of each of the next 4 years in a savings account to accumulate funds for their young daughter's college education. If the account is credited with 8 percent compound interest per year, how much of a college fund will the couple have 5 years from now? (See the time line depiction of this problem in figure 5-6.)

Set the calculator for beginning-of-period deposits. Then depress the following keys to reflect the known information: 5000, +/– (because, as we noted earlier, deposits that represent cash outflows are treated as negative numbers), PMT, 5, N, 8, I/Y, CPT, FV. The answer, the FVAD, $31,679.65, should appear on the display. If the deposits had been made at the end of each of the 5 years, the keystrokes would be identical except that you would set the calculator for end-of-period payments. The answer under this new assumption, the FVA, would be $29,333.00. You can produce this solution by pressing 2nd, BGN, 2nd, SET, 2nd, QUIT, CPT, FV, rather than reentering all the information in the problem.

If Number of Compounding Periods Exceeds Number of Deposits

Sometimes a problem will be encountered in which the number of periods during which compounding occurs exceeds the number of periods during which deposits are made. For example, assume that $500 is to be deposited at the end of each of the next 6 years in an account earning 8 percent compound annual interest. How much will be in the account at the end of 10 years? (See figure 5-7).

The simplest way to solve a problem of this type is to treat it as two separate problems and combine the results. The first step is to compute the FVA; the second is to treat that value as a single sum and compute the FVSS.

FIGURE 5-7
Time Line Representation of Problem Where Number of Compounding Periods Exceeds Number of Deposits

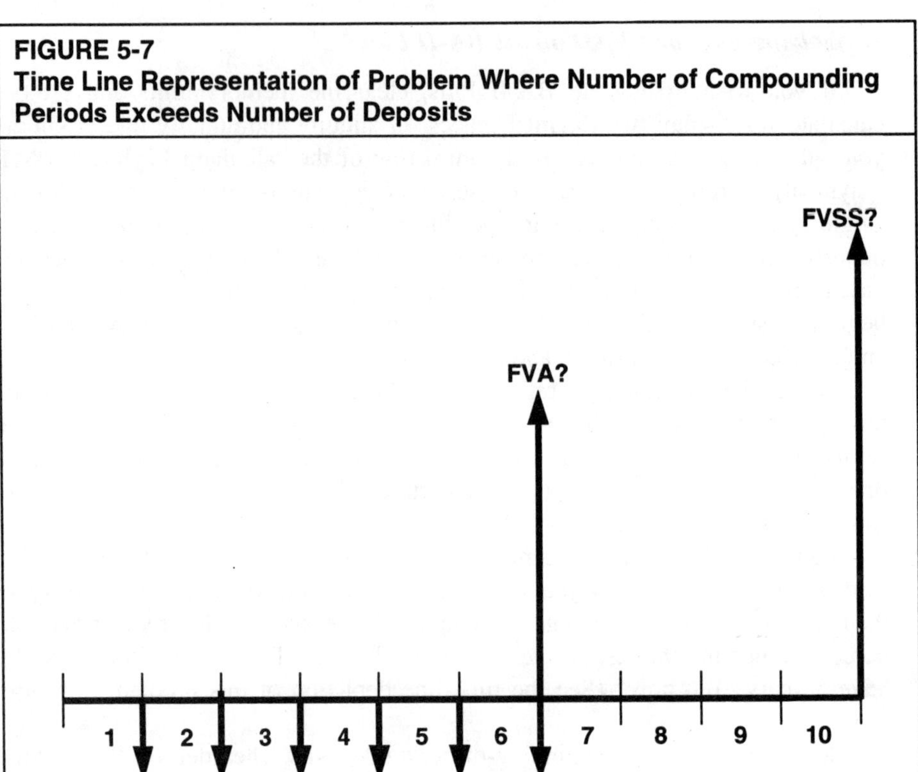

In this time line level payments are made at the end of each of 6 years. The future value of that annuity as of the end of the sixth year is then left as a single sum to accumulate until the end of the tenth year.

In this illustration, the FVA for 6 years and 8 percent interest, based on the factor from table B.3 in appendix B, is

$$\begin{aligned} \text{FVA} &= \$500 \times 7.3359 \\ &= \$3{,}667.95 \end{aligned}$$

The FVSS at 8 percent interest at the end of the remaining 4 years, using the factor from table B.1, is

$$\begin{aligned} \text{FVSS} &= \$3{,}667.95 \times 1.3605 \\ &= \$4{,}990.25 \end{aligned}$$

Solving Sinking Fund Problems

So far in this section you have learned how to compute the future value of a series of payments or deposits when the number of payments, the rate of interest, and the size of each payment are known. Sometimes, however, the facts are different, and it is the size of the periodic payment that is the unknown of the four key elements. This is often called a sinking fund payment problem.

For example, assume that a business wishes to accumulate $10,000,000 by the end of 3 years in order, at that time, to retire some of its outstanding mortgage bonds. The company plans to make three annual deposits, beginning today, into a sinking fund that will earn 9 percent compound interest. The question: How large must each of the deposits be in order to reach the target amount in 3 years?

Although the answer can, of course, be found by rearranging the FVA or FVAD formula and solving for the amount of the deposit, the use of a table or financial calculator is much more efficient. Hence only those methods will be explained here.

If you wish to use the FVA table, simply divide the target amount, the future value of the deposits, by the factor for the proper i and n. When calculating the FVA or FVAD, you *multiply* the proper factor by one of the deposits. When calculating the amount of one of the deposits, you *divide* the FVA or FVAD by the proper factor.

Since in the present illustration the sinking fund payments are to be made at the beginning of each year, you must first convert the FVA factor in table B.3 in appendix B for 3 years, 9%, which is 3.2781, into an FVAD factor. This is done by multiplying it by 1.09. The resulting FVAD factor, 3.5731, is then divided into the desired FVAD, $10,000,000, to produce the size of each deposit that will be needed to reach that goal, namely, $2,798,690.21. Three deposits of this amount, one made today and the others at the beginning of each of the next 2 years, all earning 9 percent compound annual interest, will grow to approximately $10,000,000 by the end of the third year.

Using a financial calculator is even more efficient than using table B.3, and is more precise because of a lesser problem of rounding. On the HP-12C, for example, press the following keys: 10000000, FV, 9, i, 3, n, blue g, BEG, PMT. The answer, $2,798,667.50, should be displayed on the screen (with a minus sign, in accordance with the cash flow sign convention). On the HP-17B II, set the machine for beginning-of-period payments and press 10000000, the FV menu key, 9, the I%YR menu key, 3, the N menu key, and the PMT menu key. The answer, $2,798,667.50, is displayed (with a minus sign, since these are outgoing payments). On the BA-II Plus, the same answer, again preceded by a minus sign, is found by setting the calculator for beginning-of-period payments and pressing 10000000, FV, 9, I/Y, 3, N, CPT, PMT.[13]

Variations from the foregoing sinking fund problem are problems in which the task is to compute n, the number of deposits that will be required, or i, the interest rate that must be earned on the deposits, in order to reach the target amount. For such purposes a financial calculator is the most effective tool.

Assume, for example, that you wish to accumulate $10,000 for a dream vacation in Tahiti and that you can afford to save $1,200 per year, beginning a year from now, toward that objective. If your savings earn 10 percent compound annual interest, how long will you have to wait before you can buy your airline tickets? On the HP-12C, press 10000, FV, 10, i, 1200, CHS, PMT, blue g, END, and n to produce the answer, 7 years. Or set the HP-17B II for end-of-period payments and press 10000, the FV menu key, 10, the I%YR menu key, 1200, +/–, the PMT menu key, and the N menu key. The answer, to four decimal places, is 6.3596 years. On the BA-II Plus, set the calculator for end-of-period payments and press the following keys: 10000, FV, 10, I/Y, 1200, +/–, PMT, CPT, N. The answer is 6.3596 years.[14]

On the other hand, if you insist on waiting only 5 years before going to Tahiti with your $10,000, what compound annual interest rate must you earn on your periodic deposits? On the HP-12C, press 10000, FV, 1200, CHS, PMT, 5, n, blue g, END, i. The answer, hardly encouraging, should appear after a few seconds of running time as 25.7839 percent. The HP-17B II and the BA-II Plus provide no happier an answer. With the HP-17B II set for end-of-period payments, press 10000, the FV menu key, 1200, +/–, the PMT menu key, 5, the N menu key, and the I%YR menu key. You'll have to find an investment that will earn 25.7839 percent. Or set the BA-II Plus for end-of-period payments, press 10000, FV, 1200, +/–, PMT, 5, N, CPT, I/Y to produce the answer after a few seconds, 25.7839 percent.

PRESENT VALUE OF AN ANNUITY OR ANNUITY DUE

An earlier section of this chapter contained an explanation of how to calculate the present value of a *single* sum due or needed at some time in the future. This section expands on that case and deals with the question of how to compute the present value of a *series* of level future payments. This type of problem will be referred to as a present value of an annuity (PVA) problem if the payments are to be made at the end of each period or as a present value of an annuity due (PVAD) problem if they are to be made at the beginning of each period.

To illustrate the type of problem that is the concern here, assume that an installment loan is to be repaid to you through six annual payments of $1,000 each beginning a year from now. For how much would you be willing to sell the promissory note today if you believe you can earn 8 percent compound annual interest on your money in some other investment outlet? What is the present value of this 6-year annuity discounted at 8 percent?

Assumptions

As was true in the preceding pages concerning the future value of a series of payments, it will be assumed here in the discussion of present value that each payment is made annually. This assumption will be dropped in the following chapter. In addition, it will be important to specify in each example whether the annuity payments are made at the end or at the beginning of each year. The difference in the answer can be substantial. For example, an 8-year, $1,000 annuity discounted at 6 percent has a PVA of $6,209.79, versus a PVAD of $6,582.38. (See figure 5-8.)

FIGURE 5-8
Time Line Representation of PVA and PVAD Problems

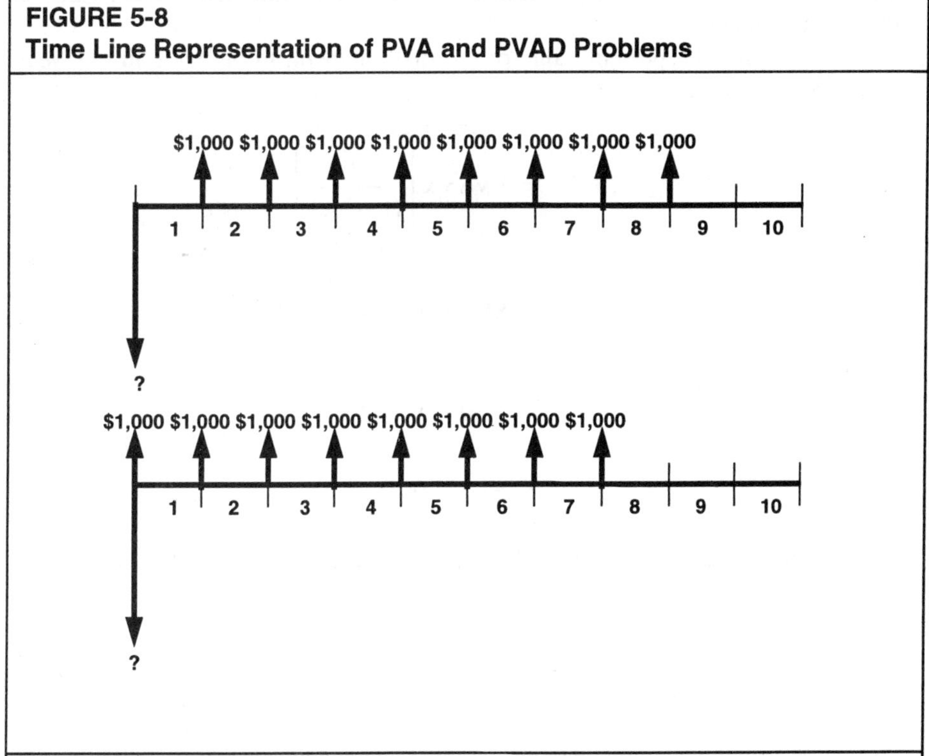

The upper time line depicts a case in which 8 annual payments of $1,000 are to be made beginning in one year, and the problem is to compute the PVA. The lower time line depicts an 8-year annuity due, in which $1,000 payments are to be made at the start of each year, and the problem is to compute the PVAD.

Using a Time-Value Formula

The basic formula for computing the present value of a single sum can also be used to compute the present value of an annuity or an annuity due. All that is needed is to calculate the PVSS for each annuity payment separately and total the results.

For example, assume that as part of a divorce settlement a father has been ordered to deposit a lump sum in trust sufficient to provide child support payments for his son. The child support payments are to be $5,000 per year for 4 years, beginning one year from today. If the amount placed in trust can be assumed to earn 7 percent compound annual interest, how much should the father place in the trust today?

Through the formula described in the discussion of the present value of a single sum, the present value of each separate payment can be found. The amount to be deposited today would be equal to the combined present value of the four payments.

Specifically, the present value of the first payment, to be made in one year, would be

$$\begin{aligned} \text{PVSS} &= \text{FVSS x} \left[\frac{1}{(1 + i)^n}\right] \\ &= \$5{,}000 \text{ x} \left[\frac{1}{1.07^1}\right] \\ &= \$5{,}000 \text{ x } .9346 \\ &= \$4{,}673.00 \end{aligned}$$

The present value of the second, third, and fourth payments would be as shown below:

$$\text{2nd} = \$5{,}000 \text{ x} \left[\frac{1}{1.07^2}\right] = \$5{,}000 \text{ x} \left[\frac{1}{1.1449}\right] = \$5{,}000 \text{ x } .8734 = \$4{,}367.00$$

$$\text{3rd} = \$5{,}000 \text{ x} \left[\frac{1}{1.07^3}\right] = \$5{,}000 \text{ x} \left[\frac{1}{1.2250}\right] = \$5{,}000 \text{ x } .8163 = \$4{,}081.50$$

$$\text{4th} = \$5{,}000 \text{ x} \left[\frac{1}{1.07^4}\right] = \$5{,}000 \text{ x} \left[\frac{1}{1.3108}\right] = \$5{,}000 \text{ x } .7629 = \$3{,}814.50$$

The sum of these present values, the PVA, would be $16,936.00 ($4,673.00 + $4,367.00 + $4,081.50 + $3,814.50). That amount, placed on deposit today at 7 percent compound annual interest, will be just enough (well, within $.07 of just enough) to provide four annual payments of $5,000 each beginning in one year. To verify this, examine what would happen to the account each year.

Year	Beginning Balance	Interest Earnings	Amount Withdrawn	Ending Balance
1	$16,936.00	$1,185.52	$5,000.00	$13,121.52
2	$13,121.52	$ 918.51	$5,000.00	$ 9,040.03
3	$ 9,040.03	$ 632.80	$5,000.00	$ 4,672.83
4	$ 4,672.83	$ 327.10	$5,000.00	($ 0.07)

If, on the other hand, the four annual payments were to be made beginning immediately, the PVAD would be as follows:

$$\text{1st PVSS} = \$5{,}000 \times \left[\frac{1}{1.07^0}\right] = \$5{,}000 \times 1.0000 = \$5{,}000.00$$

$$\text{2nd PVSS} = \$5{,}000 \times \left[\frac{1}{1.07^1}\right] = \$5{,}000 \times .9346 = \$4{,}673.00$$

$$\text{3rd PVSS} = \$5{,}000 \times \left[\frac{1}{1.07^2}\right] = \$5{,}000 \times .8734 = \$4{,}367.00$$

$$\text{4th PVSS} = \$5{,}000 \times \left[\frac{1}{1.07^3}\right] = \$5{,}000 \times .8163 = \underline{\$4{,}081.50}$$

$$\text{PVAD} = \$18{,}121.50$$

Why would a larger amount need to be deposited in trust if the payments are to begin immediately? The total interest earnings would be lower because each withdrawal to make the child support payments would occur a year earlier than under the end-of-year assumption.

As an alternative to the foregoing approach of finding PVA or PVAD by summing the present value of each of the separate annuity payments, the same result can be achieved in one step by using the following, somewhat more complex, formula:

$$\text{PVA} = \text{annual payment} \times \left[\frac{1 - \dfrac{1}{(1+i)^n}}{i}\right]$$

Note that this formula should be used only for the case where the annuity payments are made at the end of each year.

In the child support illustration, then,

$$\text{PVA} = \$5{,}000 \text{ x} \left[\frac{1 - \dfrac{1}{1.07^4}}{.07}\right]$$

$$= \$5{,}000 \text{ x} \left[\frac{1 - \dfrac{1}{1.3108}}{.07}\right]$$

$$= \$5{,}000 \text{ x} \left[\frac{.2371}{.07}\right]$$

$$= \$5{,}000 \text{ x } 3.3871$$

$$= \$16{,}935.50$$

For cases in which the payments are to be made at the beginning of each year, the same formula may be used, but with one important modification. To reflect the fact that each payment will earn one fewer year of interest before it is distributed, it is necessary to multiply the result of the preceding formula by (1 + i). That is, if the payments are made at the beginning of each year, the formula becomes

$$\text{PVAD} = \text{annual payment x} \left[\frac{1 - \dfrac{1}{(1 + i)^n}}{i}\right] \text{x } (1 + i)$$

$$= \$5{,}000 \text{ x} \left[\frac{1 - \dfrac{1}{1.07^4}}{.07}\right] \text{x } 1.07$$

$$= \$5{,}000 \text{ x} \left[\frac{.2371}{.07}\right] \text{x } 1.07$$

$$= \$16{,}935.50 \text{ x } 1.07$$

$$= \$18{,}120.99$$

As was done in converting from FVA to FVAD, then, the way to compute PVAD is to compute PVA, and then multiply the result by (1 + i).

Using a Table to Compute PVA and PVAD

By this time it should come as no surprise to the reader that the factors generated through the foregoing PVA formula for various rates of interest and numbers of years have already been calculated. They appear in table B.4 in appendix B. Excerpts from that table are presented below. To compute the PVA, simply multiply the appropriate factor in this table by the amount of one of the annuity payments. To compute the PVAD, multiply the PVA by (1 + i).

For example, assume that you have won the lottery and will be receiving $15,000 per year, beginning in one year, for the next 10 years. What is the present value of your prize if interest rates are at 9 percent? From table 5-6 or B.4, the PVA factor for 10 years, 9%, is 6.4177. This factor is multiplied by the amount of one of the payments, $15,000, to produce the PVA, $96,265.50.

One of the few things in life that would be nicer than the lottery prize you won would be if the 10 annual payments were to begin immediately, rather than 12 months from now. In this case, the PVAD would be 9 percent higher; that is, $15,000 x 6.4177 x 1.09 = $104,929.40.

TABLE 5-6
Present Value of an Annuity Factors

n/i	7%	8%	9%	10%	11%
1	0.9346	0.9259	0.9174	0.9091	0.9009
2	1.8080	1.7833	1.7591	1.7355	1.7125
3	2.6243	2.5771	2.5313	2.4869	2.4437
4	3.3872	3.3121	3.2397	3.1699	3.1024
5	4.1002	3.9927	3.8897	3.7908	3.6959
6	4.7665	4.6229	4.4859	4.3553	4.2305
7	5.3893	5.2064	5.0330	4.8684	4.7122
8	5.9713	5.7466	5.5348	5.3349	5.1461
9	6.5152	6.2469	5.9952	5.7590	5.5370
10	7.0236	6.7101	6.4177	6.1446	5.8892
11	7.4987	7.1390	6.8052	6.4951	6.2065
12	7.9427	7.5361	7.1607	6.8137	6.4924
13	8.3577	7.9038	7.4869	7.1034	6.7499
14	8.7455	8.2442	7.7862	7.3667	6.9819
15	9.1079	8.5595	8.0607	7.6061	7.1909

Using a Financial Calculator to Compute PVA and PVAD

Use of an electronic calculator with finance functions greatly eases the task of calculating the present value of an annuity or of an annuity due. The calculator is faster, less likely to produce mistakes, and allows for the selection of more values for n and i than are likely to be found in most present value tables.

Solving PVA or PVAD on the HP-12C

Assume that a woman receives $6,000 each year from a trust. She is interested in obtaining a cash sum with which to buy a fancy new sports car. Her cousin has offered to buy from her now the present value of the next four annuity payments (the first of which will be made one year from now) discounted at 8 percent compound annual interest. How much will the woman receive if she accepts the offer?

If you are using the HP-12C, clear the memory units and set the calculator to display two decimal places. Then depress the following keys to enter the known information: 6000, CHS (because we are showing payments as negative values according to the cash flow sign convention), PMT (because the problem involves a series of payments rather than a single sum), 8, i, 4, n, blue g, END (because the payments will be made at the end of each year). The calculator is now programmed to compute the PVA. Depress the PV key and the answer, $19,872.76, should be displayed on the screen.

If the facts of the problem were revised so that the four annual payments from the trust were to begin immediately, the procedure for solving it would be identical except that the BEG key would be pressed instead of the END key. You can solve it now by pressing blue g, BEG, PV. The answer, the PVAD, is $21,462.58.

Solving PVA or PVAD on the HP-17B II

Assume that you have just won the lottery and are scheduled to receive $15,000 at the end of each of the next ten years. If the going rate of interest is 7 percent, how much have you won in present-value terms?

Clear the TVM menu system and set the calculator for end-of-period payments. Then enter the known information as follows: 10, the N menu key, 15000, the PMT menu key (because the problem involves a series of payments, rather than a single sum), 7, and the I%YR menu key. Now press the PV menu key and the answer, $150,353.72, will be displayed (as a negative, because it is a present value).

Solving PVA or PVAD on the BA-II Plus

Assume that several years ago the owner of a small business borrowed $10,000 from a relative and agreed to repay the loan in 10 equal annual installments of $1,500. Six payments now remain to be made, the first of which is due in one year. The business owner now would like to pay off the remainder of the debt. What sum should the business owner propose to the lender as a payoff figure if money is presently worth 7 percent?

If you are using the BA-II Plus, clear the memory units, set the calculator to display two decimal places, and set it for end-of-period payments (because the payments will be made at the end of each year). Then depress the following keys to enter the known information: 1500, +/– (because we are showing payments as negative values), PMT (because the problem involves a series of payments, rather than a single sum), 6, N, 7, I/Y, CPT. The calculator is now programmed to compute the PVA. Depress the PV key and the answer, $7,149.81, should be displayed on the screen.

If the facts of the problem were revised so that the remaining six annual payments were to be made beginning immediately, the procedure for solving it would be identical except that the calculator should be set for beginning-of-period payments. You can solve it now by pressing 2nd, BGN, 2nd, SET, 2nd, QUIT, CPT, PV. The answer, the PVAD, is $7,650.30.

If Number of Discounting Periods Exceeds Number of Payments

Sometimes a problem will be encountered in which the number of periods during which discounting is to occur exceeds the number of periods during which annuity payments are to be made. For example, what is the present value at a 7 percent compound annual interest rate of an income stream consisting of five annual payments of $2,000 each, the first of which will be made 3 years from now? (See the time line depiction of this type of problem in figure 5-9.)

The simplest way to solve a problem of this type, called a deferred annuity problem, is to treat it as two separate problems and combine the results. The first step is to compute the PVA; the second is to treat that value as a single sum and compute its PVSS.

In the present illustration the PVA for 5 years and 7 percent, based on the factor from table B.4 in appendix B, is

$$\begin{aligned} \text{PVA} &= \$2{,}000 \times 4.1002 \\ &= \$8{,}200.40 \end{aligned}$$

The PVSS at 7 percent for the value of an annuity that commences in 2 years (even though the first payment will not be made until the end of 3 years), based on the factor from table B.2, is

$$\begin{aligned} \text{PVSS} &= \$8{,}200.40 \times .8734 \\ &= \$7{,}162.23 \end{aligned}$$

If you are using the HP-12C, HP-17B II, or BA-II Plus calculator for this type of problem, compute the PVA in the usual manner. However, be sure to then fully clear the calculator's memory units before you proceed to the second step of the problem. Then enter the PVA you just calculated as a future value, and compute its present value in the normal way.

Note that in this solution a PVA is calculated and then discounted as a single sum for 2 additional years. The same result can be achieved if the problem is viewed as entailing the calculation of a PVAD and then discounting that single sum for 3 additional years. (Re-examine figure 5-9 to verify that a 5-year PVA discounted for an additional 2 years is identical to a 5-year PVAD discounted for an additional 3 years.)

FIGURE 5-9
Time Line Depiction of PVA or PVAD Problems Where Discounting Period Exceeds Payment Period

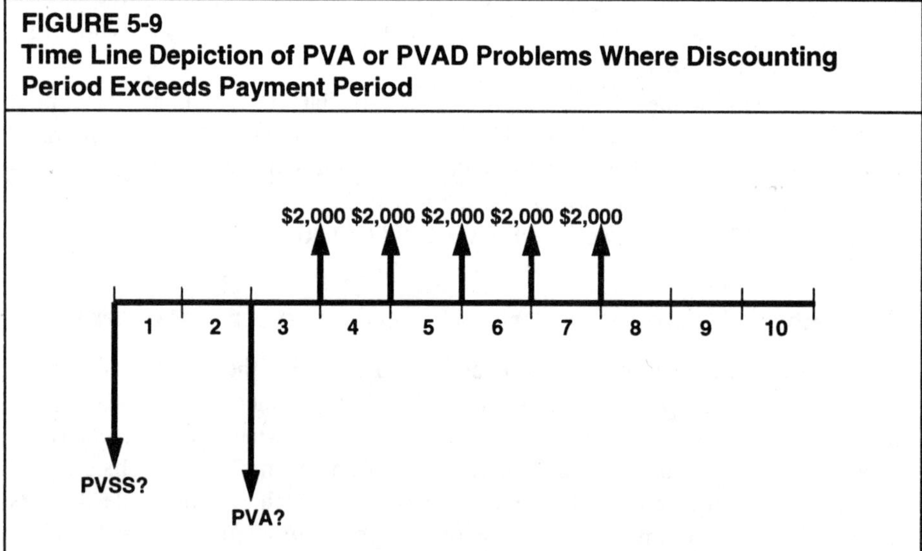

This time line depicts a case in which five annual payments of $2,000 each are to be made beginning in 3 years. The problem, which is to determine the present value of the income stream, can be divided into two parts. First determine the present value of the annuity as of the start of the annuity period, which is the beginning of year *three.* (Note: It is not the beginning of year four, even though that is when the first payment will be made.) Then compute the present value of that single sum as of today, 2 (not 3) years earlier.

Solving Debt Service/Capital Sum Liquidation Problems

Thus far you have seen how to compute the present value of a stream of equal payments when the number of payments, the rate of interest, and the size of each payment are known. Sometimes, however, it is the size of the periodic payment that is the unknown of the four key elements. A frequently encountered problem of this type is that of determining the amount of money necessary to liquidate a debt through periodic loan repayments. A similar problem is to determine how large a periodic withdrawal from a sum of capital can be in order to liquidate that sum over a given number of years.

In installment loans such as those used to finance the purchase of a house or automobile, each level periodic payment, called the debt service, consists of some repayment of the principal and some payment of interest on the remaining unpaid principal. Given the initial size of the loan, the interest rate, and the number of payments to be made, the problem is to compute the size of each required payment.[15] Such a debt service problem can be solved using PVA and PVAD factors in a manner analogous to that for solving sinking fund problems using FVA and FVAD factors as explained earlier.

For example, assume that a real estate mortgage for $50,000 bearing an 11 percent interest rate is to be repaid in 15 equal annual installments, the first to be made in one year. The question: how large must each annual installment payment be?

Although the answer can, of course, be found by rearranging the PVA formula and solving for the amount of the payment, that procedure is complex and unwieldy in comparison with using a table or financial calculator. Hence only the latter two methods are explained here.

Using the Table

In order to use the table, simply divide the original loan balance by the PVA factor for the proper i and n. When calculating the PVA, you *multiply* the proper factor by one of the payments. When calculating the amount of one of the payments, you *divide* the PVA by the proper factor.

Since in the present illustration the loan payments are to be made at the end of each year, you can use the PVA factor for 15 years and 11% shown in table B.4 in appendix B. Dividing this factor, 7.1909, into the $50,000 loan amount produces the size of the annual payment, $6,953.23. (Note, by the way, the amount of interest that will be paid on this loan. The total to be repaid will be $104,298.45, that is, 15 x $6,953.23. Since the loan principal is $50,000, the interest is $54,298.45.)

If the terms of the loan, on the other hand, had called for the first annual installment payment to be made immediately, it would be necessary first to convert the PVA factor for 15 years and 11% into a PVAD factor. This would be accomplished by multiplying 7.1909 x 1.11. The resulting PVAD factor, 7.9819, would then be divided into the $50,000 loan amount to produce the annual payment of $6,264.17. The total amount of interest to be paid in this situation would be $43,962.55, that is, ($6,264.17 x 15) – $50,000.

Using a Financial Calculator

Using a financial calculator is even more efficient, as well as being more precise, than the table because of a lesser problem of rounding. To illustrate, assume that in a negligence case a jury has awarded $125,000 to be used to support an injured child until the child reaches age 21, 11 years from now. How much will this capital sum and interest earnings thereon provide for the child per year if the fund earns 8 percent compound interest?

On the HP-12C, depress the following keys: 125000, CHS, PV, 8, i, 11, n, blue g, BEG (or END, depending on when the first withdrawal will be made), PMT. The payment under the beginning-of-year assumption is $16,212.54. Under the end-of-year assumption it is $17,509.54. Or on the HP-17B II, set the machine for beginning-of-period payments. Press 125000, +/–, the PV menu key, 8, the I%YR menu key, 11, the N menu key, and the PMT menu key. The answer is $16,212.54. Now see what the payment would be if an end-of-period assumption is used. Press the OTHER menu key, the END menu key, the EXIT key, and the PMT menu key. The answer is $17,509.54. On the BA-II Plus the same answers are found by setting the calculator for beginning- or end-of-period payments and pressing 125000, +/–, PV, 8, I/Y, 11, N, CPT, PMT.

FOCUS ON ETHICS
Ethics and the Time Value of Money

Does the concept of "ethics" apply to the time value of money? Isn't the time value of money just a mathematical formula? Do mathematical formulas have ethical values? Let's examine this issue.

It is true that mathematical formulas are amoral in and of themselves. But it is also true that these formulas, improperly used, can lead to some extremely misleading results. These errant results may lead to decisions that aren't in the client's best interests.

These formulas are dependent on interest-rate assumptions. Higher rates of return provide more optimistic results. In a competitive marketplace, it is not uncommon for projected yields to be a determining factor as the client weighs alternative courses of action. The time-value-of-money formula doesn't know one yield from another. If a salesperson offers an exaggerated yield, the formula will provide an exaggerated result. It may be decisive in making the sale. It may be decisive in leading the client into making the wrong purchase.

A $10,000 tax-deferred investment that earns 10 percent per year will grow to $67,275 in 20 years. What if a financial planner exaggerates the rate of return to 12 percent per year? The mathematical result is $96,463—a 43 percent increase in future value. Would this projection "close the sale"?

There is an old saying: "Figures don't lie, but liars figure." The ethical financial professional uses projected rates of return that are fully justified in terms of historical experience and analysis of future economic conditions.

Variations from the foregoing debt service and capital liquidation problems are problems in which the task is to compute n, the number of installment payments that will be required or possible, or i, the interest rate being charged or needed. For such purposes a financial calculator is the most effective tool.

Assume, for example, that a company plans to borrow $200,000 to expand its fleet of delivery vehicles. If the financial officer believes the company can afford to make loan repayments of $55,000 per year beginning a year from now, and if the lending institution is quoting an interest rate of 10.5 percent, how long will it take to repay the loan? On the HP-12C, press 200000, CHS, PV, 55000, PMT, blue g, END, 10.5, i, and n. The answer is five years. Or set the HP-17B II for end-of-period payments and four decimal places. Press 200000, +/–, the PV menu key, 55000, the PMT menu key, 10.5, and the I%YR menu key. Then press the N menu key to obtain the answer, 4.8172 years. On the BA-II Plus press the following keys after setting the calculator for end-of-period payments: 200000, +/–, PV, 55000, PMT, 10.5, I/Y, CPT, N. The answer is 4.8172 years.[16]

On the other hand, if the financial officer believes the company must have the loan repaid in 4 years, what interest rate must he or she obtain from the lending institution to accomplish this objective? On the HP-12C, press 200000, CHS, PV, 55000, PMT, 4, n, blue g, END, i. The answer, an unlikely 3.9245 percent, should eventually appear on the screen. Even if the borrower and lender use the HP-17B II or the BA-II Plus, they are unlikely to reach agreement on an acceptable interest rate. Set either calculator for end-of-period payments. Then on the HP-17B II press 200000, +/–, the PV menu key, 55000, the PMT menu key, 4, the N menu key, and the I%YR menu key. Or on the BA-II Plus press 200000, +/–, PV, 55000, PMT, 4, N, CPT, I/Y. After a brief delay, the 3.9245 percent rate is again displayed.

Creating an Amortization Schedule

Another useful calculation in connection with debt service problems is to generate an amortization schedule. In any installment loan, a portion of each payment is used to pay interest and the rest is applied to reduce the principal of the loan. Over the term of the loan the interest portion of the payment falls and the principal portion rises. The amortization schedule enables you to see, year by year, how much is being applied toward each.

To illustrate, assume a $1,000 loan with a compound annual interest rate of 11 percent is to be repaid in four equal annual installments beginning in one year. The amount of each payment is $322.33. How much of each year's payment will be applied to interest and how much to principal?[17]

Manual Calculation. If you are preparing the amortization schedule manually, you should set up a work sheet with column headings as shown in table 5-7.

After inserting the initial loan amount and the first year's payment, calculate the first year's interest by multiplying the 11 percent interest rate by the loan amount. This produces the figure for column (3). The balance of the payment, shown in column (4), is principal and is subtracted from the initial loan amount to produce the unpaid balance at the end of the first year, as shown in column (5). This amount is also the unpaid balance at the beginning of the second year, as shown in column (1). Again, 11 percent of this amount is the second year's interest in column (3), the remainder of the payment goes on principal in column (4), and so on through the end of the fourth and final year of the loan.

TABLE 5-7
Sample Loan Amortization Schedule

Year	(1) Unpaid Balance, Beg. of Year	(2) Payment, End of Year	(3) Interest Payment i x (1)	(4) Principal Payment (2) – (3)	(5) Unpaid Balance, End of Year (1) – (4)
1	$1,000.00	$322.33	$110.00	$212.33	$787.67
2	787.67	322.33	86.64	235.69	551.98
3	551.98	322.33	60.72	261.61	290.37
4	290.37	322.33	31.94	290.39	(.02)

Creating an Amortization Schedule with the HP-12C. If you are using the HP-12C to create an amortization schedule, note that the n key also contains a yellow AMORT (amortization) function. Note also the x $\lessgtr$ y key in the second row of the keyboard. Both of these will be used to solve the problem.

First enter the basic data about the problem in this illustration. Press 11, i, blue g, END, 1000, PV, 322.33, CHS, PMT. Now press 1 (because one payment will be made per year), yellow f, AMORT. The amount displayed, $110.00, is the first year's interest. Next press the x $\lessgtr$y key to see the principal payment, $212.33. Then press RCL (the Recall key in the bottom row of the keyboard) and PV to show the unpaid balance at the end of year one, $787.67. Repeat the sequences as shown below to see the amounts in the following years.

Year	Keystrokes	Interest	Keystrokes	Principal	Keystroke	Unpaid Balance
2	1, yellow f, AMORT	$86.64	x$\lessgtr$y	$235.69	RCL, PV	$551.98
3	1, yellow f, AMORT	$60.72	x$\lessgtr$y	$261.61	RCL, PV	$290.37
4	1, yellow f, AMORT	$31.94	x$\lessgtr$y	$290.39	RCL, PV	($ .02)

The total interest paid during the 4 years is, thus, $289.30 ($110.00 + $86.64 + $60.72 + $31.94). The principal repaid, of course, totals (except for $.02 due to rounding) $1,000.

Creating an Amortization Schedule with the HP-17B II. In order to create an amortization schedule for this problem on the HP-17B II, set the machine to display 2 decimal places. Also set it for end-of-period payments. Then enter the basic data about this problem in this illustration: 4, the N menu key, 11, the I%YR menu key, 1000, the PV menu key, 322.33, +/–, and the PMT menu key. Now press the OTHER menu key and the AMRT menu key. Next, press 1 and the #P menu key. Now you are ready to see the year-by-year results. Press the INT menu key to see that $110 of interest is paid in the first year; the PRIN menu key to see that $212.33 of principal is paid in the first year; and the BAL menu key to see that the unpaid balance at the end of the first year is $787.67. Now press the NEXT menu key; the INT menu key to see that $86.64 of interest is paid in the second year; the PRIN menu key to see that $235.69 of principal is paid in the second year; and the BAL menu key to see the unpaid balance, $551.98, at the end of the second year. Press the NEXT and INT menu keys for the third year's interest, $60.72; the PRIN menu key for the for the third year's principal payment, $261.61; and the BAL menu key to show that $290.37 is owed at the end of the third year. Complete the schedule by pressing the NEXT menu key, the INT menu key ($31.94), the PRIN menu key ($290.39), and the BAL menu key (–$.02).

If you wish to see a summary of the results for the four years, press 4, #P, the INT menu key to see that $289.30 is paid in interest. Press the PRIN and BAL menu keys to show that the loan is repaid in full. Press EXIT twice to return to the TVM menu.

Creating an Amortization Schedule with the BA-II Plus. The procedure for creating an amortization schedule on the BA-II Plus calculator requires that you leave the machine's standard calculator mode that has been used throughout this chapter and use its prompted work sheet mode. First, however, clear the memory units and set the calculator for end-of-period payments and two decimal places. Then enter the basic data about the problem in this illustration by pressing the following keys: 1000, PV, 11, I/Y, 4, N, 322.33, +/–, PMT.

Then to create the schedule you will be using the Amort (amortization) function on the PV key, the ENTER key on the top row of the keyboard, and the down-arrow key next to the ON/OFF key. Press the following keys:

2nd, Amort	(to access the amortization prompted work sheet mode),
1, ENTER, ↓, 1, ENTER,↓	(to show the unpaid loan balance after the first payment),
↓	(to show how much of the first payment was applied to principal),
↓	(to show how much of the first payment was applied to interest),

↓, ↓, 2, ENTER, ↓	(to show the unpaid loan balance after the second payment),
↓	(to show the cumulative total applied to principal to this point),
↓	(to show the cumulative total applied to interest to this point),
↓, ↓, 3, ENTER, ↓	(to show the unpaid loan balance after the third payment),
↓	(to show the cumulative total applied to principal to this point),
↓	(to show the cumulative total applied to interest to this point),
↓, ↓, 4, ENTER, ↓	(to show an unpaid loan balance of approximately zero after the fourth and final payment),
↓	(to show the approximate cumulative total applied to principal by the end of the loan period),
↓	(to show the approximate cumulative total applied as interest by the end of the loan period).

When you have completed your review of the amortization schedule, clear this prompted work sheet and all the memory registers and return to the standard calculator mode by pressing 2nd, Amort, 2nd, CLR Work, 2nd, Quit, 2nd, and CLR TVM.

CASH FLOW STRUCTURES INVOLVING SINGLE SUMS AND ANNUITIES

Earlier in this chapter we noted that, though most time-value-of-money problems involve only four variables, sometimes they involve five variables, of which four are known and the task is to solve for the fifth. For example, a problem might involve an initial deposit of $1,000 into a savings account, annual deposits of $300 at the end of years one, 2, and 3, and compound annual interest earnings of 7 percent on all the deposits. The task might be to compute the account balance at the end of the third year.

Problems such as these are simply combinations of the types of problems you have already learned to solve. Simply divide the problem into its component parts, solve each component separately, and add the solutions together.

To illustrate, the preceding problem is made up of an FVSS problem ($1,000 for 3 years at 7 percent) and an FVA problem ($300 at the end of each year for 3 years at 7 percent). If you use tables B.1 and B.3 in appendix B to solve this problem, you will find that the future value is $2,189.47, namely,

$1,000 x 1.2250	=	$1,225.00
+ $300 x 3.2149	=	964.47
Total		$2,189.47

To revise part of this problem a bit, what if the objective is to have $2,500 in the account at the end of the third year? What initial deposit is needed, together with the three annual deposits, to reach this goal? This problem involves calculating the FVA of the three $300 deposits, subtracting it from the $2,500 future goal, and computing the PVSS of the balance. Using tables B.2 and B.3 in appendix B, you will find that the answer is $1,253.45, namely,

Future amount desired		$2,500.00
– $300 x 3.2149	=	964.47
Balance		$1,535.53
$1,535.53 x .8163	=	$1,253.45

If you are using a financial calculator, the task is somewhat simpler. In the first problem, enter –$1,000 as the PV, –$300 as the end-of-period payment, 3 as the n, and 7 as the i. Then solve for FV, which should be $2,189.51. In the second problem, enter $2,500 as the FV, –$300 as the end-of-period payment, 3 as the n, and 7 as the i. Then solve for PV, which should be –$1,253.45.

A frequent situation calling for the calculation of a fifth variable on the basis of four known variables is the computation of a bond's yield to maturity. For example, what is the yield to maturity of a $1,000 face amount bond, currently selling for $920, that will mature in six years and, in the meantime, will pay $80 of interest at the end of each year?[18] Enter $1,000 as the FV, –$920 as the PV, 6 as the n, and $80 as the end-of-period payment. Then solve for i, which is 9.83%.

PROBLEMS

1. A real estate appraiser has advised you that the value of the homes in your neighborhood has been rising at a compound annual rate of about 6 percent in recent years. On the basis of this information, what is the value today of the home you bought 7 years ago for $119,500?
2. According to the rule of 72, approximately how long will it take for a sum of money to double in value if it earns a compound annual interest rate of 4 percent?
3. Although you have made no deposits or withdrawals from your emergency fund savings account at the bank, the account balance has risen during the past 3 years from $15,000 to $17,613.62.

(a) What has been the compound annual interest rate that the bank has been crediting to your account?

(b) At that rate, how many more years will be needed until your account balance reaches $20,000?

4. There is an attractive piece of undeveloped land that you are considering purchasing. You think that in 5 years it will sell for $30,000. What would you pay for it today if you want to earn a compound annual rate of return of 12 percent on your investment?

5. Your personal net worth has risen in the past 4 years from $110,000 to $260,000 due to your shrewd investing. What has been the compound annual rate of growth of your net worth during this period?

6. You hope to accumulate $45,000 as a down payment on a vacation home in the near future.

   (a) If you can set aside $38,000 now in an account that will be credited with 8 percent compound annual interest, how long will it take until you have the needed down payment?

   (b) What if you can get 9 percent per year on your money?

7. You have decided that, beginning one year from now, you are going to deposit your $1,200 annual dividend check in a savings account at the credit union to build up a retirement fund. The account will be credited with 6 percent compound annual interest.

   (a) If you plan to retire 18 years from now, how much will be in the account at that time?

   (b) If you should decide to retire 3 years earlier than that, how much will be in the account?

8. The round-the-world trip you and your spouse intend to take on your 25th wedding anniversary, 6 years from now, will cost $22,000.

   (a) How much should you set aside each year, beginning today, to reach that objective if you can earn 9 percent compound annual interest on your money?

   (b) How will the size of the annual deposit be affected if you can earn only 8 percent compound annual interest?

9. You have just started a program of depositing $2,000 at the beginning of each year in an education fund account for your newborn son. How much will be in the account

   (a) after 11 years if it earns 8.5 percent compound annual interest?

   (b) after 13 years if it earns 8.5 percent compound annual interest?

   (c) after 18 years if it earns 7.5 percent compound annual interest and you discontinue making deposits after the fifth deposit?

10. A company leases an office building you own for $25,000 each year. The next rental payment is due in one year.

   (a) For what lump sum amount would you sell the next three payments today if you could invest the proceeds at a 12.5 percent compound annual rate of return?

(b) For what amount would you sell them if the next rental payment is due later today?

11. Which would you prefer to have: $10,000 today in a lump sum or $1,000 per year for 13 years, beginning one year from now, if interest rates are
    (a) 4 percent?
    (b) 6 percent?
12. A bank is willing to lend you $15,000 to make some home improvements. The loan is to be repaid in five equal annual installments, beginning one year from now. If the interest rate on the loan is 10 percent,
    (a) what will be the size of the annual payment?
    (b) how much of the second payment will be interest?
    (c) how much of the final payment will be principal?
13. The account in which you deposited your inheritance has a present balance of $48,000. If the account is credited with 13 percent compound annual interest and if you plan to withdraw from it $7,500 per year beginning one year from now, how long will it be before the balance is zero?
14. Suppose that a bank will lend you $10,000 if you agree to repay $4,199.31 at the end of each of the next 3 years. What compound annual interest rate is the bank charging you?
15. If you deposit $1,100 in your bank account today, and add deposits of $600 to it at the end of each of the next 9 years, and if all your deposits earn 6 percent compound annual interest, how much will be in your account immediately after you make the last deposit?

SOLUTIONS

(*Note:* Solutions to most of the problems at the end of this and the next chapter have been calculated with the answers rounded to two decimal places for dollar values and four decimal places for interest rate values and values of n. Your solutions may vary slightly from those presented due to rounding differences.)

1. The house should be worth about $179,700 today. In table B.1 of appendix B, the factor to be used is 1.5036. $119,500 x 1.5036 = $179,680.20. Or using a financial calculator, $119,500 compounded at 6 percent for 7 years produces FV = $179,683.82.
2. At a 4 percent compound annual interest rate, according to the rule of 72 it will take about 18 years for a sum of money to double in value, because 72 ÷ 4 = 18. A more precise answer, found by means of a financial calculator, is n = 17.6730.
3. (a) Your account has been credited with 5.5 percent compound annual interest. $17,613.62 ÷ $15,000 = 1.1742. In table B.1 in the 3-year row the factor 1.1742 is in the 5.5% column. Or using a financial calculator with $15,000 as the PV, $17,613.62 as the FV, and 3 as the n, i = 5.5000 percent.

(b) Your account balance will reach $20,000 in a little more than 2 years. $20,000 ÷ $17,613.62 = 1.1355. In table B.1 in the 5.5% column, this FVSS factor is between those for 2 and 3 years, and is closer to that for 2 years. Through the use of a process of interpolation or use of the HP-17B II or the BA-II Plus financial calculator, you can find the precise n=2.3731 (rounded to 3 on the HP-12C calculator).

4. You should be willing to pay about $17,000 for the property today. In table B.2, the factor to be used is 0.5674. $30,000 x 0.5674 = $17,022. Or with a financial calculator, $30,000 discounted at 12 percent for 5 years produces PV = $17,022.81.
5. Your net worth has grown at a compound annual rate of almost 24 percent. $110,000 ÷ $260,000 = .4231. In table B.2 in the 4-year row, the closest factor is .4230, which is in the 24.0% column. Through a process of interpolation or the use of a financial calculator, you could calculate the precise amount, i = 23.9924 percent.
6. (a) It will take a little over 2 years to accumulate the down payment. $38,000 ÷ $45,000 = .8444. In table B.2 in the 8% column, this value lies between the factors for 2 and 3 years, and is closer to the 2-year factor. By interpolation or use of a financial calculator, you could find that the precise n = 2.1969. (Note, however, that the HP-12C produces an imprecise n = 3.)

   (b) With a higher rate, the waiting period is shortened to just under 2 years. In the 9% column of table B.2, .8444 lies between the factors for 1 and 2 years and is closer to that for 2 years. If you interpolate or use a financial calculator you will see that n = 1.9619.
7. (a) There will be about $37,087 in the account at the end of 18 years. In table B.3 the correct FVA factor is 30.9057. $1,200 x 30.9057 = $37,086.84. Or if you use a financial calculator, FVA = $37,086.78.

   (b) At the end of 15 years the account balance will be almost $27,931. From table B.3 the FVA factor of 23.2760 is multiplied by $1,200 to produce FVA = $27,931.20. If you use a financial calculator, the more precise answer is FVA = $27,931.16.
8. (a) You should set aside approximately $2,683 now and at the beginning of each of the next 5 years in order to reach the target amount. In table B.3 the factor for 9%, 6 periods, is 7.5233. To convert this to an FVAD factor, 7.5233 is multiplied by 1.09 to produce 8.2004. The target amount, $22,000, is divided by 8.2004 to produce an annuity due payment of $2,682.80. On a financial calculator, the beginning-of-year PMT = $2,682.78.

   (b) If only 8 percent compound annual interest is earned, the size of the needed annual deposit rises to about $2,777. The factor is 7.3359 x 1.08 = 7.9228. Dividing $22,000 by 7.9228 = $2,776.80. Or on the calculator, the beginning-of-year PMT = $2,776.79.

9. (a) After 11 years at 8.5 percent there will be approximately $37,099 in the account. In table B.3 the correct FVA factor is 17.0961. The correct FVAD factor is 17.0961 x 1.085 = 18.5493. $2,000 x 18.5493 = $37,098.54 FVAD. On the calculator, FVAD = $37,098.50.
   (b) After 13 years at 8.5 percent there will be about $48,198 in the account. From table B.3 the factor is 22.2109 x 1.085 = 24.0988. $2,000 x 24.0988 = $48,197.60 FVAD. On the financial calculator, replacing 11 with 13 as n produces FVAD = $48,197.73.
   (c) At the end of 5 years there will be about $12,488 in the account. The table B.3 factor is 5.8084 x 1.075 = 6.2440. Multiplying $2,000 by this factor produces $12,488.06 as the FVAD. This amount, carried forward as a single sum for 13 more years at 7.5 percent (see table B.1) will grow to $12,488.06 x 2.5604 = $31,974.43. If you use a financial calculator, $12,488.04 will be in the account at the end of 5 years. Clear the machine and reenter this as the PV, with 7.5 as the i and 13 as the n. FV = $31,974.54.
10. (a) You would be willing to sell the next three payments for about $59,533 today. In table B.4, the PVA factor for 3 years, 12.5% is 2.3813. $25,000 x 2.3813 = $59,532.50. On a financial calculator with $25,000 as the end-of-year PMT, 3 as the n, and 12.5 as the i, PVA = $59,533.61.
   (b) In this case the selling price would be higher, about $66,975. The PVAD factor is 2.3813 x 1.125, or 2.6790. $25,000 x 2.6790 = $66,975.00. If you use a financial calculator, the present value of the three beginning-of-year PMTs is $66,975.31.
11. (a) $10,000 now is preferable. In table B.4 the PVA factor for 4%, 13 years, is 9.9856. $1,000 x 9.9856 = $9,985.60 PVA. On the financial calculator, PVA = $9,985.65.
   (b) $10,000 in a lump sum now is even more preferable at the 6 percent discount rate. The PVA factor of 8.8527 multiplied by $1,000 = $8,852.70. On the financial calculator, PVA = $8,852.68.
12. (a) The PVA factor in table B.4 is 3.7908. The payment would be $15,000 ÷ 3.7908, or $3,956.95. On the financial calculator, with $15,000 as the PV, 5 as the n, and 10 as the i, the end-of-year PMT = $3,956.96.
   (b) and (c)
   It is possible, though cumbersome, to create an amortization schedule such as the following without using a financial calculator.

Year	(1) Balance, Beg. of Year	(2) Payment, End of Year	(3) Interest Payment 10% x (1)	(4) Principal Payment (2) – (3)	(5) Unpaid Balance, End of Year (1) – (4)
1	$15,000.00	$3,956.95	$1,500.00	$2,456.95	$12,543.05
2	12,543.05	3,956.95	1,254.31	2,702.64	9,840.41
3	9,840.41	3,956.95	984.04	2,972.91	6,867.50
4	6,867.50	3,956.95	686.75	3,270.20	3,597.30
5	3,597.30	3,956.95	359.73	3,597.22	.08

Thus the interest portion of the second payment will be $1,254.31 and the principal portion of the final payment will be $3,597.22. If you use the much faster financial calculator technique as described in the text with $3,956.96 as the end-of-year PMT, the second interest payment is $1,254.30 and the final principal payment is $3,597.23.

13. You could divide $48,000 by the $7,500 payment to produce a PVA factor of 6.4000. Then use the 13% column of table B.4 to find the n closest to this factor. The PVA factor for 14 years is 6.3025. The PVA factor for 15 years is 6.4624. Thus n is between 14 and 15 years, and is closer to 15. By a process of interpolation or by using a financial calculator with $7,500 as the end-of-year PMT, you can find the precise n = 14.5952.
14. First divide $10,000 by the $4,199.31 payment to produce a PVA (because the payments are to be made at the end of each year) factor of 2.3813. In the 3-year row of table B.4, this factor appears in the 12.5% column. Alternatively, enter the PV, n, and end-of-year PMT in a financial calculator to find that i = 12.5000 percent.
15. The FVSS of the $1,100 initial deposit after 9 years will be $1,858.45 ($1,100 x 1.6895). The FVA of the nine $600 deposits after the last deposit is made will be $6,894.78 ($600 x 11.4913). Thus the total account balance will be $8,753.23 ($1,858.45 + $6,894.78). Alternatively, on your financial calculator enter $1,100 as the PV, $600 as the end-of-period PMT, 9 as the n, and 6 as the i to find the FV, $8,753.22.

NOTES

1. Problems of this type are discussed briefly at the end of this chapter.
2. You should not be concerned with small differences among answers produced by the use of the table versus the formula or a calculator. Differences of a few cents often arise because of the lesser precision of the tables in the rounding process.
3. The descriptions provided for the solution of problems using the HP-12C, HP-17B II, and the BA-II Plus are for educational purposes only and should not be construed as an endorsement of them by either the author or The American College.
4. Several keys on the HP-12C calculator perform more than one function. This is accomplished by means of the yellow f key and blue g key on the bottom row of the keyboard. Pressing

yellow f and a key causes the key to perform the function printed in yellow above that key. Pressing blue g and a key causes the key to perform the function printed in blue on the lower edge of that key. For example, press the 9, ENTER, 2, and y^x keys. The number 81, which is 9 squared, appears on the display. Now press CLX, 9, ENTER, blue g, and the same y^x key. The number 3, which is the square root of 9, appears on the display. Pressing the blue g key switched the function to be performed by the y^x key from raising the number to a power (y^x), in this case squaring it, to finding its square root $\sqrt{x}$.

5. For your convenience, appendix C lists the keystrokes to be used in solving the most common types of time-value-of-money problems on the HP-12C.
6. Several keys on the HP-17B II calculator perform more than one function. This is accomplished by the colored shift key. Pressing this key and another key causes the latter key to perform the function printed in color above it. For example, press the shift key and the CLR key, which has OFF printed above it, to turn the calculator off. Turn it on again, then press 9, shift, X (which has y^x printed above it), 4, and =. The number 6,561 appears on the display screen. You have just raised the number 9 to the fourth power (9 x 9 x 9 x 9) by means of the y^x function that is activated by the shifted X key.
7. For your convenience, Appendix D lists the keystrokes to be used in performing various housekeeping functions and in solving the most common types of time-value-of-money problems on the HP-17B II.
8. Several keys on the BA-II Plus keyboard perform two separate functions. The first function is that printed on the key. The second is that printed directly above it. This latter function performed by pressing the gray key marked 2nd in the upper left-hand corner of the keyboard, followed by the key in question.
9. For your convenience, appendix E lists the keystrokes to be used in solving the most common types of time-value-of-money problems on the BA-II Plus.
10. The rule of 72 can be used for purposes of discounting as well as for compounding, as will be explained later. In this case the result of dividing the number 72 by the interest rate is the approximate number of periods it will take to produce a present value equal to one-half the original sum.
11. Specifically, the formula is as follows:

$$n = \frac{\log \left[\frac{\text{FVSS}}{\text{PVSS}} \right]}{\log (1 + i)}$$

12. In some fields, such as insurance, the terms *annuity* and *annuity due* are used to refer to a series of payments the value of which includes both compound interest *and mortality* factors. Such annuities are more accurately referred to as *life annuities* or *life annuities due.*
13. If the sinking fund payments were to be made at the end of each of the 3 years, the methods of solving the problem would be slightly different. If the table is used, divide $10,000,000 by the factor in table B.3 without first multiplying the factor by 1.09. On the HP-12C, press END after blue g, rather than BEG. On the HP-17B II or the BA-II Plus, set the machine for end-of-period payments and recompute the payment. The precise answer is $3,050,547.57. The larger deposits are necessitated, of course, by the fact that each deposit will earn interest for one year less under the end-of-year assumption.
14. Technically, this answer assumes that in the seventh year a fraction of a year's interest is earned and a fraction of one annual deposit is also added to the account. Also, as was explained earlier, the HP-12C is less precise than the BA-II Plus in solving for n. In this case, the HP-12C would give an answer of 7 years.

15. In reality, most installment loans call for monthly payments. In this chapter, however, it will be assumed that the periodic loan payments are made annually. The method for computing monthly payments will be explained in the next chapter.
16. As was explained earlier, the HP-12C is less precise than the HP-17B II or the BA-II Plus in solving for n. In this case, the HP-12C would give an answer of 5 years. Also, technically the precise answer of 4.8172 years assumes that in the final year a fraction of a year's interest is paid, as well as a fraction of a full year's loan payment.
17. The procedure for creating an amortization schedule where the loan is repaid through monthly installment payments is the same as described in this section except that (a) the figure used as the periodic payment should be the monthly payment; (b) the figure used as the interest rate should be the annual rate divided by 12; and (c) the number used as the n should be the total number of monthly payments to be made. See the discussion of simple annuities in the following chapter.
18. The solution when a bond pays interest semiannually, as is the usual case, will be explained in the next chapter.

6

Time Value of Money: Advanced Concepts and Applications

Robert M. Crowe

Chapter Outline

DEALING WITH UNEVEN CASH FLOWS

The preceding chapter included explanations of how to compute the future value and present value of an annuity (or an annuity due). By definition of the term *annuity,* the discussion dealt only with cases in which each of the payments or deposits in the series was of the same amount. This chapter begins with an explanation of how to compute the present value and future value of a stream of *uneven* payments or deposits. The ability to do so is useful in and of itself to solve several types of problems. It also is essential for evaluating various types of investments through discounted cash-flow analysis, as explained later in this chapter.

Present Value of Uneven Cash Flows

Assume that a young man will be entering college in one year. The estimated tuition is $6,000 to be paid at the start of the freshman year, $6,600 at the start of the sophomore year, $7,250 at the start of the junior year, and $8,100 at the start of the senior year. How much should be on hand today in an account earning 8.5 percent interest in order to just meet these four tuition payments as they come due? What is the present value of this series of uneven cash flows discounted at 8.5 percent?

The solution of a simple problem of this sort actually involves no techniques that have not already been covered. All that is needed is to compute the present value of each of the four tuition payments and add them together. In other words, the present value of this stream of uneven payments is simply the sum of the present values of the four single sums.

Using Time-Value Tables

Since this sequence of cash flows is fairly brief, simple tools such as a time-value formula or table can be used to compute the present value fairly quickly. Table B.2 in appendix B is used here to provide the appropriate 8.5 percent factors needed to solve the problem.

End of Year	Tuition Amount	PVSS Factor	PVSS
1	$6,000	0.9217	$ 5,530.20
2	6,600	0.8495	5,606.70
3	7,250	0.7829	5,676.03
4	8,100	0.7216	5,844.96
Total			$22,657.89

If $22,657.89 is placed on deposit today, and if 8.5 percent compound interest is earned on the account balance over the next 4 years, there will be just enough to meet each of the estimated tuition payments as they fall due. After the final payment is made, the account balance will essentially be zero. Table 6-1 shows the pattern of the account balance over the four years.

TABLE 6-1
Liquidation of a Capital Sum Compounding at 8.5% Interest Through Uneven Cash Withdrawals

Year	Beginning Balance	Interest Earnings	Cash Withdrawal	Ending Balance
1	$22,657.89	$1,925.92	$6,000	$18,583.81
2	18,583.81	1,579.62	6,600	13,563.43
3	13,563.43	1,152.89	7,250	7,466.32
4	7,466.32	634.64	8,100	0.96

This case is an illustration of so-called *ungrouped* cash flows, which means that the cash-flow sequence includes no consecutive payments of the same amount and arithmetic sign, positive or negative. Each payment, therefore, has to be discounted separately. In some situations, however, there are *grouped* cash flows, that is, some of the consecutive payments are of the same amount and flow in the same direction, either in or out. With grouped cash flows a short cut is possible in finding the present value.

A common example of an uneven cash flow where some of the payments can be grouped is a corporate bond. For example, assume that you are considering purchasing a bond that will pay you interest of $90 per year at the end of each of the next 6 years, as well as the $1,000 face amount at the end of the sixth year.[1] If you wish to earn a rate of return of 13 percent on your money, how much would you pay for the bond? That is, what is the present value, discounted at a 13 percent annual interest rate, of this income stream, which is depicted in figure 6-1?

This series of cash flows actually consists of two components: an annuity of $90 per year for 5 years and a single sum of $1,090 at the end of the sixth year (or an annuity of $90 per year for 6 years and a single sum of $1,000 at the end of the sixth year). Hence to compute the present value of the entire sequence it is necessary to (1) compute the present value of the annuity, (2) compute the present value of the single sum, and (3) add the results together.

Again, the sequence of cash flows is rather short and simple in this illustration, so the solution can be calculated fairly quickly using time-value formulas or tables. For example, table B.4 in appendix B shows a PVA factor of 3.5172 for 5 years and 13%. Multiplied by the $90 annuity payment, this produces a PVA of $316.55. Table B.2 shows a PVSS factor of .4803 for 6 years and 13%. Multiplied by $1,090 it produces a present value of the sixth year cash flow of $523.53. Thus, the present value of the total sequence of cash flows, the price you would be willing to pay for the bond, is $840.08 ($316.55 + $523.53).

To take a different situation involving some grouped cash flows, assume you loan a sum of money to a borrower today. The repayment schedule calls for the borrower to make payments to you as follows:

End of Year	Payment Amount
1	$ 0
2	2,000
3–9	3,000
10	5,000

What is the present value of this sequence of payments, which is depicted in figure 6-2, if an 11 percent interest rate is assumed?

FIGURE 6-1
Time Line Depiction of a Bond Value

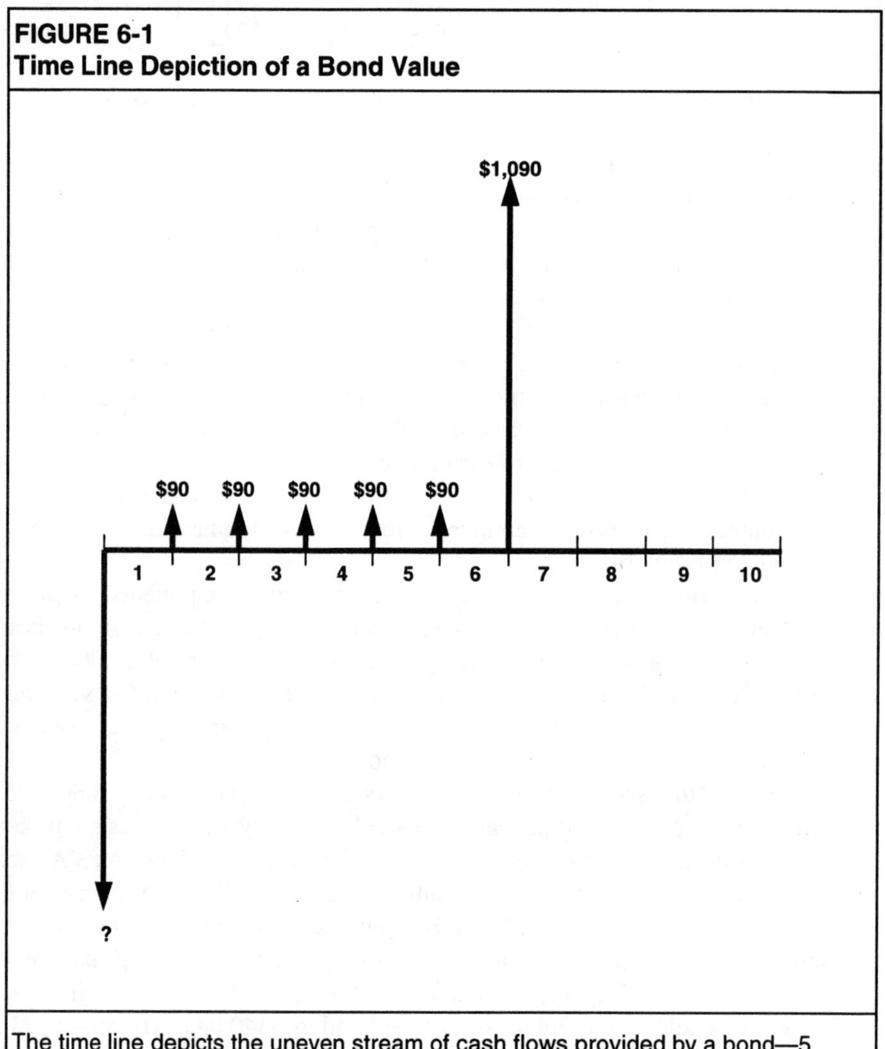

The time line depicts the uneven stream of cash flows provided by a bond—5 annual payments of $90 each and a sixth of $1,090. The problem is to compute the present value of the steam of cash flows.

FIGURE 6-2
Time Line Depiction of the Present Value of Uneven Cash Flows

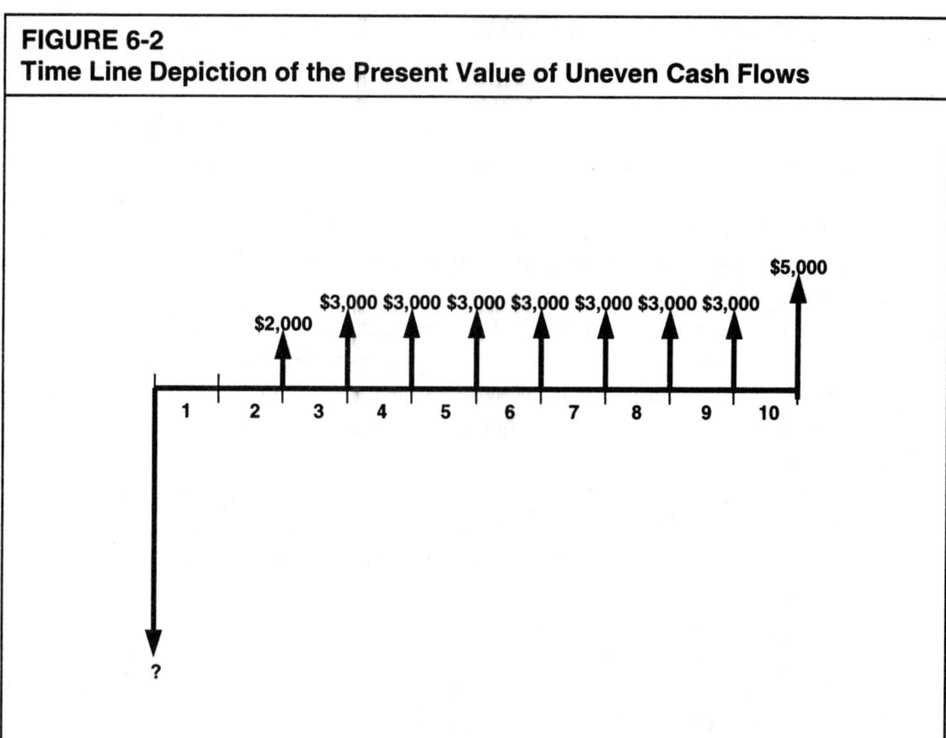

This time line shows a problem in which the task is to compute the present value of a stream of cash flows consisting of zero at the end of year 1, $2,000 at the end of year 2, $3,000 at the end of years 3 through 9, and $5,000 at the end of year 10.

The solution to this problem involves several steps. First, the $2,000 payment at the end of year 2 must be discounted. Second, the present value of a 7-year, $3,000 annuity must be computed. Third, the present value of that annuity must be further discounted as a single sum to compute its present value *today,* rather than its present value 2 years from now when the annuity begins. (Note that this annuity begins at the *start* of the third year, even though the first payment under it is not made until the *end* of the third year.) Fourth, the $5,000 payment at the end of year 10 must be discounted. Finally, the PVSS of the first payment, the twice-discounted value of the PVA of the next seven payments, and the PVSS of the ninth payment must be added together to obtain the present value of the entire series of cash flows.

Again you can use tables B.2 and B.4 to solve the problem. From the 11% column, find the appropriate factors and apply them as follows:

1. PVSS of payment at end of year 2
   $2,000 x 0.8116 = $ 1,623.20
2. PVA of payments at end of years 3–9
   $3,000 x 4.7122 = $14,136.60

3.	PVSS of PVA of payments at end of years 3–9 $14,136.60 x 0.8116 =	$11,473.26
4.	PVSS of payment at end of year 10 $5,000 x 0.3522 =	1,761.00
5.	Present value of the cash flows	$14,857.46

One last point should be made before some slightly more complex cash-flow patterns are discussed. In some problems one or more of the cash-flow amounts are negative. For example, assume you own rental property that is expected to generate net income for you of $15,000 per year at the end of each of the next 15 years, except for year 10. In that year you estimate that replacement of the heating and air conditioning units will be necessary, causing a *net cash outflow* for the year of $6,000. What is the present value of this stream of cash flow discounted at 9 percent?

In this case the only difference in procedure for finding the solution is that the present value of the net cash outflow must be *subtracted* from the aggregate present value of the net cash inflows. Specifically, in this illustration,

1.	PVA of inflows at end of years 1–9 $15,000 x 5.9952 =	$ 89,928.00
2.	PVA of inflows at end of years 11–15 $15,000 x 3.8897 = $58,345.50	
3.	PVSS of PVA of inflows at end of years 11–15 $58,345.50 x .4224 =	24,645.14
4.	Present value of cash inflows	$114,573.14
5.	PVSS of outflow at end of year 10 $6,000 x .4224 =	– 2,534.40
6.	Present value of the net cash flows	$112,038.74

As you can see, the illustrations are becoming a bit complex, and the use of tables to solve them is starting to be a little unwieldy. To reduce the difficulty, you may be able to express the cash flows of a problem in slightly different terms. For example, the preceding pattern of cash flows could be expressed as

1. an annuity of $15,000 for 15 years, and
2. an outflow of $21,000 at the end of year 10 (that is, $15,000 that needs to be subtracted out of the annuity and $6,000 that was the actual net outflow).

Calculation of the present value of this pattern of cash flows could have been completed in fewer steps than presented above.

Using a Financial Calculator to Solve Problems with Uneven Cash Flows

In the illustrative problems up to this point, the solutions were easy to find because of the short and simple patterns of payment. Tools such as time-value formulas or tables B.2 and B.4 and a simple calculator suffice in such situations for computing and totaling the present value of the individual cash flows or, in the case of groups of level cash flows, the annuities.

Often, however, a lengthy series of cash flows is involved in a problem. Frequently the series will involve many different payment amounts, some years of zero flows, and perhaps even some changes of arithmetic signs. For those cases, a financial calculator like the HP-12C, the HP-17B II, or the BA-II Plus calculator is very well suited. For problems that exceed the usually ample capacity of these calculators, a computer program may be necessary.

Ungrouped Cash Flows at End of Year. First to be explained is the use of these calculators to solve problems in which there are no consecutive cash flows of the same amount. In this circumstance, the HP-12C has the capacity to solve problems involving up to 20 cash flows that occur at the end of each year (or 21 that occur at the beginning of each year). The HP-17B II has the capacity to solve problems with up to 700 separate uneven cash flows. The BA-II Plus has the capacity, in this case, to handle up to 24 cash flows that occur at the end of each year (or 25 that occur at the beginning of each year).

To illustrate, assume an investment will produce the following pattern of net cash inflows during the next 20 years.

End of Year	Cash Flow	End of Year	Cash Flow
1	$ 500	11	$ 0
2	1,100	12	2,150
3	1,150	13	2,250
4	1,175	14	2,350
5	1,000	15	2,450
6	2,600	16	2,600
7	2,700	17	650
8	2,800	18	2,700
9	2,900	19	2,800
10	1,000	20	2,900

This set of data, together with the discount rate to be used, represents the maximum capacity that the HP-12C can handle and almost all that the BA-II Plus can handle. It barely scratches the surface of the HP-17B II's capacity. As explained below, either calculator's capacity can be expanded if some of the data consists of grouped data. Note in this problem, by the way, that some of the cash flows are of equal amounts (years 6 and 16, 7 and 18, 8 and 19, and 9 and 20).

Nevertheless, these are not grouped data because the equal amounts do not occur in consecutive years.

Using the HP-12C to Solve Problems with Uneven Cash Flows. To solve a present-value problem on the HP-12C where the cash flows are ungrouped and begin one or more periods in the future, first look at the PMT key in the top row of the keyboard. Note that it also contains a blue CFj function. (The CFj symbol stands for juxtaposed, or side-by-side, cash flows.) This function is used to enter the amount of each cash flow, including zero amounts. After all the payments in the series are entered, the discount rate is entered with the i key as usual. Finally, note that the PV key in the top row of the keyboard also contains a yellow function, NPV (net present value). The yellow f key and NPV are used to produce the solution.

To illustrate the process, assume that you have a deferred compensation agreement with your employer. Under the agreement the employer is obligated to pay you the following amounts:

End of year 1	$ 0
End of year 2	$ 75,000
End of year 3	$ 80,000
End of year 4	$ 85,000
End of year 5	$ 90,000

If you use a discount rate of 12.5 percent, what is the present value of this future income stream? Press 0, blue g, CFj. The initial year's zero value is now entered. Press 75000, blue g, CFj to reflect the amount to be received at the end of year 2. Press 80000, blue g, CFj to enter the cash inflow at the end of year 3. Enter the remaining two payments by pressing 85000, blue g, CFj, and 90000, blue g, CFj. Now enter the discount rate by pressing 12.5 and the i key. Finally, compute the present value of the income stream by pressing the yellow f key and NPV. The answer, $218,454.50, should appear on the display.

Using the HP-17B II to Solve Problems with Uneven Cash Flows. To solve a present value problem on the HP-17B II where the cash flows are uneven and occur at the end of each period, we will use the calculator's CFLO (cash flow) menu, which you will find at the same level in the menu system as the TVM menu. Press the CFLO menu key, shift, CLEAR DATA, and the YES menu key. Then press the #T? menu key. If the Time Prompting function is shown to be OFF, release the key. If not, press the #T? menu again to shut it off. Now you are ready to enter a series of ungrouped cash flows and compute their present value.

To illustrate the process, look at the brief series of cash flows in the deferred compensation agreement described in the illustration above. The HP-17B II is asking you for FLOW(0), which is the cash flow at the *start* of year one of the problem. Since there is nothing at that time in the problem you are considering, press 0 and INPUT. The calculator now is asking you for FLOW(1), which is the cash flow at the *end* of year one. Since this too is zero, press 0 and INPUT. The calculator then asks for the next cash flow, so press 75000 and INPUT. For the remaining cash flows press 80000, INPUT, 85000, INPUT, 90000, and INPUT. Now that the full series of cash flows is in the machine, press EXIT and the CALC menu key. Before you can compute the (net) present value of the series, you must tell the machine what discount rate to use. Press 12.5 and the I% menu key. Then press the NPV menu key to find the answer, $218,454.50.[2]

A sometimes useful feature of the HP-17B II is that it enables the user to check or even to alter the list of cash flows that have been entered. To review the amount of each of the flows, starting at the end of the series and proceeding back to the beginning, press the EXIT key and then press the up arrow key in the left-hand column of the keyboard several times. To change the amount of one of the cash flows, use the down or up arrow keys to display the item to be changed. Then key in the new value, press INPUT, and recompute the NPV. To delete a cash flow from the list, display the item to be eliminated and press the DELET menu key and recompute the NPV. To insert an additional cash flow, display the cash flow that follows the new one. Press the INSR menu key; then key in the new value, press INPUT, and recompute the NPV.

Using the BA-II Plus to Solve Problems with Uneven Cash Flows. If you wish to solve a present-value problem on the BA-II Plus where the cash flows are ungrouped and begin one or more periods in the future, you need to again use the prompted work sheet mode. This time, however, you do not use the amortization work sheet explained in chapter 5. Instead, you use the cash flows work sheet, which can be accessed through the CF key in the second row of the keyboard. You also use the NPV key in the same row of the keyboard to calculate the net present value of the cash flow.

To illustrate, look at the brief series of cash flows in the deferred-compensation agreement described on the previous page. If you use a 12.5 present discount rate, what is the present value of this future income stream? Press the following keys:

CF, 2nd, CLR Work	(to enter the cash flows prompted work sheet and clear it of extraneous data)
ENTER, ↓	(because there is no cash flow at the start of year one)
0, ENTER, ↓,↓	(because there is no cash flow at the end of year one and to prepare to enter the next cash flow)

75000, ENTER, ↓,↓	(to enter the first cash flow, to show that it occurred only once, and to prepare to enter the next cash flow)
80000, ENTER, ↓,↓	(to enter the second cash flow, to show that it occurred only once, and to prepare to enter the next cash flow)
85000, ENTER, ↓,↓	(to enter the third cash flow, to show that it occurred only once, and to prepare to enter the next cash flow)
90000, ENTER, ↓,↓	(to enter the final cash flow, to show that it occurred only once, and to prepare to solve the problem)
NPV, 12.5, ENTER,↓	(to tell the machine that you want to find the net present value of these cash flows discounted at 12.5 percent)
CPT	(to produce the answer)

The answer, $218,454.50, should appear on the display.

Sometimes it is useful to be able to review the cash flows that have been entered or even to revise one or more of them. To see the list again, press the CF key and move through the list by pressing the down arrow key several times. To remove a number from the list, display that number and press 2nd, DEL. Then recompute the NPV. To insert a number into the list, display the space where it is to be inserted. Press 2nd, INS, the number to be inserted, and ENTER. Then recompute the NPV.

Now you should test your skills a bit further by solving the preceding lengthy problem containing 20 cash flows. Hopefully you conclude that, if you use an 8 percent interest rate, the present value of this income stream is $16,638.51. (Did you remember to enter the zero amount in year 11?)

Solving Problems that Include Grouped Cash Flows. These three calculators can solve present value problems involving far more than 20 or 25 cash flows if the series includes some grouped data, because grouped data counts as only one cash-flow amount. For example, a cash flow of $50,000 followed by 40 annual cash flows of $2,000 involves 41 cash flows but only two cash-flow amounts. For problems that include grouped data you should enter, along with the amount of each such cash flow, the total number of times it occurs in succession, including the first time. On the HP-12C, this number is entered by means of the blue Nj function on the FV key in the center of the top row of the keyboard. On the HP-17B II, this number is entered after you have turned the #T? function to ON. On the BA-II Plus, this number is entered when you respond to the FO= prompt that appears on the display after each cash flow (other than the first one) is entered.

To illustrate the process, assume that you are considering investing in a great opportunity that yields a cash inflow to you starting next year of $6,000 per year for 5 years, followed by $4,000 per year for 10 years, followed by $2,000 per year for 15 years, followed by a lump-sum payment of $25,000. Compute the present value of this income stream utilizing an 8 percent discount rate.

On the HP-12C, begin by entering the amount of the initial inflow: 6000, blue g, CFj. Since it occurs a total of five times (including the first), press 5, blue g, Nj. Now enter the next group of inflows: 4000, blue g, CFj; and the number of times this amount occurs: 10, blue g, Nj. Enter the third group of inflows by pressing 2000, blue g, CFj, and 15, blue g, Nj. Then enter the 31st and final inflow: 25000, blue g, CFj. Finally, enter the interest rate by pressing 8 and the i key. Compute the answer by pressing yellow f, NPV and the answer, $49,920.35, should appear on the screen. You can revise the interest rate if you wish simply by entering the new rate and pressing i, yellow f, NPV.

If you are using the HP-17B II, enter the cash flow mode by pressing the CFLO menu key and clear its memory. Press the #T? menu key once or twice to turn the function that prompts you to tell how many times a particular cash flow occurs to ON. Next, press 0 and INPUT to tell the machine that there is no cash flow at the start of the first year. Now press 6000, INPUT, 5, and INPUT to tell the machine that the first cash flow is $6,000 and that it occurs for five consecutive periods. Then press 4000, INPUT, 10, and INPUT to enter the next set of cash flows. Complete the series by pressing 2000, INPUT, 15, INPUT, 25000, INPUT, 1, and INPUT. Now press EXIT, the CALC menu key, 8, the I% menu key, and the NPV menu key to produce the answer, $49,920.35. You can revise the interest rate if you wish by simply entering the new rate and pressing the I% and the NPV menu keys.

The present value of this same great opportunity can be solved with the BA-II Plus by pressing the following keys:

CF, 2nd, CLR Work, ENTER,↓	(to clear the work sheet, to show that there is no cash flow at the start of the first year, and to prepare to enter the first set of cash flows)
6000, ENTER,↓ , 5, ENTER,↓	(to enter the first set of 5 cash flows)
4000, ENTER, ↓, 10, ENTER,↓	(to enter this set of 10 cash flows)
2000, ENTER, ↓, 15, ENTER, ↓	(to enter this set of 15 cash flows)
25000, ENTER, ↓,↓	(to enter the final lump-sum payment and to prepare to solve the problem)
NPV, 8, ENTER, ↓, CPT,	(to calculate the answer at the specified discount rate)

The answer is $49,920.35. You can revise the interest rate if you wish by pressing NPV, the new interest rate, ENTER, ↓, CPT.

Cash Flows at Beginning of Year. Each of the preceding illustrations of how to use the HP-12C, the HP-17B II, and BA-II Plus involve cash flows that occur at the end of the year. If the cash flows occur at the beginning of the year, only a slight change in procedure is needed to find the present value of the payment stream. If you are using the HP-12C, take another look at the PV key, and note that it has a blue CFo function. If the problem to be solved entails cash flows at the beginning of each year, the first such flow (or group of consecutive cash inflows or outflows of equal amount) is entered by means of this blue CFo function. (The symbol CFo stands for original cash flow.) Subsequent cash flows are then entered via the CFj function in the manner described above.[3]

If you are using the HP-17B II, notice that when you enter the cash flow made by pressing the CFLO menu key, the calculator asks for the FLOW(0), the original cash flow, the cash flow at the start of the first year. If this cash flow is ungrouped data, enter the first cash flow here and proceed in the manner described above to enter the size and number of each of the subsequent cash flows. However, if the first cash flow constitutes grouped data, for example, $1,000 at the beginning of years one, two, three, and four, this data must be treated as two separate cash flows, $1,000 occurring at the start of the first year followed by a group of three additional cash flows of $1,000 each.

If you are using BA-II Plus, the procedure is a bit more complex. Notice that when you enter the cash flow prompted work sheet, the calculator asks for the CFo, the original cash flow. If this cash flow is ungrouped data, insert the first cash flow and proceed in the manner described above to enter the size and number of each of the subsequent cash flows. However, if the first cash flow constitutes grouped data, for example, $1,000 at the beginning of years 1, 2, 3, and 4, this data must be treated as two separate cash flows—$1,000 occurring at the start of year one followed by a group of three additional cash flows of $1,000 each.

To illustrate, if a 12 percent discount rate is used, what is the present value of the following series of cash flows?

Beginning of Year	Amount
1–5	$3,500
6–10	2,500
11	1,500
12	500

On the HP-12C, enter the first five cash flows by pressing 3500, blue g, CFo, 5, blue g, Nj. The next five cash flows are entered by pressing 2500, blue g, CFj, 5, blue g, Nj. The last two cash flows are entered by pressing 1500, blue g, CFj, 500, blue g, CFj. The solution is found by entering the discount rate (12 and

i) and pressing yellow f, NPV. The answer, \$20,484.67, should appear on the display.

On the HP-17B II, after entering the cash flow menu system and clearing CFLO of any old data, turn on the #T? function. Enter the cash flows by pressing 3500, INPUT, 3500, INPUT, 4, INPUT, 2500, INPUT, 5, INPUT, 1500, INPUT, 1, INPUT, 500, INPUT, 1, and INPUT. Next, press EXIT the CALC menu key, 12, the I% menu key, and NPV. The answer, \$20,484.67, will be displayed.

On the BA-II Plus, after entering the cash flow prompted work sheet and clearing it of any old data, enter the first five cash flows by pressing 3500, ENTER, ↓, 3500, ENTER, ↓, 4, ENTER,↓. The next five cash flows are then entered by pressing 2500, ENTER, ↓, 5, ENTER,↓. The last two cash flows are entered by pressing 1500, ENTER, ↓,↓ , 500, ENTER, ↓,↓. The solution is then found by pressing NPV, 12, ENTER,↓ , CPT. The answer, \$20,484.67, should appear on the display.

Payments Growing by a Constant Percentage

In many cases time-value-of-money problems involve the need to discount to their present value a stream of payments that grows by a constant annual percentage. Adjusting for an assumed inflation rate is often the underlying motivation.

For example, assume that you wish to have an income stream of \$25,000 per year in *constant purchasing power* for the next 10 years, starting immediately. (That is, a total of ten payments with the first one occurring right now.) How large a capital sum would you need to set aside today to meet this objective if the annual inflation rate is assumed to be 5 percent and if the principal sum to be liquidated can be assumed to produce a rate of return of 8 percent per year? What is the present value, discounted at 8 percent, of this 10-year stream of payments that rises by 5 percent per year?

You could, of course, calculate the amount of each of the 10 payments, discount each of them for the appropriate number of years, and add up the results. There is, however, a better way to produce the answer to this problem. If done manually, it involves using the following formula:

$$\text{PV} = \text{amount of 1st payment x } \frac{1 - \left[\dfrac{(1 + \text{growth rate})}{(1 + \text{i})}\right]^{\text{n}}}{(\text{i} - \text{growth rate})} \text{ x } (1 + \text{i})$$

In the present illustration, the answer is

$$= \$25{,}000 \text{ x } \frac{1 - \left[\frac{1.05}{1.08}\right]^{10}}{(.08 - .05)} \text{ x } 1.08$$

$$= \$25{,}000 \text{ x } \frac{1 - .7545}{.03} \text{ x } 1.08$$

$$= \$25{,}000 \text{ x } 8.1836 \text{ x } 1.08$$

$$= \$220{,}957.20$$

If the first $25,000 payment is to be made after one year, rather than immediately, the answer found through this formula is divided by (1 + i). In this case the present value is $204,590.00 ($220,957.20 ÷ 1.08).

Rather than laboring through the formula, you may prefer to use the HP-12C or BA-II Plus calculator to solve this problem. On the HP-12C, the keystrokes are as follows for the beginning-of-year approach:

blue g, BEG, 25000, PMT	(to enter the first payment, which is to occur immediately)
1.08, ENTER, 1.05, ÷, 1, –, 100, x, i	(to enter the adjusted discount rate)
10, n, PV	(to enter the n and produce the solution)

The answer, $220,955.95, should appear on the display. Dividing this result by 1.08 produces the end-of-year solution, $204,588.85.

If you are using the HP-17B II, return to the TVM menu system by pressing shift, MAIN, the FIN menu key, and the TVM menu key. Set the calculator for beginning-of-period payments. Then press the following keys: 25000, the PMT menu key, 1.08, ÷, 1.05, –, 1, x, 100, =. and the I%YR menu key. You have now entered the initial payment and the inflation-adjusted discount rate. Now press 10, the N menu key, and the PV menu key to produce the solution, $220,955.95. If you want to see the answer under the assumption of end-of-period payments, divide this answer by 1.08. Press ÷, 1.08, =, and the revised answer, $204,588.85, will appear on the display.

On the BA-II Plus, return to the standard calculator mode by pressing 2nd and QUIT. Set the calculator for beginning-of-year payments. Clear the calculator of extraneous data by pressing 2nd and CLR TVM. Then the keystrokes for the beginning-of-year solution are as follows:

25000, PMT	(to enter the first payment)
1.08, ÷, 1.05, –, 1, x, 100, =, I/Y	(to enter the adjusted discount rate)
10, N, CPT, PV	(to enter the n and produce the solution)

The answer, $220,995.95, should appear on the display. Dividing this result by 1.08 produces the end-of-year solution, $204,588.85.

Future Value of Uneven Cash Flows

The following pages deal with the reverse of the previous set of problems and explain how to calculate the future value of a series of uneven cash flows. The explanation is brief because the approach to solving such problems parallels that for solving present-value problems.

Assume that a business plans to make the following series of contributions to fund certain obligations under its pension plan:

End of Year	Amount
1	$30,000
2	40,000
3–5	50,000
6–10	60,000

If these contributions are credited with 10 percent interest per year, how much will be in the fund at the end of the 10th year? What is the future value of this series of uneven cash flows?

The solution of this problem entails compounding each payment from the time it is made until the end of the 10th year and totaling the results. Thus the first $30,000 should be compounded for 9 years at 10 percent to produce its FVSS. The second should be compounded for 8 years, the third for 7 years, and so on. The final $60,000 payment, of course, earns no interest because it is made at the end of the 10th year.

Using Time-Value Tables to Calculate Future Value of Uneven Cash Flows

If, as in the present illustration, the sequence of cash flows is brief and straightforward, the basic future-value formulas or tables can be used to produce a solution. For example, table B.1 in appendix B can provide the nine FVSS factors to be applied to the various payments. Alternatively, since this illustrative problem includes two sets of grouped data ($50,000 per year for 3 years and $60,000 per year for 5 years), table B.3 can be used to provide FVA factors. It must be remembered, however, that the FVA of the three payments at the end of years 3, 4, and 5 must be further compounded by means of an FVSS factor to produce the future value of these three contributions as of the end of the 10th year.

Specifically, then, the future value of this series of uneven cash flows at 10 percent can be found as shown:[4]

1. FVSS of payment at end of year 1
   $30,000 x 2.3579 — $ 70,737.00
2. FVSS of payment at end of year 2
   $40,000 x 2.1436 — 85,744.00

3.	FVA of payments at end of years 3–5 $50,000 x 3.3100 = $165,500	
4.	FVSS of FVA of payments at end of years 3–5 $165,500 x 1.6105	266,537.75
5.	FVA of payments at end of years 6–10 $60,000 x 6.1051	366,306.00
6.	Future value of the cash flows	$789,324.75

Using a Financial Calculator to Calculate the Future Value of Uneven Cash Flows

The HP-12C and BA-II Plus calculators are not constructed to directly compute the future value of a series of uneven cash flows. However, since they do have the capability to compute the present value of a series of uneven cash flows, you can compute the single sum that is the present value of the cash flows and then compute the future value of that single sum. This provides the same result as if you calculated the future value of the cash flows directly. The HP-17B II, unlike the other machines, can produce the answer directly.

For example, assume the following sequence of cash flows:

End of Year	Amount
1	$500
2–5	600
6–8	700

Calculate the future value as of the end of year 8 using a 7 percent interest rate.

Using the HP-12C. On the HP-12C, begin by computing the present value of these cash flows as explained earlier. Press the keys as shown below.

500, blue g, CFj
600, blue g, CFj, 4, blue g, Nj
700, blue g, CFj, 3, blue g, Nj
7, i, yellow f, NPV

The present value, $3,676.43, should appear on the display. Now carry this present value forward as a single sum to the end of year 8 using the same 7 percent interest rate by pressing the following keys:

ENTER, CHS, PV, 8, n, 7, i, FV

The future value of this series of uneven cash flows, $6,316.79, should appear on the display.

Using the BA-II Plus. If you are using the BA-II Plus, compute the present value of the cash flows by pressing the following keys:

CF, 2nd, CLR Work, ENTER, ↓,
500, ENTER, ↓,↓ ,
600, ENTER, ↓, 4, ENTER, ↓,
700, ENTER, ↓, 3, ENTER, ↓,
NPV, 7, ENTER, ↓, CPT

The present value, $3,676.43, should appear on the display. Now carry this present value forward as a single sum to the end of year 8 using the same 7 percent interest rate by pressing the following keys:

STO, 1	(to store this present value in a memory register)
2nd, QUIT, 2nd, CLR TVM	(to leave the prompted work sheet mode, return to the standard calculator mode, and clear the calculator of extraneous data)
RCL, 1, +/–, PV	(to recall the stored value and enter it as the present value)
8, N, 7, I/Y	(to insert the rest of the information needed to find the future value)
CPT, FV	(to produce the answer)

The future value, $6,316.79, should appear on the display. If the cash flows in this problem had occurred at the beginning of each year, rather than the end, use the same procedure, but multiply the answer by (1 plus the interest rate).

Using the HP-17B II. On the HP-17B II, solving a future-value-of-uneven-cash-flows problem is less cumbersome. Enter the CFLO mode and clear the CFLO memory of any extraneous data. Turn the #T? function to ON. Then press the following keys:

0, INPUT
500, INPUT, 1, INPUT,
600, INPUT, 4, INPUT,
700, INPUT, 3, INPUT,
EXIT, the CALC menu key,
7, the I% menu key, and the NFV menu key

The answer, $6,316,79, will appear on the display. If the cash flows in this problem had occurred at the beginning of each year, rather than the end, use the same procedure, but multiply the answer by (1 plus the interest rate).

Deposits Growing by a Constant Percentage

Now instead of dealing with the future value of cash flows that change in an irregular manner we take up the case of the future value of cash flows with amounts that increase each year by a constant percentage. This type of problem frequently arises when someone sets up a savings plan for the attainment of a financial goal and the amount to be saved each year rises at the same rate as the person's income is expected to grow.

For example, assume that you plan to begin a program of annual saving, beginning with a $500 deposit now. Assume also that you expect your income and, hence, the amount you can save to rise by about 10 percent per year. If your savings generate a 7 percent annual rate of return, how much will be in your account at the end of 5 years? What is the future value, compounded at 7 percent interest, of this 5-year stream of deposits that rises by 10 percent per year?

You could, of course, calculate the amount of each of the five deposits, compound each of them for the appropriate number of years, and add up the results. There is, however, a faster way. This type of problem can be solved through the use of the following formula where the first deposit is made immediately:

$$\text{FV} = \text{amount of first deposit x} \left[\frac{(1 + i)^n - (1 + \text{growth rate})^n}{(i - \text{growth rate})} \right] \text{x } (1 + i)$$

In the present example, the answer is

$$= \$500 \text{ x} \left[\frac{1.07^5 - 1.10^5}{.07 - .10} \right] \text{x } 1.07$$

$$= \$500 \text{ x} \left[\frac{1.4026 - 1.6105}{-.03} \right] \text{x } 1.07$$

$$= \$500 \text{ x } 6.9300 \text{ x } 1.07$$

$$= \$3{,}707.55$$

If the first $500 deposit is made after one year, rather than immediately, the answer found through this formula is divided by (1 + i). In this case the future value is $3,465.000 ($3,707.55 ÷ 1.07).

If instead of using the formula you prefer a financial calculator for solving this type of problem, the HP-12C, HP-17B II, or BA-II Plus can be used. However, they can compute the solution only in the indirect manner described earlier in this chapter for calculating the future value of uneven cash flows. First compute the present compounding period.

Using the HP-12C. The HP-12C keystrokes needed to solve the present problem, based on the beginning-of-year approach, are as follows:

blue g, BEG, 500, PMT	(to enter the first deposit)
1.07, ENTER, 1.10, ÷, 1, –, 100, x, i	(to enter the adjusted discount rate)
5, n, PV	(to enter the n and produce the present value)
STO, 1, yellow f, FIN	(to preserve the present value while clearing out the financial registers)
RCL, 1, PV, 7, i, 5, n, FV	(to produce the solution)

The answer, $3,708.59, should appear on the display. Dividing the result by 1.07 produces the end-of-year solution, $3,465.97.

Using the HP-17B II. Enter the TVM menu system, clear any extraneous data, and set the machine for the beginning-of-period mode. Then press the following keys:

500, the PMT menu key	(to enter the first deposit),
1.07, ÷, 1.10, –, 1, x, 100, =, the I%YR menu key	(to enter the inflation-adjusted discount rate),
5, the N menu key, the PV menu key	(to enter the number of payments and produce the present value),
STO, 1, shift, CLEAR DATA	(to preserve the present value while clearing out the extraneous data),
RCL, 1, the PV menu key, 7, the I%YR menu key, 5, the N menu key, the FV menu key	(to produce the solution).

The answer, $3,708.59, will appear on the display. Dividing this result by 1.07 will produce the end-of-period solution, $3,465.97.

Using the BA-II Plus. On the BA-II Plus, begin by clearing the TVM registers and setting the calculator for beginning-of-period deposits or payments. Then press these keys:

500, PMT	(to enter the first deposit)
1.07, ÷, 1.10, –, 1, x, 100, =, I/Y	(to enter the adjusted discount rate)
5, N, CPT, PV	(to enter the n and produce the present value)
STO, 1, 2nd, CLR TVM	(to preserve the present value while clearing out any extraneous data)
RCL, 1, PV, 7, I/Y, 5, N, CPT, FV	(to produce the solution)

The answer, $3,708.59, should appear on the display. Dividing this result by 1.07 produces the end-of-year solution, $3,465.97.

EVALUATING AN INVESTMENT THROUGH DISCOUNTED CASH-FLOW ANALYSIS

One of the most common personal and business applications of time-value-of-money principles and techniques is the evaluation of a proposed investment. For example, assume that you are considering the purchase of a bond that involves a cash outlay now (the purchase price) and a series of cash inflows over several time periods in the future (the interest payments and the face amount). Or perhaps you are considering construction of an apartment building that involves a cash outlay now and perhaps again next year (the construction costs), after which you anticipate a series of cash inflows for a period of years (the rental payments). Or perhaps the investment under consideration is the purchase (cash outflow) of a piece of equipment that reduces expenses (cash inflow) over some future period.

In all of these situations there is a tradeoff: one or more cash outflows in return for one or more cash inflows. The questions: Are the inflows to be received worth the outflows expended—is it a good investment? By this point you surely understand that these questions cannot be adequately answered without taking into account the time value of money. Discounted cash-flow analysis assists you to evaluate an investment by making comparable the time value of the cash outflows and the time value of the cash inflows. It can be used to assist in deciding (1) whether a proposed investment project is an acceptable one and (2) how to rank several competing investment opportunities in terms of their relative acceptability.

Of course there is more to evaluating an investment than simply crunching some numbers through various time-value-of-money formulas, tables, or calculator functions. The degree of certainty in amount, timing, and duration associated with various cash outflows and inflows, as well as the tax aspects, must also be considered. Evaluation of tax elements is beyond the scope of this chapter. Risk considerations, however, are incorporated in the interest rate that is used in discounted cash-flow analysis.

As you will see, the mechanics of discounted cash-flow analysis are quite straightforward when the pattern of the cash outflows and inflows is simple. Calculations become more complex when the amounts vary from year to year, and still more complex when cash flows are positive in some years and negative in others. This chapter deals with simple discounted cash-flow analysis situations first, followed by gradually more complicated cases.

Discounted Cash-Flow Techniques Defined

There are two commonly used techniques for discounted cash-flow analysis: calculation of an investment's net present value (NPV) and its internal rate of return (IRR).

Net Present Value

The *net present value* of an investment is defined as the present value of the stream of cash inflows minus the present value of the stream of cash outflows, with both present values calculated on the basis of an appropriate rate of interest. The discount rate used might be the minimum rate of return that is acceptable to an investor in light of his or her assessment of the riskiness of the investment; the cost of capital the investor has to raise in order to make the investment; or the rate available on an alternative acceptable investment involving a similar degree of risk.

If the result of the NPV calculation is positive, that is, if the present value of the inflow stream exceeds the present value of the outflow stream, the investment is a good one. It provides a net addition to the wealth (in a time-value sense) of the investor in the amount of the positive remainder. A positive NPV means that the rate of return provided by the investment (whatever that rate is) exceeds the discount rate being used as the benchmark. If the NPV is negative, the reverse is true and the investment will result in a net reduction in the wealth (in a time-value sense). And if the NPV is zero, the investment neither adds to nor subtracts from the investor's wealth (in a time-value sense), so that it is a matter of indifference as to whether the investment should be made.

Internal Rate of Return

The *internal rate of return* on an investment is the interest rate that equates the present value of the stream of cash inflows to the present value of the stream of cash outflows. If that rate is larger than the minimum rate deemed acceptable by the investor, the investment is a good one and should be pursued. If not, it should be rejected. Criteria for determining an acceptable minimum rate of return are the same as those described in connection with the net present value technique.

Similarity of the NPV and IRR Techniques

Note that the NPV and IRR methods of evaluating an investment are very similar. In computing NPV the investor specifies the minimum acceptable interest rate and determines whether at that rate the present value of the inflows exceeds the present value of the outflows. In computing IRR the investor computes the interest rate that makes the present value of the inflows equal to the present value of the outflows; that is, the investor computes the interest rate that produces an NPV of zero.

As a general rule, when used to evaluate a particular investment the two techniques will lead the investor to the same conclusion if the same data is used. If the NPV is positive, the IRR normally is acceptable and the investment is an attractive one. Conversely, if the NPV is negative, the IRR normally is unacceptable and the investment should be rejected. When used to rank several investments as to their relative acceptability, however, there are situations in which the NPV and IRR techniques produce different results using the same data. In most cases the NPV method is more reliable for ranking several competing investment possibilities. The project with the largest NPV should be ranked first, the one with the next largest NPV should be second, and so on.

Computing Net Present Value: Simple Problems

Consider this very simple investment: You are evaluating the purchase of a piece of equipment that costs $10,000. It provides a net cash flow of $4,000 per year at the end of each of the next 4 years, after which it will have no value. Is this a worthwhile investment if your cost of capital is 10 percent per year?[5]

Depicted on a time line, the cash flows associated with this project appear as shown in the upper half of figure 6-3 on the following page. The single component of cash outflow, $10,000 occurs immediately, so its present value is $10,000. The four inflows of $4,000, totaling $16,000, constitute a 4-year annuity to be discounted at 10 percent. You have already learned how to calculate a PVA by several methods. For example, using table B.4 in appendix B you can find the 10%, 4-year PVA factor of 3.1699. Multiplying this factor by the $4,000 annuity payment produces a PVA of $12,679.60. Subtracting the present value of the outflow, $10,000, you find that the project has a positive NPV of $2,679.60. Your wealth will increase (in a time-value sense) by this amount if you invest in the project. So far, then, calculation of NPV involves nothing that you have not already learned.

If the problem is made a bit more complex by involving uneven cash flows, the calculation is still similar to the procedures explained earlier. The lower half of figure 6-3 shows a modification to the preceding case by including a pattern of increasing cash inflows totaling $16,000. The present value of the income stream, discounted at 10 percent, can be found by one of the methods described earlier. For example, using the basic formula to compute a PVSS, you can find the present value of each inflow and total them to produce the solution.

$$\text{Amount x } \frac{1}{(1 + i)^n} = \text{PVSS}$$

$$\$2{,}500 \text{ x } \frac{1}{1.10} = \$\ 2{,}272.73$$

$$\$3{,}500 \text{ x } \frac{1}{1.10^2} = 2{,}892.56$$

$$\$4{,}500 \text{ x } \frac{1}{1.10^3} = 3{,}380.92$$

$$\$5{,}500 \text{ x } \frac{1}{1.10^4} = \underline{3{,}756.57}$$

$$\text{Total} \qquad \$12{,}302.78$$

Subtracting the present value of the outflow stream, $10,000, you find that this investment has a positive net present value of $2,302.78. (It should not be surprising that the NPV with the increasing pattern of cash inflows, $2,302.78, is less than the NPV for the previous case of level cash inflows, $2,679.60, that totaled the same amount, $16,000.)

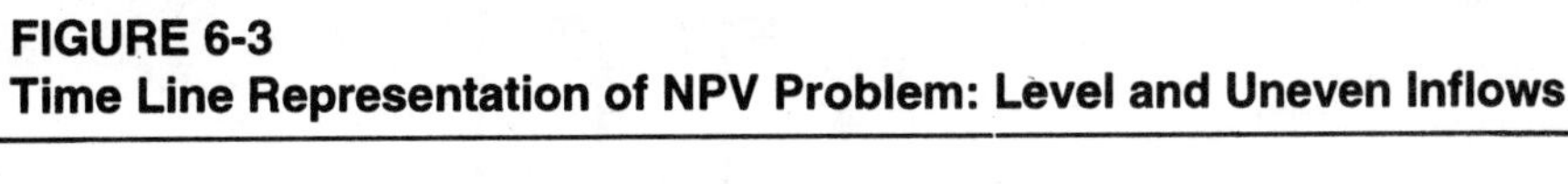

FIGURE 6-3
Time Line Representation of NPV Problem: Level and Uneven Inflows

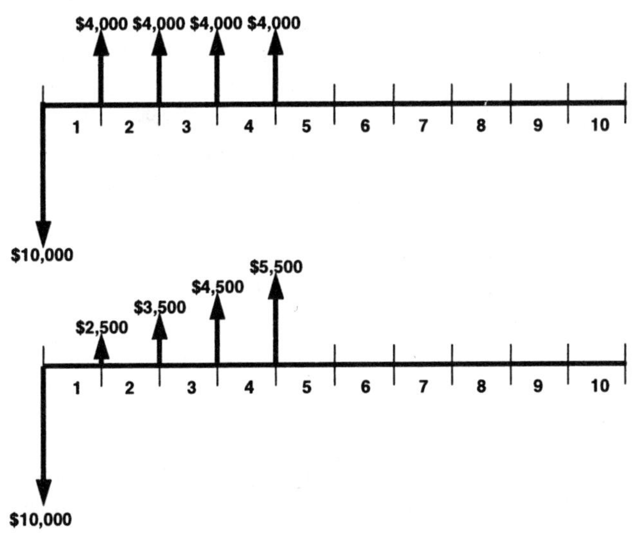

The upper time line depicts an investment that entails an initial cash outflow of $10,000 and a level stream of four $4,000 cash inflows. In the lower time line the initial cash outflow is the same but the four cash inflows follow an increasing pattern over time.

An additional level of complexity is introduced into the problem if it is assumed that a series of cash outflows is required before the series of cash inflows begins. See, for example, figure 6-4 below, in which the top time line depicts a project calling for 3 years of uneven cash outflows ($2,000, $1,000, and $500), followed by 5 years of cash inflows ($500, $1,000, $2,000, $2,000 and $3,000). Here the only new procedure is that you must subtract the present value of the series of outflows from the present value of the series of inflows. Note also from the time line when the outflows are assumed to occur (at the *beginning* of years one, 2, and 3) and when the inflows are assumed to occur (at the *end* of years 3, 4, 5, 6, and 7).

FIGURE 6-4
Time Line Representation of NPV Problem: Series of Outflows and Inflows and Years of Zero Outflows or Inflows

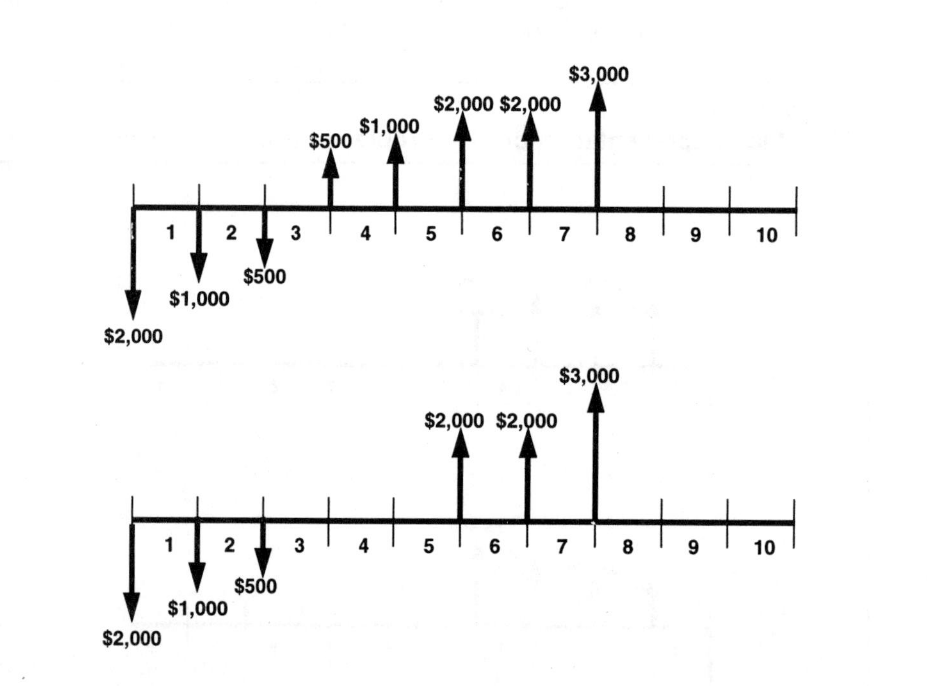

The top line depicts an investment that entails a decreasing series of cash outflows followed by an increasing series of cash inflows. The lower line depicts a similar situation except that there is a gap of 3 years between the last outflow and the first inflow.

Based on the use of table B.2 in appendix B, the procedure for finding the solution to this problem, with a discount rate of 8 percent, for example, is as follows:

1. Calculate and sum the present value, discounted at 8 percent, of each of the inflows:

\$ 500 (in 3 years)	x .7938	=	\$ 396.90
\$1,000 (in 4 years)	x .7350	=	735.00
\$2,000 (in 5 years)	x .6806	=	1,361.20
\$2,000 (in 6 years)	x .6302	=	1,260.40
\$3,000 (in 7 years)	x .5835	=	1,750.50
Total			\$5,504.00

2. Calculate and sum the present value, discounted at 8 percent, of each of the outflows.

\$2,000 (in 0 years)	x 1.0000	=	\$2,000.00
\$1,000 (in 1 year)	x .9259	=	925.90
\$ 500 (in 2 years)	x .8573	=	428.65
Total			\$3,354.55

3. Subtract the result of step two from that of step one to produce the positive NPV of \$2,149.45.

One more complicating factor may be the presence of one or more years in which there is no cash outflow or inflow. This does not change the procedure for solving the problem, but it does require a little extra care to make sure the inflows and outflows are being discounted for the correct number of years. For example, if the last illustration is changed so that there is no cash inflow at the end of years 3 and 4 (see the bottom time line in figure 6-4), the NPV, on the basis of an 8 percent discount rate, is as follows:

1. Present value of inflows

\$2,000 (in 5 years) x .6806	=	\$1,361.20
\$2,000 (in 6 years) x .6302	=	1,260.40
\$3,000 (in 7 years) x .5835	=	1,750.50
Total		\$4,372.10

2. Present value of outflows

\$2,000 (in 0 years) x 1.0000	=	\$2,000.00
\$1,000 (in 1 year) x .9259	=	925.90

$ 500 (in 2 years) x .8573	=	428.65
Total		$3,354.55

3. Net present value $1,017.55

The final bit of complexity to be introduced at this point is the presence of one or more cash outflows after the stream of cash inflows has begun. Any inflows and outflows that occur in the same year should be netted against each other. This may result in: a net cash inflow that is smaller than it otherwise would have been; a net cash inflow that is zero; or a net cash outflow. The first two results involve no new procedures in finding the NPV. The third result requires a little extra work. (As you will see later, this result may greatly complicate the task of computing an internal rate of return.)

Consider, for example, an investment that calls for the following pattern of cash flows (see figure 6-5):

Beginning of Year	Cash Flow
1	$3,000 outflow
2	$2,000 outflow
3	$ 0
4	$1,000 inflow
5	$2,000 outflow
6	$3,000 inflow
7	$3,000 inflow
8	$3,000 inflow

In this case the only new procedure for solving the problem is that you must remember to add the present value of the initial outflows in years one and 2 to the present value of the outflow that occurs at the beginning of year 5. If, for instance, a 7 percent discount rate is assumed, the present values based on table B.2 in appendix B are as shown below:

1. Present value of inflows

$1,000 (in 3 years) x .8163	=	$ 816.30
$3,000 (in 5 years) x .7130	=	2,139.00
$3,000 (in 6 years) x .6663	=	1,998.90
$3,000 (in 7 years) x .6227	=	1,868.10
Total		$6,822.30

2. Present value of outflows

$3,000 (in 0 years) x 1.0000	=	$3,000.00
$2,000 (in 1 year) x .9346	=	1,869.20

$2,000 (in 4 years) x .7629	=	1,525.80
Total		$6,395.00

3. Net present value $ 427.30

In the net present value illustrative problems up to this point, the solutions were fairly easy to find because of the short pattern of cash flows. As explained earlier, tools such as the time-value formulas or tables B.2 and B.4 in appendix B and a simple calculator suffice for computing and totaling the present values of the individual cash flows or, in the case of a series of level cash flows, the annuity.

As net present value problems start to become more involved, however, the use of formulas or tables starts to be cumbersome. At that point a calculator like the HP-12C, the HP-17B II, or the BA-II Plus, or perhaps even a computer, becomes necessary.

FIGURE 6-5
Time Line Representation of NPV Problem: Series of Outflows followed by Year of Zero Flow followed by Series of Inflows Interrupted by Outflow

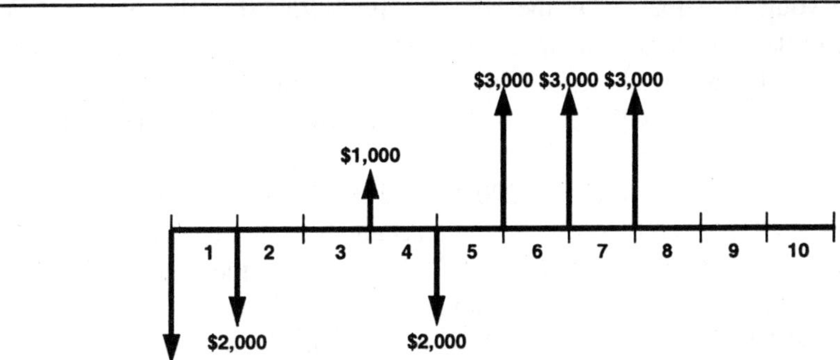

This line shows a series of decreasing cash outflows followed by one year in which there is no net inflow or outflow. Thereafter comes one year of a net cash inflow and one of a net cash outflow. Finally, 3 years of level net cash inflows occur.

Computing Net Present Value: Complex Problems

Ungrouped Cash Flows

Now we will take up somewhat more complicated problems. First explained is the use of calculators to solve NPV problems in which there are no consecutive cash flows of the same amount and sign. To solve an NPV problem on the HP-12C where the cash flows are ungrouped, the procedure is the same as that explained earlier in this chapter. You use the blue CFo and CFj keys in the top row of the keyboard. In addition, you need to use the CHS key to enter outflows as negative numbers. You enter the discount rate using the i key as usual. Finally, you use the yellow f key and the NPV function to produce the solution. To solve the same type of problem on the HP-17B II or the BA-II Plus, you use the cash flow prompted work sheet explained earlier in this chapter. In addition, however, you use the +/– key to enter outflows as negative numbers. You enter the discount rate into the work sheet just as before and use the CPT and NPV keys to produce the answer.

To illustrate the process, assume you have been asked to make a $75,000 loan. The borrower agrees to the following repayment schedule:

End of year 1	$ 0
End of year 2	$15,000
End of year 3	$20,000
End of year 4	$25,000
End of year 5	$30,000

Should you enter into this loan if you insist on a rate of return of at least 11 percent on your investment? On the HP-12C, press 75000, CHS, blue g, CFo. The initial outlay (at the beginning of the first year) has now been entered as a negative amount. Press 0, blue g, CFj to reflect the fact that in the first year following the initial outlay there is no net cash inflow or outflow. Press 15000, blue g, and CFj to enter the positive cash inflow at the end of year 2. Enter the remaining three inflows by pressing 20000, blue g, CFj; 25000, blue g, CFj; and 30000, blue g, CFj. Now enter the minimum acceptable rate of return by pressing 11 and the i key. Finally, compute the NPV by pressing the yellow f key and NPV. The answer, –$13,930.02, should appear on the display.

On the HP-17B II, enter the CFLO menu system and turn off the #T? function. Then press 75000, +/–, and INPUT. The initial outlay (at the beginning of the first year) has now been entered as a negative amount. Press 0 and INPUT to reflect the fact that in the first year following the initial outlay, there is no net cash inflow or outflow. Press 15000, and INPUT to enter the positive cash inflow at the end of year two. Enter the remaining three inflows by pressing 20000, INPUT, 25000, INPUT, 30000, and INPUT. Now press EXIT and the CALC menu key. Enter the minimum acceptable rate of return by pressing 11 and the I% menu key. Finally, press the NPV menu key to produce the answer, –$13,930.02.

If you use the BA-II Plus, press CF, 2nd, CLR Work. Then press 75000, +/–, ENTER,↓. The initial outlay (at the start of the first year) has now been entered as a negative amount. Press 0, ENTER, ↓, ↓ to reflect the fact that at the end of the first year there is no net cash inflow or outflow. Then enter each of the remaining cash inflows by pressing 15000, ENTER, ↓, ↓, 20000, ENTER, ↓, ↓,

25000, ENTER, ↓, ↓, and 30000, ENTER, ↓,↓. Now press NPV, 11, ENTER, ↓, CPT. The answer, –$13,930.02, should appear on the display.

Obviously this project should be rejected since, in light of the time value of money, it would cost you almost $14,000. This project would be unacceptable even if you were willing to settle for as little as a 5 percent rate of return. On the HP-12C press 5, i, yellow f, NPV; on the HP-17B II, press 5, the I% menu key, and the NPV menu key; or on the BA-II Plus press NPV, 5, ENTER, ↓, CPT. Note that the net present value even at this rate is negative $44.46.

Grouped Cash Flows

These financial calculators can solve NPV problems involving more cash flows if there is grouped data. As explained earlier in this chapter, for such problems you should enter, along with the amount of each cash flow, the total number of times it occurs in succession, including the first time.

To illustrate the process, assume that you are considering investing in an oil exploration limited partnership that you believe will entail the following cash flows:

Initial outlay	$50,000
Inflows at end of years 1–5	0
Inflows at end of years 6–9	$ 6,000
Inflow at end of year 10	$60,000

Is this investment acceptable if you insist on a rate of return of at least 12 percent per year?

After clearing the HP-12C, begin by entering the amount of the initial outflow: 50000, CHS, blue g, CFo. Now enter the first group of inflows by pressing 0, blue g, CFj. Since this amount will occur a total of five times (including the first), press 5, blue g, Nj. Now enter the next group of inflows: 6000, blue g, CFj, and the number of times it occurs: 4, blue g, Nj. Then enter the last inflow, 60000, blue g, CFj. Finally, enter the required interest rate by pressing 12 and i. Compute the answer by pressing yellow f and NPV and the answer, –$20,340.76, should appear on the screen. Another investment to be avoided!

If you are using the HP-17B II, enter the CFLO menu system and turn on the #T? function. Now enter the initial outflow by pressing 50000, +/–, and INPUT. Then enter the first group of inflows by pressing 0 and INPUT. Since this will occur a total of five times (including the first), press 5 and INPUT. Now enter the next group of inflows: 6000, INPUT, 4, and INPUT. Then enter the last inflow: 60000, INPUT, 1, and INPUT. Then press EXIT, the CALC menu key, 12, and the I% menu key. Press the NPV menu key to produce the answer, –$20,340.76. This is a "great" investment that you definitely don't need!

Or if you are using the BA-II Plus, enter the cash flow prompted work sheet and clear it of extraneous data. (You didn't have to be reminded, did you?) Then press the following keys:

50000, +/–, ENTER, ↓, 0, ENTER, ↓, 5, ENTER, ↓, 6000, ENTER, ↓, 4, ENTER, ↓, 60000, ENTER, ↓, 1, ENTER, ↓, NPV, 12, ENTER, ↓, CPT

The answer, –$20,340.76, should appear on the screen. An investment you can get along without!

Computing Internal Rate of Return

Recall the definition of the second technique for discounted cash-flow analysis. The internal rate of return generated by an investment is the interest rate that equates the present value of the cash inflows and outflows, producing a net present value of zero. If the IRR exceeds the investor's minimum desired rate of return, the investment is an attractive one. If it equals the minimum desired rate, the investor should be neutral toward the project. If the IRR is below the minimum desired rate, the investment is unattractive.

The mathematics of computing the IRR of an investment are extremely complex. The process is essentially one of trial and error. To solve the problem manually, you must begin with an estimate of what the IRR might be.[6] (Some authors suggest that a 10 or 15 percent rate is usually a reasonable starting point.) Discount the cash inflows and outflows to their present values using that rate and compare. If the present value of the inflows exceeds the present value of the outflows (that is, if there is a positive NPV at that rate), the rate being used is below the actual IRR, so you must select a higher rate and repeat the calculations. (Remember the present values move in a direction opposite than that of interest rates. Here you are looking for a smaller net present value, namely, zero, so you must increase the interest rate being used.) On the other hand, if with a given interest rate the discounted cash outflows exceed the discounted cash inflows (that is, if there is a negative NPV), you must select a lower interest rate and repeat the calculations. Continue this trial and error process, using higher and lower interest rates to discount the cash flows, until the resulting NPV is equal to or very close to zero. The rate producing this result is the IRR, which is an average rate of return over the period under consideration, weighted to reflect the amount and timing of the various cash flows.

Using a Time-Value Table

Time-value tables can be used to solve only very simple IRR problems. To illustrate, assume that an investment today of $10,000 will produce cash inflows of $2,739.80 at the end of each of the next 5 years. What is the internal rate of return on this investment?

Begin with a guess that it is 10 percent. At that rate, using table B.4 in appendix B you can find that the present value of the annuity in this problem is \$10,386.03 (\$2,739.80 x 3.7908). The net present value is positive (namely, \$386.03), so you need to raise the discount rate and redo the calculation. At a rate of 12.5 percent the PVA is \$9,755.33 (\$2,739.80 x 3.5606), so the NPV is now negative. Try 11 percent, and you find that the NPV is \$126.03 (\$2,739.80 x 3.6959 – \$10,000). You are getting closer, so try a rate of 11.5 percent. Here the present value of the inflows is \$10,000.00 (\$2,739.80 x 3.6499). Bingo! The internal rate of return is 11.5 percent.

Obviously the process of computing the internal rate of return is extremely tedious if done in this manner. Imagine, for example, if the project involves a series of uneven cash outflows, a lengthy series of uneven cash inflows, and an occasional year of zero inflows or outflows. By the time you finish doing and redoing all the computations, the investment opportunity will have passed you by.

Also, of course, it is impossible to calculate very precise IRR answers using tables B.2 and B.4. They show an array of interest rates only in intervals of half percentage points. A process of interpolation is necessary to come closer to the precise IRR if an interest rate doesn't happen to fall neatly on one of the tabular rates.

Using Financial Calculators to Solve IRR Problems

The procedure for solving IRR problems with financial calculators is very similar to that for NPV problems. The only differences in the procedure are as follows:

1. When solving for IRR you do not need to enter a discount rate, since this is what you are trying to find. Therefore skip the next-to-last portion of the NPV sequence.
2. On the HP-12C, instead of pressing yellow f and the NPV function after all the data have been entered, press yellow f and the IRR function, which is located on the FV key.
3. On the HP-17B II, instead of pressing the NPV menu key after all the data have been entered, press the IRR% menu key, which is immediately to the left of the I% menu key.
4. On the BA-II Plus, instead of pressing NPV, the discount rate, ENTER, ↓, CPT after all the cash flows have been entered, simply press IRR in the second row of the keyboard and CPT.

For example, to solve an earlier illustrative problem (a single outflow of \$10,000 followed by five inflows of \$2,739.80 each), set the calculator to display four decimal places. Then on the HP-12C press the following keys: 10000, CHS, blue g, CFo, 2739.80, blue g, CFj, 5, blue g, Nj, yellow f, IRR. Or on the

HP-17B II, turn the #T? function on and press 10000, +/–, INPUT, 2739.80, INPUT, 5, INPUT, EXIT, the CALC menu key, and the IRR% menu key. On the BA-II Plus press 10000, +/–, ENTER, ↓, 2739.80, ENTER, ↓, 5, ENTER, ↓, IRR, CPT. (Normally it is necessary for you to wait for several seconds for the answer to appear because the complex mathematical characteristics of the IRR calculation.) Eventually the answer, 11.4997 percent, should be displayed on the screen. (Note the added precision of the financial calculators versus table B.4. In fact, if you set any of the calculators to display eight decimal places, the maximum capacity in this case, you will see that the IRR is 11.49974092 percent.)

To take a more involved example, assume that an investment you are considering involves a $60,000 initial outlay and the following series of cash flows:

End of Year	Cash Flow	End of Year	Cash Flow
1	$2,000 inflow	6	$10,000 outflow
2	$9,000 inflow	7	$11,000 inflow
3	$9,000 inflow	8	$ 0
4	$9,000 inflow	9	$12,000 inflow
5	$9,000 inflow	10	$30,000 inflow

The keystrokes on the HP-12C are as follows:

Initial outlay	60000, CHS, blue g, CFo,
year 1	2000, blue g, CFj,
years 2–5	9000, blue g, CFj, 4, blue g, Nj,
year 6	10000, CHS, blue g, CFj,
year 7	11000, blue g, CFj,
year 8	0, blue g, CFj,
year 9	12000, blue g, CFj,
year 10	30000, blue g, CFj

Then press the yellow f key and IRR. After the machine runs for several seconds, the answer, 4.6664 percent, should be displayed.

The keystrokes on the HP-17B II, with the #T? function turned on, would be as follows:

initial outlay	60000, +/–, INPUT,
year 1	2000, INPUT, 1, INPUT,
years 2–5	9000, INPUT, 4, INPUT,
year 6	10000, +/–, INPUT, 1, INPUT,
year 7	11000, INPUT, 1, INPUT,
year 8	0, INPUT, 1, INPUT,
year 9	12000, INPUT, 1, INPUT,
year 10	30000, INPUT, 1, INPUT

Then press EXIT, the CALC menu key, and the IRR% menu key. The answer will be displayed very quickly as 4.6664%.

The keystrokes on the BA-II Plus, after entering CF, 2nd, and CLR Work, are as follows:

Initial outlay	60000, +/–, ENTER, ↓,
year 1	2000, ENTER, ↓, ↓,
years 2–5	9000, ENTER, ↓, 4, ENTER, ↓,
year 6	10000, +/–, ENTER, ↓, ↓,
year 7	11000, ENTER, ↓, ↓,
year 8	0, ENTER, ↓, ↓,
year 9	12000, ENTER, ↓, ↓,
year 10	30000, ENTER,↓

Then press IRR and CPT. After a few seconds the answer, 4.6664 percent, should be displayed.

Problems in Decision Making Based on IRR

The internal rate of return provided by potential investments must be used with caution as a basis for decision making. This is especially true when the IRR is used as a means of ranking competing investment opportunities.

One situation in which an evaluation based solely on comparative IRRs may lead to an incorrect decision is the case of mutually exclusive investment projects that are of substantially different magnitudes. Assume, for example, that you can invest in either of two pieces of equipment for your business, but the investment in one eliminates the possibility of investing in the other for some technical reason. Assume also that you have or can borrow enough money so that you are free to invest in either piece of equipment. The total cash flows from the two projects, A and B, are shown below. Neither piece of equipment has any salvage value.

Beginning of Year	Cash Flow (A)	Cash Flow (B)
1	$5,000 outflow	$50,000 outflow
2	$3,000 inflow	$25,000 inflow
3	$4,000 inflow	$35,000 inflow
4	$5,000 inflow	$45,000 inflow

The IRR from project A is 54.0603 percent, while that from project B is only 42.9811 percent. Does this mean that project A is preferable? Not necessarily. For example, if the money to meet the initial outflow is borrowed at a 10 percent rate of interest, it may be preferable to invest in project B. On the basis of a 10 percent discount rate, the NPV of project B is $35,462.06, whereas that of project A is only $4,789.63. In other words, project B increases your wealth (in a time-value sense) by more than seven times the amount project A provides. A more modest rate of return on a large project may be preferable to a higher rate of return on a small project. (Note, however, that this illustration deals with *mutually exclusive* projects. In other cases, the wise decision might be to invest in both projects.)

A second situation in which a decision based solely on IRR may be incorrect is when mutually exclusive potential investment projects entail substantially different cash-flow patterns. Assume that two competing investment opportunities, C and D, are expected to produce the total cash flows shown below. Assume also that the two projects are mutually exclusive because you are able to borrow only $30,000, the amount of the initial cash outlay for each. The interest rate the lender charges and therefore the discount rate you decide to use in evaluating the two projects is 12 percent per year.

Beginning of Year	Cash Flow (C)	Cash Flow (D)
1	$30,000 outflow	$30,000 outflow
2–5	$11,000 inflow	$ 5,000 inflow
6–20	$ 0	$ 5,000 inflow

The IRR from project C is 17.2968 percent, while that from project D is only 15.6071 percent. The NPV of project D, however, is $6,828.88 at a discount rate of 12 percent, whereas it is only $3,410.84 for project C. Once again, the project with the lower IRR provides a greater addition to your wealth (in a time-value sense).

If all of this isn't sufficiently confusing, assume a different discount rate, such as 19 percent, for the calculation of the NPV of the two projects. Under that assumption, project C has both the better IRR and the better (actually, the less bad) NPV.[7]

There is also a difficulty in relying solely on IRRs when deciding between investment opportunities that have substantially different durations. The IRR method includes no explicit assumption about how the rate of return funds released from a short duration project can be reinvested. In the preceding example, project D generates an annual IRR of over 15 percent for 19 years. Project C provides an annual IRR of a bit over 17 percent, but for only 4 years. Assume that the rates of return available on investments of comparable risk fall substantially during the next few years. This means that the heavy early cash inflows from project C have to be reinvested at rates so unattractive that the combined IRR from project C and its successor(s) over the full 19 years will be less than its 4-year IRR, and perhaps even less than the 19-year IRR of project D.

Another limitation of the IRR method for comparing investment projects involves the question of financing costs of cash outflows that may be associated with one or both of the projects. Consider the following set of cash flows from investment projects E and F.

Beginning of Year	Cash Flow (E)	Cash Flow (F)
1	$10,000 outflow	$10,000 outflow
2	$ 1,000 inflow	$ 0
3	$ 5,000 outflow	$ 0
4	$ 5,000 inflow	$ 0
5	$ 5,000 inflow	$ 0
6	$ 5,000 inflow	$ 3,000 inflow
7	$ 5,000 inflow	$13,000 inflow

On the surface, project E appears to be clearly preferable. Its IRR is 9.7283 percent versus 8.4315 percent for project F. And if a reasonable discount rate is used, such as 8 percent, for calculating NPV, project E wins again, $837.31 versus $233.95.

But notice that project E requires a $5,000 cash outflow at the beginning of year 3. Presumably that amount will have to be borrowed at some rate of interest or taken out of another investment where it is earning a rate of return. In either case there is a cost to the investor, either a direct cost or an opportunity cost, arising from the need to cover the cash outflow. If interest rates should rise substantially during the first 2 years of the project, that cost alone might be sufficient to drive the actual IRR of project E below that of project F.

A final problem to be discussed here concerning the IRR method is that it is possible for a project to have more than one IRR, each of which is mathematically correct. It is also possible that an investment may have no IRR within the realm of real numbers. A mathematical explanation of how these results can be produced is beyond the scope of this book. They can arise, however, whenever the stream of outflows and inflows involves more than one change of sign between negative and positive (for example, one or more outflows followed by one or more inflows followed by one or more outflows, as is the case in connection with project E).

How can you tell whether an investment may have more than one internal rate of return? Look over the pattern of net cash outflows and inflows. Often there is only one change of sign in these net flows over the lifetime of the investment. The sequence might begin with one or a few periods of net cash outflows (minus signs) that are followed by a series of net cash inflows (plus signs), perhaps with an occasional net inflow of zero (still a plus sign), until the project is concluded. Where there is only one sign change, there is only one internal rate of return. If there is more than one sign change, however, there *may* be more than one IRR, or there may be no IRR at all. A number of answers may be mathematically correct—but none of them will be of much help as a basis of making an intelligent decision.[8]

If you are using the HP-12C, HP-17B II, or BA-II Plus to compute the IRR of an investment, the calculator will usually let you know if it is having trouble computing the one-and-only correct internal rate of return and will display an error message.

What should you do about these problems of using IRR as a basis for deciding about an investment? One simple solution is to punt. Perhaps you should forget about trying to use IRR as a method of evaluating the particular investment. Rather, use the NPV method. Another approach is to use one of several *modified* IRR methods. Many textbooks on investments and managerial finance contain explanations of these modified IRR methods.

Modified Internal Rate of Return (MIRR)

A modified internal rate of return calculation entails (a) reducing a series of cash flows having multiple sign changes to one that has only one sign change; and (b) specifying the reinvestment rate that will apply, rather than assuming that the project's IRR will be the applicable reinvestment rate. In these ways, MIRR may be superior to IRR, while still expressing the solution as the familiar yield or rate of return that decision makers sometimes prefer to the fuzzy notion of NPV.

The first step in computing a project's MIRR is to select a rate, usually a conservative (low) one, at which it is safe to assume that the project's cash inflows can be reinvested until the end of the project. The second step is to compute the future value (sometimes called the *terminal value*) of all those inflows as of the end of the project's life. The third step is to discount (find the present value of) all the project's outflows back to the origination point of the project. The final step is to compute the annual rate of return represented by the difference between the present value of the outflows and the future or terminal value of the inflows over the life of the project.

To illustrate, assume that a proposed investment is likely to entail the following series of cash flows:

Initial outlay	$1,500,000
Inflow at end of year 1	125,000
Outflow at end of year 2	150,000
Inflow at end of year 3	0
Inflow at end of year 4	200,000
Inflow at end of year 5	1,900,000

If a safe reinvestment rate of 5 percent is assumed, what is this investment's MIRR?

(a) The future or terminal value of the inflows at 5 percent is $125,000 for four years plus $200,000 for one year plus $1,900,000, or a total of $2,261,938.28.

(b) The present value of the outflows at 5 percent is $1,500,000 plus $150,000 for two years, or a total of $1,636,054.42.

(c) The life of the project is five years.

(d) In the calculator, insert $2,261,938.28 as the FV, $1,636,054.42 as the negative PV, and 5 as the n. Solve for i, which is 6.6932%. This is the modified IRR based on an assumed 5 percent reinvestment rate.

The use of MIRR doesn't solve all the problems that arise when comparing mutually exclusive projects. For example, an investment with a high MIRR and a low NPV might be less desirable than one with a lower MIRR and a higher NPV. Therefore, NPV is still the most reliable tool for ranking competing investments. MIRR is often, however, an improvement over IRR in such circumstances.

INCREASING THE COMPOUNDING, DISCOUNTING, OR PAYMENT FREQUENCY

All the explanations and illustrations so far in this and the preceding chapter are based on the assumption that compounding and discounting occur once per year. In reality, however, compounding and discounting often occur more frequently than annually. For example, a certificate of deposit may be credited with compound interest on a monthly basis. A NOW (negotiable order of withdrawal) account may earn daily compound interest. The present value of the income from a corporate bond typically is computed on a semiannual discounting basis.

In addition, all of the explanations of problems involving periodic payments thus far have been based on the assumption that payments are made annually. Often, however, such payments occur more than once per year. Installment loan payments, for example, are frequently made monthly. Bond interest payments are usually made every 6 months. Deposits into the savings accounts of many people are made weekly.

The remainder of this chapter examines the effect on the interest rate and therefore on the time value of money resulting from compounding or discounting more often than annually. It also contains an explanation of how to solve problems involving a series of level payments that occur more often than once per year, regardless of how often compounding or discounting takes place.

Nominal versus Effective Interest Rates

As you know, compounding results in the conversion of interest earnings into principal. For example, if $100 is deposited today and subsequently credited with $7.00 of compound interest, the principal on which future interest is credited rises to $107. The $7.00 of interest converts into principal.

If compounding occurs annually, when does interest convert into principal and begin to earn interest on itself? Obviously the conversion and thus the capacity for increased interest earnings occur after one year, again after 2 years, and so on. If, on the other hand, compounding occurs on a monthly basis, when does interest convert to principal and thus begin to earn interest on itself? The conversions occur after one month has elapsed, again after 2 months, 3 months, and so on.

Of course the greater the frequency in which compounding occurs, the smaller the dollar amount of interest earned and converted into principal on the occasion of each compounding. Naturally the amount of interest a given amount of principal can earn in a week is less than it can earn in a month at any given stated or nominal annual interest rate. Nevertheless, all other things being equal, the more frequently compounding occurs per year, the greater the *total* amount of interest credited to an account during the year. To illustrate, table 6-2 shows the amount of interest credited during one year to a $5,000 deposit with a stated or nominal 9 percent annual interest rate applied with various frequencies during the year.

TABLE 6-2
Total Interest Credited to a $5,000 Deposit during One Year at 9% Stated Annual Interest Rate and Various Compounding Frequencies

Compounding Frequency	Interest Earnings
Annually	$450.00
Semiannually	460.13
Quarterly	465.42
Monthly	469.03
Weekly	470.45
Daily*	470.81

*Based on 360 days per year[9]

Technically, of course, compounding can occur even more frequently than daily—every hour, every minute, every second, or even more frequently than that. And as the frequency continues to increase, so does the total interest credited. The upper limit of the total interest credited to a sum of money for a particular stated or nominal annual interest rate occurs in the case of continuous compounding, wherein interest is compounded an infinite number of times per year, rather than at discrete time intervals. Continuous compounding is a theoretical concept useful principally in the study of advanced financial topics, but it also has some practical applications since financial institutions occasionally credit interest to customer accounts on a continuous basis.

From the figures in table 6-2 it should be obvious that a stated or nominal annual interest rate does not necessarily reflect the true or effective interest rate. You have seen that a 9 percent nominal annual rate produces any of six separate interest earnings in a year, depending on the frequency in which compounding occurs. Hence it is important to distinguish between the nominal or stated annual rate (9 percent in this illustration) and the true or effective annual rate (also known in some instances as the yield, or the annual percentage rate or APR).

When compounding occurs once per year, the nominal and effective annual rates are identical. In table 6-2, when annual compounding is applied, the $5,000 deposit earns $450, exactly 9 percent. In all other cases it earns more than $450 (more than 9 percent) because compounding occurs more than once per year.

The *effective annual interest rate* is defined as the annual rate that produces in one compounding the same amount of interest as does the nominal annual rate with its compounding frequency. For instance, the 9 percent nominal annual rate in table 6-2 when compounded quarterly produces $465.42 of interest. Thus the effective annual interest rate is 9.3084 percent ($465.42 ÷ $5,000). Similarly, the 9 percent nominal annual rate compounded daily generates $470.81 of interest. Thus the effective annual rate is 9.4162 percent ($470.81 ÷ $5,000).

Calculating the Effective Annual Rate

The effective annual interest rate can be computed for any nominal rate and compounding frequency by the following formula:[10]

$$i_{eff} = \left[1 + \frac{i_{nom}}{f}\right]^{f} - 1$$

where i_{eff} is the effective annual rate,
i_{nom} is the nominal annual rate, and
f is the compounding frequency per year

Thus, for example, a 9 percent nominal annual rate compounded monthly represents an effective annual rate of

$$i_{eff} = \left[1 + \frac{.09}{12}\right]^{12} - 1$$
$$= 9.3807\%$$

As an alternative to using this formula, you can calculate the effective interest rate for any nominal annual rate and compounding frequency by using the HP-12C, HP-17B II, or BA-II Plus calculators. To illustrate, assume that a 7 percent nominal rate is to be compounded weekly. Set the HP-12C calculator to display four decimal places. Then press the following keys:

blue g, END, 7, ENTER	(to enter the nominal rate)
52, n, ÷, i	(to enter the weekly frequency of compounding)
100, CHS, ENTER, PV, FV, +	(to produce the effective rate)

The answer, 7.2458 percent, should appear on the display.

If you are using the HP-17B II, set it to display four decimal places. Then enter the interest rate conversion menu system by pressing the ICNV menu key, which is next to the TVM menu key. Then press the PER menu key, since in this, and almost all problems, compounding is periodic, rather than continuous. Then press 7 and the NOM% menu key to enter the nominal rate; 52 and the P menu key to enter the weekly frequency of compounding; and the EFF% menu key to produce the effective annual rate, 7.2458 percent.

If you use the BA-II Plus, set the calculator to display four decimal places. Then press 2nd and I Conv, which is located on the number 2 key. Press 2nd, CLR Work to remove any extraneous data. Then press 7, ENTER, ↓, ↓ (to put the nominal rate into the machine), 52, ↑ (to put the number of compounding periods per year into the machine) and CPT. The answer, 7.2458 percent, should appear on the display.

For those who do not wish to use either a formula or a financial calculator to determine the effective interest rate, appendix F will be of some help. It contains a table showing the effective annual interest rates that correspond to a number of nominal annual rates and commonly used compounding frequencies. The table also includes the effective rate for the unusual case of continuous compounding.

To illustrate further the difference between the nominal and effective annual rates of interest, the following list shows the effective rate for a nominal rate of 7 percent with various compounding frequencies:

7% annually	=	7.0000% effective rate
7% semiannually	=	7.1225% effective rate
7% quarterly	=	7.1859% effective rate
7% monthly	=	7.2290% effective rate
7% weekly	=	7.2458% effective rate
7% daily (360)	=	7.2501% effective rate

Again it is clear that, for a particular nominal annual interest rate, the true or effective rate rises as the frequency of compounding per year increases. Note, however, that the increase in the effective rate becomes smaller and smaller with each increase in compounding frequency. In the above list, for example, the change from annual to semiannual compounding increased the effective rate by .1225 percentage points (7.1225–7.0000). The change from semiannual to quarterly compounding changed the effective rate by only .0634 percentage points (7.1859–7.1225); and the change from quarterly to monthly compounding increased it by only .0432 percentage points (7.2290–7.1859).

Another point worth noting concerning nominal versus effective annual interest rates is that sometimes a low nominal rate with a high compounding frequency produces a higher effective rate than a high nominal rate with a low compounding frequency. For example, assume that you plan to deposit $10,000 in an interest-bearing account for one year. Bank A pays interest of 8 percent compounded semiannually. Bank B pays 7.9 percent compounded daily (360 days per year). Where should you put your money? If you use the formula described earlier or a financial calculator, you will find that the effective rate in Bank A is 8.1600 percent. Bank B, on the other hand, pays an effective rate of 8.2195 percent. That is an extra $5.95 credited to your $10,000 deposit if you go to Bank B.

Impact of Compounding Frequency on Future Values

Because the effective interest rate rises as the frequency of compounding increases, so does the future value of a single sum. The same is true of other future values described in this and the previous chapter. For example, the future value of an annual annuity or of a series of annual uneven cash flows rises as compounding frequency increases. Conversely in sinking fund problems the size of the annual payment needed to reach a targeted future amount diminishes as the frequency of compounding and the effective interest rate increase. Finally, the number of years or annual payments needed to reach a particular future value decreases as the frequency of compounding and the effective interest rate increase.

Impact of Discounting Frequency on Present Values

You probably have already guessed that increasing the frequency of discounting has the opposite effect on present values than increasing the frequency of compounding has on future values. This again follows from the preceding discussion of nominal versus effective interest rates.

To illustrate, calculate the present value of $100 due in one year at 7 percent. Discounted annually, you know that the effective rate is 7 percent. The present value of $100 for one year at 7 percent is $93.46. Discounted quarterly, however, the effective rate is 7.1859 percent. The present value of $100 for one year at 7.1859 percent is $93.30. And discounted monthly the effective rate is 7.2290 percent, which produces a present value of $93.26. Generalizing from these results, then, you can conclude that, all other things being equal, an increase in the frequency of discounting increases the effective interest rate and, therefore, reduces the present value of a single sum. The same is true of the present value of an annual annuity or of a series of annual uneven cash flows. Conversely, in debt services problems, an increase in the frequency of charging interest per year, all other things being equal, increases the amount of the loan payments per year. Finally, the number of years it takes to pay off a loan or to liquidate a principal sum increases as the frequency of charging or crediting interest per year increases, all other things being equal.

Calculating Future and Present Values

When you encounter a time-value-of-money problem in which the interest rate is compounded or discounted more than once per year, there are two basic ways of solving it: (1) use the effective rate or (2) adjust the nominal rate and number of periods.

Using the Effective Rate

The first basic approach is to solve the problem by computing the effective interest rate as explained earlier. Then use the effective rate in the same way you have learned to use the nominal annual interest rate throughout this and the preceding chapter.

To illustrate, \$500 will grow to what amount in 3 years at 6 percent interest compounded quarterly? The effective rate is 6.13636 percent. Therefore you can use this rate in place of 6 percent in the FVSS formula:

$$\begin{aligned} \text{FVSS} &= \$500 \times 1.0613636^3 \\ &= \$500 \times 1.19562 \\ &= \$597.81 \end{aligned}$$

Or what is the present value of a 5-year annuity of \$2,000 if it is discounted at 8 percent weekly? The effective rate is 8.32205 percent. Therefore you can use this rate in place of 8 percent in the PVA formula:

$$\begin{aligned} \text{PVA} &= \$2{,}000 \times \frac{1 - \dfrac{1}{1.0832205^5}}{.0832205} \\ &= \$2{,}000 \times \frac{1 - \dfrac{1}{1.49137}}{.0832205} \\ &= \$2{,}000 \times \frac{1 - .67053}{.0832205} \\ &= \$2{,}000 \times 3.9590 \\ &= \$7{,}918 \end{aligned}$$

Instead of using a formula, you can solve these problems by means of your financial calculator. Again, however, first calculate the effective rate. Then follow the normal series of keystrokes for the particular type of problem inserting the effective rate, rather than the nominal rate, as the interest rate.

Using a present-value or future-value table usually is infeasible if you follow this first method. Most tables, including those in appendix B of this book, fail to provide the needed factors for the fine gradations of effective interest rates. For example, there is no set of FVSS factors in table B.1 for an interest rate of 6.13636 percent. Similarly, there is no set of PVA factors in table B.4 for an interest rate of 8.32205 percent.

Adjusting the Nominal Rate and Number of Periods

The second basic way of solving these kinds of problems involves using the nominal annual rate, rather than the effective rate. In this case, two adjustments must be made. First, the problem's nominal annual interest rate must be *divided* by the number of compounding or discounting periods per year. This reflects the fact that only a fraction of the annual rate will be applied each time compounding or discounting occurs during the year. Second, the number of years in the problem must be *multiplied* by the number of compounding or discounting periods per year. This reflects the total number of times that compounding or discounting of the fractional annual rate occurs. Note, then, that if this approach is used, the number that is divided into i and the number that is multiplied by n are always the same (four for quarterly compounding or discounting, 12 for monthly, 360 for daily, etc.).

To illustrate this approach of solving time-value problems, compute the FVSS of \$100 at 8 percent compounded quarterly for 20 years. Instead of the usual formula

$$\text{FVSS} = \$100 \times 1.08^{20} = \$466.10$$

the formula is

$$\text{FVSS} = \$100 \times 1.02^{80} = \$487.54$$

That is, the 8 percent annual rate is divided by 4 and the 20-year period is multiplied by 4.

If you wish to calculate by means of the formula the present value of \$3,000 due 6 years hence with a discount rate of 12 percent applied monthly, the usual formula

$$\text{PVSS} = \$3{,}000 \times \left[\frac{1}{1.12^6}\right] = \$1{,}519.89$$

is replaced by

$$\text{PVSS} = \$3{,}000 \times \left[\frac{1}{1.01^{72}}\right] = \$1{,}465.49$$

The 12 percent annual rate is divided by 12 and the 6-year period is multiplied by 12.

If you prefer to use tables rather than formulas to calculate present and future values, the same two adjustments must be made. For example, if the nominal annual interest rate in a problem is 6 percent compounded quarterly for one year, use the tabular factor not for 6 percent and one period but for 1.5 percent (6% ÷ 4) and four periods (1 x 4). Or if a problem involves a nominal rate of 9 percent discounted semiannually for 8 years, use the tabular factor not for 9 percent and 8 periods but for 4.5 percent (9% ÷ 2) and 16 periods (8 x 2).

One difficulty you may encounter in attempting to use tables in this way is that the adjusted nominal rate may not be listed. For example, an 11 percent rate that is compounded monthly would require a set of factors for an adjusted nominal rate of 9.1667 percent. A 12 percent nominal rate that is compounded weekly would require a set of factors for an adjusted nominal rate of .2308 percent. There is no easy way to overcome this difficulty.

A second difficulty you may encounter in using the tables is that when n is multiplied by the number of compounding or discounting periods in a year, the resulting number of periods may be greater than those shown in the table. For example, assume you wish to calculate the future value of $2,000 at the end of 5 years at 18 percent interest compounded monthly. The factor needed from table B.1 is for 1.5 percent (18% ÷ 12) and 60 periods (5 x 12). The table, however, shows factors for only 50 periods. This difficulty is overcome simply by multiplying factors for any 2 years in the 1.5 percent column in which the combined number of periods equals the desired number of periods. For example, multiply the factor for 50 years by that for 10 years to produce a 60-year FVSS factor at 1.5 percent of 2.4431 (2.1052 x 1.1605). This, multiplied by $2,000, produces the FVSS, $4,886.17. The same technique may be used in conjunction with table B.2 to compute the factor for any number of periods needed to solve a PVSS problem. *It cannot be used in this way, however, to solve annuity problems through tables B.3 or B.4.*

Assume that instead of formulas or tables you wish to use a financial calculator. The only new procedure when using financial calculators for problems involving compounding more often than annually is to make the two adjustments referred to above: (1) divide the nominal annual i by the compounding frequency and (2) multiply the number of years by the compounding frequency. These adjustments may be made mentally before data is entered or they may be made on the calculator itself as part of the data entry process. The latter approach is illustrated here because the numbers are a bit too complex to compute mentally.

How can you calculate the amount to which $15,000 will grow in 4 years at an 8 percent nominal annual interest rate if compounding occurs on a weekly basis? The solution process entails entering the initial sum as a present value, entering 4 years of weekly compounding as the number of periods, and entering 1/52 of 8 percent as the weekly interest rate.

The sequence of keystrokes for solving this problem on the HP-12C is as follows:

15000, CHS, PV	(to enter the initial deposit)
4, ENTER, 52, x, n	(to enter the number of compounding periods)
8, ENTER, 52, ÷, i	(to enter the weekly interest rate)
FV	(to produce the solution)

The answer, $20,651.84, should be displayed.

The HP-12C has one additional feature that provides a useful shortcut when solving problems involving monthly compounding (or discounting). Note that the n key also has a blue 12x function and the i key has a blue 12÷ function. These serve to automatically adjust n and i to a monthly basis.

To illustrate, assume you wish to calculate the payment amount at the end of each month on a $9,000, 4-year automobile loan carrying a nominal annual interest rate of 8.8 percent compounded monthly. Press the following keys:

blue g, END	(to set the payment mode to the end of the month)
9000, CHS, PV	(to enter the loan amount)
8.8, blue g, i	(to enter the monthly interest rate)
4, blue g, n	(to enter the number of payments)
PMT	(to produce the solution)

The answer, $223.11, should appear on the display.

Users of the HP-17B II will recall from chapter 5 that they were instructed to set the calculator for one payment per year and one compounding period per year and not to change this setting—ever! But now we are dealing with payments that occur and compounding that takes place more than once per year. Should the calculator setting be changed? Though doing so will produce a correct answer, we recommend strongly against it. Our experience has been that users of the calculator often forget to change the settings back to once per year/once per year after solving a problem, and they forget to check these settings for accuracy the next time they try solving a problem, with the result that solutions to subsequent problems are wildly incorrect. Therefore, we prefer to set the calculator for one payment per year and one compounding period per year and not to change that setting—ever!

How, then, does one deal with payments and compounding that occur more frequently than annually? The answer is to enter the number of periods, not the number of years, as the value of N, and the periodic interest rate, not the nominal annual rate, as the value of I%YR. For example, to find the future value of $15,000 in four years at 8 percent compounded weekly, the keystrokes on the HP-17B II in the TVM menu system are as follows:

15000, +/–, the PV menu key	(to enter the initial deposit),
4, x, 52, =, the N menu key	(to enter the number of compounding periods),
8, ÷, 52, =, the I%YR menu key	(to enter the weekly interest rate),
the FV menu key	(to produce the solution).

The answer, $20,651.84, is displayed.

Those who are using the BA-II Plus calculator will recall from chapter 5 that they were instructed to set the calculator for one payment per year and one compounding period per year and not to change this setting—ever! But now we are dealing with payments that occur and compounding that takes place more than once per year. Should the calculator setting be changed? Though doing so will produce a correct answer, we recommend strongly against it. Our experience has been that users of the calculator often forget to change the settings back to once per year/once per year after solving a problem, and they forget to check these settings for accuracy the next time they try solving a problem, with the result that solutions to subsequent problems are wildly incorrect. Therefore, we prefer to set the calculator for one payment per year and one compounding period per year and not to change that setting—ever!

How, then, does one deal with payments and compounding that occur more frequently than annually? The answer is to enter the number of periods, not the number of years, as the value of N, and the periodic interest rate, not the nominal annual rate, as the value of I/Y. For example, to find the future value of $15,000 in four years at 8 percent compounded weekly, press the following keys:

15000, +/–, PV	(to enter the initial deposit)
4, x, 52, =, N	(to enter the number of compounding periods)
8, ÷, 52, =, I/Y	(to enter the weekly interest rate)
CPT, FV	(to produce the solution)

The answer, $20,651.84, should appear on the display screen.

Interpreting the Results of the Calculations

When the solution to a time-value-of-money problem is a value for i, I/Y, n, N, or PMT, remember that these are *periodic* values. Therefore, if the compounding or discounting frequency is other than annual, these solutions are also other-than-annual values. To convert the solution to an annual basis, therefore, it must be adjusted by, in the case of monthly results, a factor of 12. For example, if a monthly payment is $800, the amount paid per year is $800 x 12 = $9,600. Similarly, if the number of monthly payments is 24, the number of years during which payments will be made is 24 ÷ 12 = 2.

Also, if the solution to a time-value-of-money problem is a value for i, I%YR, or I/Y, it too is a *periodic* value. If its frequency is other-than-annual, such as monthly, it too should be converted to an annual basis. However, it is insufficient to merely multiply the periodic interest rate value by, in this case, 12, since the result of such a multiplication would be a *nominal* annual rate (often called the APR, or annual percentage rate, by financial institutions). A more accurate result is found by then converting that nominal annual rate to an effective annual rate as described earlier.

Assume you wish to compute the annual interest rate on a $1,000 loan that calls for 12 monthly payments of $99, beginning one month from the date of the loan. When you enter the data into your calculator, you initially find as the solution a rate of 2.7553 percent. This, however, is a monthly rate. Multiply it by 12 to find the annual rate, 33.0631 percent. Then convert this to an effective annual rate as explained earlier. The effective annual rate on this loan is 38.5634 percent.

FOCUS ON ETHICS
The Impact of Inflation

The financial planner must never lose track of the impact of inflation. If a couple planning to retire in 20 years projects its annual needs at $50,000, that projection is in the current year's dollars. If inflation is estimated at 3 percent per year, at the retirement date the inflation-adjusted needs will be $90,000! Twenty years into retirement (40 years from today), the adjusted income needs at 3 percent annual inflation would be $163,000! Viewed another way, a $50,000 income in 40 years will have purchasing power equal to only $15,000 in today's dollars.

Often planners supply future projections of mutual fund or insurance cash values with specific rate-of-return assumptions. Often the projected accumulation is extremely large, and the client is lulled into a dangerous complacency because inflation is ignored.

Unfortunately, fully informing the client of the perils of inflation often (unintentionally and ironically) results in scaring the client into inaction. This may mean a loss of income for the planner. Regardless of this possibility, the planner's ethical responsibility is clear. Inflation is a critical factor that must be addressed in any financial projections. Withholding this information is the same as misinforming the client.

Annuity Payments Occurring Other Than Annually

Thus far we have examined problems in which compounding or discounting occurs more frequently than once per year. A related but separate topic is the question of annuity payments that occur more frequently than once per year.

(Uneven cash flows that occur other than annually are not dealt with in this book.)

Simple Annuities and Simple Annuities Due

A *simple annuity* or *annuity due* is one in which the frequency of payments and the frequency of compounding or discounting are identical. An example of a simple annuity is a series of six quarterly deposits credited with interest quarterly, beginning 3 months from now. Likewise, a simple annuity due is a series of 15 monthly payments discounted on a monthly basis, beginning immediately. All of the annuity topics discussed so far involved simple annuities or simple annuities due because both the payment frequency and the compounding or discounting frequency were identical, once per year.

The calculation of the present or future value of a simply annuity or a simple annuity due when payments are more frequent than annual involves the same tools and procedures as you have already learned. The same formulas you use for computing FVA, FVAD, PVA, and PVAD can be used; the same FVA and PVA tables can be used; the same keystrokes can be used on the HP-12C, HP-17B II, or the BA-II Plus—*except for two adjustments.* First, the figure you use as the n should always be the total number of *payments* in the problem, not the number of years. Second, the figure you use as the i should always be the *periodic* interest rate, not the annual rate. For example, in a problem that involves 3 years of quarterly payments and a 16 percent interest rate compounded quarterly, n is 12 and i is 4 percent. Or in one that involves 5 years of monthly payments and a 6 percent interest rate compounded monthly, n is 60 and i is .5 percent.

A corporate bond is a frequently encountered security that includes a simple annuity with payments occurring other than annually. For example, assume that a bond provides semiannual interest payments of $40 for ten years, beginning six months from now, as well as payment of the $1,000 principal sum at the end of the tenth year. If bonds with a similar degree of riskiness are yielding 11 percent, what should you pay for this bond? The present value of 20 payments of $40 each should be found based on a 5.5 percent discount rate. To this should be added the present value of the $1,000 final payment, also discounted at 5.5 percent for 20 periods. On a financial calculator, enter 40 as the end-of-period PMT, 1000 as the FV, 5.5 as the i, 20 as the n, and find the PV, or intrinsic value of this bond, $820.74.[11]

Now assume that you buy this bond for $821 and hold it for three years, at which time it is called by the issuing corporation for $1,040. What has been your annual yield to the call date? On a financial calculator, enter 821 as the PV, 1040 as the FV, 40 as the end-of-period PMT, and 6 as the n. Find i, the period interest rate, 8.47%. Now convert this periodic rate to an effective annual rate. Find the nominal annual rate by doubling 8.47 to 16.94 percent. The effective annual yield to call of a nominal annual 16.94 percent received semiannually is 17.66 percent.

You can also calculate the n, i, or PMT in a simple annuity or annuity due involving other-than-annual payments. Use the same tools you would use if the payments were annual. Again, however, the item you input or compute as n is always the total number of payments, not the total number of years. The item you input or compute as i is always the periodic interest rate, not the annual rate. And the item you input or compute as PMT is always the single periodic payment, not the sum of the payments per year.

Complex Annuities and Complex Annuities Due

A *complex annuity* or *annuity due* is one in which the frequency of payments and the frequency of compounding or discounting are different. For example, a complex annuity due is a series of 14 monthly deposits that are credited with interest daily, beginning immediately. Likewise, a complex annuity is a series of 10 semiannual lease payments that are discounted on an annual basis, beginning 6 months from now.

The mathematics of solving problems involving complex annuities are fairly complicated and generally beyond the scope of this book. Here we deal with only two types of complex annuity problems, computing the FVA or FVAD and the PVA or PVAD. The tool described for finding the solution to each is a formula, although a calculator is also needed, especially to facilitate raising certain numbers to a power.

In order to solve problems involving complex annuities, it is necessary to introduce one new variable that has not been used in any of the problems heretofore. That new variable, which we shall label as "c," is the number of times that compounding or discounting occurs in *each payment interval.* The value of c is found by dividing the frequency of compounding or discounting per year by the frequency of the payments per year. For example, if compounding occurs monthly and annuity payments are made quarterly, c = 3. Or if discounting occurs semiannually and annuity payments are made weekly, c = 1/26.

The formula for computing the future value of a complex annuity is presented below. In it, as in simple annuities, i is the periodic interest rate and n is the total number of annuity payments.

$$\text{FVA} = \left[\frac{(1 + i)^{n \times c} - 1}{(1 + i)^{c} - 1} \right] \text{x amount of one deposit}$$

To illustrate, assume that $70 is deposited into a savings account every 6 months for 5 years. The first deposit is made 6 months from now. Interest is credited to the account at a 12 percent nominal annual rate, compounded monthly. How much will be in the account at the end of 5 years? Substituting in the formula, we have

$$\text{FVA} = \left[\frac{1.01^{10 \times 6} - 1}{1.01^{6} - 1}\right] \times \$70$$

$$= \left[\frac{.8167}{.0615}\right] \times \$70$$

$$= 13.2797 \times \$70$$

$$= \$929.58$$

If in this illustration the first deposit is made immediately rather than 6 months from now (if the problem called for finding FVAD), one further step is necessary. The value of the FVA has to be increased in a manner analogous to that used for annual annuities due. Specifically, the adjustment to be made is

$$\text{FVAD} = \text{FVA} \times (1 + i)^{c}$$

Again, remember to use the periodic interest rate for i in making this adjustment. In this illustration, then,

$$\begin{aligned} \text{FVAD} &= \$929.58 \times 1.01^{6} \\ &= \$929.58 \times 1.0615 \\ &= \$986.75 \end{aligned}$$

That is, the account balance is 6.15 percent higher because an extra 6 months of interest is earned at a 12 percent nominal annual rate compounded monthly.

Next we turn to calculating the present value of a complex annuity. The formula is presented below. As before, n is the total number of payments, i is the periodic interest rate, and c is the discounting frequency per payment interval.

$$\text{PVA} = \text{amount of one payment} \times \left[\frac{1 - \dfrac{1}{(1 + i)^{n \times c}}}{(1 + i)^{c} - 1}\right]$$

To illustrate, assume that during the first 3½ years after you retire you want to have interest income of $250 per month, beginning one month after your retirement date. Also assume that the principal sum to be liquidated in order to provide this income can be invested at a nominal annual rate of 6 percent, compounded quarterly. How large a principal sum will you need on the date you retire? What is the present value of this complex annuity? Substituting in the formula, we have

$$\text{PVA} = \$250 \text{ x} \left[\frac{1 - \dfrac{1}{1.015^{42 \text{ x } 1/3}}}{1.015^{1/3} - 1} \right]$$

$$= \$250 \text{ x} \left[\frac{1 - .8118}{1.0050 - 1} \right]$$

$$= \$250 \text{ x } 37.64$$

$$= \$9{,}410.00$$

If the $250 of monthly income is to begin on your retirement date, rather than one month later (if the problem called for calculating the PVAD rather than the PVA), one further step is necessary. The value of the PVA has to be increased in a manner analogous to that used for annual annuities due. Specifically, the adjustment is

$$\text{PVAD} = \text{PVA x } (1 + i)^c$$

Again, remember to use the periodic interest rate in making this adjustment. In this illustration, then,

$$\begin{aligned} \text{PVAD} &= \$9{,}410 \text{ x } 1.015^{1/3} \\ &= \$9{,}410 \text{ x } 1.0050 \\ &= \$9{,}457.05 \end{aligned}$$

The principal sum has to be about .5 percent higher because one month of interest earnings is lost on a 6 percent annual rate compounded quarterly.

PROBLEMS

1. The divorce is final and you have been awarded the following alimony: $5,000 at the end of each of the next 3 years, plus $6,000 at the end of each of the following 5 years, plus $7,000 at the end of each of the following 10 years. If you remarry, however, you receive no further alimony. Measured in terms of present value and a discount rate of 6.5 percent, what will your wedding cost if you remarry today?
2. To convince yourself of the wisdom of your recent decision to quit smoking (and this time you really mean it), you plan at the end of each of the next 5 years to put into a savings account earning 6 percent compound annual interest the money you would have spent on cigarettes. You anticipate that the amounts of the five deposits will be $400, $450, $500, $550, and $600. If all goes according to plan, how much will be in your account after 5 years?
3. Which of the following income streams would you rather have if interest rates currently are 7 percent?

Beginning of Year	Cash Flow		End of Year	Cash Flow
1	$2,000		1	0
2	$2,500		2	0
3	$3,000	OR	3	$5,500
4	$3,000		4	$5,500
5	$3,000		5	$5,500

4. Your race horse is a sure thing to win $60,000 for you at the end of each of the next 3 years, after which you believe that the horse will be able to earn about $10,000 per year in stud fees at the end of each of 5 years. If you insist on a compound annual rate of return of at least 20 percent, what would you accept for the horse today?
5. Tuition at the university your daughter will be attending next year is expected to be $11,000 at that time and to rise by about 8 percent per year thereafter. You plan to set aside today a capital sum that, invested at 6 percent interest, will be just sufficient to pay her tuition in full at the start of each of the 4 years. How large a capital sum is needed to accomplish this objective?
6. Your goal is to have accumulated a capital sum of $75,000 when you retire 12 years from now. You plan to make an initial deposit of $2,000 today, and on each of the following 11 annual anniversary dates you will deposit an amount that is 10 percent higher than the previous year's deposit. If your deposits earn 7 percent interest per year, will you reach your goal?
7. You have just made a loan of $85,000 to a friend, who has agreed to the following repayment schedule:

End of year 1	$ 5,000
End of year 2	$ 10,000
End of year 3	0
End of year 4	0
End of year 5	$100,000

(a) What is your internal rate of return?

(b) What is the net present value of this investment if 10 percent is your minimum acceptable compound annual rate of return?

8. Tax reform legislation notwithstanding, you have located an exotic tax-sheltered investment opportunity. For an initial outlay of $50,000 and an additional $10,000 5 years from now, you will receive the following income stream:

End of years 1–4	$ 7,500
End of years 6–10	$ 8,000

What is the internal rate of return on this investment?

9. You are debating whether to invest $100,000 in a piece of equipment that will produce the following cost savings for your business:

End of years 1–3	$ 30,000
End of year 4	($ 10,000)
End of years 5–7	$ 20,000

(a) What is the internal rate of return?

(b) What is the net present value if you discount the cash flows at the 8 percent compound annual interest rate you would have to pay in order to finance the purchase of the equipment?

10. Use the formula or your financial calculator to compute the effective annual interest rate when a nominal annual rate of 18 percent is compounded

(a) semiannually

(b) quarterly

(c) monthly

Check your answers by comparing them with table F in appendix F.

11. Where should you put your money: in a certificate of deposit that will earn 9.75 percent compounded daily (360 days) or in one that will earn 10 percent compounded semiannually?

12. (a) Show which is the larger amount: the future value of a 10-year, $2,000 annual annuity growing at a nominal annual interest rate of 5 percent compounded weekly or one growing at a nominal annual interest rate of 5 percent compounded monthly.

(b) Show which is the larger amount: the present value of a 6-year, $3,000 annual annuity discounted at 11 percent applied monthly or one discounted at 11 percent applied quarterly.

13. Assume that you plan to save for Junior's college education by depositing $200 per month for the next 12 years in a savings account, beginning immediately. The account is expected to earn a nominal annual rate of 6 percent, compounded monthly. How much will be in the account at the end of the 12th year?
14. What is the present value of a stream of 10 quarterly payments of $500 each, beginning 3 months from now, if an annual discount rate of 16 percent is applied semiannually?

SOLUTIONS

1. Not counting the cost of the gown, the organist, the flowers, the photographer, and so on, the wedding will cost you $64,287.34 in lost alimony, computed as shown below, using factors in tables B.2 and B.4.

The present value of the first series of payments is $13,242.50.	($5,000 x 2.6485 = $13,242.50)
The present value of the second series of payments as of the beginning of year 4 is $24,934.20.	($6,000 x 4.1557 = $24,934.20)
The present value of this amount as of the beginning of year one is $20,640.53.	($24,934.20 x .8278 = $20,640.53)
The present value of the third series of payments as of the beginning of year 9 is $50,321.60.	($7,000 x 7.1888 = $50,321.60)
The present value of this amount as of the beginning of year one is $30,404.31.	($50,321.60 x .6042 = $30,404.31)
The total present value of the three series of payments is $64,287.34.	($13,242.50 + $20,640.53 + $30,404.31 = $64,287.34)

If you used a financial calculator, the present value of these uneven cash flows is $64,290.04.

2. The future values of these five items of ungrouped data, based on FVSS factors in table B.1, are as follows:

$400 x 1.2625 = $ 505.00

$450 x 1.1910	=	535.95
$500 x 1.1236	=	561.80
$550 x 1.0600	=	583.00
$600 x 1.0000	=	600.00
Total future value		$2,785.75

Use of a financial calculator in the way described in this chapter would produce a future value of the same amount.

3. Using PVSS and PVA factors from tables B.2 and B.4, you can compute the present value of the income stream on the left as $11,694.02.

$2,000 x 1.0000	=	$ 2,000.00
$2,500 x .9346	=	2,336.50
$3,000 x 2.6243 x 1.07 x .8734	=	7,357.52
Total present value		$11,694.02

The present value of the income stream on the right is higher, $12,606.35.

$5,500 x 2.6243 x .8734 = $12,606.35

If you use a financial calculator, the income stream on the left is worth $11,694.34 and that on the right is worth $12,606.99.

4. Based on the appropriate PVA and PVSS factors from tables B.2 and B.4, the horse's present value is

$60,000 x 2.1065	=	$126,390.00
$10,000 x 2.9906 x .5787	=	17,306.60
Total present value		$143,696.60

This would be your minimum selling price. (On the HP-12C, HP-17B II, or BA-II Plus, the answer is $143,695.67).

5. The answer may be found through the formula for calculating the present value of a series of payments that grow by a constant percentage. Specifically,

$$PV = \$11{,}000 \times \left[\frac{1 - \left[\frac{1.08}{1.06}\right]^4}{(.06 - .08)}\right] \times 1.06$$

$$= \$11{,}000 \times \left[\frac{1 - 1.0776}{-.02}\right] \times 1.06$$

$$= \$11{,}000 \times 3.8817 \times 1.06$$

$$= \$45{,}260.62$$

But since the first payment is not due for one year, this result should be divided by 1.06 to produce the answer, \$42,698.70. Alternatively, if you use the appropriate keystrokes on the HP-12C, HP-17B II, or the BA-II Plus, the answer that appears on the display is \$45,261.02. Dividing this by 1.06 produces the answer, \$42,699.08.

6. You will not reach the \$75,000 goal with the planned funding pattern. The answer may be found through the formula for calculating the future value of a series of deposits that grow by a constant percentage and that begin immediately. Specifically,

$$FV = \$2{,}000 \times \left[\frac{1.07^{12} - 1.10^{12}}{.07 - .10}\right] \times 1.07$$

$$= \$2{,}000 \times \left[\frac{2.2522 - 3.1384}{-.03}\right] \times 1.07$$

$$= \$2{,}000 \times 29.5400 \times 1.07$$

$$= \$63{,}215.60$$

Or if you use the appropriate keystrokes on the HP-12C, HP-17B II, or BA-II Plus, the answer that appears on the display is \$63,218.22.

7. (a) Even for a fairly simple set of cash flows such as this one, a financial calculator is the most practical means of calculating the IRR. <u>The keystrokes for the HP-12C</u> are as follows: 85000, CHS, blue g, CFo, 5000, blue g, CFj, 10000, blue g, CFj, 0, blue g, CFj, 2, blue g, Nj, 100000, blue g, CFj, yellow f, IRR. <u>On the HP-17B II</u>, with the #T? function turned off, the keystrokes in the CFLO menu system are as follows: 85000, +/–, INPUT, 5000, INPUT, 1, INPUT, 10000, INPUT, 1, INPUT, 0, INPUT, 2, INPUT, 100000, INPUT, 1, INPUT, EXIT, the CALC menu key, and the IRR% menu key. <u>The keystrokes for the BA-II Plus</u> are as follows: 85000, +/–, ENTER, ↓, 5000, ENTER, ↓, ↓,

10000, ENTER, ↓, ↓, 0, ENTER, ↓, 2, ENTER, ↓, 100000, ENTER, ↓, IRR, CPT. The answer is 6.9171%.

(b) With the above data still in the machine, on the HP-12C press 10, i, yellow f, NPV. On the HP-17B II, press 10, the I% menu key, and the NPV menu key. Or on the BA-II Plus press NPV, 10, ENTER, ↓, CPT. The answer is –$10,097.95.
Alternatively, the NPV can be found by using present value factors from table B.2.

$5,000 x .9091	=	$ 4,545.50
$10,000 x .8264	=	8,264.00
$100,000 x .6209	=	62,090.00
Present value of inflows		$74,899.50
Present value of outflows		–85,000.00
Net present value		–$10,100.50

8. On the HP-12C press 50000, CHS, blue g, CFo, 7500, blue g, CFj, 4, blue g, Nj, 10000, CHS, blue g, CFj, 8000, blue g, CFj, 5, blue g, Nj, yellow f, IRR. On the HP-17B II, the keystrokes in the CFLO menu system with the #T? function turned on are as follows: 50000, +/–, INPUT, 7500, INPUT, 4, INPUT, 10000, +/–, INPUT, 1, INPUT, 8000, INPUT, 5, INPUT, EXIT, the CALC menu key, and the IRR% menu key. On the BA-II Plus press 50000, +/–, ENTER, ↓, 7500, ENTER, ↓, 4, ENTER, ↓, 10000, +/–, ENTER, ↓, ↓, 8000, ENTER, ↓, 5, ENTER, ↓, IRR, CPT. The answer probably is 3.3231%. Because the income stream involves more than one sign change, however, there may also be a negative IRR, though this is unlikely.
9. (a) The internal rate of return may be found on the HP-12C by pressing 100000, CHS, blue g, CFo, 30000, blue g, CFj, 3, blue g, Nj, 10000, CHS, blue g, CFj, 20000, blue g, CFj, 3, blue g, Nj, yellow f, IRR. If you are using the HP-17B II, you can find the IRR by entering the CFLO menu system, turning on the #T? function, and pressing the following keys: 100000, +/–, INPUT, 30000, INPUT, 3, INPUT, 10000, +/–, INPUT, 1, INPUT, 20000, INPUT, 3, INPUT, EXIT, the CALC menu key and the IRR% menu key. Or you can find the IRR on the BA-II Plus by pressing 100000, +/–, ENTER, ↓, 30000, ENTER, ↓, 3, ENTER, ↓, 10000, +/–, ENTER, ↓, ↓, 20000, ENTER, ↓, 3, ENTER, ↓, IRR, CPT. The answer is 10.6118% (but see solution 8 above).

   (b) With the above data still in the HP-12C, press 8, i, yellow f, NPV. On the HP-17B II, with the above data still in the machine, press 8, the I% menu key, and the NPV menu key. Or if you use the BA-II Plus, with the above data still in the machine press NPV, 8, ENTER, ↓, CPT. The answer is \$7,847.48. Alternatively, the NPV can be found by using PVSS and PVA factors from tables B.2 and B.4.

\$30,000 x 2.5771	=	\$ 77,313.00
\$20,000 x 2.5771 x .7350	=	37,883.37
Present value of inflows		\$115,196.37
\$100,000 x 1.0000	=	\$100,000.00
\$10,000 x .7350	=	7,350.00
Present value of outflows		\$107,350.00
Net present value		\$ 7,846.37

10.

$$\text{(a)} \left[1 + \frac{.18}{2}\right]^2 - 1 = 18.81000\%$$

$$\text{(b)} \left[1 + \frac{.18}{4}\right]^4 - 1 = 19.25186\%$$

$$\text{(c)} \left[1 + \frac{.18}{12}\right]^{12} - 1 = 19.56182\%$$

11. Take the 10 percent rate. The 9.75 percent CD pays an effective rate of

$$\left[1 + \frac{.0975}{360}\right]^{360} - 1 = 10.2397\%$$

whereas the 10 percent CD pays an effective rate of

$$\left[1 + \frac{.10}{2}\right]^2 - 1 = 10.2500\%$$

12. (a) Weekly compounding will produce the larger FVA because the effective annual interest rate is 5.12458 percent, versus 5.11619 percent for monthly compounding. Substituting these effective rates in the FVA formula, we have

$$\$2{,}000 \text{ x} \left[\frac{1.0512458^{10} - 1}{.0512458}\right] = \$25{,}302.55$$

versus

$$\$2{,}000 \text{ x} \left[\frac{1.0511619^{10} - 1}{.0511619}\right] = \$25{,}292.63$$

(b) Discounting on a quarterly basis will produce the larger PVA. The effective rate for quarterly discounting is 11.46213 percent, versus 11.57188 percent for monthly discounting. Substituting these effective rates in the PVA formula, we have

$$\$3{,}000 \text{ x} \left[\frac{1 - \left[\frac{1}{1.1146213^{6}}\right]}{.1146213}\right] = \$12{,}524.44$$

versus

$$\$3{,}000 \text{ x} \left[\frac{1 - \left[\frac{1}{1.1157188^{6}}\right]}{.1157188}\right] = \$12{,}485.23$$

13. If you use the FVAD formula, the answer for this simple annuity is

$$= \$200 \text{ x} \left[\frac{1.005^{144} - 1}{.005}\right] \text{x } 1.005$$

$$= \$200 \text{ x} \left[\frac{1.0508}{.005}\right] \text{x } 1.005$$

$$= \$200 \text{ x } 210.16 \text{ x } 1.005$$

$$= \$42{,}242.16$$

Table B.2 cannot be used to solve the problem because it does not contain a factor in the .5% column for an n of 144.

The HP-12C, HP-17B II, or the BA-II Plus can also be used. Remember that n or N is 144 and i or I/Y is .5. The answer displayed will be $42,240.18.

14. In this problem the annuity is a complex annuity. The value of c is 2 ÷ 4, or ½. Substituting in the formula for the PVA of a complex annuity, we have

$$= \$500 \text{ x } \left[\frac{1 - \left[\frac{1}{1.08^{10 \text{ x } 1/2}} \right]}{1.08^{1/2} - 1} \right]$$

$$= \$500 \text{ x } \left[\frac{1 - .6806}{.0392} \right]$$

$$= \$500 \text{ x } 8.1480$$

$$= \$4{,}074.00$$

NOTES

1. Most corporate bonds pay interest semiannually. For purposes of simplicity, however, annual payments are assumed here. A later section of this chapter deals with compounding and discounting where cash flows occur more frequently than once per year.
2. In some cases you might at this point want to calculate an annuity, that is, a series of level payments, that would have the same net present value as the uneven cash flows in the machine. If so, simply press the NUS (net uniform series) menu key to produce the answer, $61,353.83. A five-year annuity of this amount, discounted as 12.5 percent, has a present value of $218,454.50.
3. Alternatively, you could compute the present value under the end-of-year approach referred to in note 1, and multiply the result by (1 + i).
4. You may have noticed that this cash flow can be restated in terms that are easier to handle if you are using tables.

   $30,000 for 10 years
   +$10,000 for 9 years
   +$10,000 for 8 years
   +$10,000 for 5 years
   Compute the future value of each annuity and add them together.
5. In this and in all investment opportunities being evaluated, care must be exercised to be sure that all relevant elements of the cash inflow and outflow streams are considered and discounted property. Don't forget to include, when appropriate, such items as shipping and installation costs of a proposed new piece of equipment, maintenance costs, income taxes, salvage value, and so on. In the illustrations in this portion of the chapter it is assumed that all such considerations have already been accounted for in the numbers being used.
6. As seen later in this chapter, this is not usually necessary when using the HP-12C, HP-17B II, or BA-II Plus calculator's IRR function.
7. For more on this phenomenon, review the subject of NPV profiles in college-level financial management textbooks.
8. For an interesting example of multiple IRRs, see Roger H. Allen, *Real Estate Investment and Taxation,* 2d ed. (Cincinnati: South-Western Publishing Co., 1984), p. 205. An illustration developed by Robert J. Doyle, formerly of the faculty of The American College, is presented showing an investment that has several internal rates of return. The cash flows used in the

illustration are ($1,000), $3,600, ($4,310), and $1,716. An investment with this set of cash flows has IRRs of 10 percent, 20 percent, and 30 percent. Each of those rates, when used to discount the cash flows, produces an NPV of zero.

9. Financial institutions typically use a 360-day year as the basis for daily compounding calculations. This produces a slightly smaller annual interest, all other things being equal, than if they were to use a 365-day year.
10. The mathematics of calculating the effective rate manually when compounding is continuous are too complex to be dealt with in this book. The procedure for calculating it by using the HP-12C or BA-II Plus calculators, however, is included in appendixes C and E.
11. The three financial calculators dealt with in this text also have separate systems for computing various bond values. Consult the owner's manual for details.

7

Risk Tolerance in Financial Decisions

Michael J. Roszkowski

Chapter Outline

INTRODUCTION

Investments are characterized by different levels of risk and potential return. Both ethical and regulatory principles require that the financial planner recommend only those products and investment strategies that are *suitable* given the client's investment objectives, financial capacity to absorb a loss, and psychological propensity for risk taking. The goal is to deliver the most return for the amount of tolerable risk. Proper asset allocation requires a determination of the client's risk tolerance.

At the 1995 IAFP Conference for Advanced Planners, Eleanor Blayney, a member of the IAFP Ethics Committee, reported that 90 percent of the cases under review by her committee involved suitability. Ms. Blayney stated that: "In every case, no risk-tolerance instrument was ever used," adding, "I have to wonder how much more favorably disposed I would have been if I could have seen a documented effort to make that risk assessment."

It is encouraging to see that there is growing recognition of the need to understand the psychological factors involved in investment decisions. For example, the *Journal of Financial Planning* now has a regular feature called "Money & Soul" that examines the behavioral issues in financial planning. A recent (March 1997) cover story, titled "Inside the Minds of Clients," dealt with the processes investors use to make financial decisions. James G. Powers, in his *Best's Review* article (December 1996), proposed that a source of problems with life insurance policy illustrations could be avoided if an agent considers the client's risk tolerance needs in the life insurance selling process. He argues that the further one deviates from a guaranteed rate of return, the more likely the policy will underperform.

Financial services professionals of all types, therefore, need to understand risk tolerance and convey to their clients its significance in reaching proper investment decisions. Determining a client's level of risk tolerance, while extremely important, is also one of the most difficult tasks facing the financial planner. Done properly, however, it will improve relationships with clients and could lessen the possibility of litigation by those who have invested beyond their comfort level.

Although it may appear to be a rather simple topic, risk tolerance is an extremely complex phenomenon. It is an area of interest for many academic disciplines—notably economics, psychology, finance, and management science. Each field has a different tradition and approaches risk tolerance from a different perspective. This chapter integrates the relevant research from all these disciplines and thereby reveals areas of professional disagreement. (More information appears in the references listed at the end of this chapter.)

Specifically, this chapter examines how people view risk and how they process information about risk factors. It explores the reasons people either minimize or maximize the objective level of risk in a situation. It also identifies demographic and personality characteristics that have been linked to risk tolerance. Finally it considers various approaches to assessing a client's risk-taking propensity and notes their relative merits and drawbacks.

Hopefully, after completing this study, financial planners will better understand why clients accept or refuse risk, and they will be able to use this information to serve their clients more effectively.

RISK AVERSION, RISK SEEKING, AND RISK INDIFFERENCE

It is generally accepted that people react differently to risk. Some are always willing to accept it; others are always ready to reject it. It is best to think of reactions to risk as a *continuum.* Individuals on the one end are known as "risk seekers" (or risk tolerant), while those on the other end are known as "risk averters" (or risk rejecters). People in the middle are referred to as "risk indifferent." Frequently the terms *aggressive* and *conservative* are used to describe investors who are, respectively, risk seeking and risk averse. According to conventional wisdom, investment decisions involve a trade-off between risk and expected return. Risk-averse investors prefer low risks and are therefore willing to sacrifice some expected return in order to reduce the variation in possible outcomes.

The *majority* of the population is thought to be closer to the risk-averter end of the continuum. For example, a study conducted by the Life Insurance Marketing and Research Association (LIMRA) asked survey participants if they would be willing to take risks for higher yields. The answers were to be given on a 10-point scale where 1 indicated "not willing" and 10 stood for "very willing." Whereas 45 percent of the people rated themselves 1, 2, or 3, only 11 percent rated themselves 8, 9, or 10. The remaining 44 percent used the middle values (4 through 7) to describe themselves. Security is a fundamental human need, as revealed in various surveys conducted over the years.

The generally negative view people hold about exposing themselves to the risk of a loss is, in fact, the basis for all sorts of consumer warranties. Is it any wonder that advertisements allowing for a "risk-free 30-day examination period" are so appealing for all products, including insurance policies?

Why are some people more willing than others to take risks? Various factors contribute to the attitude of risk acceptance. They include biological makeup, upbringing, and other life experiences.

Loss Aversion

People's unwillingness to accept losses is a fundamental part of their attitude toward risk. Although it is typically stated that most people are *risk* averse, it is really more appropriate to say that they are *loss* averse.

In finance and related disciplines risk aversion means the preference for certain outcomes over uncertain outcomes. Conversely, risk seeking refers to a preference for uncertain outcomes over certain outcomes. Studies have demonstrated conclusively that people are indeed cautious when faced with a choice between certain and uncertain gains. That is, they most often select the certain gain, even if it is smaller. However, when the two alternatives are a choice between a relatively small but certain loss and a relatively larger but only probable loss, most people are risk takers. In other words, they are willing to risk a large loss rather than accept a smaller but certain loss. For illustrative purposes, consider the following problems posed by psychologists A. Tversky and D. Kahneman. First look at problem 1, which consists of the following two choices, A and B.

A: a sure win of $3,000

B: an 80 percent chance to win $4,000 (and a corresponding 20 percent chance of winning nothing)

Most people take choice A. That is, offered a choice between a relatively smaller but certain gain, and a relatively larger but nonguaranteed gain, most people elect the smaller but certain prize. Choice A is considered the risk-averse alternative, whereas choice B is the risk-seeking alternative.

Now look at problem 2, which consists of choices C and D.

C: a sure loss of $3,000

D: an 80 percent chance of losing $4,000 (and a corresponding 20 percent chance of losing nothing)

Note that the only difference between problem 2 and problem 1 is that problem 2 deals with losses. That is, the probabilities and money involved remain the same as in problem 1. Here, alternative C is the certain (risk-averse) choice, while D is the uncertain (risk-seeking) choice. Under the possibility of loss, most people revise their preferences; they now elect choice D. When both alternatives are unpleasant, most people are inclined to take the 20 percent gamble that they will lose nothing even though the odds are against them. In problem 2, then, they prefer uncertainty to certainty or, in other words, they are risk-seeking.

Both the preference for A and the preference for D are a manifestation of the same psychological mechanism, namely, a reluctance to sustain a loss. It is really the prospect of loss that makes one risk averse in the first problem and risk seeking in the second problem. In both cases, people don't want to give up any money. For most people, the extent of risk seeking that occurs when faced with a choice between losses is much greater than the extent of risk avoidance that occurs when the choice is between gains.

These laboratory findings have been confirmed by observing real-life activities. At racetracks, a person will gamble more money and place more bets on longshots when he or she has been losing that day. Likewise, companies take greater risks when they are in financial trouble, as when their returns are below target.

FORMAL CONCEPT OF RISK AND PEOPLE'S INTUITIVE PERCEPTION

The term *risk* has many definitions. Psychologists and other scientists have compared these definitions to people's intuitive understanding of the concept of risk. There are some striking differences.

In the field of finance, the conventional measures of investment risk are statistical concepts of variability such as standard deviation, covariance, and beta. High variability in past (and projected future) returns is equated with risk.

To the average person unsophisticated about investment matters, however, the most important factor in evaluating the riskiness of an investment is the historical trend line in the return generated by the investment. If the trend is *upward*, the investment is perceived as less risky than if the trend is *downward*. Fluctuations in the return are only a *secondary* consideration.

Intuitively, then, people do accept variability of investment returns as a measure of risk, but the evidence shows that many do not treat uncertainty about *positive* outcomes as an aspect of risk. Rather, most people focus on the probability of negative returns in defining a risk. Generally people regard the word risk to mean danger or possible loss. A survey of public opinion regarding the term risk by the Insurance Information Institute further corroborates this point. Asked to indicate what the word risk connotes, most people said "danger" (84 percent) and "possible loss" (77 percent). Risk is thought to increase as bad outcomes become more likely.

With respect to investments, the danger lies in either getting less than the expected return or sustaining a loss of the principal. Surveys have demonstrated that portfolio managers and professionals who must routinely deal with capital budgeting tend to incorporate the probability of not achieving an expected (that is, target) return on an investment into their personal definition of a risky investment. However, in most other people's minds, the loss of principal is closest to their intuitive understanding of the word risk. For example, a recent study reported in the *Financial Analysts Journal* (March/April 1997) compared the definitions of investment risk held by professional portfolio managers and individual investors. The top two definitions for both groups included references to (a) a large loss and (b) return rates below target. However, the primary definition for the portfolio managers was return below target, whereas for the individual investors it was a large loss. The table below provides the details of the results, indicating factors that the respondents said came to mind first when they thought about a "risky" investment.

Percentage of Portfolio Managers and Individual Investors Thinking of Each Characteristic First

Characteristic Category	Portfolio Mangers	Individual Investors
Large Loss	22%	40%
Return below target	25%	20%
Business risk	22%	18%
Liquidity	15%	8%
Knowledge about firm	7%	10%
Economic uncertainty	9%	4%
Note: The median number of attributes mentioned per respondent was three		

Therefore any investment product promising no loss of principal will appear safe to most consumers. Some individuals tend to draw a distinction between investing and speculating. According to this view, investments assure the safety of principal whereas speculations do not. It is no accident that mutual funds guaranteeing the return of the principal appeared after the October 1987 stock market crash.

Another difference between people's intuitive understanding of the word risk and some formal definitions of this term involves the distinction between risk and uncertainty. About 58 percent of the people questioned in the previously noted survey indicated that they associated risk with the word *uncertainty*. However, in the decision sciences, risk and uncertainty are not considered the same. There, risk refers to situations in which (1) the various consequences of each alternative are known and (2) their exact probabilities can be specified. Uncertainty, in contrast, is said to exist when the possible alternatives and their associated probabilities of occurrence are unknown.

For illustrative purposes, consider the possible outcomes that students face when they take a pass-fail examination. There are only two possible outcomes—passing or failing. Assume for a moment that someone is asked to estimate his or her chances of passing the course. If he or she can assign a probability to this event (for example, 60 percent chance of passing/40 percent chance of failing), then the exam represents a risk. If, however, the person has no way of assigning odds (being unfamiliar with the instructor's grading policies), then the exam represents an uncertainty.

Perceived versus Objective Risk

In essence, there are four dimensions to a choice involving risk: (1) the potential amount to be gained, (2) the probability of achieving this gain, (3) the amount that could potentially be lost, and (4) the probability of this loss occurring. Whether a person accepts or rejects a risk depends on his or her analysis of these four elements. In analyzing the risk, people tend to focus more on some of these dimensions than on others. Some people look most closely at the probability of winning, while others focus on the probability of losing. Still others are mainly concerned with the amounts involved.

It has been demonstrated repeatedly that the objective riskiness of a situation and one's interpretation of it, called "perceived risk," are not necessarily the same. Different people exposed to the same information interpret it differently. The objective odds are either lowered or heightened depending on the person's experiences, inclinations toward risk taking, and the particular circumstances surrounding a given situation.

LIMITATIONS IN RATIONAL THINKING

Debates abound regarding the extent of rationality shown in people's economic behavior. While some continue to view people's financial actions as *always* totally rational, recent evidence suggests less than totally rational behavior. At best, human beings act within what the Nobel prize-winning economist and psychologist Herbert Simon calls "bounded" rationality. That is, there are bounds or limits to how rational people can be. Their choices in financial matters are shaped not only by knowledge and rational thinking but also by their values and emotions.

Challenges to rationality are often reported in the behavior of the stock market. Certain research suggests that much of the volatility in the stock market is due to fads and mass psychology (that is, people doing something because others are doing it) rather than to changes in the economy or the fundamental soundness of the companies issuing the stocks. It has been observed that attitudes about the economy change faster than the economy itself. Some have likened the spread of enthusiasm and disenchantment about a given stock to the spread of an epidemic. For instance, in October 1984, a woman in New York City claimed that she found glass slivers in Gerbers baby food. Gerbers Products' stock fell 15 percent in two days. But not long thereafter it bounced back. The market crash of October 1987 can be attributed to numerous factors, but there is no doubt that investors mimicked the behavior of others in the selling frenzy.

Psychologists have conducted studies on how people perceive and process information about uncertain events. Most studies have found that people tend to violate rationality to some degree. These flaws in judgment are due in part to people's limited abilities to process information and in part to the interference of their emotions.

With respect to risky decisions, many people do not understand the laws of probability, and their ability to combine two or more probabilities is especially flawed. For example, in one study many people preferred a lottery in which they were allowed one draw out of 10 tickets to another lottery in which they were allowed 20 draws out of 100 tickets. (The 20-draw lottery is, of course, a better deal.) When processing information about probability, most people do it intuitively, rather than mathematically. Few people know how to make optimal decisions using mathematical decision rules.

Overconfidence in Intuitive Judgments

Most people, laymen and professionals alike, tend to be overconfident in their judgment, as shown in studies that ask people to make a choice and then estimate their probability of being right. These research findings indicate that if a person believes he or she has an 80 percent chance of being right, in reality this probability is only 70 percent. In other words, people are right in their judgment 7 out of 10 times rather than 8 out of 10. Errors are frequent even when one is totally certain about something. In one study, when people said something *always* happened, it actually occurred only 80 percent of the time. Likewise, when these individuals indicated that something *never* happened, it occurred about 20 percent of the time.

Typically, people use fewer clues to make a decision than they claim. The importance of minor clues is overestimated in most instances. Presenting people with more facts seems to make people feel more *confident* about their decisions, but generally the accuracy of their decisions is not enhanced greatly.

Nonrepresentative Quality of Short-Run Trends

Most people disregard "the Law of Large Numbers." They are willing to make their risk assessments on the basis of very small samples, not realizing that what is true in the *long run* may not occur in the *short run*. Some analysts believe that many investors overvalue short-run economic developments. Recent events get undue emphasis in people's decision making.

The following experiment illustrates people's failure to appreciate the significance of small versus large samples. In this experiment, people were asked to indicate which of the following is more likely to be an honest coin—coin A or coin B. Remember, in a single flip of an *honest* coin there is a 50-50 chance of the coin falling on its head or tail.

Coin A: 8 heads in 10 flips
Coin B: 70 heads in 100 flips

The honest coin is more likely to be A, but many people say B because the distribution of heads and tails is closer to 50-50 for coin B. These individuals are in error, however, because they fail to appreciate the small number of flips that took place with coin A. In the *short run*, an outcome that defies what one would expect in the long run is quite possible.

Failure to Correctly Evaluate Exposure

Most people have a particularly hard time evaluating the true magnitude of a risk that is not constant. In one study, the participants were asked to estimate the magnitude of risks that varied in both extent of potential harm and exposure time (that is, long-duration high risk; long-duration low risk; short-duration high risk; short-duration low risk). It was discovered that people fail to factor exposure time correctly into their estimates of risk. They tend to *overestimate* the impact of short-duration high-risk events. Being in danger for a very short time is seen as much more dangerous than it really is.

Denial of Risk

High risk taking could be due to either a failure to assess the level of danger or simply a willingness or desire to engage in the activity regardless of the level of danger. The evidence suggests that people engaging in risky behaviors on a *voluntary* basis often fail to appreciate the true level of danger in the situation. They may know the statistical odds but refuse to believe that these odds apply to them personally.

As an example, consider the results of a study sponsored by the Insurance Infonnation Institute. It was discovered that only 58 percent of people who smoke in bed consider it to be a very risky activity, whereas 92 percent of those who do not smoke in bed find it to be so. Similar patterns were identified for activities such as gambling (35 versus 63 percent), driving a car (27 versus 39 percent), skiing (13 versus 33 percent), and investing in the stock market (26 versus 39 percent).

Frequently, people claim that there is less risk in their own personal case because their skills reduce the risky aspects of the situation. For instance, many sky divers deny that their sport is risky. To them, it is risky only if one "does not know what he or she is doing." Similar attitudes have been documented among people who speculate in the stock market and real estate. A sharp distinction is drawn by such individuals between taking risks and being foolhardy. In many cases, people have unwarranted confidence in their skill levels.

Other people deny the risk because they feel especially lucky. They believe that the odds can be beaten. Even if the odds of success are only 10 in 100, such individuals are apt to think, "Somebody has to be in that 10 percent, so why shouldn't it be me?" When the objective probability of an event is unknown, people tend to *overestimate* the probability of a desired outcome and *underestimate* the probability of an undesired outcome. Many an individual who felt that the odds could be beaten has traveled to Las Vegas in a $15,000 car and indeed has come home in a $100,000 vehicle. Unfortunately, in a majority of such cases the $100,000 vehicle was not a new car but a bus.

People's reluctance to buy insurance stems in part from such unrealistic optimism. Some agents present actuarial data to their prospects on the probability of death, disability, and hospitalization, but most prospects feel that such statistics don't really apply to them personally. Most people believe that they are less likely than average to die prematurely, be hospitalized, or become disabled. In a recent study people were presented with the statistic that during a given year approximately 19 out of every 1,000 persons would sustain a disability lasting over 3 months. (In other words, the odds of disability were 19 in 1,000.) The group was then asked to estimate their personal odds of sustaining a disability. On average, the subjects felt their personal odds to be much lower—only 6 in 1,000.

Findings indicate that people tend to especially discount very small negative probabilities, treating them as if they were nonexistent. Due to this bias in the processing of risk information, many people are reluctant to insure against low-probability events even if a catastrophic loss potential exists and the insurance is underpriced (in relation to the actuarial risk). For example, flood insurance, despite being federally subsidized, is not easy to sell. Sales do increase after a flood occurs, but only for a few months. Psychologists have examined the style of thinking that supports this undue optimism. It has been found that people tend to overgeneralize from their previous experiences. The person's thinking reflects "It hasn't happened to me yet, so it probably never will."

Two techniques might encourage the purchase of insurance coverage for underestimated perils. One, the insurance should be sold as part of a comprehensive package rather than as a separate policy. Two, a partial refund can be offered to the policyholder during years in which no claims occur.

The refunding concept can be used with other coverages as well. For instance, some companies offer accidental death protection that offers a refund of the full premium paid if, after a certain number of years of continuous coverage (for example, 15 years), no claim is made. The same concept is being used by others to market a fully refundable homeowners insurance, even if claims have been made. The plan, of course, requires a single lump-sum, up-front premium payment that is higher than the standard annual premiums would have been.

Complete Elimination versus Reduction in Risk

Research comparing how people react to a *reduction* in a risk relative to its complete *elimination* suggests that most people place a disproportionately high value on the latter. This mindset might also have implications for the marketing of insurance products.

The high value placed on the elimination of risk may explain why many people get the low deductibles on property and casualty coverages, despite the relatively high premiums. Furthermore, this bias implies that the way a particular coverage's degree of protection is described to a client is very important. For instance, an insurance policy guarding against a particular peril, like fire, may be viewed as either *full* protection against the specific risk or a reduction in the overall probability of property loss. Based on the observed preference for the elimination of a risk compared to its reduction, there is a distinct marketing advantage in focusing on the coverage's *full* protection aspect. Telling a prospective client that buying the policy will lower his or her chances of suffering property damage will have a lower inducement value than will stressing to the client that he or she has *full* protection against fire.

Availability Bias

The most well-documented bias altering people's estimates of risk is called "availability bias." It refers to the fact that events that are easy to imagine or recall will be judged as more probable than they actually are. Events that are dramatic and vivid or that receive heavy media attention are easily available to one's mind and are therefore overestimated. In contrast, events that are dull or abstract are underestimated. A few examples should help explain this particular bias.

- When asked to estimate whether the letter "K" occurs more frequently as the first letter or the third letter in an English word, most people say first. In actuality, the letter "K" appears three times more frequently in the third position of a word. The reason why most people believe otherwise is because it is a lot easier for them to think of words that start with "K."
- Which is more frequent, homicide or suicide? Most people believe that homicide is five times more frequent. Yet suicides are 30 percent more common. People tend to believe that the opposite is true because homicides are reported in the news, whereas suicides are generally not reported (unless the suicide involves a well-known personality).
- People overestimate the probability of dying from accidents in comparison to dying from illnesses. Again, this is because the media devotes more coverage to deaths resulting from events like airplane crashes than to deaths resulting from heart attacks.
- Seeing the movie *Jaws* made the public much more wary of going into the ocean than the actual probabilities of being attacked by a shark warranted.
- People who watch TV frequently tend to overestimate the degree of violence in society because of the violence that occurs on both shows and the news.
- People tend to be more influenced by personal experiences because they are more vivid. Thus research shows that people overestimate the probability of death from diseases that killed people they knew personally. Similarly people tend to be influenced more by anecdotal evidence provided by their friends than by more representative and

trustworthy information contained in statistical reports. Consequently most people when they are in the market for a car will rely more heavily on the experiences of a friend than on a consumer survey report. Accordingly, many individuals who failed to wear a seat belt, despite repeated warnings from various governmental agencies, started to wear one when a friend or neighbor was hurt or killed because a seat belt was not worn. It was only after this personal experience that they began to wear a seat belt. (On a more positive note, because they make information much more vivid, sales presentations incorporating slides or other graphics have proven to be much more successful than purely oral presentations.)

Familiarity Bias

Most people dread the unknown. Risks that are familiar are feared less than risks that are unfamiliar. For example, investors see greater risk in foreign equities than warranted based on historical returns. This sensed fear occurs because they know less about other countries than their own country. In other words, people tend to perceive less risk in things they know. The more a person knows about a country, company, product, or situation, the lower will be his or her perception of risk. For instance, it has been reported that sophisticated investors are more risk tolerant than naive investors. Educating clients about unfamiliar investments may lower their inherent fears.

Typically, people overreact to unexpected news. Studies show that both securities analysts and the lay public overreact to recent information, giving the new (that is, unfamiliar) information more importance than it really deserves. The impact of familiarity can be discerned clearly in both the financial industry's and investors' reactions to the October 1987 stock market drop of 508 points as compared to the drop of 200 points in October 1989. Despite reports after the "miniplunge" of 1989 that the market was fragile, most investors and their advisers were unfazed by the drop, and few advisers received any panicky telephone calls from their clients. A random survey by the publication *Financial Services Week,* conducted after the October 1989 drop, revealed a very unconcerned attitude. One financial adviser who was interviewed in the *Financial Services Week* survey summarized the situation in the following terms:

> I was so disappointed. . . . Not only did I not get any calls from clients, but Monday morning I called up a bunch of clients—I was going to calm them down and let them know that the world had not ended and their consensus was "big deal, so what?"

Illusion of Control Bias

People tend to underestimate the risk involved in activities under their control, like driving a car, relative to activities in which the control is given over to someone else, like flying as a passenger in an airplane. Ironically, the chance of being involved in a car accident driving to the airport to catch a flight is greater than the chance of the airplane crashing.

Time Horizon

In investments, differences can exist between short-run and long-run strategies to maximize return. Therefore it is critical that a time horizon be specified. It has been reported that for most decisions involving an element of risk, the length of the time elapsing between making the decision and the knowledge of the eventual outcome is very crucial. If the time span between these two events is long, the person is more likely to accept the risk than if the time span is relatively short. In other words, if something is imminent, there is an increased sense of danger.

People tend to psychologically overemphasize short-term risks. Some authorities have suggested that people start smoking because the threat of cancer is so far in the future. The long-term risk, although quite threatening, does not seem real to them. (This refusal to consider future risks seriously can be seen in Mark Twain's reaction to being told that, by giving up smoking and drinking, he could add another 5 years to his life. Twain's reaction was that without smoking and drinking another 5 years of living would not be worth it.)

Fortunately, there may be some synergy between people's willingness to bear risk under a broad time horizon and the performance of the riskier investment products. Analysis of historical data has shown that, from a long-term perspective, many of these products were not risky. While they show great volatility in the short run, they are less volatile in the long run. In other words, they are safer when viewed within a broadened investment time horizon.

Unfortunately for their financial well-being, people typically have a short-range rather than long-range planning horizon. The tendency to be myopic about one's investment planning horizon is well illustrated in a study conducted by psychologist R. J. Herrnstein. Herrnstein presented a group of people with the following situation: Let's suppose that you win a lottery that gives you two alternative ways, A and B, of collecting your winnings.

A: You can collect $100 tomorrow.
B: You can collect $115 a week from tomorrow.

Most of the group selected option A, despite the fact that by waiting only one more week they would have been able to earn 15 percent. (There are few investments that would pay 15 percent *per week* interest.)

Next, the people who selected choice A were presented with another hypothetical lottery, in which the two payment schedules were C and D.

C: You can collect $100 in 52 weeks from today.
D: You can collect $115 in 53 weeks from today.

Interestingly, almost all of those who selected payment schedule A now selected payment schedule D. If they were consistent in their behavior, they would have chosen C. There was the same one-week difference between A and B as between C and D. However, the one-week difference meant much more in the present than it did in the future.

Research-based evidence shows that 10 to 15 years is the longest time horizon that most people consider to be practical for planning purposes. Surveys of the general public continue to find that people do recognize that upon retirement they may not have enough income to live in their present style, but they fail to do anything to remedy the situation. The reason typically offered as justification is that they have a more pressing *immediate* crisis or concern. Many people who purchase term insurance instead of permanent insurance, intending to invest the difference in premiums, never do so because more immediate concerns always arise.

Mood

Psychologists have been studying the impact of a person's mood on his or her willingness to undertake a risk. The relationship between mood and risk tolerance is quite complex, given the results of various studies. The research shows that a good mood leads to more positive expectations and lower perceived risk. Conversely, a bad mood leads to increased estimates of risk. However, when it comes to actual behavior, a good mood does not necessarily lead to greater risk taking. While a good mood does increase willingness to take relatively *low risks*, it decreases the person's willingness to accept *high risks*. Perhaps this is because the person does not want to jeopardize his or her good mood.

Some theoreticians attribute the generally lower stock prices on Monday as compared to Friday (known as the weekend effect) to differences in people's moods on Mondays as opposed to Fridays. Monday is said to be an unpleasant day for most people, since it is the start of a work week. On Friday, though, most people are in a pleasant mood because they are anticipating the weekend. These differences in mood are believed to be reflected in stock prices. The same explanation can be extended to the observation that stock returns are generally high in January (the January effect). Since January marks the beginning of a new year, people are generally optimistic, which again shows up in higher prices.

Effects of Alcohol on Risk Taking

Studies have shown that alcohol consumption causes people to become reckless and take greater risks than they would ordinarily. An intriguing result of such experiments is that even those people who *believed* that they were drinking alcoholic beverages—when in reality they were not—also increased their risk-taking behaviors.

Parties Bearing the Consequences of a Decision

The answer to the question "Who will be affected by the consequences of my actions?" is a strong determinant of whether a risk will be acceptable or unacceptable. A decision is most risk averse in nature if its outcomes will have consequences for both the individual making the decision and those the individual cares about. A decision is somewhat less risk averse if only the individual decision maker is affected. The *most* risk-prone decisions are made if only others will bear the consequences of the decision. For instance, managers take more risks when they invest their company's money than when they invest their own personal funds. Studies of stock market trading reveal a similar pattern. If the money being invested is his or her own, the investor requires more information before making a transaction and makes significantly fewer trades.

Group Dynamics of Risk Taking

A phenomenon studied for about 30 years concerns the difference between individual and group reactions to risk. Originally called the "risky shift," today this phenomenon is also known as the "choice shift." It refers to the finding that a group decision is usually more extreme than a decision favored by most members of the group when they are polled individually (before the discussion). Generally the shift is toward more risky action, although in some instances the shift is toward a more cautious attitude. (Hence, the more neutral term *choice shift* is preferred today.)

Several studies on the choice shift phenomenon bear directly on financial planning. In one study people were asked to identify the investment products that they would be willing to buy. The investments available to them ranged from low risk (no variability in their historical return patterns) to high risk (very variable, with low returns in certain years and high returns in other years). First, each person made his or her selection individually. Next, they took part in a group discussion to reach a consensus regarding their choices. While on an individual basis most members of the group wanted the less risky products, the group decision was in favor of the riskier products. There were similar results in another study where the group's task was the selection of an automobile physical damage coverage. When polled individually, the participants were willing to pay, on average, about another $48 in premiums in order to get collision coverage. As a result of the group discussion, however, the consensus was that they would be willing to pay less—only $31—for this particular coverage. In other words, the group was willing to bear more of the risk.

Possible explanations for the shift in the risky direction include the following:

- The responsibility for a decision is shared by the group, so no one person feels totally responsible if it turns out to have been the wrong one.

- The risk-tolerant members in the group are influential.
- As a result of the discussion, the group members become more *familiar* with the situation, and this lessens their inherent fears.

Mental Accounts

Various psychological experiments have been conducted to illustrate how "mental accounts" operate in people's evaluation of monetary gains and losses. One such study shows that the opportunity to save a given amount of money will be viewed quite differently, depending on what mental account a person uses to evaluate the psychological value of this money. Psychologists Daniel Kahneman and Amos Tversky asked people what they would do if they went out to buy a $125 jacket and a $15 calculator, and upon arrival at the main store they were informed by the sales clerk that the calculator was on sale for $10 at a branch store 20 minutes away. Under these circumstances, 68 percent of people were willing to drive 20 minutes to save $5.

In a second version of this same story, the $5 in savings was on the jacket rather than the calculator. (That is, the price of the jacket was $120 at the branch store and $125 at the main store. The price of the calculator was $15 at both stores.) The percentage of people willing to drive 20 minutes to save $5 under the second set of circumstances was only 29 percent.

Five dollars would be saved either way, yet the number of people willing to save this amount of money was substantially different. Why? The simple reason is that people maintain different mental accounts for the prices of jackets and calculators. Money to be gained or lost is not evaluated in a vacuum. Rather, there is always some *subjective standard* that is employed as a yardstick to gauge the value.

The concept of mental accounts has many implications for financial services practitioners. The amount of pleasure or displeasure that the appreciation or depreciation in the value of a certain asset will bring to a client is not necessarily determined by the simple dollar amounts lost or gained. Other factors will influence the client's assessment of the event. For example, did the client's neighbor (or brother or sister) do better or worse? How did a different security that the client considered purchasing fare?

It is necessary for financial services professionals to recognize that because of mental accounts their clients may have different risk-tolerance levels for different funds, depending on how they acquired the money and what they intend to do with it. Inherited versus earned money is one factor that may account for different risk-tolerance levels. Some people who inherit hard-earned money from a loved relative refuse to risk losing the principal. With money they earned personally, however, they may have less fear of potential loss. For others, the reverse may be true.

People's mental accounting for posting gains and losses does not treat money earned and money lost as equal units. Money lost carries a much heavier psychological value. For instance, making $5,000 on an investment, provided that this return is equal to what was expected, will make a client happy. Conversely, losing $5,000 on an investment will make a client unhappy. Research shows, however, that the unhappiness experienced at losing the $5,000 is greater than the happiness felt at earning $5,000. Therefore clients are apt to be more upset about a given loss than pleased about an equivalent gain. Similarly most investors feel worse if they sell a security that shortly thereafter increases in value than if they failed to buy the security in the first place.

Mental accounting may also be the underlying cause for the finding that most investors prefer cash dividends over capital gains. Dividends and capital gains are placed into separate mental accounts according to some theorists.

RISK TAKING: SITUATION-SPECIFIC OR GENERAL PERSONALITY TRAIT

Some financial planners tend to describe people as risk takers or risk averters, without considering the type of behaviors on which they base such classifications. It is as if they expect people to act in a similar manner in all aspects of life. Yet psychologists are still debating whether most people have a consistent pattern of risk taking in all realms of their lives or whether the degree of risk they are willing to assume depends on the nature of the situation. Although some evidence suggests that there is a *slight* predisposition to act in either a risk-taking or risk-averse manner in different situations, this predisposition is weak for most persons. Only persons with the personality type that psychologists call the "thrill seeker" (also known as the "sensation" or "arousal" seeker) seem to be relatively consistent.

In general, the more similar any two situations are, the greater is the consistency in risk-taking behavior in these two situations. Research has shown that essentially four major types of life situations involve risk taking:

- *Monetary* situations involve such risks as investments, gambling, or job changes.
- *Physical* situations involve risks that could result in bodily harm, such as mountain climbing or skydiving.
- *Social* situations involve risks that could lead to loss of self-esteem or another person's respect.
- *Ethical* situations involve risks in which one is faced with the prospect of compromising one's moral or religious standards or society's legal standards. (For example, trading on insider information involves an ethical risk.)

These four risk contexts have been described, based on their consequences, as the potential loss of capital (monetary risk), the potential loss of life (physical risk), the potential loss of face (social risk), and the potential loss of freedom (ethical risk).

Cases in which the level of risk taking is quite different across different contexts are not hard to find, as many people change their behavior from situation to situation. The author was told of one, a Navy pilot who had been decorated for heroism during the Vietnam War. After his discharge from the service, this individual was encouraged to begin a career in life insurance sales. His new career proved to be both financially and emotionally unrewarding, however, because he was uncomfortable with prospecting. This came as a surprise to the person's manager since there was clear-cut evidence of fearlessness and risk taking in the person's war record. The ex-pilot and his manager had a discussion about his fear of prospecting. During the course of the conversation, it became evident to the manager that it was actually a low level of social risk tolerance that accounted for this person's high physical risk tolerance during the war. The individual related that what kept him flying was the fear of disapproval by others. As he put it, whenever he got jittery about a mission and thought of turning back, all he had to do was picture the look of disapproval from his commander and fellow pilots. In this case, low tolerance for social risk was, in part, responsible for high physical risk tolerance.

One should be careful in using risk taking in nonfinancial matters to infer a level of risk tolerance for investments. Knowing that someone is a risk taker in a certain physical activity provides clues about how the individual will react in other situations that involve potential bodily harm. However, this information provides little insight as to whether this person will be willing to invest in a financially risky venture. The latter information is best determined from a knowledge of the person's typical behavior in monetary risk-taking situations. Therefore a financial planner who promotes an "aggressive" mutual fund to a skydiving club should not be surprised if the responses to the ad are not dramatically greater than responses from the general public. The best predictor of an investor's risk tolerance in a financial matter is his or her risk preference in other financial matters, rather than how the person reacts to risk in sports, social situations, and so on.

The client's risk tolerance in financial matters should be of primary concern to the financial planner, since this is the aspect of the client's situation that is within the planner's purview. However, there may be some value in looking at the client's total risk-taking disposition. First, the client could learn that he or she may not necessarily have the same propensity for risk in money matters as in physical activities or social activities. Often clients assume that they have a general predisposition to take on the same level of risk in all spheres of life. Second, consistency across different contexts may alert the financial planner to whether the individual is someone who is a thrill seeker (discussed later in this chapter).

Physical risk taking could be a relevant issue when determining a client's insurance needs. It has been shown that risk taking in the physical realm is a major factor in various types of accidents. Therefore people who have high levels of physical risk tolerance are more apt to die from accidental causes or to suffer disabling injuries from an accident. According to the *Statistical Bulletin* published by the Metropolitan Life Companies, accidents are the *leading* cause of death among children and young adults. When the U.S. population is considered as a whole, accidental death is third in line after death due to cardiovascular diseases or cancer. Deaths from motor vehicle accidents account for approximately half of the accidental deaths reported in this country. Accidental death riders and disability income insurance may be of interest to the physical risk taker, especially if the individual has, at the same time, a low level of monetary risk tolerance.

Physical risk taking is also a contributing factor in death from nonaccidental causes. Consequently risk taking in health-related matters is of increasing concern to insurance companies. It is now standard for insurance carriers to charge lower premiums for nonsmokers, and an emergent trend may be to extend similar premium reductions to people who avoid other health risks as well. Because of the AIDS epidemic, a growing area of research—some sponsored by the insurance industry—is concerned with risk taking in sexual behaviors (a form of physical risk taking).

LIFESTYLE OF THE RISK TAKER

Most of the early studies on the personality of the typical risk taker assumed that risk taking was a general personality trait rather than being specific to a particular context. Therefore the measures of risk taking used in these studies did not differentiate between attitudes toward physical, social, ethical, and monetary risk taking. As such, one needs to exercise caution in utilizing these findings in financial planning since they may apply more to one of the other categories of risk taking than to monetary risk taking in particular.

For example, the following life experiences that some researchers identify as typical of the risk taker probably apply more to physical risk takers than monetary risk takers:

- took dares as a child
- drank and smoked at an early age
- was sexually active at a young age
- enjoys dangerous leisure activities, such as mountain climbing, surfing, hang gliding, scuba diving, racing a car, motorcycling, or skydiving
- is likely to hold a job as a pilot, soldier, fireman, or policeman

Likewise, the following characteristics of risk takers may be related mostly to social risk taking:

- has a social presence
- is self-accepting
- is self-confident
- is aggressive
- is independent
- is irresponsible
- is status-seeking
- has strong leadership abilities
- is unaccepting of other people's opinions

Similarly, the finding that risk takers feel low levels of guilt for wrongdoing probably applies more to the ethical risk taker than to the physical, monetary, or social risk taker.

Other characteristics identified in this type of research may, however, also apply to monetary risk takers. Among these are the following:

- emphasizes merit rather than seniority in job promotions
- enjoys work that involves decision making
- requires little time to make a major decision
- completes tests that have a time limit very quickly, attempting to compensate for more mistakes by answering more questions
- takes a chance and guesses on tests that impose a penalty for guessing (such as the Scholastic Aptitude Test)
- is optimistic, seeing mistakes as setbacks, not personal failures
- has a low need for an ordered environment
- is able to handle stress
- is persistent

The following characteristics may also distinguish between monetary risk averters and risk takers in their outlook on life:

Risk Averter	Risk Taker
• sees risk as danger	• sees risk as challenge or opportunity
• overestimates risk	• underestimates risk
• prefers low variability	• prefers high variability
• adopts the worst-case scenario (emphasizes the probability of loss)	• adopts the best-case scenario (emphasizes the probability of a win)

• is pessimistic	• is optimistic
• likes structure	• likes ambiguity
• dislikes change	• enjoys change
• prefers certainty to uncertainty	• prefers uncertainty to certainty

Few studies have focused on the biographical and psychological characteristics of monetary risk takers per se. Research conducted by psychologist Frank Farley is an exception. His studies indicate that monetary risk takers are good money managers who spend considerable time reading about investments and related financial matters and express confidence in their money-making abilities. In contrast to the monetary risk averters, who stated that their long-term goal was happiness, the monetary risk takers listed success as their primary goal. Farley also found that monetary risk takers tend to possess leadership skills and good sales skills. For many monetary risk takers, money is the center of their lives

A 1993 study of mutual fund shareholders, sponsored by the mutual fund industry trade association, indicates that investors with high risk tolerance have clear financial goals. They were also more likely to be raised in homes that had an interest in investing, discussed such matters, and actually invested. In describing the outcomes of their families' investments, the high risk takers were more likely to indicate that it was successful. High-risk-tolerant mutual fund owners made their own first investment at an earlier age than their low-risk-tolerant counterparts, and their first investment was more likely to be an individual stock. The first investment for low-risk-tolerant mutual fund owners was more likely to be real estate.

Compared to low and moderate risk takers, high-risk-tolerant shareholders in this study were more apt to have confidence in their ability to make their own investment decisions, rather than relying on the advice of professionals. They used magazines and newspapers as their primary source of investment information to make these decisions. High-risk-tolerant shareholders were also more likely to read the mutual funds prospectus for investing information (that is, 38 percent of the high risk takers versus 25 percent of the moderate risk takers and 13 percent of the low risk takers). The same pattern was found in the readership of investment newsletters (26 percent, 19 percent, and 15 percent respectively for high, moderate, and low risk takers.) Low risk takers, in contrast, indicated that they were confused by the multitude of investment choices, and therefore relied on others for advice; their most frequent sources of information were friends, family, and business associates. The high-risk-tolerant investors were more likely to actually adapt a long-term view of their investments, even though the low and moderate risk takers agree just as strongly that a long-term strategy leads to the best results. Low risk takers seem overly concerned about short-term fluctuations. (See figure 7-1.)

FIGURE 7-1
Sources of Financial Information by Level of Risk Tolerance

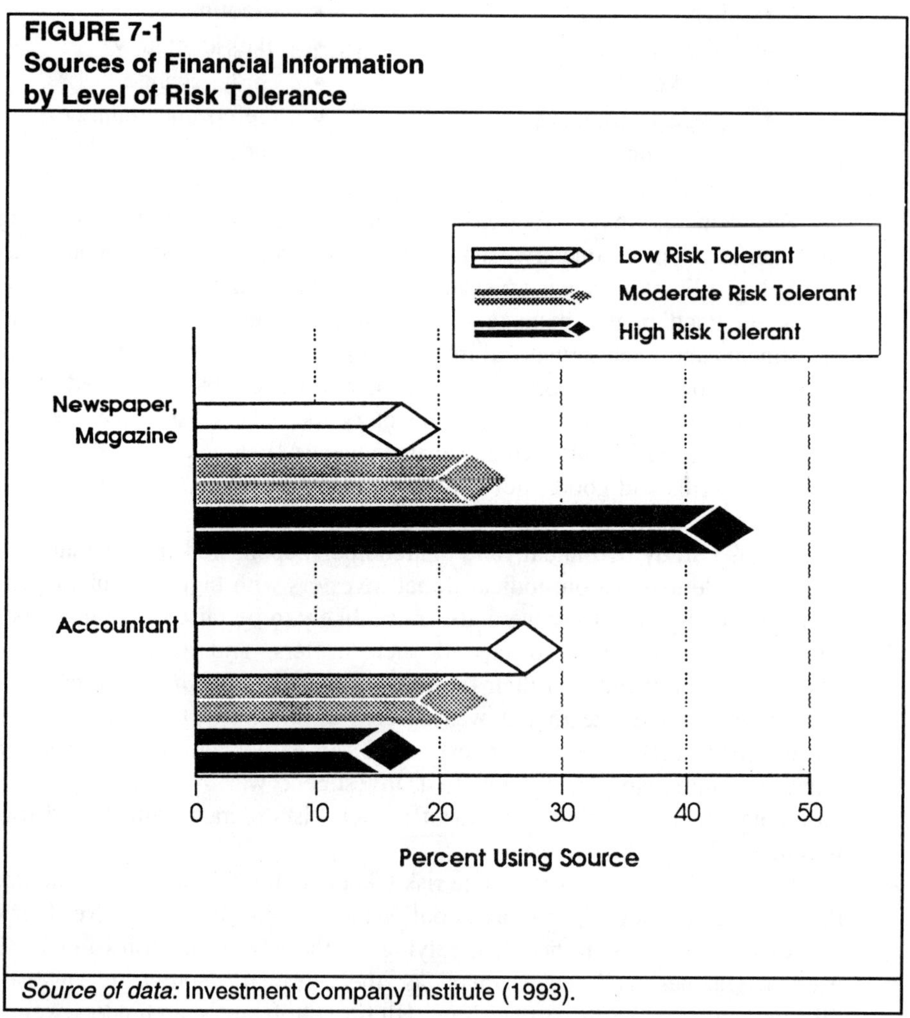

Source of data: Investment Company Institute (1993).

The groups were also compared on their knowledge of investment principles, and as one might expect, the high-risk-tolerant group showed the best understanding of the subject.

Another significant survey comparing the investment attitudes of risk-tolerant and risk-intolerant investors concerns their satisfaction with the returns they previously received on their investments. Whereas risk-averse investors are generally satisfied, those who are risk tolerant tend to feel that they were not adequately compensated.

THE THRILL SEEKER

The thrill seeker is the personality type most likely to be *consistently* risk seeking across all dimensions of life, including financial matters. Sometimes a distinction is made between physical thrill seekers and mental thrill seekers. However, all thrill seekers abhor routine, be it mental or physical. These individuals are always on the lookout for experiences that offer novelty, ambiguity, complexity, and intensity. If a thrill seeker can't find excitement, he or she will create it. "In-and-out" trading in the stock market, for instance, provides many such quick thrills. For the thrill seeker, the uncertainty of an investment decision may hold as much enticement, perhaps even more, than the anticipated payoff. To the thrill seeker, money made from a safe investment does not hold as much value as the same amount of money made from a risky investment. There is some research showing that thrill seekers have a biologically based need for greater than normal levels of arousal.

Thrill seeking can have either very constructive or very destructive outlets. For example, constructive mental outlets are available in the arts or sciences, fields that reward the creative thinking characteristic of the thrill seeker. Crime, in turn, provides a common destructive outlet for both mental and physical thrill seeking. Even in prison, thrill seekers are a problem, because they continually try to escape.

It is important to realize that not everyone who takes many risks is necessarily a thrill seeker, although by definition, every thrill seeker must be considered a risk taker. How can a financial planner spot the thrill seeker? To a certain extent, the thrill seeker is a caricature of a risk taker, showing many of the same basic characteristics, but in a markedly exaggerated form. In addition to the characteristics already mentioned in defining the thrill-seeking personality, the financial planner should be alert to those that follow.

Thrill seeking is more common among men than women. Thrill seekers enjoy loud parties. They tend to be outgoing, spontaneous, and fast decision makers. In looking for a history of sensation seeking, the planner needs to check to see if the person participates in risky sports and likes to gamble, especially at blackjack. A history of traffic violations is common. Thrill seekers may associate with unconventional persons and have an intense dislike for people they perceive as boring. The thrill seeker seeks variety in his or her sex life. If the thrill seeker uses recreational drugs, a variety of drugs rather than just one drug are taken.

Thrill seekers may appear to be perfect candidates for risky investments, given their obviously high tolerance for risk. But this very desire for novel, intense, and varied experiences, may lead the thrill seeker to pursue legal action against the planner for suggesting an overly risky product if the investment does not produce the expected returns. With this type of client, the planner must take particular care in documenting due diligence.

DEMOGRAPHIC CHARACTERISTICS

Numerous studies have been conducted over the years in which risk tolerance was related to such things as birth order, age, wealth, education, age, gender, marital status, and occupation. The results of this research are discussed below.

Wealth

Do wealthy individuals take more risks with their money? First, a distinction must be drawn between *absolute* and *relative* risk tolerance. Absolute risk tolerance is gauged by the *amount* of wealth one allocates to risky assets. Relative risk tolerance, in contrast, is measured by the *proportion* of one's wealth allocated to risky assets. It is generally accepted that absolute risk tolerance increases with wealth, since the wealthy have more money to spend on *everything*. There is some disagreement, though, about whether relative risk tolerance increases with wealth. Several studies have addressed this question by examining people's investment portfolios. One such study, conducted by R. A. Cohn and his colleagues, found that relative risk tolerance does increase with wealth—the wealthier a person was, the greater the proportion of total wealth that person put in risky assets. For instance, if the individual's assets were above $175,000, on average, 62 percent of his or her investments were risky. If the total value of assets was below $175,000, only 42 percent of the investments were of the risky type. This pattern held even after sex, age, and marital status were taken into account. However, this relationship between wealth and risk tolerance was strongest among male investors and married investors.

Some researchers have been unable to find such relationships. One reason for the discrepancy is attributable to differences in the type of assets considered and how these assets were classified (safe versus risky). The way the primary residence is treated seems to be especially critical. Relative risk tolerance goes up with increasing wealth if housing is either excluded from the definition of wealth or classified as a riskless asset.

There is further support for a positive relationship between relative risk tolerance and wealth in studies using questionnaires as the basis for determining the degree of risk tolerance. In the survey sponsored by the Insurance Information Institute cited at the beginning of this chapter, it was reported that the wealthy were more likely to associate the word *risk* with the word *opportunity* than the other respondents. Similarly, a study of the upper affluent sponsored by CIGNA found that the risk takers in this group were more likely to have higher incomes and were much more likely to be millionaires. The "chicken and egg" question still remains—did the wealthy become so because of their greater willingness to assume risk, or is it that they are more risk taking now that they are wealthy? That is, does having money make one more risk seeking?

How money was acquired may also be a factor in the risk-taking propensity characteristic of the wealthy. Differences in risk tolerance have been reported between those who inherited their wealth and those who made their fortune themselves. Namely, people who earned their own wealth are more risk tolerant than those who inherited their wealth.

Some evidence suggests that a majority of the millionaires alive today did not inherit their wealth. In an interview with *Financial Services Week* (March 5, 1990), consultant Steve Moeller reports that 60 percent of millionaires made their fortunes by starting their own businesses. According to Moeller, the profile of the average millionaire is as follows: married, male, 57 years old, some college education, blue-collar family background, annual income of $130,000. Millionaires who acquired their own wealth prefer to make their own decisions, so Moeller recommends that financial planners present such individuals with a variety of investment options. Other evidence indicates that those who inherit their money are more receptive to financial planning advice than those who made their money themselves.

Education

Numerous studies have found that financial risk tolerance increases with degree of formal education. Riley and Chow, for instance, looked at the percentage of total wealth held in risky assets by individuals with differing levels of education and made the following observations.

Education	Percentage of Wealth in Risky Assets
Less than high school	2.0%
High school diploma	3.4%
Some college	5.2%
College degree	7.9%
Post graduate	8.0%

Among the mutual fund shareholders studied by the Investment Company Institute, the percentage of investors with at least a 4-year college degree increases with risk tolerance (39 percent among the low risk tolerant, 57 percent among the moderate risk tolerant, and 66 percent among the high risk tolerant). The reason for this relationship is not entirely clear, however. Because education is correlated with income and wealth, it could be that it is the latter two variables that account for the greater risk tolerance among the better educated, rather than education *per se.* It is also possible that people with higher levels of education become familiar with the range of investment options available to them.

Age

Recently, mutual fund investors were asked whether they agree or disagree with the statement, "The older people get, the less willing they are to take investment risk." Ratings were to be made on a scale from 0 to 10, with 0 indicating no agreement and 10 indicating strong agreement. Mostly, people agree with this statement, since the average rating was 7.6. Low-risk-tolerant, moderate-risk-tolerant, and high-risk-tolerant shareholders were compared on their opinions about this issue, and surprising differences were noted. The low-risk-tolerant investors were most likely to agree with this statement (average rating = 8.6), while the high-risk-tolerant investors were least likely to agree with it (average rating = 6.7). The moderate risk takers fell in the middle (average rating = 7.5).

Who is correct? A substantial body of research exists on the relationship between age and risk taking in all sorts of activities, financial as well as nonfinancial. The bulk of this research points to a negative or inverse relationship between age and willingness to take risks. That is, as one gets older, one becomes more cautious. For instance, the 1993 Investment Company Institute Study of Risk Tolerance (cited previously) found that the average ages of their low-, moderate-, and high-risk-tolerant investors were 60, 51, and 42 years, respectively.

The observed relationship between financial risk taking and age has been linked to biological factors. An article published in the *Financial Analysts Journal* (November/December 1990), titled "Understanding and Assessing Financial Risk Tolerance: A Biological Perspective," reported that an enzyme, monoamine oxidase (MAO) is found in higher concentrations among the risk averse, and that MAO levels increase with age. (It was noted in jest in a review of this article in the *CFA Journal* that a practical application of this research could be a blood test to determine the client's level of risk tolerance.)

Some qualifiers are in order, however. This relationship between more advanced age and increased caution may not be as strong for monetary risks as it is for physical risks. Moreover, the relationship between monetary risk tolerance and age may be weaker among the wealthy, according to some studies. It has been suggested that when looking at the impact of age on risk taking one also needs to consider the client's particular circumstances. For instance, some financial planners report that they have encountered middle-aged couples who were previously very conservative investors but who now take an interest in aggressive investing because their obligations to raise and educate their children are at an end.

Gender

The study of psychological differences between men and women has a long history. Almost all research prior to the women's movement indicates that men are more risk tolerant than women in most aspects of life. Both biologically based and psychologically based explanations have been offered. One psychological explanation is that women have been socialized to be more dependent and risk-averse.

The results of more recent studies are mixed. Some newer studies encourage consideration of age and income when looking at sex differences in monetary risk taking. While older married women are less likely to accept financial risks than their husbands, the differences in financial risk taking between younger men and women with comparable incomes are either small or nonexistent.

Recent polls also reveal the changing attitudes toward financial risks among women. For instance, a *Ms. Magazine* poll conducted in 1977 found that only 26 percent of their readers would invest a cash windfall rather than keep it in a savings account. When the same poll was repeated in 1988, 40 percent of the respondents indicated that they would be willing to take risks in order to obtain a higher potential return. Also stock ownership in this group increased. About 33 percent of the 1988 respondents owned stocks, compared to 24 percent of the 1977 respondents.

Other gender-related differences between men and women have also been declining. For example, a recent review of the literature found that the difference favoring males in mathematics skills was larger in studies published before 1974 than in studies published after that date.

Birth Order

Although there is only limited research on the topic, it appears that birth order is related to risk taking. Namely, the firstborn child tends to be less willing to take risks than the later-born children in the same family. The favorite explanation is that parents exert greater control over the early life of the firstborn child and instill in him or her the need to be dependable and act responsibly. To the child, this means not taking unnecessary chances.

Marital Status

Single individuals appear more risk tolerant than married individuals in some studies, and more risk averse in other studies. The reason for the conflicting results is a failure to consider whether both spouses are employed. The key is the presence of dependents, rather than marital status per se. If the individual feels that his or her actions might have negative consequences for dependents, then he or she is likely to be more cautious. In dual-income families, the spouse's level of risk tolerance may be no less than that of a single person, because neither party is the dependent under these circumstances. In fact, a dual income may increase the level of risk tolerance. For example, a study of mutual fund shareholders found that among married low-risk-tolerant investors, 61 percent of the spouses worked, compared to 73 percent of the high-risk-tolerant married households.

Other research indicates that widowed and separated people are more risk-averse than either never-married persons or persons who are currently married.

Occupation

Most people spend much of their adult life working. Certainly the types of jobs they hold in some way relate to risk tolerance. Several aspects related to occupation and risk tolerance have been studied and are discussed below.

Public-Sector versus Private-Sector Employment

One important manifestation of financial risk-taking propensity is the need for job security—the greater the probability of becoming unemployed, the greater the financial riskiness in that occupation. Thus one would expect monetarily risk-averse individuals to gravitate toward jobs that offer security, even if the pay is lower. It is generally accepted that the public sector offers greater job security. A number of studies have compared the monetary risk-taking propensities of private-sector and public-sector employees. This research points to greater risk aversion among public-sector employees.

Professionals versus Nonprofessionals

According to the results of some studies, professionals (physicians, lawyers, managers, and so on) tend to be more risk taking in investment decisions than nonprofessionals (farmers, unskilled and skilled laborers, clerical workers, and so on). This disparity is perhaps due to differences in the level of sophistication about investment matters. As mentioned earlier, risk tolerance tends to increase with increased knowledge and familiarity.

Risk tolerance differences within a given profession cannot be explained in these terms, however. Certain reports indicate that professionals in private practice or professionals working for small firms are more risk tolerant than individuals in the same profession who are employed by large firms. Among physicians, differences have also been observed between surgeons and physicians in other specialties (internists, for example). Specifically, surgeons reportedly are more likely to be risk tolerant than other physicians.

Length of Job Tenure

Chances of advancement decrease the longer a person remains in one position. Remaining with the same company at the same job especially lowers one's future advancement opportunities. Again, many financially risk-averse people remain in positions that offer few possibilities for upward mobility because of financial security needs. Financial risk takers, in contrast, change jobs quite frequently (that is, they are *job hoppers*).

Management Level

Studies comparing the risk-tolerance levels of managers at different levels within an organization usually find that the risk takers hold more senior level positions, earn higher incomes, and have greater authority. Risk takers are also more likely to work as managers in small rather than large firms.

Salary versus Commission

A recent study examined the personality characteristics of job seekers and how these characteristics related to the compensation system preferred by the job seeker. It was determined that risk-averse individuals were more attracted to positions and organizations that offered a fixed rather than a contingent (upon performance) pay system. Moreover, risk-averse individuals did not consider pay level to be as important a criterion in the job they were seeking.

Monetary risk takers are well represented in occupations in which all or a substantial portion of the earnings depend on commissions. Moreover, the more successful performers in such jobs generally take higher risks. It has been found, for example, that the risk-taking individual is more likely to pursue one or two large accounts instead of a large number of small accounts.

Entrepreneurship

According to the Small Business Administration, about 75 percent of new business ventures fail within 5 years. Given the financial risks involved, one would naturally expect people who are successful entrepreneurs to be high risk takers. Surprisingly, however, research points to only a moderate propensity for taking risks among entrepreneurs. In other words, risk taking is not the characteristic that differentiates entrepreneurs from nonentrepreneurs. Rather, it seems to be the need for independence—to be one's own boss—and a need to achieve. This pattern of motivation may explain the preference for moderate levels of risk over low and high levels of risk. People with a strong need to achieve prefer moderate levels of risk where skill can have a marked influence on the outcome. In low-risk situations, everyone can achieve the desired outcome, whereas in high-risk situations, it becomes more a matter of luck than skill.

COMMUNICATING PROBABILITY STATEMENTS VERBALLY

Poor communication between client and financial adviser is responsible for many of the allegations of investment unsuitability filed against financial services professionals. Typically, the client claims that the risks of the investment were not conveyed adequately. This brings us to the issue of communicating probabilities of success and failure to one's clients.

Research indicates that people prefer to obtain information about the probability of an event in numerical form, yet are generally more comfortable describing the probability of an event to others in words rather than in numbers. Perhaps it is because in everyday situations it is not always possible to assign an exact probability to outcomes. But what does it mean to clients if their financial planner tells them that a certain investment will *probably* double their money in 6 years, while another investment offers only a *low chance* of producing this rate of appreciation?

It has been suggested that at least 282 words and phrases can be used to report the likelihood of something happening. A number of researchers have attempted to quantify these expressions by asking people questions like: "If you were told that an outcome was ______ [the blank being filled in by a word or phrase], what percentage would best represent the probability of that outcome occurring?" Table 7-1 shows the percentages that were assigned to the 18 most commonly used expressions. The intent is to provide the financial planner with a basis for determining how these terms would be understood by clients if he or she were to use them in communicating estimates of the probabilities of various investment opportunities. For example, on average, "almost impossible" is

TABLE 7-1
Correspondence between Numerical Probability and Verbal Probability Statements

Numerical	Verbal
2%	Almost impossible
5	Very improbable
10	Very unlikely; very low chance
15	Improbable; unlikely
20	Low chance
40	Possible
50	Medium chance; even chance
70	Probable; likely
80	Very possible; very probable; high chance
85	Very likely
90	Very high chance; almost certain

Source of data: Reagan, Mosteller, and Youtz (1989).

understood as having a 2 percent (2 in 100) chance of occurring. The phrases "medium chance" and "even chance," in turn, are understood to represent about a 50 percent chance of occurring. Research conducted in 1993 by the Investment Company Institute dealt with how much risk certain investment terms connoted for mutual fund shareholders. Participants in this study were asked to indicate, on a scale of 0 (no risk) to 10 (great risk), how much risk they associated with an investment described by the particular term. The mean ratings for the terms can be found in figure 7-2. These ratings ranged from 7.2 to 3.2, with "high yield" conveying the greatest risk and "guaranteed investment" connoting the lowest risk. Other terms suggesting high risk were "emerging growth" (6.9), "maximum return" (6.7), and "international" (6.6). Other terms suggesting low risk were "fixed rate" (3.5) and "tax free" (3.7).

FIGURE 7-2
Degree of Risk Connoted by Selected Investment Terms

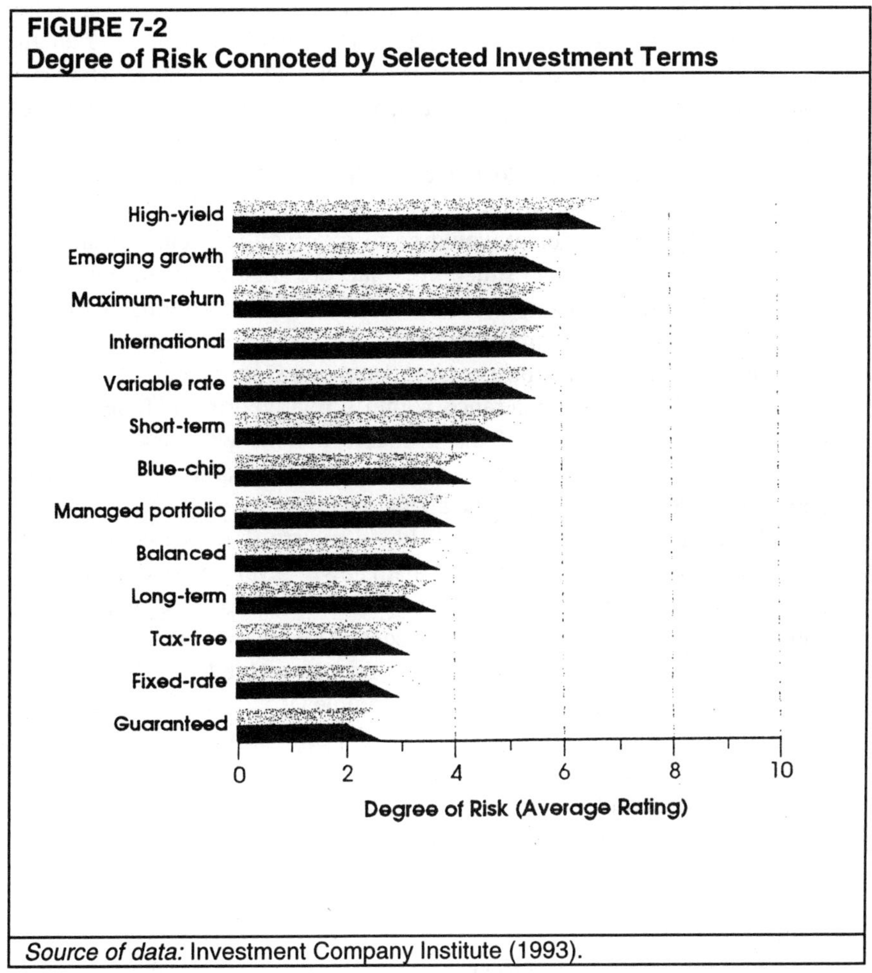

Source of data: Investment Company Institute (1993).

It was reported that low, moderate, and high risk-taking shareholders did not vary much in their assessment, other than for the term "maximum return" and "international." "Maximum return" implied *less* risk for low-risk-tolerant investors than for moderate or high-risk-tolerant investors, whereas "international" connoted more risk for the low-risk-tolerant investors relative to the other two groups.

When communicating with clients, planners need to be aware of differences in linguistic style between men and women. In the *Harvard Business Review* (September-October 1995), Deborah Tannen reports the finding that women tend to downplay their certainty about things whereas men tend to minimize their doubts.

ASSESSMENT OF THE CLIENT'S RISK TOLERANCE

Purpose of Assessment

So far, some of the factors that exert an influence of one sort or another on a person's willingness to undertake a risky course of action have been examined. Now comes the issue of assessment. How does one measure a client's *typical* level of risk tolerance? By typical, we mean the level at which the aforementioned distortions do not cause the client to make decisions that are either riskier or safer than would generally be characteristic of that individual.

The best way, of course, would be to observe the client repeatedly over an extended time period in situations that are likely to reveal his or her characteristic risk-tolerance level. Of course, this is not really feasible since it would be unreasonably time-consuming for the financial planner and would constitute an unwarranted intrusion for the client. Consequently there is a need to estimate the client's risk tolerance within a relatively short time period. In the sections that follow, some of the available options will be considered. All of these options call for sensitivity to appropriate cues and an ability to integrate them into a total impression of the client.

Whatever method is used, one should realize the assessment process; it is meant to help clients *understand* their own level of risk tolerance. Quite frequently, clients are not aware of how risk-tolerant or risk-averse they are. To them risk tolerance is a vague concept that requires both explanation and exploration. The purpose of assessment is not to enable the planner to *impose* his or her perceptions on the client. For example, it is inappropriate to advise the client that the choice is between "eating" (risky investments) and "sleeping" (nonrisky investments). In the end, it is the client who must decide what constitutes an acceptable level of risk. The planner's role is to help the client learn enough about himself or herself to be able to make an informed decision.

Assessment Methods

Many practitioners fail to appreciate the complexity of the task facing them in trying to determine a client's risk tolerance accurately. Considerable time and effort are required to do it correctly. The primary problem is that, frequently, the various techniques do not give the same picture of a particular person's level of risk tolerance. All too often the individual may appear to be a risk taker when assessed with one technique and a risk averter when assessed with another. For example, in one study employing 16 different assessment procedures, the percentage of people who could be classified as risk takers ranged from 0 percent to 94 percent, depending on the technique used. Practically, this means that more than one approach should be employed for an accurate assessment of a client's risk-taking propensity.

Contrasts between Qualitative and Quantitative Assessment

The assessment process can be either *qualitative* or *quantitative* in its orientation. When one relies on a qualitative approach, one typically collects the necessary information primarily through conversations with the client, without assigning numbers to the information gathered. The information is collected in an unstructured format and is evaluated on an intuitive or impressionistic basis, based on the planner's training and experience. A quantitative approach, in contrast, relies on the use of a structured format—questionnaires, for example—that allows one to translate observations into some type of numerical score. These scores are then used to interpret the client's risk-taking propensities.

Most planners do not rely on one approach to the exclusion of the other. For example, few quantitatively oriented planners are willing to surrender their professional judgment to the results of a questionnaire. It is really a matter of degree of how qualitative or quantitative one planner is compared to another. One can use a primarily qualitative approach and still not forfeit some of the advantages of quantifiable information. Questionnaires and other quantitative devices can be valuable tools in the hands of any skilled financial planner.

Often a questionnaire, or similar device, used to assess a client's risk tolerance can facilitate the beginning of a dialogue between the planner and the client. The content of the questionnaire highlights issues that the client may not have thought about. Another advantage is that a quantitative approach allows one to standardize the assessment process.

A number of limitations are inherent in a strictly qualitative approach—one in which the financial planner relies solely on the verbal comments made by a client and interprets their significance on an intuitive basis. One study found that financial planners (like all people) are overconfident about their ability to make intuitive judgments. The planners, presented with various statements that clients could make, were asked to evaluate the level of risk tolerance these statements implied on a 10-point scale, where 1 indicated low risk tolerance and 10 indicated high risk tolerance.

It is understandable that an ambiguous statement such as "Taking calculated risks is different from being rash" would receive ratings as low as 4 and as high as 8. (The average was 6.7.) However, even on more straightforward statements there was also a lack of consensus. The statement "I like to speculate on my investments," if made by a client, was interpreted, on average, as an 8.5. However, again there was diversity of opinion about its meaning. Some financial planners saw the statement as meriting only a rating of 5 whereas others assigned it a rating of 10. "Rubber yardsticks" of this type can be minimized in a quantitative-assessment approach.

When using a qualitative orientation to the assessment of risk tolerance, the planner should be familiar with good interviewing skills. There are standards for quantitative assessment procedures as well, most of which are beyond the scope of this chapter. Suffice it to say that a quantitative measurement device, such as a test or even a questionnaire, needs to be constructed very carefully. The questions should be written in such a way that they do not lead or bias the individual to answer them in a certain way. Moreover, evidence must be provided to demonstrate that the test or questionnaire does, in fact, assess the attributes it is meant to measure and that it measures them accurately on a consistent basis.

Provided that they are accurate, the best quantitative measurement devices are ones that allow the planner to compare the standing of a particular individual to a representative group. A measurement device of this sort is said to have "norms." Using such norms, one can compare the individual to the public at large, or to some subgroup. For instance, using a normed measure of risk tolerance, it is possible to see whether the client is more or less risk tolerant than people in general or to compare the client to other people of the same age and sex.

Unfortunately, most of the tests, inventories, scales, checklists, and questionnaires employed today by financial planners to measure their clients' risk tolerance have not been developed under such strict standards. A majority were created for in-house use by individual planners, brokerage houses, or mutual funds. Many of the developers of these assessment devices are probably unaware of such requirements. There is a critical need for well-constructed questionnaires that provide some evidence to support their use as measures of risk tolerance.

Most of the available assessment devices suffer from the same problems. In some, the wrong questions are asked, or they are presented in an incorrect format. Many devices are too short, thereby failing to contain an adequate representation of questions. It has been demonstrated repeatedly that answers to similar questions about risk tolerance may not concur. In order to avoid being misled by the answer to any one question, the financial planner needs to ask a *series* of questions. Some answers may underestimate the client's true level of risk tolerance, whereas others may overestimate the true level of this attribute. Other things being equal, the more questions that are used to measure a psychological characteristic, the more precise are the results.

Some questionnaires do not separate the different contexts of risk taking, so that a high score on such a questionnaire is probably better at identifying tendencies toward thrill seeking rather than high risk tolerance for investment matters. For all these reasons, one must exercise caution in using questionnaires. It is strongly recommended that the financial planner examine the content of the questionnaire. A "questionnaire" or "checklist" or "inventory" purporting to assess risk tolerance may, in fact, be measuring some other attribute.

Many techniques can be used to assess a client's risk tolerance. Some lend themselves more to a qualitative approach, whereas others call for a more quantitative approach. In the section that follows, a brief overview of the most common approaches is provided. In essence, such techniques consist of looking at the client's

- investment objectives
- preferences for various investment vehicles
- real-life choices involving risk
- attitudes toward risk
- preferences for different probabilities and payoff levels

Examination of Client Investment Objectives

Frequently clients are asked to identify their financial objectives. For example, the client may be asked to indicate how important the following are to him or her: liquidity, safety of principal, appreciation, protection from inflation, current income, and tax reduction. The client's level of risk tolerance is inferred from the answers. If the client's primary concerns are safety of principal and/or liquidity, then risk aversion is assumed. If, however, the main objectives are protection from inflation or tax relief, then the inference is that the client is risk tolerant.

Objectives, however, must not be confused with risk tolerance. There are many individuals who desire tax relief yet are quite risk-averse. One's stated objectives may, in fact, be quite incompatible with one's level of risk tolerance. In many cases the client may be unaware of this incongruity. In a sense, the client's level of risk tolerance should be the basis for evaluating how reasonable the client's objectives are. However, using objectives for the purpose of gauging risk tolerance, without any further attempts to assess actual risk tolerance, is a mistake. To do so is to have "the tail wag the dog."

Preferences for Various Investment Products

This is the most direct approach to measuring a client's risk tolerance. With this method, the client indicates the products that he or she prefers as investments. Several variations of this procedure exist. In its simplest form, the client is presented with the available alternatives and is then asked how he or she wishes to distribute available assets among these options. The products are usually presented in some rank order, ranging from very safe investments to very risky investments. Either actual (real) or imaginary funds can be used. For the latter variation of this task, the client is asked something like, "What would you do if you got a windfall?" Naturally people tend to be more daring with imaginary money than with actual money. A third variation of this approach is to ask the client to rank the products from most preferred to least preferred or to assign to each product some rating that represents the client's level of preference (for example, low, medium, or high).

The accuracy of this procedure (in all its variants) rests on the client's knowledge of the actual risk-return potential of the various investments. Preferably these differences are explained and specified to the client, since many clients may lack even basic knowledge. One should never assume that clients are highly knowledgeable about financial matters. Surveys of the general public, including the wealthy, reveal a startling level of financial ignorance.

Real-Life Choices Involving Risks

As with investment products, a person's past performance is no guarantee of future performance. But it has been observed that the best predictor of future behavior is typically past behavior. This notion underlies the real-life choices approach to risk-tolerance assessment. That is, factual information about the client's life is gathered and evaluated. The following lifestyle characteristics can be used to gauge a client's disposition toward monetary risk.

- *composition of present investment portfolio.* How risky is it? What percentage of total assets are in passbook savings accounts, Treasury notes, mutual funds, stocks, options and commodities, and so on? If stocks are owned, does the person use short selling and margin buying? If an annuity is owned, is it of the fixed or variable type? How satisfied or dissatisfied is the client with this type of portfolio? If changes were made to a previous portfolio, were these changes in a more conservative or more aggressive direction?
- *debt ratio.* The ratio of the client's liabilities to his or her gross assets has been used as a measure of risk tolerance. It has been suggested by some that a debt ratio over 23 percent reflects risk taking, under 8 percent is characteristic of risk aversion, and 8 percent to 23 percent suggests a risk-neutral attitude.
- *ratio of life insurance to annual salary.* The assumption is that the larger the resulting ratio, the higher the client's level of risk aversion.
- *the size of deductibles on property-liability coverage.* It has been observed that as the amount of wealth allocated to risky securities rises, so does the size of the deductible on the client's insurance coverages. Risk-tolerant individuals elect larger deductibles.
- *percentage of net wealth used for recreational gambling.* The larger the ratio is, the more risk seeking the individual is considered.
- *job tenure.* The willingness to make a voluntary job change is considered an indicator of a willingness to take financial risks. Therefore clients can be asked how many job changes they have made during the last 15 years. Over three changes is considered by some as a sign of a risk-taking attitude. Quitting a job before one has found a replacement is particularly significant. Job changes at middle age may also be especially noteworthy.
- *variations in income.* Risk-taking individuals may show greater variations in their annual income from year to year, and not always in an

upward direction. The financial adviser should also look at the duration of unemployment if the client was ever unemployed. Did the individual take the first job offer he or she received during this period of unemployment or did he or she wait until a job to his or her liking was found? What was the salary of the new job the client took after the period of unemployment? If it was lower than that of the previous job, it could indicate risk aversion.

- *type of mortgage.* A willingness to undertake a variable rather than a fixed mortgage could be a sign of monetary risk taking. If the client has chosen a fixed mortgage, did he or she lock in on a guaranteed rate before settlement? Locking in is a sign of risk aversion.

Attitudes toward Risk

A method frequently used to obtain information about a client's degree of risk tolerance involves eliciting his or her attitude toward risk. Attitudes toward risk can be elicited by using either a quantitative or a qualitative approach. Questions can take on many different forms. First, clients can be asked *global* questions such as whether they view themselves as risk averters or risk takers. For example, "On a 10-point scale, where 1 is an ultimate risk averter and 10 is an ultimate risk taker, where would you place yourself?"

Second, clients can be asked about their *specific* reactions to risk. For example, does the client experience the following:

- can't sleep after making a risky investment
- has persisting second thoughts about the investment
- views risk as an opportunity rather than a danger
- gets more pleasure from making $3,000 on a risky investment than $3,000 on a safe investment
- is afraid of losing what he or she has
- is willing to borrow money to make a good investment
- believes that it is impossible to get ahead without taking chances
- agrees with the saying, "Better safe than sorry"

Earlier it was noted that many questions must be asked in order to assess risk tolerance accurately. This is especially true in the case of the attitude approach to measurement. It has been found that the reason why many attitudes, as measured through questionnaires or other scales of that type, fail to predict actual behavior is because not enough questions were asked. When the number of questions was increased, there was a much better correspondence between attitude and behavior.

A major problem with the attitude approach to risk-tolerance assessment is that people want to present themselves in the best possible light to others. Any characteristic that is valued is likely to be overstated. In America it is considered more desirable to be risk-taking than risk-averse. Clients are therefore likely to exaggerate their willingness to take risks. Consequently discrepancies between verbally expressed attitudes and behavior are frequent, even if numerous questions are asked. When using this approach, one needs to ascertain how well the expressed attitudes agree with other evidence, such as factual information about the person's risk-taking proclivities.

Probability and Payoff Preferences

A variety of assessment techniques fall under this classification. Three types will be considered:

- preferences for certain versus probable gambles
- minimal required probability of success
- minimal required return

All of these methods rely on a manipulation of at least one of the four elements found in any gamble: probability of loss, probability of gain, amount to be lost, and amount to be gained. Consequently the techniques falling under this classification are best used in a quantitative approach to assessment.

Anyone using the probability and payoff-preferences approach to measuring a client's risk tolerance needs to be aware of how framing a question affects the answer, lest he or she be misled by the results. Framing refers to the finding that the same objective facts can be described either in terms of the probability of gaining or the probability of losing. Although it may not seem that—to use an analogy—describing a bottle as half empty or half full should have any marked consequences on one's choices in a risky situation, the evidence shows otherwise. To illustrate, consider research in which one group of people is informed that there is a 50 percent chance of success in a particular venture. Another group is told that this same venture has a 50 percent chance of failure. Logically, the same proportion of people in each group should be willing to take this risk. Yet this was not the case. When the risk was described (framed) in terms of the probability of success, more people were willing to take it than when this same risk was described in terms of the chances of failure. Other related research has shown that describing ground meat in terms of how lean versus how fat the product was made a big difference. To shoppers, ground meat described as 90 percent lean was seen as a better buy than the same ground meat described as 10 percent fat.

Another consideration is the "unpacking effect." This principle refers to the finding that the perceived likelihood of an event is influenced by how specifically it is described. The more specific the description becomes, the more likely it is judged to be. For example, Stanford University undergraduate students were asked to estimate the frequency of different causes of death. When asked to estimate the probability of death from a natural cause, on average, the answer was 58 percent. However, when they were requested to estimate the probability of death from a list of three possible natural causes of death—cancer, heart disease, and other natural causes—the probabilities assigned to these respective events were 22 percent, 18 percent, and 33 percent. Together, they sum up to 73 percent (22% + 18% + 33%), which is higher than the first estimate, 58 percent. In other words, the sum of the components was greater than the whole. This type of effect has been observed among both novices and experts, and in different professions, including professional options traders estimating the closing price of Microsoft stock.

Preferences for Certain versus Probable Gambles. Gambles are abstract representations of real-life situations. One very common technique is to present the client with two alternatives. One choice is a certain win, whereas the other choice offers only some probability of winning. A series of such pairs of gambles is presented. For example, the person is asked to indicate whether he or she would choose

A: a sure gain of $1,000
B: a 50 percent chance of gaining $2,000

Persons who are risk-averse chose options similar to A, whereas risk-taking individuals chose options similar to B.

On some questionnaires, these choices are woven around a story line. For example, an item of this type may be "Imagine that you are a winning contestant on a game show. Which of the following actions would you take?"

A: Stop playing with a certain prize of $8,000 in cash.
B: Go another round with a 50 percent chance of winning $16,000 and a 50 percent chance of winning nothing.

Minimum Probability of Success Required before Undertaking a Risky Action. A good example of a procedure relying on this approach is the "choice dilemma" questionnaire (Kogan and Wallach, 1964), often used to study the risky shift phenomenon discussed earlier. This questionnaire presents 12 situations. For each situation, two alternatives are described. One choice is risky and the other is safe. In every case, the risky course of action offers a larger potential payoff. Five odds are given for the chance of success for the risky course of action, namely 1 in 10, 3 in 10, 5 in 10, 7 in 10, and 9 in 10. The person answering the questionnaire is asked to select the odds that would make it worthwhile to take the risky alternative instead of the safe one. The situations involve a broad range of dilemmas, such as job change, heart operation, football game, marriage decision, and so on. One such question involves a business investment decision:

> Mr. E is president of a light metals corporation in the United States. The corporation is quite prosperous and has strongly considered the

possibilities of business expansion by building an additional plant in a new location. The choice is between building another plant in the U.S., where there would be a moderate return on the initial investment, or building a plant in a foreign country. Lower labor costs and easy access to raw materials in that country would mean a much higher return on the initial investment. On the other hand, there is a history of political instability and revolution in the foreign country under consideration. In fact, the leader of a small minority party is committed to nationalizing, that is, taking over all foreign investments.

Imagine that you are advising Mr. E. Listed below are several probabilities or odds of continued political stability in the foreign country under consideration.

Please check the lowest probability that you would consider acceptable for Mr. E's corporation to build a plant in that country.

- The chances are 1 in 10 that the country will remain politically stable.
- The chances are 3 in 10 that the country will remain politically stable.
- The chances are 5 in 10 that the country will remain politically stable.
- The chances are 7 in 10 that the country will remain politically stable.
- The chances are 9 in 10 that the country will remain politically stable.
- Place a check here if you think Mr. E's corporation should not build a plant in the foreign country, no matter what the probabilities.

The higher the odds of success the person requires, the greater the level of risk aversion. The choice dilemma is a research instrument with well-known measurement properties. However, its appropriateness for assessing monetary risk taking is questionable because this questionnaire looks at risk taking in all contexts (for example, it looks at risk taking as if it was a unitary—which it is not, as noted in the earlier discussion of the subject). Only a few of the 12 situations are concerned with financial risk taking. Furthermore, some of the items are quite dated. Nonetheless, some researchers have found it to be useful in differentiating between investors who are risk-taking from those who are risk-averse.

Minimum Return Required before Undertaking a Risky Action. An example of a question that requires an answer in terms of amount to be gained rather than in terms of probability (as was the case in the choice dilemma task) is: "You are faced with an investment opportunity in which you stand a 50 percent chance of losing half of your personal net wealth and a 50 percent chance of making a certain amount of money. How much of a return would you require in order to take this risk?" (The answers are evaluated in relation to the person's net wealth.)

Guidelines on Assessment

The following guidelines are based on the preceding discussion of assessment, taking into consideration the information presented about risk and situational influences on risk-taking propensity:

- Focus on monetary risk taking.
- Assume the client is risk-averse, unless evidence to the contrary can be obtained.
- Remember that people are more likely to *overstate* than *understate* their risk-taking propensity.
- Keep in mind that even risk-averse individuals may be risk-seeking in situations where the choices are between losses. People are reluctant to cut their losses.
- Start your assessment by looking at the client's demographic characteristics and personality makeup. However, remember you are dealing with an individual rather than a group. Just because a person belongs to a group that is more risk-tolerant or risk-averse than average, it does not mean that the client facing you today will necessarily follow the group pattern. The differences in risk tolerance between demographic groups are usually small, so there will be many people who do not fit the stereotype. Do not judge the individual merely by the group to which he or she belongs. Group differences simply provide you with some hunches that can be explored through the assessment process; you still need to assess the *individual* client.
- Look for quantitative-assessment devices that are accurate and allow you to compare the client's performance to a norm group.
- Consider the results from a questionnaire or other measurement device as only an approximation of the client's actual risk tolerance. No assessment procedure is perfect; they are all susceptible to some error.
- Diversify your methods of assessment. This will allow you to draw on the strengths of the various techniques.
- Use the information you collect to start a dialogue with the client about risk tolerance. Be sure to remember that assessing the client's risk tolerance is a cooperative venture. When an agreement is reached, ask the client to provide a written confirmation of the results of this assessment.
- Realize that biases may be operating on the client's risk perceptions (for example, familiarity, availability, and so on), which may be inflating or deflating the client's true level of risk tolerance.
- Remember that a client's propensity for risk taking does not necessarily remain constant throughout his or her lifetime. As noted throughout this chapter, changes in personal circumstances such as age, wealth, and number of dependents can produce shifts. Likewise, world events can

either increase or decrease a person's level of risk tolerance. Therefore it is prudent to periodically reassess the client's risk tolerance.

EPILOGUE

One needs to recognize that knowledge about risk tolerance is still evolving. The amount of information that is available is substantial, even though many unanswered questions remain.

Even the existing body of knowledge is useless if it is not actually applied by financial planners in their dealings with clients. Loren Dunton, one of the early leaders in the development of the financial planning profession, writes that he is frequently asked by the media to describe the difference between the approach used by financial planners and that used by other financial services practitioners. In his reply, Dunton makes the following comment about financial planners: "Most of them, and all the good ones, will first find out the risk tolerance of the individual or couple they might be going to counsel" (Dunton, p. 71).

REFERENCES

Arrow, K. J. "Risk Perception in Psychology and Economics." *Economic Inquiry*, 1982, vol. 20, pp. 1–9.

Baker, M. W., and E. Kramer. *Success in America: The CIGNA Study of the Upper-Affluent*. Louis Harris and Assoc., Inc., 1987.

Barnewall, M. M. "Examining the Psychological Traits of Passive and Active Affluent Investors." *Journal of Financial Planning,* October 1988, vol. 1, no. 2, pp. 70–74.

Bellante, D., and A. N. Link. "Are Public Sector Workers More Risk Averse Than Private Sector Workers?" *Industrial and Labor Relations Review,* 1981, vol. 34, pp. 408–412.

Bjorkman, M. "Decision Making, Risk Taking and Psychological Time: Review of Empirical Findings and Psychological Theory." *Scandinavian Journal of Psychology,* 1984, vol. 25, pp. 31–49.

Blayney, E. "IAFP Conference for Advanced Planners Roundup." *Investment* Advisor, June 1995, pp. 30–37.

Blum, S. H. "Investment Preferences and the Desire for Security: A Comparison of Men and Women." *American Journal of Psychology,* 1976, vol. 94, pp. 87–91.

Bonieki, G. "What Are the Limits to Man's Time and Space Perspectives: Toward a Definition of a Realistic Planning Horizon." *Technological Forecasting and Social Change,* 1980, vol. 17, pp. 161–175.

Brockhaus, R. H., Sr. "Risk-Taking Propensity of Entrepreneurs." *Academy of Management Journal,* 1980, vol. 23, pp. 509–520.

Brown, M. S. "Communicating Information about Workplace Hazards: Effects on Worker Attitudes toward Risks." *Social and Cultural Construction of*

Risk, edited by B. B. Johnson and V. T. Covello. Norwell, Mass.: Kluver Academic Publishers, 1987.

Cable, D. M., and T. A. Judge. "Pay Preferences and Job Search Decisions: A Person-Organization Fit Perspective." *Personnel Psychology,* 1994, vol. 47, pp. 317–348.

Cohn, R. A., W. G. Lewellen, R. C. Lease, and G. G. Schlarbaum. "Individual Investor Risk Aversion and Investment Portfolio Composition." *Journal of Finance,* 1975, vol. 30, pp. 605–620.

Crum, R. L., D. J. Laughhunn, and J. W. Payne. "Risk-Seeking Behavior and Its Implications for Financial Models." *Financial Management,* Winter 1981, pp. 20–27.

DeBondt, W. M. F., and R. Thaler. "Does the Stock Market Overreact?" *The Journal of Finance,* 1985, vol. 40, pp. 793–808.

Deets, M. K., and G. C. Hoyt. "Variance Preferences and Variance Shifts in Group Investment Decisions." *Organizational Behavior and Human Performance,* 1970, vol. 5, pp. 378–386.

Dickson, G. C. A. "A Comparison of Attitudes towards Risk among Business Managers." *Journal of Occupational Psychology,* 1981, vol. 54, pp. 157–164.

Dowling, G. R. "Perceived Risk: The Concept and Its Measurement." Psychology and Marketing, 1986, vol. 3, pp. 193–210.

Dunton, L. *About Your Future.* San Diego: The National Center for Financial Education, 1988.

Erev, I., and B. L. Cohen, "Verbal versus Numerical Probabilities: Efficiency, Biases, and the Preference Paradox." *Organizational Behavior and Human Decision Processing,* 1990, vol. 45, pp. 1–18.

Farrelly, G. "A Behavioral Science Approach to Financial Research." *Financial Management,* 1980, vol. 9, no. 3, pp. 15–22.

Feinberg, R. M. "Risk Aversion, Risk, and the Duration of Unemployment." Review of Economics & Statistics, 1977, vol. 59, pp. 264–271.

Fischoff, B., and R. Beyth. "I Knew It Would Happen—Remembered Probabilities of Once-Future Things." *Organizational Behavior and Human Performance,* 1975, vol. 13, pp. 1–16.

Gooding, A. E. "Quantification of Investors' Perceptions of Common Stocks: Risk and Return Dimensions." *The Journal of Finance,* 1975, vol. 30, pp. 1301–1316.

Grey, R. J., and C. E. Gordon. "Risk-Taking Managers: Who Gets the Top Jobs?" *Management Review,* 1978, vol. 67, pp. 8–13.

Grossberg, S., and W. E. Gutowski. "Neural Dynamics of Decision Making under Risk: Affective Balance and Cognitive-Emotional Interactions." *Psychological Review,* 1987, vol. 94, pp. 300–318.

Harlow, W. V., and K. C. Brown. "Understanding and Assessing Financial Risk Tolerance: A Biological Perspective." *Financial Analysts Journal,* Nov./Dec. 1992, pp. 51–62.

Harris, L., and Associates. *Public Attitudes toward Risk.* Study No. 837008, conducted for the Insurance Information Institute, 1983.

Heflin, T. L., M. L. Power, and W. L. Dellva. "Choice Shift: Implications for Insurance Application." *The Journal of Insurance: Issues and Practices,* 1988, vol. 2, pp. 68–82.

Hensley, W. E. "Probability, Personality, Age and Risk Taking." *Journal of Psychology,* 1977, vol. 95, pp. 139–145.

Herrnstein, R. J. "Rational Choice Theory: Necessary but Not Sufficient." *American Psychologist,* 1990, vol. 45, pp. 356–367.

Hisrich, R. D. "Entrepreneurship/Intrapreneurship." *American Psychologist,* 1990, vol. 45, no. 2, pp. 209–222.

Hogarth, R. *Judgment and Choice: The Psychology of Decisions.* New York: John Wiley & Sons, 1987.

Hunter, J. E., and T. D. Coggin. "Analyst Judgment: The Efficient Market Hypothesis versus a Psychological Theory of Human Judgment." *Organizational Behavior and Human Decision Processes,* 1988, vol. 42, pp. 284–302.

Investment Company Institute. "Piecing Together Shareholder Perceptions of Investment Risk," Spring 1993.

Isen, A. M., and R. Patrick. "The Effect of Positive Feelings on Risk Taking: When the Chips Are Down." *Organizational Behavior and Human Performance, 1983,* vol. 31, pp. 194–202.

Isen, A.M., T. E. Nygren, and F. G. Ashby. "Influence of Positive Affect on the Subjective Utility of Gains and Losses: It Is Just Not Worth the Risk." *Journal of Personality and Social Psychology,* 1988, vol. 55, pp. 710B717.

Jackson, D. N., L. Hourany, and N. J. Vidmar. "A Four-Dimensional Interpretation of Risk Taking." *Journal of Personality,* 1972, vol. 40, no. 3, pp. 483–501.

Jamison, K. S. "Upscale Consumers in a Changing Marketplace." *Managers Magazine,* August 1988, pp. 20–24.

Johnson, E. J., and A. Tversky. "Affect, Generalization, and the Perception of Risk." *Journal of Personality and Social Psychology,* 1983, vol. 45, pp. 20–31.

Jones, C. P., and J. W. Wilson. "An Analysis of the January Effect in Stocks and Interest Rates under Varying Monetary Regimes." *The Journal of Finance,* 1989, vol. 12, pp. 341–354.

Kahle, L. R., and P. Kennedy. "Using the List of Values (LOV) to Understand Consumers." *The Journal of Consumer Marketing,* 1989, vol. 6, no. 3, pp. 5–12.

Kahneman, D., and A. Tversky. "Choices, Values and Frames." *American Psychologist,* 1984, vol. 39, pp. 341–350.

Kogan, N., and M. Wallach. *Risk Taking: A Study in Cognition and Personality.* New York: Holt, Rinehart and Winston, 1964.

Levin, I. P., R. D. Johnson, C. P. Russo, and P. J. Deldin. "Framing Effects in Judgment Tasks with Varying Amounts of Information." Organizational *Behavior and Human Decision Processes,* 1985, vol. 36, pp. 362–377.

Levin, I. P., M. A. Snyder, and D. P. Chapman. "The Interaction of Experimental and Situational Factors and Gender in a Simulated Risky Decision-Making Task." *The Journal of Psychology,* 1988, vol. 122, pp. 173–181.

Ludwig, L. D. "Elation-Depression and Skill as Determinants of Desire and Excitement." Journal of Personality, 1975, vol. 43, pp. 1–22.

Lupfer, M. "The Effects of Risk-Taking Tendencies and Incentive Conditions on the Performance of Investment Groups." *Journal of Social Psychology,* 1970, vol. 82, pp. 135–136.

MacCrimmon, K. R., D. A. Wehrung, and W. T. Stanbury. Taking Risks: The *Management of Uncertainty*. New York: Free Press, 1986.

MacDonald, J. G., and R. E. Stehle. "How Do Institutional Investors Perceive Risk?" *Journal of Portfolio Management,* 1975, vol. 2, no. 1, pp. 11–16.

Mann, L., and C. Ball. "The Relationship between Search Strategy and Risking Choice." *Australian Journal of Psychology,* 1994, vol. 46, pp. 131–136.

March, J. G., and Z. Shapira. "Managerial Perspectives on Risk and Risk Taking." *Management Science,* 1987, vol. 33, pp. 1404–1418.

Markese, J. D., and G. W. Perritt. "Investment Attitudes and Portfolio Decisions of Individual Investors." *The Mid-Atlantic Journal of Business,* 1985, vol. 23, no. 2, pp. 21–31.

Masters, R. "Study Examines Investors' Risk-Taking Propensities." *Journal of Financial Planning,* July 1989, pp. 151–155.

Masters, R., and R. Meier. "Sex Differences and Risk-Taking Propensity of Entrepreneurs." *Journal of Small Business Management,* 1988, vol. 26, no. 1, pp. 31–35.

Milburn, T. W., and R. S. Billings. "Decision-Making Perspectives from Psychology." *American Behavioral Scientist,* 1976, vol. 20, no. 1, pp. 111–126.

Mongrain, S., and L. Standing. "Impairment of Cognition, Risk-Taking, and Self-Perception by Alcohol." *Perceptual and Motor Skills,* 1989, vol. 69, pp. 199–210.

Morgan, R. L., "Risk Preference as a Function of the Number of Wins and the Amount Won." *American Journal of Psychology,* 1983, vol. 96, pp. 469–475.

Morin, R. A., and A. F. Suarez. "Risk Aversion Revisited." *The Journal of Finance,* 1983, vol. 38, pp. 1201–1216.

Okun, M. A. "Adult Age and Cautiousness in Decision: A Review of the Literature." *Human Development,* 1976, vol. 19, pp. 220–233.

Olsen, R. A. "Investment Risk: The Experts' Perspective." *Association for Investment and Research,* 1997, pp. 62–66.

Plax, T. G., and L. B. Rosenfeld. "Correlates of Risky Decision Making." *Journal of Personality Assessment,* 1976, vol. 40, pp. 413–418.

Powers, J. G. "Risky Business: One Size Does Not Fit All." *Best's Review,* December 1997, pp. 84–86.

Rachlin, H., A. W. Logue, J. Gibbon, and M. Frankel. "Cognition and Behavior in Studies of Choice." *Psychological Review,* 1986, vol. 93, pp. 33–45.

Rapoport, A. "Effects of Wealth on Portfolios under Various Investment Conditions." *Acta Psychologica,* 1984, vol. 55, pp. 31–51.

Reagan, R. T., F. Mosteller, and C. Youtz. "Quantitative Meanings of Verbal Probability Expressions." *Journal of Applied Psychology,* 1989, vol. 74, pp. 433–442.

Riley, W. B., and K. V. Chow. "Asset Allocation and Individual Risk Aversion." *Financial Analysts Journal,* Nov./Dec. 1992, pp. 32–37.

Rim, Y. "Personality and Risky Shift in a Passive Audience." *Personality and Individual Differences,* 1982, vol. 3, pp. 465–467.

Roszkowski, M. J., and G. E. Snelbecker. "Effects of `Framing' on Measures of Risk Tolerance: Financial Planners Are Not Immune." *Journal of Behavioral Economics,* 1990, vol. 19, no. 2, pp. 237–246.

"How Much Risk Can a Client Stand?" *Best's Review,* August 1989, pp. 44–46, 118–119.

Schaninger, C. M. "Perceived Risk and Personality." *Journal of Consumer Research,* 1976, vol. 3, pp. 95–100.

Schoemaker, P. J. H. "The Role of Statistical Knowledge in Gambling Decisions: Moment vs. Risk Dimension Approaches." *Organizational Behavior and Human Performance,* 1979, vol. 24, pp. 1–17.

Schooley, D. "Risk Aversion Measures: Company Attitude and Asset Allocation." *Financial Service Review,* vol. 5, no.2, 1996, pp. 87–99.

Schwager, J. D. *Market Wizards—Interviews with Top Traders.* New York: Simon & Schuster, 1989.

Sciortino, J. J., J. H. Huston, and R. W. Spencer. "Risk and Income Distribution." *Journal of Economic Psychology,* 1988, vol. 9, pp. 399–408.

Shefrin, H., and M. Statman. "The Disposition to Sell Winners Too Early and Ride Losers Too Long: Theory and Evidence." *The Journal of Finance,* 1985, vol. 40, pp. 777–792.

Sinn, H. "Psychophysical Laws in Risk Theory." *Journal of Economic Psychology, 1985,* vol. 6, pp. 185–206.

Slovic, P. "Information Processing, Situation Specificity and the Generality of Risk-Taking Behavior." *Journal of Personality and Social Psychology,* 1972, vol. 21, no. 1, pp. 128–134.

Slovic, P., B. Fischoff, S. Lichtenstein, B. Corrigan, and B. Combs. "Preference for Insuring against Probable Small Losses: Insurance Implications." *Journal of Risk and Insurance,* 1977, vol. 44, pp. 237–258.

Snelbecker, G. E., M. J. Roszkowski, and N. E. Cutler. "Investors' Risk Tolerance and Return Aspirations, and Financial Advisors' Interpretations: A Conceptual Model and Exploratory Data." *Journal of Behavioral Economics,* 1990, vol. 19, no. 2, pp. 377–393.

Sutton, N. A. "An Illusion of Control." *Best's Review: Life/Health Insurance Edition,* July 1987, pp. 54–58.

Svenson, O. "Cognitive Strategies in a Complex Judgment Task: Analyses of Concurrent Verbal Reports and Judgments of Cumulated Risk over Different Exposure Times." *Organizational Behavior and Human Decision Processes,* 1985, vol. 36, pp. 1–15.

— "Time Perception and Long Term Risk." *Canadian Journal of Operations Research and Information Processing,* 1984, vol. 22, pp. 196–214.

Tannen, D. "The Power of Talk: Who Gets Heard and Why." *Harvard Business Review,* September-October 1995, pp. 138–148.

Taylor, R. N. "Psychological Determinants of Bounded Rationality: Implications for Decision-Making Strategies." *Decision Sciences,* 1973, vol. 6, pp. 409–429.

Tharp, V. K. "Winners and Losers: Attitude Makes the Difference." *Futures,* 1984, vol. 12, no. 12, pp. 54–56.

Tversky, A., and C. Heath. "Preferences and Beliefs: Ambiguity and Competence in Choice under Uncertainty." *Journal of Risk and Uncertainty,* 1991, vol. 4, pp. 5–28.

Tversky, A., and D. J. Koehler. "Support Theory: A Nonextensional Representation of Subjective Probability." *Psychological Review,* 1994, vol. 101, pp. 547–567.

Tversky, A., S. Sattath, and P. Slovic. "Contingent Weighting in Judgment and Choice." *Psychological Review,* 1988, vol. 95, pp. 371–384.

Watson, J. S. "Volunteer and Risk-Taking Groups Are More Homogeneous on Measures of Sensation Seeking Than Control Groups." *Perceptual and Motor Skills,* 1985, vol. 62, pp. 471–475.

Weinstein, N. D. "Why It Won't Happen to Me: Perceptions of Risk Factors and Susceptibility." *Health Psychology,* 1984, vol. 3, pp. 431–457.

Wicker, F. W., D. Hamman, A. S. Hagen, J. Lynn. "Studies of Loss Aversion and Perceived Necessity." *Journal of Psychology,* 1995, vol. 129, pp. 75–89.

Wiegman, O., and J. M. Gutteling. "Risk Appraisal and Risk Communication: Some Empirical Data from the Netherlands Reviewed. *Basic and Applied Social Psychology,* 1995, vol. 16, pp. 227–249.

Wiener, J. L., J. W. Gentry, and R. K. Miller. "The Framing of the Insurance Purchase Decision." *Advances in Consumer Research,* 1986, pp. 251–256.

Winger, B. J., and N. K. Mohan. "Investment Risk and Time Diversification." *Journal of Financial Planning,* 1988, vol. 1, no. 1, pp. 45–48.

Zuckerman, M. "Sensation Seeking: A Comparative Approach to a Human Trait." *Behavioral and Brain Sciences,* 1984, vol. 7, pp. 413–471.

Zuckerman, M., M. S. Buchsbaum, and D. L. Murphy. "Sensation Seeking and Its Biological Correlates." *Psychological Bulletin,* 1980, vol. 88, pp. 187–214.

Appendix A

Preparing Financial Statements

David M. Cordell and Stephan R. Leimberg

The preparation of organized financial information is an important but often-ignored aspect of personal financial planning. Like businesses, individuals must often prepare financial information for external use. Banks and other lending institutions rarely make loans to individuals without first analyzing their current financial position and future ability to repay the loan. However, the primary use of financial information in personal financial planning is for internal purposes.

Financial analysis, planning, and control are important planning techniques, whether conducted by the individual alone or by the individual assisted by a professional. The focus of this appendix is on financial statements useful for such internal purposes. It is difficult, if not impossible, to identify financial objectives and formulate strategies for their achievement without knowing a client's current financial situation and resources. In addition, the ongoing analysis of personal financial information is crucial in monitoring whether financial objectives are being achieved.

Two primary pieces of client information used by planners are the current financial position (represented by the *financial position statement,* or *balance sheet*) and the cash-flow status (represented by the *cash-flow statement*). Before each is discussed in greater detail, a few general comments introduce this topic.

While it is common to see personal financial statements that have been prepared only at the end of a calendar or fiscal year, both the timing and frequency of financial statements often vary. When a lending institution needs personal financial information for loan purposes, it usually requires that the information be prepared as of the date of the loan application. Similarly, a financial planner needs financial information at the time the planning process begins and at the time of each subsequent review of a client's financial plan. If reviews take place every 6 months, it is necessary to update personal financial statements at these same intervals. In other words, personal financial statements are not prepared at arbitrary times, but rather when the information is needed for the financial planning process.

The financial position and cash-flow status relate to what has occurred in the past. For financial planning, it is necessary to prepare pro forma (or projected) balance sheets and cash-flow statements. These pro formas illustrate future financial statements if certain activities are implemented under specified assumptions. Finally actual financial statements can be compared with past projections to see if the client's financial plan was realized.

FINANCIAL POSITION STATEMENT

The financial position statement shows an individual's (or family's) wealth at a specified time. It reflects the results of the individual's past financial activities and contains three basic classifications: assets, liabilities, and net worth. These three categories make up the basic accounting equation:

ASSETS = LIABILITIES + NET WORTH

Financial planners can choose from many different formats for the financial position statement since there is no standard. Usually, statements group the items that make up assets and liabilities into subclassifications that better enable the planner to analyze the components of the client's total financial situation and to evaluate the mix of assets in relation to the client's objectives. Table A-1 shows John and Mary Sample's financial position in a typical format.

TABLE A-1
Financial Position Statement—John and Mary Sample

ASSETS		LIABILITIES AND NET WORTH	
Cash and Cash Equivalents		LIABILITIES	
Cash	$ 12,000	Credit card balances	$ 2,000
Money market fund	50,000	Consumer loans	4,000
Life insurance cash value	18,000	Automobile loans	12,000
	$ 80,000	Mortgage loans	220,000
		TOTAL LIABILITIES	$238,000
Other Financial Assets			
Stock	$150,000	NET WORTH	$692,000
Bonds, taxable	90,000		
Bonds, tax-exempt	80,000		
Vested pension and 401(k)	120,000		
	$440,000		
Personal Assets			
Residence	$300,000		
Automobiles	30,000		
Household furnishings, possessions, jewelry, art	80,000		
	$410,000		
TOTAL ASSETS	$930,000	TOTAL LIABILITIES AND NET WORTH	$930,000

Assets

Assets are items the client owns. It is immaterial whether the item was purchased for cash, financed by borrowing, or received as a gift or inheritance. Items that the client possesses but does not own, such as rented apartments or leased automobiles, are not shown as assets.

It is common practice for personal financial position statements to show assets at their current fair market values. These values may vary considerably from the original purchase prices. In contrast, business financial statements must list many assets on the basis of adjusted historical costs, net of depreciation.

At a minimum, assets should be subdivided into two categories: financial assets and personal (or nonfinancial) assets. Many statement formats include other categories such as use assets, nonuse assets, personal assets, investment assets, and retirement assets, among others. The financial position statement in table A-1 uses three major categories of assets by separating total assets into (1) cash and cash equivalents, (2) other financial assets, and (3) personal assets. Other financial assets are sometimes further subdivided, according to their relative liquidity, income characteristics, tax status, or growth characteristics.

Liabilities

Liabilities are the debts of the client. While the financial position statement in table A-1 does not separate liabilities into major subcategories, it is not unusual to see liabilities grouped by the time period in which they must be repaid. For example, the statement might show subtotals for short-term liabilities (due in one year or less), intermediate-term liabilities (due in one to 5 years), and long-term liabilities (due in more than 5 years).

In theory, the liabilities section of the financial position statement should show all liabilities as of the date of the statement—even if the client has not received a formal bill. This process may require the client to make estimates for such items as taxes due, utility charges owed, and credit-card obligations. In practice, clients and planners often ignore relatively small accruals for unaudited statements.

Net Worth

Net worth measures the client's wealth or equity at the date of the financial position statement. It is calculated by restating the basic accounting equation as follows:

NET WORTH = TOTAL ASSETS – TOTAL LIABILITIES

In other words, net worth is what remains if all the client's assets are sold at their fair market values and all debts are paid. If a client has a negative net worth, the client is considered to be bankrupt. However, such clients can avoid formal bankruptcy proceedings if cash flow is sufficient to service all financial obligations.

By itself, net worth reveals little about the nature of the assets or liabilities. A client with considerable net worth may have all his or her assets tied up in nonincome-producing assets, such as homes, automobiles, and other personal possessions. Conversely, a client with a modest net worth may hold most assets in the form of financial assets that may be generating income, capital appreciation, or both. Further, it is possible for a client to have a positive cash balance with a negative net worth or to have a zero cash balance with a very high net worth. The key to understanding net worth is to recognize that it is simply a residual—the difference between total assets and total liabilities.

A client's net worth may increase or decrease during a period of time. Other things being equal, a client's net worth will increase as a result of any one of the following:

- appreciation in the value of assets
- addition to assets through retaining income
- addition of assets through gifts or inheritances
- decrease in liabilities through forgiveness

The following are examples of actions that have no effect on net worth:

- paying off a debt. The cash account declines by the same amount that the liability declines, leaving the difference between total assets and total liabilities unchanged.
- buying an asset with cash. Total assets remain unchanged because cash declines by the same amount that the other asset category increases. However, commissions and other transaction costs cause net worth to decline because the cash that pays these costs is not reflected in the value of the purchased asset.

The Format of the Financial Position Statement

Obviously, any financial statement should be in a format that is understandable, and uniformity is desirable. However, the actual format is really secondary to the quality of the information. It should be noted that the format of a financial position statement (and a cash-flow statement) is often determined by the software system used by the financial planner for analyzing data and producing reports.

Financial position statements have traditionally been presented in two columns—one containing assets, the other containing liabilities and net worth. The term *balance sheet* is derived from the fact that these two sides must balance according to the accounting equation (total assets = total liabilities + net worth).

It is now more common in personal financial planning to present financial position statements in a single-column format. The major advantage of the single-column format is that it facilitates the preparation of pro forma financial position statements and the comparison of consecutive statements over time.

CASH-FLOW MANAGEMENT

Cash-flow management is one of the most basic tools in financial planning. Ironically, practitioners frequently find that clients resist the management process more than any other technique even though it is critical to reaching a goal. Communicating the importance of cash-flow management and talking the client through the process are among the practitioner's greatest services.

Although the well-heeled client sometimes considers cash-flow management as an activity for the less fortunate, the advantages cut across income levels. Cash-flow management is always beneficial and is especially useful when the client needs to accomplish any of the following objectives:

- measure periodic progress toward the achievement of specific goals (a) within a defined time frame and (b) within the confines of limited resources
- monitor especially complex elements of economic activity
- provide guidelines for evaluating the economic performance of elements constituting the client's cash flow
- communicate a planning strategy to those affected by the budget
- provide incentive (goals) for the performance of individuals involved
- control household expenses
- achieve desired wealth accumulation/savings goals, such as retirement or children's education
- monitor the performance of a specific investment, such as a securities portfolio, rental property, or a closely held business
- reposition assets to improve the likelihood of accomplishing goals

What Is Cash-Flow Management?

Cash-flow management is essentially a euphemism for the budget planning and control process. Financial planners adopted the change in terminology partly because cash-flow management is more inclusive than budgeting. More importantly, the word *budget* carries negative connotations for many clients, making them less likely to participate in the process.

Cash-flow management consists of three basic components: cash-flow analysis, cash-flow planning, and budgeting. In practice, many planners mix aspects of each of the three and consider them as a single process.

Cash-Flow Analysis

Cash-flow analysis, or revenue and expense analysis, is the process of gathering data concerning the client's cash-flow situation, presenting the data in an organized format (the cash-flow statement), and identifying strengths, weaknesses, and important patterns. Cash-flow analysis is the starting point for the client and the financial counseling team to develop objectives. It also reveals inefficient, ineffective, or unusual utilization of resources, highlights alternative courses of action, motivates the client, and makes family members aware of the need to conserve resources.

Cash-Flow Planning

Cash-flow planning involves identifying courses of action that will help optimize *net discretionary cash flow.* Net discretionary cash flow is defined as the difference between income and expenses. Positive cash flow is available for any use, whether for consumption, investment, or gifting. However, in most financial planning situations, the primary benefit of net discretionary cash flow is to provide a source of investable funds.

Note that the goal is to optimize rather than to maximize. Maximizing net discretionary cash flow means to make it as large as possible. Pursuit of this goal suggests increasing income in any way possible. Presumably this mandate includes working longer hours, finding a second job, or seeking employment for the non-earning spouse. On the expense side, maximization implies having a less expensive home and automobile, quitting the club, and discontinuing vacations and eating out. Clearly these approaches represent changes in lifestyle and standard of living, not to mention family relationships. In contrast, optimization means seeking the best, not necessarily the largest, net discretionary income.

Optimal net discretionary income implies a balance between investing for the future and maintaining and/or improving the current lifestyle. While the distinction between maximizing and optimizing may seem arcane, the difference is important not only in substance, but also in style. Optimization holds greater appeal to clients because it puts wealth accumulation in perspective. It also gives clients greater control since they ultimately decide their own funds allocation according to their own personal preferences.

Cash-flow planning is interwoven through almost all aspects of personal financial planning. At the extreme, each of the following is a factor or a tool in cash-flow planning:

- income tax planning
- investment planning
- insurance planning
- estate planning
- retirement planning

- employee benefits
- saving/investment vehicles

Some practitioners believe that cash-flow planning includes each of the six steps in financial planning (see chapter 1) in a sort of microcosm of the larger process. Some even view cash management as the framework within which other planning functions are employed.

The more common approach is simply to use cash-flow planning as an extension of cash-flow analysis in an iterative process that involves other planning areas. For example cash-flow analysis reveals opportunities for increasing net discretionary income by addressing income and expense factors. Cash-flow planning then considers what to do with the increase in discretionary net income. The result may include an insurance or investment alternative that represents a financial commitment. Typically, the commitment raises expenses, thus lowering net discretionary income calculated in the cash-flow analysis. Based on this new level, the client may consider another alternative for the remaining net discretionary income.

Budgeting

Budgeting is the process of creating and following an explicit plan for spending and investing the resources available to the client. In simplest terms, the process works via the establishment of a working budget model followed by a comparison of actual and expected results. By constantly monitoring the budget, the practitioner and client can recognize problems as they occur and even anticipate problems. Budgeting provides both a means of financial self-evaluation and a guideline to measure actual performance.

Budgeting does have some disadvantages, however. For example, many individuals have a psychological aversion to the record keeping required and may not maintain sufficient information for the budget to be useful. Obviously, to the extent the data utilized are inaccurate, the conclusions drawn from the budget may be misleading. For some clients a rote dependence on budgeting numbers inhibits creativity, stifles risk taking, and encourages mechanical thinking. Such clients may forfeit investment opportunities or fail to minimize losses.

Here are some guidelines for establishing a budget:

- Make the budget flexible enough to deal with emergencies, unexpected opportunities, or other unforeseen circumstances.
- Keep the budget period long enough to utilize an investment strategy and a workable series of investment procedures—typically one calendar year.
- Make the budget simple and brief.
- Follow the form and content of the budget consistently.

- Eliminate extraneous information.
- Estimate especially with insignificant items.
- Tailor the budget to specific goals and objectives.
- Remember that a budget is also a guideline against which actual results are to be measured. Unexpected results should be analyzed: they may be the norm and deserve to be incorporated in a revised budget.
- Pinpoint, in advance, variables that may influence the amounts of income and expenditures. Income items include expected annual raises and increases or decreases in interest or dividend rates. Expenditures include costs, changing tastes or preferences, or changes in family circumstances.

Creating the Cash-Flow Statement and Budget

Budgeting requires looking to the future, but for most clients the best place to start is the past. The basic sources of budget information are personal financial statements, prior years' tax returns, canceled checks, and projections of income and expenditures for the target period. Once initial estimates have been made, they must be adjusted in light of special circumstances or considerations. Usually, practitioners use a cash-flow worksheet in assembling the data and input the data in a computer program to create the cash-flow statement.

A family budget should project income and expenditures for any planning period that is convenient or appropriate for a specific purpose. Most planners budget for 12 months at a time, usually coinciding with a calendar year. Generally, the budget is calculated on a month-by-month basis since some cash flows occur only in specific months.

It is often appropriate to budget for longer periods of time, such as a 4-year period of college education. However, for long-range budgeting, keep in mind that the budget's accuracy decreases as the length of the period covered increases.

Constructing a cash-flow statement or a cash budget is largely a mechanical process involving very specific steps. Although some clients present unusual situations, the majority fit into the following framework.

STEP 1—Estimate the Family's Annual Income

Identify fixed amounts of income expected from each of the following:

- salary
- bonus
- self-employment
- real estate
- dividends—close corporations
- dividends—publicly traded corporations

- interest—savings accounts
- interest—taxable bonds
- interest—tax-free bonds
- trust income
- other fixed-payment income
- variable sources of income

The client's income can be affected by salary increases, bonuses, dividend or interest-rate changes, proceeds from the sale of stocks or other assets, inheritances, and many other events.

If a family experiences an irregular income flow or extreme variations of income, two income estimates should be developed. One estimate should be based on the lowest amount of income that might be received, while the other should be based on a higher but still reasonable estimated figure.

STEP 2—Develop Estimates for Both Fixed and Discretionary Expenses

Annual expenditures can be classified as either fixed or discretionary. However, "fixed" applies only in the short run and can often be changed without imposing a radical shift in the client's lifestyle. Even the most fixed of all expenditures, housing, can be changed if necessary.

Discretionary expenditures, by definition, can be prevented or timed through proper budgeting so that sufficient income is available.

Canceled checks and charge account receipts serve as a good basis for developing the following expenditure estimates:

- fixed expenses
  –housing (mortgage or rental payments)
  –utilities
  –food, groceries, etc.
  –clothing and cleaning
  –income taxes
  –social security
  –property taxes
  –transportation
  –medical and dental
  –debt repayments
  –household supplies and maintenance
  –life and disability insurance
  –property and liability insurance
  –current school expenses
- discretionary expenses
  –vacations, travel, etc.
  –gifts and contributions

–household furnishings
–education fund
–savings
–investments
–other

Note that a client's expenditures can vary as a result of increased costs of living, unexpected business expenses, financial catastrophes (such as uninsured theft or fire losses), changes in tastes or preferences, and large-scale expenses (such as college or retirement).

STEP 3—Determine the Excess or Shortfall of Income within the Budget Period

Subtracting total expenses from total income reveals the client's net cash flow. Discretionary expenses already include listings for savings, investments, and an education fund. If projected net cash flow is positive, the client can allocate even more to these categories (although most clients are more adept at finding ways to spend the money).

Individuals, like businesses, commonly project some months with positive net income and others with negative. In practice, cash or cash-equivalent balances simply grow in positive months and shrink in negative months.

STEP 4—Consider Available Methods of Increasing Income or Decreasing Expenses

If net cash flow is negative, either income must increase or expenses must decrease. This is bad news for the client, but it is better to recognize the situation early.

Clients should be realistic in identifying categories for revision—blind optimism is counterproductive. Practitioners should encourage clients to avoid lowering the savings, investment, and education-planning figures, unless there is no alternative.

STEP 5—Calculate Income and Expenses as a Percentage of the Total to Determine a Better Allocation of Resources

Many clients benefit from a comparison of their spending patterns to those of the general population. However, practitioners must recognize that the ratios can vary dramatically according to age, income, family structure, geography, and other factors.

As noted earlier, an organized cash-flow planning approach is useful in evaluating the potential of major adjustments in cash flows and portfolio characteristics.

Other Considerations

Families who experience difficulty in predicting income or who have highly variable cash outflows should consider two budgets—one based on the lowest income and highest expenditures expected (worst-case budget), and the second based on the client's reasonable expectations of income and expenses (average-case budget).

In some cases it also makes sense to prepare a budget based on the highest possible income and lowest possible expenditures (best-case budget). This third alternative budget is often used to ascertain whether the cost of a "hoped for" expenditure, such as a new car, is within reach if everything falls into place.

Another conservative approach is to base the budget on only fixed and certain income. Limiting expenditures to this conservative estimate ensures that fixed and expected costs will be covered. Any excess income can then be used for investment or discretionary spending, or placed in a *contingency fund.*

Budgeting should allocate cash reserves for such contingencies as (a) liquidity needs, (b) emergencies, (c) scheduled expenditures, and (d) investment opportunities. These cash reserves should be invested according to the speed at which they will be needed. In other words, funds should be placed in investments suitable for the needs to be satisfied.

Short-term reserves to meet liquidity needs—day-to-day transactions—should be placed in an interest-bearing checking account. Clients should maintain balances that are large enough to qualify for payment of interest and, if available, waiver-of-service fees. However, they should not allow excessive amounts to accumulate in the checking account since the interest rate is very low. The optimal size depends on numerous factors, such as monthly cash flow, timing of receipts and payments, and the client's comfort level. Practitioners often advise retaining intermediate reserves equal to 3 to 6 months of expenses in a money market account as an emergency fund. Some families, rather than building emergency funds, have lines of credit through various banks or credit cards. This enables them to invest any excess income, or use it to increase their standard of living. There are two drawbacks to using this technique. First, the interest charged on credit-card borrowing is usually high. Second, the client must have sufficient income to repay the loan. If the emergency is a lost job, for example, payment becomes problematic.

Sample Pro Forma Cash-Flow Statement

Figure A-2 is an illustration of the Sample family's budget, or pro forma cash-flow statement, reflecting $5,800 excess of income over expenditures for the year. With this estimate of the year's expected financial results available early in the year, the Sample family can then plan its investment or spending of the projected excess.

However, as the illustration in figure A-3 indicates, if Mr. Sample does not receive his expected bonus of $15,000, the family will experience a budgeted shortfall of $4,500. This is so even after projected reductions in income taxes of $4,500 (from $28,000 to $23,500) and in medicare taxes of $200 (from $7,700 to $7,500) as a result of not receiving the bonus. On this basis, the Sample family must modify its spending and investing plans for the year. This example illustrates the importance of preparing budgets that reflect conservative as well as optimistic results.

TABLE A-2
Pro Forma Cash-Flow Statement—John and Mary Sample (With Bonus)

Annual Income	Amount	% of Total Income
Salary/Bonus—John	$125,000	74.4%
Salary/Bonus—Mary	30,000	17.9
Self-Employment (Business)	0	0.0
Dividends—Close Corporation Stock	0	0.0
Dividends—Investments	3,000	1.8
Interest on Savings Accounts	2,000	1.2
Interest on Bonds, Taxable	5,000	3.0
Interest on Bonds, Exempt	3,000	1.8
Trust Income	0	0.0
Rental Income	0	0.0
Other	0	0.0
Total Annual Income	$ 168,000	100.1%*
Fixed Expenses		
Housing (Mortgage/Rent)	$ 15,500	9.2%
Utilities & Telephone	7,000	4.2
Food, Groceries, Etc.	10,500	6.3
Clothing and Cleaning	7,000	4.2
Income Taxes	28,000	16.7
Social Security and Medicare Taxes	7,700	4.6
Real Estate Taxes	5,000	3.0
Transportation	8,000	4.8
Medical/Dental Expenses	8,000	4.8
Debt Repayment	5,000	3.0
Housing Supplies/Maint.	6,000	3.6
Life Insurance	8,000	4.8
Prop. & Liability Ins.	5,000	3.0
Current School Exp.	4,500	2.7
Total Fixed Expenses	$ 125,200	74.9%
Variable Expenses		
Vacations, Travel, Etc.	$ 4,000	2.4%
Recreation/Entertainment	5,000	3.0
Contributions, Gifts	7,500	4.5
Household Furnishings	5,000	3.0
Education Fund	5,000	3.0
Savings	3,000	1.8
Investment	2,500	1.5
Other	5,000	3.0
Total Variable Expenses	$ 37,000	22.2%
Total Expenses	$ 162,200	97.1%
Net Cash Flow	$ 5,800	3.0%

*Discrepancies in totals are due to rounding.

Adapted with permission from *Financial Planning* TOOLKIT, Financial Data Center (610-527-5216).

TABLE A-3
Pro Forma Cash-Flow Statement—John and Mary Sample (No Bonus)

	Amount	% of Total Income
Annual Income		
Salary/Bonus—John	$110,000	71.9%
Salary/Bonus—Mary	30,000	19.6
Self-Employment (Business)	0	0.0
Dividends—Close Corporation Stock	0	0.0
Dividends—Investments	3,000	2.0
Interest on Savings Accounts	2,000	1.3
Interest on Bonds, Taxable	5,000	3.3
Interest on Bonds, Exempt	3,000	2.0
Trust Income	0	0.0
Rental Income	0	0.0
Other	0	0.0
Total Annual Income	$153,000	100.1%
Fixed Expenses		
Housing (Mortgage/Rent)	$ 15,500	10.1%
Utilities & Telephone	7,000	4.6
Food, Groceries, Etc.	10,500	6.9
Clothing and Cleaning	7,000	4.6
Income Taxes	23,500	15.4
Social Security and Medicare Taxes	7,500	4.9
Real Estate Taxes	5,000	3.3
Transportation	8,000	5.2
Medical/Dental Expenses	8,000	5.2
Debt Repayment	5,000	3.3
Housing Supplies/Maint.	6,000	3.9
Life Insurance	8,000	5.2
Prop. & Liability Ins.	5,000	3.3
Current School Exp.	4,500	2.9
Total Fixed Expenses	$120,500	78.8%
Variable Expenses		
Vacations, Travel, Etc.	$ 4,000	2.6%
Recreation/Entertainment	5,000	3.3
Contributions, Gifts	7,500	4.9
Household Furnishings	5,000	3.3
Education Fund	5,000	3.3
Savings	3,000	2.0
Investments	2,500	1.6
Other	5,000	3.3
Total Variable Expenses	$ 37,000	24.3%
Total Expenses	$ 157,500	103.1%
Net Cash Flow	$ –4,500	–3.0%

Adapted with permission from *Financial Planning* TOOLKIT, Financial Data Center (610-527-5216).

APPENDIX B

Time Value of Money Tables

Appendix B
Time Value of Money Tables

TABLE B.1
FUTURE VALUE OF A SINGLE SUM FACTORS
FVSS Factor = $(1 + i)^n$ where i = rate and n = periods

i =	0.5%	1%	1.5%	2%	2.5%	3%	3.5%	4%	4.5%	5%
n = 1	1.0050	1.0100	1.0150	1.0200	1.0250	1.0300	1.0350	1.0400	1.0450	1.0500
2	1.0100	1.0201	1.0302	1.0404	1.0506	1.0609	1.0712	1.0816	1.0920	1.1025
3	1.0151	1.0303	1.0457	1.0612	1.0769	1.0927	1.1087	1.1249	1.1412	1.1576
4	1.0202	1.0406	1.0614	1.0824	1.1038	1.1255	1.1475	1.1699	1.1925	1.2155
5	1.0253	1.0510	1.0773	1.1041	1.1314	1.1593	1.1877	1.2167	1.2462	1.2763
6	1.0304	1.0615	1.0934	1.1262	1.1597	1.1941	1.2293	1.2653	1.3023	1.3401
7	1.0355	1.0721	1.1098	1.1487	1.1887	1.2299	1.2723	1.3159	1.3609	1.4071
8	1.0407	1.0829	1.1265	1.1717	1.2184	1.2668	1.3168	1.3686	1.4221	1.4775
9	1.0459	1.0937	1.1434	1.1951	1.2489	1.3048	1.3629	1.4233	1.4861	1.5513
10	1.0511	1.1046	1.1605	1.2190	1.2801	1.3439	1.4106	1.4802	1.5530	1.6289
11	1.0564	1.1157	1.1779	1.2434	1.3121	1.3842	1.4600	1.5395	1.6229	1.7103
12	1.0617	1.1268	1.1956	1.2682	1.3449	1.4258	1.5111	1.6010	1.6959	1.7959
13	1.0670	1.1381	1.2136	1.2936	1.3785	1.4685	1.5640	1.6651	1.7722	1.8856
14	1.0723	1.1495	1.2318	1.3195	1.4130	1.5126	1.6187	1.7317	1.8519	1.9799
15	1.0777	1.1610	1.2502	1.3459	1.4483	1.5580	1.6753	1.8009	1.9353	2.0789
16	1.0831	1.1726	1.2690	1.3728	1.4845	1.6047	1.7340	1.8730	2.0224	2.1829
17	1.0885	1.1843	1.2880	1.4002	1.5216	1.6528	1.7947	1.9479	2.1134	2.2920
18	1.0939	1.1961	1.3073	1.4282	1.5597	1.7024	1.8575	2.0258	2.2085	2.4066
19	1.0994	1.2081	1.3270	1.4568	1.5987	1.7535	1.9225	2.1068	2.3079	2.5270
20	1.1049	1.2202	1.3469	1.4859	1.6386	1.8061	1.9898	2.1911	2.4117	2.6533
21	1.1104	1.2324	1.3671	1.5157	1.6796	1.8603	2.0594	2.2788	2.5202	2.7860
22	1.1160	1.2447	1.3876	1.5460	1.7216	1.9161	2.1315	2.3699	2.6337	2.9253
23	1.1216	1.2572	1.4084	1.5769	1.7646	1.9736	2.2061	2.4647	2.7522	3.0715
24	1.1272	1.2697	1.4295	1.6084	1.8087	2.0328	2.2833	2.5633	2.8760	3.2251
25	1.1328	1.2824	1.4509	1.6406	1.8539	2.0938	2.3632	2.6658	3.0054	3.3864
26	1.1385	1.2953	1.4727	1.6734	1.9003	2.1566	2.4460	2.7725	3.1407	3.5557
27	1.1442	1.3082	1.4948	1.7069	1.9478	2.2213	2.5316	2.8834	3.2820	3.7335
28	1.1499	1.3213	1.5172	1.7410	1.9965	2.2879	2.6202	2.9987	3.4297	3.9201
29	1.1556	1.3345	1.5400	1.7758	2.0464	2.3566	2.7119	3.1187	3.5840	4.1161
30	1.1614	1.3478	1.5631	1.8114	2.0976	2.4273	2.8068	3.2434	3.7453	4.3219
35	1.1907	1.4166	1.6839	1.9999	2.3732	2.8139	3.3336	3.9461	4.6673	5.5160
40	1.2208	1.4889	1.8140	2.2080	2.6851	3.2620	3.9593	4.8010	5.8164	7.0400
45	1.2516	1.5648	1.9542	2.4379	3.0379	3.7816	4.7024	5.8412	7.2482	8.9850
50	1.2832	1.6446	2.1052	2.6916	3.4371	4.3839	5.5849	7.1067	9.0326	11.4674

TABLE B.1 (CONTINUED)
FUTURE VALUE OF A SINGLE SUM FACTORS
FVSS Factor = $(1 + i)^n$ where i = rate and n = periods

i =	5.5%	6%	6.5%	7%	7.5%	8%	8.5%	9%	9.5%	10%
n = 1	1.0550	1.0600	1.0650	1.0700	1.0750	1.0800	1.0850	1.0900	1.0950	1.1000
2	1.1130	1.1236	1.1342	1.1449	1.1556	1.1664	1.1772	1.1881	1.1990	1.2100
3	1.1742	1.1910	1.2079	1.2250	1.2423	1.2597	1.2773	1.2950	1.3129	1.3310
4	1.2388	1.2625	1.2865	1.3108	1.3355	1.3605	1.3859	1.4116	1.4377	1.4641
5	1.3070	1.3382	1.3701	1.4026	1.4356	1.4693	1.5037	1.5386	1.5742	1.6105
6	1.3788	1.4185	1.4591	1.5007	1.5433	1.5869	1.6315	1.6771	1.7238	1.7716
7	1.4547	1.5036	1.5540	1.6058	1.6590	1.7138	1.7701	1.8280	1.8876	1.9487
8	1.5347	1.5938	1.6550	1.7182	1.7835	1.8509	1.9206	1.9926	2.0669	2.1436
9	1.6191	1.6895	1.7626	1.8385	1.9172	1.9990	2.0839	2.1719	2.2632	2.3579
10	1.7081	1.7908	1.8771	1.9672	2.0610	2.1589	2.2610	2.3674	2.4782	2.5937
11	1.8021	1.8983	1.9992	2.1049	2.2156	2.3316	2.4532	2.5804	2.7137	2.8531
12	1.9012	2.0122	2.1291	2.2522	2.3818	2.5182	2.6617	2.8127	2.9715	3.1384
13	2.0058	2.1329	2.2675	2.4098	2.5604	2.7196	2.8879	3.0658	3.2537	3.4523
14	2.1161	2.2609	2.4149	2.5785	2.7524	2.9372	3.1334	3.3417	3.5629	3.7975
15	2.2325	2.3966	2.5718	2.7590	2.9589	3.1722	3.3997	3.6425	3.9013	4.1772
16	2.3553	2.5404	2.7390	2.9522	3.1808	3.4259	3.6887	3.9703	4.2719	4.5950
17	2.4848	2.6928	2.9170	3.1588	3.4194	3.7000	4.0023	4.3276	4.6778	5.0545
18	2.6215	2.8543	3.1067	3.3799	3.6758	3.9960	4.3425	4.7171	5.1222	5.5599
19	2.7656	3.0256	3.3086	3.6165	3.9515	4.3157	4.7116	5.1417	5.6088	6.1159
20	2.9178	3.2071	3.5236	3.8697	4.2479	4.6610	5.1120	5.6044	6.1416	6.7275
21	3.0782	3.3996	3.7527	4.1406	4.5664	5.0338	5.5466	6.1088	6.7251	7.4002
22	3.2475	3.6035	3.9966	4.4304	4.9089	5.4365	6.0180	6.6586	7.3639	8.1403
23	3.4262	3.8197	4.2564	4.7405	5.2771	5.8715	6.5296	7.2579	8.0635	8.9543
24	3.6146	4.0489	4.5331	5.0724	5.6729	6.3412	7.0846	7.9111	8.8296	9.8497
25	3.8134	4.2919	4.8277	5.4274	6.0983	6.8485	7.6868	8.6231	9.6684	10.8347
26	4.0231	4.5494	5.1415	5.8074	6.5557	7.3964	8.3401	9.3992	10.5869	11.9182
27	4.2444	4.8223	5.4757	6.2139	7.0474	7.9881	9.0490	10.2451	11.5926	13.1100
28	4.4778	5.1117	5.8316	6.6488	7.5759	8.6271	9.8182	11.1671	12.6939	14.4210
29	4.7241	5.4184	6.2107	7.1143	8.1441	9.3173	10.6528	12.1722	13.8998	15.8631
30	4.9840	5.7435	6.6144	7.6123	8.7550	10.0627	11.5583	13.2677	15.2203	17.4494
35	6.5138	7.6861	9.0623	10.6766	12.5689	14.7853	17.3796	20.4140	23.9604	28.1024
40	8.5133	10.2857	12.4161	14.9745	18.0442	21.7245	26.1330	31.4094	37.7194	45.2593
45	11.1266	13.7646	17.0111	21.0025	25.9048	31.9204	39.2951	48.3273	59.3793	72.8905
50	14.5420	18.4202	23.3067	29.4570	37.1897	46.9016	59.0863	74.3575	93.4773	117.391

TABLE B.1 (CONTINUED)
FUTURE VALUE OF A SINGLE SUM FACTORS
FVSS Factor = $(1 + i)^n$ where i = rate and n = periods

i =	10.5%	11%	11.5%	12%	12.5%	13%	13.5%	14%	14.5%	15%
n = 1	1.1050	1.1100	1.1150	1.1200	1.1250	1.1300	1.1350	1.1400	1.1450	1.1500
2	1.2210	1.2321	1.2432	1.2544	1.2656	1.2769	1.2882	1.2996	1.3110	1.3225
3	1.3492	1.3676	1.3862	1.4049	1.4238	1.4429	1.4621	1.4815	1.5011	1.5209
4	1.4909	1.5181	1.5456	1.5735	1.6018	1.6305	1.6595	1.6890	1.7188	1.7490
5	1.6474	1.6851	1.7234	1.7623	1.8020	1.8424	1.8836	1.9254	1.9680	2.0114
6	1.8204	1.8704	1.9215	1.9738	2.0273	2.0820	2.1378	2.1950	2.2534	2.3131
7	2.0116	2.0762	2.1425	2.2107	2.2807	2.3526	2.4264	2.5023	2.5801	2.6600
8	2.2228	2.3045	2.3889	2.4760	2.5658	2.6584	2.7540	2.8526	2.9542	3.0590
9	2.4562	2.5580	2.6636	2.7731	2.8865	3.0040	3.1258	3.2519	3.3826	3.5179
10	2.7141	2.8394	2.9699	3.1058	3.2473	3.3946	3.5478	3.7072	3.8731	4.0456
11	2.9991	3.1518	3.3115	3.4785	3.6532	3.8359	4.0267	4.2262	4.4347	4.6524
12	3.3140	3.4985	3.6923	3.8960	4.1099	4.3345	4.5704	4.8179	5.0777	5.3503
13	3.6619	3.8833	4.1169	4.3635	4.6236	4.8980	5.1874	5.4924	5.8140	6.1528
14	4.0464	4.3104	4.5904	4.8871	5.2016	5.5348	5.8877	6.2613	6.6570	7.0757
15	4.4713	4.7846	5.1183	5.4736	5.8518	6.2543	6.6825	7.1379	7.6222	8.1371
16	4.9408	5.3109	5.7069	6.1304	6.5833	7.0673	7.5846	8.1372	8.7275	9.3576
17	5.4596	5.8951	6.3632	6.8660	7.4062	7.9861	8.6085	9.2765	9.9929	10.7613
18	6.0328	6.5436	7.0949	7.6900	8.3319	9.0243	9.7707	10.5752	11.4419	12.3755
19	6.6663	7.2633	7.9108	8.6128	9.3734	10.1974	11.0897	12.0557	13.1010	14.2318
20	7.3662	8.0623	8.8206	9.6463	10.5451	11.5231	12.5869	13.7435	15.0006	16.3665
21	8.1397	8.9492	9.8350	10.8038	11.8632	13.0211	14.2861	15.6676	17.1757	18.8215
22	8.9944	9.9336	10.9660	12.1003	13.3461	14.7138	16.2147	17.8610	19.6662	21.6447
23	9.9388	11.0263	12.2271	13.5523	15.0144	16.6266	18.4037	20.3616	22.5178	24.8915
24	10.9823	12.2392	13.6332	15.1786	16.8912	18.7881	20.8882	23.2122	25.7829	28.6252
25	12.1355	13.5855	15.2010	17.0001	19.0026	21.2305	23.7081	26.4619	29.5214	32.9190
26	13.4097	15.0799	16.9491	19.0401	21.3779	23.9905	26.9087	30.1666	33.8020	37.8568
27	14.8177	16.7386	18.8982	21.3249	24.0502	27.1093	30.5414	34.3899	38.7033	43.5353
28	16.3736	18.5799	21.0715	23.8839	27.0564	30.6335	34.6644	39.2045	44.3153	50.0656
29	18.0928	20.6237	23.4948	26.7499	30.4385	34.6158	39.3441	44.6931	50.7410	57.5755
30	19.9926	22.8923	26.1967	29.9599	34.2433	39.1159	44.6556	50.9502	58.0985	66.2118
35	32.9367	38.5749	45.1461	52.7996	61.7075	72.0685	84.1115	98.1002	114.338	133.176
40	54.2614	65.0009	77.8027	93.0510	111.199	132.782	158.429	188.884	225.019	267.864
45	89.3928	109.530	134.082	163.988	200.384	244.641	298.410	363.679	442.840	538.769
50	147.270	184.565	231.070	289.002	361.099	450.736	562.073	700.233	871.514	1083.66

TABLE B.1 (CONTINUED)
FUTURE VALUE OF A SINGLE SUM FACTORS
FVSS Factor = $(1 + i)^n$ where i = rate and n = periods

i =	16%	17%	18%	19%	20%	22%	24%	26%	28%	30%
n = 1	1.1600	1.1700	1.1800	1.1900	1.2000	1.2200	1.2400	1.2600	1.2800	1.3000
2	1.3456	1.3689	1.3924	1.4161	1.4400	1.4884	1.5376	1.5876	1.6384	1.6900
3	1.5609	1.6016	1.6430	1.6852	1.7280	1.8158	1.9066	2.0004	2.0972	2.1970
4	1.8106	1.8739	1.9388	2.0053	2.0736	2.2153	2.3642	2.5205	2.6844	2.8561
5	2.1003	2.1924	2.2878	2.3864	2.4883	2.7027	2.9316	3.1758	3.4360	3.7129
6	2.4364	2.5652	2.6996	2.8398	2.9860	3.2973	3.6352	4.0015	4.3980	4.8268
7	2.8262	3.0012	3.1855	3.3793	3.5832	4.0227	4.5077	5.0419	5.6295	6.2749
8	3.2784	3.5115	3.7589	4.0214	4.2998	4.9077	5.5895	6.3528	7.2058	8.1573
9	3.8030	4.1084	4.4355	4.7854	5.1598	5.9874	6.9310	8.0045	9.2234	10.6045
10	4.4114	4.8068	5.2338	5.6947	6.1917	7.3046	8.5944	10.0857	11.8059	13.7858
11	5.1173	5.6240	6.1759	6.7767	7.4301	8.9117	10.6571	12.7080	15.1116	17.9216
12	5.9360	6.5801	7.2876	8.0642	8.9161	10.8722	13.2148	16.0120	19.3428	23.2981
13	6.8858	7.6987	8.5994	9.5964	10.6993	13.2641	16.3863	20.1752	24.7588	30.2875
14	7.9875	9.0075	10.1472	11.4198	12.8392	16.1822	20.3191	25.4207	31.6913	39.3738
15	9.2655	10.5387	11.9737	13.5895	15.4070	19.7423	25.1956	32.0301	40.5648	51.1859
16	10.7480	12.3303	14.1290	16.1715	18.4884	24.0856	31.2426	40.3579	51.9230	66.5417
17	12.4677	14.4265	16.6722	19.2441	22.1861	29.3844	38.7408	50.8510	66.4614	86.5042
18	14.4625	16.8790	19.6733	22.9005	26.6233	35.8490	48.0386	64.0722	85.0706	112.455
19	16.7765	19.7484	23.2144	27.2516	31.9480	43.7358	59.5679	80.7310	108.890	146.192
20	19.4608	23.1056	27.3930	32.4294	38.3376	53.3576	73.8641	101.721	139.380	190.050
21	22.5745	27.0336	32.3238	38.5910	46.0051	65.0963	91.5915	128.169	178.406	247.065
22	26.1864	31.6293	38.1421	45.9233	55.2061	79.4175	113.574	161.492	228.360	321.184
23	30.3762	37.0062	45.0076	54.6487	66.2474	96.8894	140.831	203.480	292.300	417.539
24	35.2364	43.2973	53.1090	65.0320	79.4968	118.205	174.631	256.385	374.144	542.801
25	40.8742	50.6578	62.6686	77.3881	95.3962	144.210	216.542	323.045	478.905	705.641
26	47.4141	59.2697	73.9490	92.0918	114.475	175.936	268.512	407.037	612.998	917.333
27	55.0004	69.3455	87.2598	109.589	137.371	214.642	332.955	512.867	784.638	1192.53
28	63.8004	81.1342	102.967	130.411	164.845	261.864	412.864	646.212	1004.34	1550.29
29	74.0085	94.9271	121.501	155.189	197.814	319.474	511.952	814.228	1285.55	2015.38
30	85.8499	111.065	143.371	184.675	237.376	389.758	634.820	1025.93	1645.50	2620.00
35	180.314	243.503	327.997	440.701	590.668	1053.40	1861.05	3258.14	5653.91	9727.86
40	378.721	533.869	750.378	1051.67	1469.77	2847.04	5455.91	10347.2	19426.7	36118.9
45	795.444	1170.48	1716.68	2509.65	3657.26	7694.71	15994.7	32860.5	66749.6	134106.8
50	1670.70	2566.22	3927.36	5988.91	9100.44	20796.6	46890.4	104358.4	229349.9	497929.2

TABLE B.2
PRESENT VALUE OF A SINGLE SUM FACTORS
PVSS FACTOR = $1/(1 + i)^n$ where i = rate and n = periods

i =	0.5%	1%	1.5%	2%	2.5%	3%	3.5%	4%	4.5%	5%
n = 1	0.9950	0.9901	0.9852	0.9804	0.9756	0.9709	0.9662	0.9615	0.9569	0.9524
2	0.9901	0.9803	0.9707	0.9612	0.9518	0.9426	0.9335	0.9246	0.9157	0.9070
3	0.9851	0.9706	0.9563	0.9423	0.9286	0.9151	0.9019	0.8890	0.8763	0.8638
4	0.9802	0.9610	0.9422	0.9238	0.9060	0.8885	0.8714	0.8548	0.8386	0.8227
5	0.9754	0.9515	0.9283	0.9057	0.8839	0.8626	0.8420	0.8219	0.8025	0.7835
6	0.9705	0.9420	0.9145	0.8880	0.8623	0.8375	0.8135	0.7903	0.7679	0.7462
7	0.9657	0.9327	0.9010	0.8706	0.8413	0.8131	0.7860	0.7599	0.7348	0.7107
8	0.9609	0.9235	0.8877	0.8535	0.8207	0.7894	0.7594	0.7307	0.7032	0.6768
9	0.9561	0.9143	0.8746	0.8368	0.8007	0.7664	0.7337	0.7026	0.6729	0.6446
10	0.9513	0.9053	0.8617	0.8203	0.7812	0.7441	0.7089	0.6756	0.6439	0.6139
11	0.9466	0.8963	0.8489	0.8043	0.7621	0.7224	0.6849	0.6496	0.6162	0.5847
12	0.9419	0.8874	0.8364	0.7885	0.7436	0.7014	0.6618	0.6246	0.5897	0.5568
13	0.9372	0.8787	0.8240	0.7730	0.7254	0.6810	0.6394	0.6006	0.5643	0.5303
14	0.9326	0.8700	0.8118	0.7579	0.7077	0.6611	0.6178	0.5775	0.5400	0.5051
15	0.9279	0.8613	0.7999	0.7430	0.6905	0.6419	0.5969	0.5553	0.5167	0.4810
16	0.9233	0.8528	0.7880	0.7284	0.6736	0.6232	0.5767	0.5339	0.4945	0.4581
17	0.9187	0.8444	0.7764	0.7142	0.6572	0.6050	0.5572	0.5134	0.4732	0.4363
18	0.9141	0.8360	0.7649	0.7002	0.6412	0.5874	0.5384	0.4936	0.4528	0.4155
19	0.9096	0.8277	0.7536	0.6864	0.6255	0.5703	0.5202	0.4746	0.4333	0.3957
20	0.9051	0.8195	0.7425	0.6730	0.6103	0.5537	0.5026	0.4564	0.4146	0.3769
21	0.9006	0.8114	0.7315	0.6598	0.5954	0.5375	0.4856	0.4388	0.3968	0.3589
22	0.8961	0.8034	0.7207	0.6468	0.5809	0.5219	0.4692	0.4220	0.3797	0.3418
23	0.8916	0.7954	0.7100	0.6342	0.5667	0.5067	0.4533	0.4057	0.3634	0.3256
24	0.8872	0.7876	0.6995	0.6217	0.5529	0.4919	0.4380	0.3901	0.3477	0.3101
25	0.8828	0.7798	0.6892	0.6095	0.5394	0.4776	0.4231	0.3751	0.3327	0.2953
26	0.8784	0.7720	0.6790	0.5976	0.5262	0.4637	0.4088	0.3607	0.3184	0.2812
27	0.8740	0.7644	0.6690	0.5859	0.5134	0.4502	0.3950	0.3468	0.3047	0.2678
28	0.8697	0.7568	0.6591	0.5744	0.5009	0.4371	0.3817	0.3335	0.2916	0.2551
29	0.8653	0.7493	0.6494	0.5631	0.4887	0.4243	0.3687	0.3207	0.2790	0.2429
30	0.8610	0.7419	0.6398	0.5521	0.4767	0.4120	0.3563	0.3083	0.2670	0.2314
35	0.8398	0.7059	0.5939	0.5000	0.4214	0.3554	0.3000	0.2534	0.2143	0.1813
40	0.8191	0.6717	0.5513	0.4529	0.3724	0.3066	0.2526	0.2083	0.1719	0.1420
45	0.7990	0.6391	0.5117	0.4102	0.3292	0.2644	0.2127	0.1712	0.1380	0.1113
50	0.7793	0.6080	0.4750	0.3715	0.2909	0.2281	0.1791	0.1407	0.1107	0.0872

TABLE B.2 (CONTINUED)
PRESENT VALUE OF A SINGLE SUM FACTORS
PVSS FACTOR = $1/(1 + i)^n$ where i = rate and n = periods

i =	5.5%	6%	6.5%	7%	7.5%	8%	8.5%	9%	9.5%	10%
n = 1	0.9479	0.9434	0.9390	0.9346	0.9302	0.9259	0.9217	0.9174	0.9132	0.9091
2	0.8985	0.8900	0.8817	0.8734	0.8653	0.8573	0.8495	0.8417	0.8340	0.8264
3	0.8516	0.8396	0.8278	0.8163	0.8050	0.7938	0.7829	0.7722	0.7617	0.7513
4	0.8072	0.7921	0.7773	0.7629	0.7488	0.7350	0.7216	0.7084	0.6956	0.6830
5	0.7651	0.7473	0.7299	0.7130	0.6966	0.6806	0.6650	0.6499	0.6352	0.6209
6	0.7252	0.7050	0.6853	0.6663	0.6480	0.6302	0.6129	0.5963	0.5801	0.5645
7	0.6874	0.6651	0.6435	0.6227	0.6028	0.5835	0.5649	0.5470	0.5298	0.5132
8	0.6516	0.6274	0.6042	0.5820	0.5607	0.5403	0.5207	0.5019	0.4838	0.4665
9	0.6176	0.5919	0.5674	0.5439	0.5216	0.5002	0.4799	0.4604	0.4418	0.4241
10	0.5854	0.5584	0.5327	0.5083	0.4852	0.4632	0.4423	0.4224	0.4035	0.3855
11	0.5549	0.5268	0.5002	0.4751	0.4513	0.4289	0.4076	0.3875	0.3685	0.3505
12	0.5260	0.4970	0.4697	0.4440	0.4199	0.3971	0.3757	0.3555	0.3365	0.3186
13	0.4986	0.4688	0.4410	0.4150	0.3906	0.3677	0.3463	0.3262	0.3073	0.2897
14	0.4726	0.4423	0.4141	0.3878	0.3633	0.3405	0.3191	0.2992	0.2807	0.2633
15	0.4479	0.4173	0.3888	0.3624	0.3380	0.3152	0.2941	0.2745	0.2563	0.2394
16	0.4246	0.3936	0.3651	0.3387	0.3144	0.2919	0.2711	0.2519	0.2341	0.2176
17	0.4024	0.3714	0.3428	0.3166	0.2925	0.2703	0.2499	0.2311	0.2138	0.1978
18	0.3815	0.3503	0.3219	0.2959	0.2720	0.2502	0.2303	0.2120	0.1952	0.1799
19	0.3616	0.3305	0.3022	0.2765	0.2531	0.2317	0.2122	0.1945	0.1783	0.1635
20	0.3427	0.3118	0.2838	0.2584	0.2354	0.2145	0.1956	0.1784	0.1628	0.1486
21	0.3249	0.2942	0.2665	0.2415	0.2190	0.1987	0.1803	0.1637	0.1487	0.1351
22	0.3079	0.2775	0.2502	0.2257	0.2037	0.1839	0.1662	0.1502	0.1358	0.1228
23	0.2919	0.2618	0.2349	0.2109	0.1895	0.1703	0.1531	0.1378	0.1240	0.1117
24	0.2767	0.2470	0.2206	0.1971	0.1763	0.1577	0.1412	0.1264	0.1133	0.1015
25	0.2622	0.2330	0.2071	0.1842	0.1640	0.1460	0.1301	0.1160	0.1034	0.0923
26	0.2486	0.2198	0.1945	0.1722	0.1525	0.1352	0.1199	0.1064	0.0945	0.0839
27	0.2356	0.2074	0.1826	0.1609	0.1419	0.1252	0.1105	0.0976	0.0863	0.0763
28	0.2233	0.1956	0.1715	0.1504	0.1320	0.1159	0.1019	0.0895	0.0788	0.0693
29	0.2117	0.1846	0.1610	0.1406	0.1228	0.1073	0.0939	0.0822	0.0719	0.0630
30	0.2006	0.1741	0.1512	0.1314	0.1142	0.0994	0.0865	0.0754	0.0657	0.0573
35	0.1535	0.1301	0.1103	0.0937	0.0796	0.0676	0.0575	0.0490	0.0417	0.0356
40	0.1175	0.0972	0.0805	0.0668	0.0554	0.0460	0.0383	0.0318	0.0265	0.0221
45	0.0899	0.0727	0.0588	0.0476	0.0386	0.0313	0.0254	0.0207	0.0168	0.0137
50	0.0688	0.0543	0.0429	0.0339	0.0269	0.0213	0.0169	0.0134	0.0107	0.0085

TABLE B.2 (CONTINUED)
PRESENT VALUE OF A SINGLE SUM FACTORS
PVSS FACTOR = $1/(1 + i)^n$ where i = rate and n = periods

i =	10.5%	11%	11.5%	12%	12.5%	13%	13.5%	14%	14.5%	15%
n = 1	0.9050	0.9009	0.8969	0.8929	0.8889	0.8850	0.8811	0.8772	0.8734	0.8696
2	0.8190	0.8116	0.8044	0.7972	0.7901	0.7831	0.7763	0.7695	0.7628	0.7561
3	0.7412	0.7312	0.7214	0.7118	0.7023	0.6931	0.6839	0.6750	0.6662	0.6575
4	0.6707	0.6587	0.6470	0.6355	0.6243	0.6133	0.6026	0.5921	0.5818	0.5718
5	0.6070	0.5935	0.5803	0.5674	0.5549	0.5428	0.5309	0.5194	0.5081	0.4972
6	0.5493	0.5346	0.5204	0.5066	0.4933	0.4803	0.4678	0.4556	0.4438	0.4323
7	0.4971	0.4817	0.4667	0.4523	0.4385	0.4251	0.4121	0.3996	0.3876	0.3759
8	0.4499	0.4339	0.4186	0.4039	0.3897	0.3762	0.3631	0.3506	0.3385	0.3269
9	0.4071	0.3909	0.3754	0.3606	0.3464	0.3329	0.3199	0.3075	0.2956	0.2843
10	0.3684	0.3522	0.3367	0.3220	0.3079	0.2946	0.2819	0.2697	0.2582	0.2472
11	0.3334	0.3173	0.3020	0.2875	0.2737	0.2607	0.2483	0.2366	0.2255	0.2149
12	0.3018	0.2858	0.2708	0.2567	0.2433	0.2307	0.2188	0.2076	0.1969	0.1869
13	0.2731	0.2575	0.2429	0.2292	0.2163	0.2042	0.1928	0.1821	0.1720	0.1625
14	0.2471	0.2320	0.2178	0.2046	0.1922	0.1807	0.1698	0.1597	0.1502	0.1413
15	0.2236	0.2090	0.1954	0.1827	0.1709	0.1599	0.1496	0.1401	0.1312	0.1229
16	0.2024	0.1883	0.1752	0.1631	0.1519	0.1415	0.1318	0.1229	0.1146	0.1069
17	0.1832	0.1696	0.1572	0.1456	0.1350	0.1252	0.1162	0.1078	0.1001	0.0929
18	0.1658	0.1528	0.1409	0.1300	0.1200	0.1108	0.1023	0.0946	0.0874	0.0808
19	0.1500	0.1377	0.1264	0.1161	0.1067	0.0981	0.0902	0.0829	0.0763	0.0703
20	0.1358	0.1240	0.1134	0.1037	0.0948	0.0868	0.0794	0.0728	0.0667	0.0611
21	0.1229	0.1117	0.1017	0.0926	0.0843	0.0768	0.0700	0.0638	0.0582	0.0531
22	0.1112	0.1007	0.0912	0.0826	0.0749	0.0680	0.0617	0.0560	0.0508	0.0462
23	0.1006	0.0907	0.0818	0.0738	0.0666	0.0601	0.0543	0.0491	0.0444	0.0402
24	0.0911	0.0817	0.0734	0.0659	0.0592	0.0532	0.0479	0.0431	0.0388	0.0349
25	0.0824	0.0736	0.0658	0.0588	0.0526	0.0471	0.0422	0.0378	0.0339	0.0304
26	0.0746	0.0663	0.0590	0.0525	0.0468	0.0417	0.0372	0.0331	0.0296	0.0264
27	0.0675	0.0597	0.0529	0.0469	0.0416	0.0369	0.0327	0.0291	0.0258	0.0230
28	0.0611	0.0538	0.0475	0.0419	0.0370	0.0326	0.0288	0.0255	0.0226	0.0200
29	0.0553	0.0485	0.0426	0.0374	0.0329	0.0289	0.0254	0.0224	0.0197	0.0174
30	0.0500	0.0437	0.0382	0.0334	0.0292	0.0256	0.0224	0.0196	0.0172	0.0151
35	0.0304	0.0259	0.0222	0.0189	0.0162	0.0139	0.0119	0.0102	0.0087	0.0075
40	0.0184	0.0154	0.0129	0.0107	0.0090	0.0075	0.0063	0.0053	0.0044	0.0037
45	0.0112	0.0091	0.0075	0.0061	0.0050	0.0041	0.0034	0.0027	0.0023	0.0019
50	0.0068	0.0054	0.0043	0.0035	0.0028	0.0022	0.0018	0.0014	0.0011	0.0009

TABLE B.2 (CONTINUED)
PRESENT VALUE OF A SINGLE SUM FACTORS
PVSS FACTOR = $1/(1 + i)^n$ where i = rate and n = periods

i =	16%	17%	18%	19%	20%	22%	24%	26%	28%	30%
n = 1	0.8621	0.8547	0.8475	0.8403	0.8333	0.8197	0.8065	0.7937	0.7813	0.7692
2	0.7432	0.7305	0.7182	0.7062	0.6944	0.6719	0.6504	0.6299	0.6104	0.5917
3	0.6407	0.6244	0.6086	0.5934	0.5787	0.5507	0.5245	0.4999	0.4768	0.4552
4	0.5523	0.5337	0.5158	0.4987	0.4823	0.4514	0.4230	0.3968	0.3725	0.3501
5	0.4761	0.4561	0.4371	0.4190	0.4019	0.3700	0.3411	0.3149	0.2910	0.2693
6	0.4104	0.3898	0.3704	0.3521	0.3349	0.3033	0.2751	0.2499	0.2274	0.2072
7	0.3538	0.3332	0.3139	0.2959	0.2791	0.2486	0.2218	0.1983	0.1776	0.1594
8	0.3050	0.2848	0.2660	0.2487	0.2326	0.2038	0.1789	0.1574	0.1388	0.1226
9	0.2630	0.2434	0.2255	0.2090	0.1938	0.1670	0.1443	0.1249	0.1084	0.0943
10	0.2267	0.2080	0.1911	0.1756	0.1615	0.1369	0.1164	0.0992	0.0847	0.0725
11	0.1954	0.1778	0.1619	0.1476	0.1346	0.1122	0.0938	0.0787	0.0662	0.0558
12	0.1685	0.1520	0.1372	0.1240	0.1122	0.0920	0.0757	0.0625	0.0517	0.0429
13	0.1452	0.1299	0.1163	0.1042	0.0935	0.0754	0.0610	0.0496	0.0404	0.0330
14	0.1252	0.1110	0.0985	0.0876	0.0779	0.0618	0.0492	0.0393	0.0316	0.0254
15	0.1079	0.0949	0.0835	0.0736	0.0649	0.0507	0.0397	0.0312	0.0247	0.0195
16	0.0930	0.0811	0.0708	0.0618	0.0541	0.0415	0.0320	0.0248	0.0193	0.0150
17	0.0802	0.0693	0.0600	0.0520	0.0451	0.0340	0.0258	0.0197	0.0150	0.0116
18	0.0691	0.0592	0.0508	0.0437	0.0376	0.0279	0.0208	0.0156	0.0118	0.0089
19	0.0596	0.0506	0.0431	0.0367	0.0313	0.0229	0.0168	0.0124	0.0092	0.0068
20	0.0514	0.0433	0.0365	0.0308	0.0261	0.0187	0.0135	0.0098	0.0072	0.0053
21	0.0443	0.0370	0.0309	0.0259	0.0217	0.0154	0.0109	0.0078	0.0056	0.0040
22	0.0382	0.0316	0.0262	0.0218	0.0181	0.0126	0.0088	0.0062	0.0044	0.0031
23	0.0329	0.0270	0.0222	0.0183	0.0151	0.0103	0.0071	0.0049	0.0034	0.0024
24	0.0284	0.0231	0.0188	0.0154	0.0126	0.0085	0.0057	0.0039	0.0027	0.0018
25	0.0245	0.0197	0.0160	0.0129	0.0105	0.0069	0.0046	0.0031	0.0021	0.0014
26	0.0211	0.0169	0.0135	0.0109	0.0087	0.0057	0.0037	0.0025	0.0016	0.0011
27	0.0182	0.0144	0.0115	0.0091	0.0073	0.0047	0.0030	0.0019	0.0013	0.0008
28	0.0157	0.0123	0.0097	0.0077	0.0061	0.0038	0.0024	0.0015	0.0010	0.0006
29	0.0135	0.0105	0.0082	0.0064	0.0051	0.0031	0.0020	0.0012	0.0008	0.0005
30	0.0116	0.0090	0.0070	0.0054	0.0042	0.0026	0.0016	0.0010	0.0006	0.0004
35	0.0055	0.0041	0.0030	0.0023	0.0017	0.0009	0.0005	0.0003	0.0002	0.0001
40	0.0026	0.0019	0.0013	0.0010	0.0007	0.0004	0.0002	0.0001	<0.0001	<0.0001
45	0.0013	0.0009	0.0006	0.0004	0.0003	0.0001	0.0001	<0.0001	<0.0001	<0.0001
50	0.0006	0.0004	0.0003	0.0002	0.0001	<0.0001	<0.0001	<0.0001	<0.0001	<0.0001

TABLE B.3
FUTURE VALUE OF AN ANNUITY FACTORS
FVA Factor = $((1 + i)^n - 1)/i$ where i = rate and n = periods

i =	0.5%	1%	1.5%	2%	2.5%	3%	3.5%	4%	4.5%	5%
n = 1	1.0000	1.0000	1.0000	1.0000	1.0000	1.0000	1.0000	1.0000	1.0000	1.0000
2	2.0050	2.0100	2.0150	2.0200	2.0250	2.0300	2.0350	2.0400	2.0450	2.0500
3	3.0150	3.0301	3.0452	3.0604	3.0756	3.0909	3.1062	3.1216	3.1370	3.1525
4	4.0301	4.0604	4.0909	4.1216	4.1525	4.1836	4.2149	4.2465	4.2782	4.3101
5	5.0503	5.1010	5.1523	5.2040	5.2563	5.3091	5.3625	5.4163	5.4707	5.5256
6	6.0755	6.1520	6.2296	6.3081	6.3877	6.4684	6.5502	6.6330	6.7169	6.8019
7	7.1059	7.2135	7.3230	7.4343	7.5474	7.6625	7.7794	7.8983	8.0192	8.1420
8	8.1414	8.2857	8.4328	8.5830	8.7361	8.8923	9.0517	9.2142	9.3800	9.5491
9	9.1821	9.3685	9.5593	9.7546	9.9545	10.1591	10.3685	10.5828	10.8021	11.0266
10	10.2280	10.4622	10.7027	10.9497	11.2034	11.4639	11.7314	12.0061	12.2882	12.5779
11	11.2792	11.5668	11.8633	12.1687	12.4835	12.8078	13.1420	13.4864	13.8412	14.2068
12	12.3356	12.6825	13.0412	13.4121	13.7956	14.1920	14.6020	15.0258	15.4640	15.9171
13	13.3972	13.8093	14.2368	14.6803	15.1404	15.6178	16.1130	16.6268	17.1599	17.7130
14	14.4642	14.9474	15.4504	15.9739	16.5190	17.0863	17.6770	18.2919	18.9321	19.5986
15	15.5365	16.0969	16.6821	17.2934	17.9319	18.5989	19.2957	20.0236	20.7841	21.5786
16	16.6142	17.2579	17.9324	18.6393	19.3802	20.1569	20.9710	21.8245	22.7193	23.6575
17	17.6973	18.4304	19.2014	20.0121	20.8647	21.7616	22.7050	23.6975	24.7417	25.8404
18	18.7858	19.6147	20.4894	21.4123	22.3863	23.4144	24.4997	25.6454	26.8551	28.1324
19	19.8797	20.8109	21.7967	22.8406	23.9460	25.1169	26.3572	27.6712	29.0636	30.5390
20	20.9791	22.0190	23.1237	24.2974	25.5447	26.8704	28.2797	29.7781	31.3714	33.0660
21	22.0840	23.2392	24.4705	25.7833	27.1833	28.6765	30.2695	31.9692	33.7831	35.7193
22	23.1944	24.4716	25.8376	27.2990	28.8629	30.5368	32.3289	34.2480	36.3034	38.5052
23	24.3104	25.7163	27.2251	28.8450	30.5844	32.4529	34.4604	36.6179	38.9370	41.4305
24	25.4320	26.9735	28.6335	30.4219	32.3490	34.4265	36.6665	39.0826	41.6892	44.5020
25	26.5591	28.2432	30.0630	32.0303	34.1578	36.4593	38.9499	41.6459	44.5652	47.7271
26	27.6919	29.5256	31.5140	33.6709	36.0117	38.5530	41.3131	44.3117	47.5706	51.1135
27	28.8304	30.8209	32.9867	35.3443	37.9120	40.7096	43.7591	47.0842	50.7113	54.6691
28	29.9745	32.1291	34.4815	37.0512	39.8598	42.9309	46.2906	49.9676	53.9933	58.4026
29	31.1244	33.4504	35.9987	38.7922	41.8563	45.2189	48.9108	52.9663	57.4230	62.3227
30	32.2800	34.7849	37.5387	40.5681	43.9027	47.5754	51.6227	56.0849	61.0071	66.4388
35	38.1454	41.6603	45.5921	49.9945	54.9282	60.4621	66.6740	73.6522	81.4966	90.3203
40	44.1588	48.8864	54.2679	60.4020	67.4026	75.4013	84.5503	95.0255	107.030	120.800
45	50.3242	56.4811	63.6142	71.8927	81.5161	92.7199	105.782	121.029	138.850	159.700
50	56.6452	64.4632	73.6828	84.5794	97.4843	112.797	130.998	152.667	178.503	209.348

TABLE B.3 (CONTINUED)
FUTURE VALUE OF AN ANNUITY FACTORS
FVA Factor = $((1 + i)^n - 1)/i$ where i = rate and n = periods

i =	5.5%	6%	6.5%	7%	7.5%	8%	8.5%	9%	9.5%	10%
n = 1	1.0000	1.0000	1.0000	1.0000	1.0000	1.0000	1.0000	1.0000	1.0000	1.0000
2	2.0550	2.0600	2.0650	2.0700	2.0750	2.0800	2.0850	2.0900	2.0950	2.1000
3	3.1680	3.1836	3.1992	3.2149	3.2306	3.2464	3.2622	3.2781	3.2940	3.3100
4	4.3423	4.3746	4.4072	4.4399	4.4729	4.5061	4.5395	4.5731	4.6070	4.6410
5	5.5811	5.6371	5.6936	5.7507	5.8084	5.8666	5.9254	5.9847	6.0446	6.1051
6	6.8881	6.9753	7.0637	7.1533	7.2440	7.3359	7.4290	7.5233	7.6189	7.7156
7	8.2669	8.3938	8.5229	8.6540	8.7873	8.9228	9.0605	9.2004	9.3426	9.4872
8	9.7216	9.8975	10.0769	10.2598	10.4464	10.6366	10.8306	11.0285	11.2302	11.4359
9	11.2563	11.4913	11.7319	11.9780	12.2298	12.4876	12.7512	13.0210	13.2971	13.5795
10	12.8754	13.1808	13.4944	13.8164	14.1471	14.4866	14.8351	15.1929	15.5603	15.9374
11	14.5835	14.9716	15.3716	15.7836	16.2081	16.6455	17.0961	17.5603	18.0385	18.5312
12	16.3856	16.8699	17.3707	17.8885	18.4237	18.9771	19.5492	20.1407	20.7522	21.3843
13	18.2868	18.8821	19.4998	20.1406	20.8055	21.4953	22.2109	22.9534	23.7236	24.5227
14	20.2926	21.0151	21.7673	22.5505	23.3659	24.2149	25.0989	26.0192	26.9774	27.9750
15	22.4087	23.2760	24.1822	25.1290	26.1184	27.1521	28.2323	29.3609	30.5402	31.7725
16	24.6411	25.6725	26.7540	27.8881	29.0772	30.3243	31.6320	33.0034	34.4416	35.9497
17	26.9964	28.2129	29.4930	30.8402	32.2580	33.7502	35.3207	36.9737	38.7135	40.5447
18	29.4812	30.9057	32.4101	33.9990	35.6774	37.4502	39.3230	41.3013	43.3913	45.5992
19	32.1027	33.7600	35.5167	37.3790	39.3532	41.4463	43.6654	46.0185	48.5135	51.1591
20	34.8683	36.7856	38.8253	40.9955	43.3047	45.7620	48.3770	51.1601	54.1222	57.2750
21	37.7861	39.9927	42.3490	44.8652	47.5525	50.4229	53.4891	56.7645	60.2638	64.0025
22	40.8643	43.3923	46.1016	49.0057	52.1190	55.4568	59.0356	62.8733	66.9889	71.4027
23	44.1118	46.9958	50.0982	53.4361	57.0279	60.8933	65.0537	69.5319	74.3529	79.5430
24	47.5380	50.8156	54.3546	58.1767	62.3050	66.7648	71.5832	76.7898	82.4164	88.4973
25	51.1526	54.8645	58.8877	63.2490	67.9779	73.1059	78.6678	84.7009	91.2459	98.3471
26	54.9660	59.1564	63.7154	68.6765	74.0762	79.9544	86.3546	93.3240	100.914	109.182
27	58.9891	63.7058	68.8569	74.4838	80.6319	87.3508	94.6947	102.723	111.501	121.100
28	63.2335	68.5281	74.3326	80.6977	87.6793	95.3388	103.744	112.968	123.094	134.210
29	67.7114	73.6398	80.1642	87.3465	95.2553	103.966	113.562	124.135	135.788	148.631
30	72.4355	79.0582	86.3749	94.4608	103.399	113.283	124.215	136.308	149.688	164.494
35	100.251	111.435	124.035	138.237	154.252	172.317	192.702	215.711	241.688	271.024
40	136.606	154.762	175.632	199.635	227.257	259.057	295.683	337.882	386.520	442.593
45	184.119	212.744	246.325	285.749	332.065	386.506	450.530	525.859	614.519	718.905
50	246.217	290.336	343.180	406.529	482.530	573.770	683.368	815.084	973.445	1163.91

TABLE B.3 (CONTINUED)
FUTURE VALUE OF AN ANNUITY FACTORS
FVA Factor = $((1 + i)^n - 1)/i$ where i = rate and n = periods

i =	10.5%	11%	11.5%	12%	12.5%	13%	13.5%	14%	14.5%	15%
n = 1	1.0000	1.0000	1.0000	1.0000	1.0000	1.0000	1.0000	1.0000	1.0000	1.0000
2	2.1050	2.1100	2.1150	2.1200	2.1250	2.1300	2.1350	2.1400	2.1450	2.1500
3	3.3260	3.3421	3.3582	3.3744	3.3906	3.4069	3.4232	3.4396	3.4560	3.4725
4	4.6753	4.7097	4.7444	4.7793	4.8145	4.8498	4.8854	4.9211	4.9571	4.9934
5	6.1662	6.2278	6.2900	6.3528	6.4163	6.4803	6.5449	6.6101	6.6759	6.7424
6	7.8136	7.9129	8.0134	8.1152	8.2183	8.3227	8.4284	8.5355	8.6439	8.7537
7	9.6340	9.7833	9.9349	10.0890	10.2456	10.4047	10.5663	10.7305	10.8973	11.0668
8	11.6456	11.8594	12.0774	12.2997	12.5263	12.7573	12.9927	13.2328	13.4774	13.7268
9	13.8684	14.1640	14.4663	14.7757	15.0921	15.4157	15.7468	16.0853	16.4317	16.7858
10	16.3246	16.7220	17.1300	17.5487	17.9786	18.4197	18.8726	19.3373	19.8142	20.3037
11	19.0387	19.5614	20.0999	20.6546	21.2259	21.8143	22.4204	23.0445	23.6873	24.3493
12	22.0377	22.7132	23.4114	24.1331	24.8791	25.6502	26.4471	27.2707	28.1220	29.0017
13	25.3517	26.2116	27.1037	28.0291	28.9890	29.9847	31.0175	32.0887	33.1997	34.3519
14	29.0136	30.0949	31.2207	32.3926	33.6126	34.8827	36.2048	37.5811	39.0136	40.5047
15	33.0600	34.4054	35.8110	37.2797	38.8142	40.4175	42.0925	43.8424	45.6706	47.5804
16	37.5313	39.1899	40.9293	42.7533	44.6660	46.6717	48.7750	50.9804	53.2928	55.7175
17	42 4721	44.5008	46.6362	48.8837	51.2493	53.7391	56.3596	59.1176	62.0203	65.0751
18	47.9317	50.3959	52.9993	55.7497	58.6554	61.7251	64.9681	68.3941	72.0132	75.8364
19	53.9645	56.9395	60.0942	63.4397	66.9873	70.7494	74.7388	78.9692	83.4551	88.2118
20	60.6308	64.2028	68.0051	72.0524	76.3608	80.9468	85.8286	91.0249	96.5561	102.444
21	67.9970	72.2651	76.8257	81.6987	86.9058	92.4699	98.4154	104.768	111.557	118.810
22	76.1367	81.2143	86.6606	92.5026	98.7691	105.491	112.701	120.436	128.732	137.632
23	85.1311	91.1479	97.6266	104.603	112.115	120.205	128.916	138.297	148.399	159.276
24	95.0699	102.174	109.854	118.155	127.130	136.831	147.320	158.659	170.917	184.168
25	106.052	114.413	123.487	133.334	144.021	155.620	168.208	181.871	196.699	212.793
26	118.188	127.999	138.688	150.334	163.023	176.850	191.916	208.333	226.221	245.712
27	131.597	143.079	155.637	169.374	184.401	200.841	218.825	238.499	260.023	283.569
28	146.415	159.817	174.535	190.699	208.452	227.950	249.366	272.889	298.726	327.104
29	162.789	178.397	195.607	214.583	235.508	258.583	284.031	312.094	343.041	377.170
30	180.881	199.021	219.101	241.333	265.946	293.199	323.375	356.787	393.782	434.745
35	304.159	341.590	383.879	431.663	485.660	546.681	615.640	693.573	781.644	881.170
40	507.252	581.826	667.850	767.091	881.592	1013.70	1166.14	1342.03	1544.96	1779.09
45	841.836	986.639	1157.23	1358.23	1595.07	1874.16	2203.04	2590.56	3047.17	3585.13
50	1393.05	1668.77	2000.61	2400.02	2880.79	3459.51	4156.10	4994.52	6003.54	7217.72

TABLE B.3 (CONTINUED)
FUTURE VALUE OF AN ANNUITY FACTORS
FVA Factor = $((1 + i)^n-1)/i$ where i = rate and n = periods

i =	16%	17%	18%	19%	20%	22%	24%	26%	28%	30%
n = 1	1.0000	1.0000	1.0000	1.0000	1.0000	1.0000	1.0000	1.0000	1.0000	1.0000
2	2.1600	2.1700	2.1800	2.1900	2.2000	2.2200	2.2400	2.2600	2.2800	2.3000
3	3.5056	3.5389	3.5724	3.6061	3.6400	3.7084	3.7776	3.8476	3.9184	3.9900
4	5.0665	5.1405	5.2154	5.2913	5.3680	5.5242	5.6842	5.8480	6.0156	6.1870
5	6.8771	7.0144	7.1542	7.2966	7.4416	7.7396	8.0484	8.3684	8.6999	9.0431
6	8.9775	9.2068	9.4420	9.6830	9.9299	10.4423	10.9801	11.5442	12.1359	12.7560
7	11.4139	11.7720	12.1415	12.5227	12.9159	13.7396	14.6153	15.5458	16.5339	17.5828
8	14.2401	14.7733	15.3270	15.9020	16.4991	17.7623	19.1229	20.5876	22.1634	23.8577
9	17.5185	18.2847	19.0859	19.9234	20.7989	22.6700	24.7125	26.9404	29.3692	32.0150
10	21.3215	22.3931	23.5213	24.7089	25.9587	28.6574	31.6434	34.9449	38.5926	42.6195
11	25.7329	27.1999	28.7551	30.4035	32.1504	35.9620	40.2379	45.0306	50.3985	56.4053
12	30.8502	32.8239	34.9311	37.1802	39.5805	44.8737	50.8950	57.7386	65.5100	74.3270
13	36.7862	39.4040	42.2187	45.2445	48.4966	55.7459	64.1097	73.7506	84.8529	97.6250
14	43.6720	47.1027	50.8180	54.8409	59.1959	69.0100	80.4961	93.9258	109.612	127.913
15	51.6595	56.1101	60.9653	66.2607	72.0351	85.1922	100.815	119.347	141.303	167.286
16	60.9250	66.6488	72.9390	79.8502	87.4421	104.935	126.011	151.377	181.868	218.472
17	71.6730	78.9792	87.0680	96.0218	105.931	129.020	157.253	191.735	233.791	285.014
18	84.1407	93.4056	103.740	115.266	128.117	158.405	195.994	242.585	300.252	371.518
19	98.6032	110.285	123.414	138.166	154.740	194.254	244.033	306.658	385.323	483.973
20	115.380	130.033	146.628	165.418	186.688	237.989	303.601	387.389	494.213	630.165
21	134.841	153.139	174.021	197.847	225.026	291.347	377.465	489.110	633.593	820.215
22	157.415	180.172	206.345	236.438	271.031	356.443	469.056	617.278	811.999	1067.28
23	183.601	211.801	244.487	282.362	326.237	435.861	582.630	778.771	1040.36	1388.46
24	213.978	248.808	289.494	337.010	392.484	532.750	723.461	982.251	1332.66	1806.00
25	249.214	292.105	342.603	402.042	471.981	650.955	898.092	1238.64	1706.80	2348.80
26	290.088	342.763	405.272	479.431	567.377	795.165	1114.63	1561.68	2185.71	3054.44
27	337.502	402.032	479.221	571.522	681.853	971.102	1383.15	1968.72	2798.71	3971.78
28	392.503	471.378	566.481	681.112	819.223	1185.74	1716.10	2481.59	3583.34	5164.31
29	456.303	552.512	669.447	811.523	984.068	1447.61	2128.96	3127.80	4587.68	6714.60
30	530.312	647.439	790.948	966.712	1181.88	1767.08	2640.92	3942.03	5873.23	8729.99
35	1120.71	1426.49	1816.65	2314.21	2948.34	4783.64	7750.23	12527.4	20189.0	32422.9
40	2360.76	3134.52	4163.21	5529.83	7343.86	12936.5	22728.8	39793.0	69377.5	120393
45	4965.27	6879.29	9531.58	13203.4	18281.3	34971.4	66640.4	126383	238388	447019
50	10435.6	15089.5	21813.1	31515.3	45497.2	94525.3	195373	401374	819103	1659761

TABLE B.4
PRESENT VALUE OF AN ANNUITY FACTORS
PVA Factor = $(1 - (1/(1 + i)^n))/i$ where i = rate and n = periods

i =	0.5%	1%	1.5%	2%	2.5%	3%	3.5%	4%	4.5%	5%
n = 1	0.9950	0.9901	0.9852	0.9804	0.9756	0.9709	0.9662	0.9615	0.9569	0.9524
2	1.9851	1.9704	1.9559	1.9416	1.9274	1.9135	1.8997	1.8861	1.8727	1.8594
3	2.9702	2.9410	2.9122	2.8839	2.8560	2.8286	2.8016	2.7751	2.7490	2.7232
4	3.9505	3.9020	3.8544	3.8077	3.7620	3.7171	3.6731	3.6299	3.5875	3.5460
5	4.9259	4.8534	4.7826	4.7135	4.6458	4.5797	4.5151	4.4518	4.3900	4.3295
6	5.8964	5.7955	5.6972	5.6014	5.5081	5.4172	5.3286	5.2421	5.1579	5.0757
7	6.8621	6.7282	6.5982	6.4720	6.3494	6.2303	6.1145	6.0021	5.8927	5.7864
8	7.8230	7.6517	7.4859	7.3255	7.1701	7.0197	6.8740	6.7327	6.5959	6.4632
9	8.7791	8.5660	8.3605	8.1622	7.9709	7.7861	7.6077	7.4353	7.2688	7.1078
10	9.7304	9.4713	9.2222	8.9826	8.7521	8.5302	8.3166	8.1109	7.9127	7.7217
11	10.6770	10.3676	10.0711	9.7868	9.5142	9.2526	9.0016	8.7605	8.5289	8.3064
12	11.6189	11.2551	10.9075	10.5753	10.2578	9.9540	9.6633	9.3851	9.1186	8.8633
13	12.5562	12.1337	11.7315	11.3484	10.9832	10.6350	10.3027	9.9856	9.6829	9.3936
14	13.4887	13.0037	12.5434	12.1062	11.6909	11.2961	10.9205	10.5631	10.2228	9.8986
15	14.4166	13.8651	13.3432	12.8493	12.3814	11.9379	11.5174	11.1184	10.7395	10.3797
16	15.3399	14.7179	14.1313	13.5777	13.0550	12.5611	12.0941	11.6523	11.2340	10.8378
17	16.2586	15.5623	14.9076	14.2919	13.7122	13.1661	12.6513	12.1657	11.7072	11.2741
18	17.1728	16.3983	15.6726	14.9920	14.3534	13.7535	13.1897	12.6593	12.1600	11.6896
19	18.0824	17.2260	16.4262	15.6785	14.9789	14.3238	13.7098	13.1339	12.5933	12.0853
20	18.9874	18.0456	17.1686	16.3514	15.5892	14.8775	14.2124	13.5903	13.0079	12.4622
21	19.8880	18.8570	17.9001	17.0112	16.1845	15.4150	14.6980	14.0292	13.4047	12.8212
22	20.7841	19.6604	18.6208	17.6580	16.7654	15.9369	15.1671	14.4511	13.7844	13.1630
23	21.6757	20.4558	19.3309	18.2922	17.3321	16.4436	15.6204	14.8568	14.1478	13.4886
24	22.5629	21.2434	20.0304	18.9139	17.8850	16.9355	16.0584	15.2470	14.4955	13.7986
25	23.4456	22.0232	20.7196	19.5235	18.4244	17.4131	16.4815	15.6221	14.8282	14.0939
26	24.3240	22.7952	21.3986	20.1210	18.9506	17.8768	16.8904	15.9828	15.1466	14.3752
27	25.1980	23.5596	22.0676	20.7069	19.4640	18.3270	17.2854	16.3296	15.4513	14.6430
28	26.0677	24.3164	22.7267	21.2813	19.9649	18.7641	17.6670	16.6631	15.7429	14.8981
29	26.9330	25.0658	23.3761	21.8444	20.4535	19.1885	18.0358	16.9837	16.0219	15.1411
30	27.7941	25.8077	24.0158	22.3965	20.9303	19.6004	18.3920	17.2920	16.2889	15.3725
35	32.0354	29.4086	27.0756	24.9986	23.1452	21.4872	20.0007	18.6646	17.4610	16.3742
40	36.1722	32.8347	29.9158	27.3555	25.1028	23.1148	21.3551	19.7928	18.4016	17.1591
45	40.2072	36.0945	32.5523	29.4902	26.8330	24.5187	22.4955	20.7200	19.1563	17.7741
50	44.1428	39.1961	34.9997	31.4236	28.3623	25.7298	23.4556	21.4822	19.7620	18.2559

TABLE B.4 (CONTINUED)
PRESENT VALUE OF AN ANNUITY FACTORS
PVA Factor = $(1 - (1/(1 + i)^n))/i$ where i = rate and n = periods

i =	5.5%	6%	6.5%	7%	7.5%	8%	8.5%	9%	9.5%	10%
n =	0.9479	0.9434	0.9390	0.9346	0.9302	0.9259	0.9217	0.9174	0.9132	0.9091
2	1.8463	1.8334	1.8206	1.8080	1.7956	1.7833	1.7711	1.7591	1.7473	1.7355
3	2.6979	2.6730	2.6485	2.6243	2.6005	2.5771	2.5540	2.5313	2.5089	2.4869
4	3.5052	3.4651	3.4258	3.3872	3.3493	3.3121	3.2756	3.2397	3.2045	3.1699
5	4.2703	4.2124	4.1557	4.1002	4.0459	3.9927	3.9406	3.8897	3.8397	3.7908
6	4.9955	4.9173	4.8410	4.7665	4.6938	4.6229	4.5536	4.4859	4.4198	4.3553
7	5.6830	5.5824	5.4845	5.3893	5.2966	5.2064	5.1185	5.0330	4.9496	4.8684
8	6.3346	6.2098	6.0888	5.9713	5.8573	5.7466	5.6392	5.5348	5.4334	5.3349
9	6.9522	6.8017	6.6561	6.5152	6.3789	6.2469	6.1191	5.9952	5.8753	5.7590
10	7.5376	7.3601	7.1888	7.0236	6.8641	6.7101	6.5613	6.4177	6.2788	6.1446
11	8.0925	7.8869	7.6890	7.4987	7.3154	7.1390	6.9690	6.8052	6.6473	6.4951
12	8.6185	8.3838	8.1587	7.9427	7.7353	7.5361	7.3447	7.1607	6.9838	6.8137
13	9.1171	8.8527	8.5997	8.3577	8.1258	7.9038	7.6910	7.4869	7.2912	7.1034
14	9.5896	9.2950	9.0138	8.7455	8.4892	8.2442	8.0101	7.7862	7.5719	7.3667
15	10.0376	9.7122	9.4027	9.1079	8.8271	8.5595	8.3042	8.0607	7.8282	7.6061
16	10.4622	10.1059	9.7678	9.4466	9.1415	8.8514	8.5753	8.3126	8.0623	7.8237
17	10.8646	10.4773	10.1106	9.7632	9.4340	9.1216	8.8252	8.5436	8.2760	8.0216
18	11.2461	10.8276	10.4325	10.0591	9.7060	9.3719	9.0555	8.7556	8.4713	8.2014
19	11.6077	11.1581	10.7347	10.3356	9.9591	9.6036	9.2677	8.9501	8.6496	8.3649
20	11.9504	11.4699	11.0185	10.5940	10.1945	9.8181	9.4633	9.1285	8.8124	8.5136
21	12.2752	11.7641	11.2850	10.8355	10.4135	10.0168	9.6436	9.2922	8.9611	8.6487
22	12.5832	12.0416	11.5352	11.0612	10.6172	10.2007	9.8098	9.4424	9.0969	8.7715
23	12.8750	12.3034	11.7701	11.2722	10.8067	10.3711	9.9629	9.5802	9.2209	8.8832
24	13.1517	12.5504	11.9907	11.4693	10.9830	10.5288	10.1041	9.7066	9.3341	8.9847
25	13.4139	12.7834	12.1979	11.6536	11.1469	10.6748	10.2342	9.8226	9.4376	9.0770
26	13.6625	13.0032	12.3924	11.8258	11.2995	10.8100	10.3541	9.9290	9.5320	9.1609
27	13.8981	13.2105	12.5750	11.9867	11.4414	10.9352	10.4646	10.0266	9.6183	9.2372
28	14.1214	13.4062	12.7465	12.1371	11.5734	11.0511	10.5665	10.1161	9.6971	9.3066
29	14.3331	13.5907	12.9075	12.2777	11.6962	11.1584	10.6603	10.1983	9.7690	9.3696
30	14.5337	13.7648	13.0587	12.4090	11.8104	11.2578	10.7468	10.2737	9.8347	9.4269
35	15.3906	14.4982	13.6870	12.9477	12.2725	11.6546	11.0878	10.5668	10.0870	9.6442
40	16.0461	15.0463	14.1455	13.3317	12.5944	11.9246	11.3145	10.7574	10.2472	9.7791
45	16.5477	15.4558	14.4802	13.6055	12.8186	12.1084	11.4653	10.8812	10.3490	9.8628
50	16.9315	15.7619	14.7245	13.8007	12.9748	12.2335	11.5656	10.9617	10.4137	9.9148

TABLE B.4 (CONTINUED)
PRESENT VALUE OF AN ANNUITY FACTORS
PVA Factor = $(1 - (1/(1 + i)^n))/i$ where i = rate and n = periods

i =	10.5%	11%	11.5%	12%	12.5%	13%	13.5%	14%	14.5%	15%
n = 1	0.9050	0.9009	0.8969	0.8929	0.8889	0.8850	0.8811	0.8772	0.8734	0.8696
2	1.7240	1.7125	1.7012	1.6901	1.6790	1.6681	1.6573	1.6467	1.6361	1.6257
3	2.4651	2.4437	2.4226	2.4018	2.3813	2.3612	2.3413	2.3216	2.3023	2.2832
4	3.1359	3.1024	3.0696	3.0373	3.0056	2.9745	2.9438	2.9137	2.8841	2.8550
5	3.7429	3.6959	3.6499	3.6048	3.5606	3.5172	3.4747	3.4331	3.3922	3.3522
6	4.2922	4.2305	4.1703	4.1114	4.0538	3.9975	3.9425	3.8887	3.8360	3.7845
7	4.7893	4.7122	4.6370	4.5638	4.4923	4.4226	4.3546	4.2883	4.2236	4.1604
8	5.2392	5.1461	5.0556	4.9676	4.8820	4.7988	4.7177	4.6389	4.5621	4.4873
9	5.6463	5.5370	5.4311	5.3282	5.2285	5.1317	5.0377	4.9464	4.8577	4.7716
10	6.0148	5.8892	5.7678	5.6502	5.5364	5.4262	5.3195	5.2161	5.1159	5.0188
11	6.3482	6.2065	6.0697	5.9377	5.8102	5.6869	5.5679	5.4527	5.3414	5.2337
12	6.6500	6.4924	6.3406	6.1944	6.0535	5.9176	5.7867	5.6603	5.5383	5.4206
13	6.9230	6.7499	6.5835	6.4235	6.2698	6.1218	5.9794	5.8424	5.7103	5.5831
14	7.1702	6.9819	6.8013	6.6282	6.4620	6.3025	6.1493	6.0021	5.8606	5.7245
15	7.3938	7.1909	6.9967	6.8109	6.6329	6.4624	6.2989	6.1422	5.9918	5.8474
16	7.5962	7.3792	7.1719	6.9740	6.7848	6.6039	6.4308	6.2651	6.1063	5.9542
17	7.7794	7.5488	7.3291	7.1196	6.9198	6.7291	6.5469	6.3729	6.2064	6.0472
18	7.9451	7.7016	7.4700	7.2497	7.0398	6.8399	6.6493	6.4674	6.2938	6.1280
19	8.0952	7.8393	7.5964	7.3658	7.1465	6.9380	6.7395	6.5504	6.3701	6.1982
20	8.2309	7.9633	7.7098	7.4694	7.2414	7.0248	6.8189	6.6231	6.4368	6.2593
21	8.3538	8.0751	7.8115	7.5620	7.3256	7.1016	6.8889	6.6870	6.4950	6.3125
22	8.4649	8.1757	7.9027	7.6446	7.4006	7.1695	6.9506	6.7429	6.5459	6.3587
23	8.5656	8.2664	7.9845	7.7184	7.4672	7.2297	7.0049	6.7921	6.5903	6.3988
24	8.6566	8.3481	8.0578	7.7843	7.5264	7.2829	7.0528	6.8351	6.6291	6.4338
25	8.7390	8.4217	8.1236	7.8431	7.5790	7.3300	7.0950	6.8729	6.6629	6.4641
26	8.8136	8.4881	8.1826	7.8957	7.6258	7.3717	7.1321	6.9061	6.6925	6.4906
27	8.8811	8.5478	8.2355	7.9426	7.6674	7.4086	7.1649	6.9352	6.7184	6.5135
28	8.9422	8.6016	8.2830	7.9844	7.7043	7.4412	7.1937	6.9607	6.7409	6.5335
29	8.9974	8.6501	8.3255	8.0218	7.7372	7.4701	7.2191	6.9830	6.7606	6.5509
30	9.0474	8.6938	8.3637	8.0552	7.7664	7.4957	7.2415	7.0027	6.7778	6.5660
35	9.2347	8.8552	8.5030	8.1755	7.8704	7.5856	7.3193	7.0700	6.8362	6.6166
40	9.3483	8.9511	8.5839	8.2438	7.9281	7.6344	7.3607	7.1050	6.8659	6.6418
45	9.4173	9.0079	8.6308	8.2825	7.9601	7.6609	7.3826	7.1232	6.8810	6.6543
50	9.4591	9.0417	8.6580	8.3045	7.9778	7.6752	7.3942	7.1327	6.8886	6.6605

TABLE B.4 (CONTINUED)
PRESENT VALUE OF AN ANNUITY FACTORS
PVA Factor = $(1 - (1/(1 + i)^n))/i$ where i = rate and n = periods

i =	16%	17%	18%	19%	20%	22%	24%	26%	28%	30%
n = 1	0.8621	0.8547	0.8475	0.8403	0.8333	0.8197	0.8065	0.7937	0.7813	0.7692
2	1.6052	1.5852	1.5656	1.5465	1.5278	1.4915	1.4568	1.4235	1.3916	1.3609
3	2.2459	2.2096	2.1743	2.1399	2.1065	2.0422	1.9813	1.9234	1.8684	1.8161
4	2.7982	2.7432	2.6901	2.6386	2.5887	2.4936	2.4043	2.3202	2.2410	2.1662
5	3.2743	3.1993	3.1272	3.0576	2.9906	2.8636	2.7454	2.6351	2.5320	2.4356
6	3.6847	3.5892	3.4976	3.4098	3.3255	3.1669	3.0205	2.8850	2.7594	2.6427
7	4.0386	3.9224	3.8115	3.7057	3.6046	3.4155	3.2423	3.0833	2.9370	2.8021
8	4.3436	4.2072	4.0776	3.9544	3.8372	3.6193	3.4212	3.2407	3.0758	2.9247
9	4.6065	4.4506	4.3030	4.1633	4.0310	3.7863	3.5655	3.3657	3.1842	3.0190
10	4.8332	4.6586	4.4941	4.3389	4.1925	3.9232	3.6819	3.4648	3.2689	3.0915
11	5.0286	4.8364	4.6560	4.4865	4.3271	4.0354	3.7757	3.5435	3.3351	3.1473
12	5.1971	4.9884	4.7932	4.6105	4.4392	4.1274	3.8514	3.6059	3.3868	3.1903
13	5.3423	5.1183	4.9095	4.7147	4.5327	4.2028	3.9124	3.6555	3.4272	3.2233
14	5.4675	5.2293	5.0081	4.8023	4.6106	4.2646	3.9616	3.6949	3.4587	3.2487
15	5.5755	5.3242	5.0916	4.8759	4.6755	4.3152	4.0013	3.7261	3.4834	3.2682
16	5.6685	5.4053	5.1624	4.9377	4.7296	4.3567	4.0333	3.7509	3.5026	3.2832
17	5.7487	5.4746	5.2223	4.9897	4.7746	4.3908	4.0591	3.7705	3.5177	3.2948
18	5.8178	5.5339	5.2732	5.0333	4.8122	4.4187	4.0799	3.7861	3.5294	3.3037
19	5.8775	5.5845	5.3162	5.0700	4.8435	4.4415	4.0967	3.7985	3.5386	3.3105
20	5.9288	5.6278	5.3527	5.1009	4.8696	4.4603	4.1103	3.8083	3.5458	3.3158
21	5.9731	5.6648	5.3837	5.1268	4.8913	4.4756	4.1212	3.8161	3.5514	3.3198
22	6.0113	5.6964	5.4099	5.1486	4.9094	4.4882	4.1300	3.8223	3.5558	3.3230
23	6.0442	5.7234	5.4321	5.1668	4.9245	4.4985	4.1371	3.8273	3.5592	3.3254
24	6.0726	5.7465	5.4509	5.1822	4.9371	4.5070	4.1428	3.8312	3.5619	3.3272
25	6.0971	5.7662	5.4669	5.1951	4.9476	4.5139	4.1474	3.8342	3.5640	3.3286
26	6.1182	5.7831	5.4804	5.2060	4.9563	4.5196	4.1511	3.8367	3.5656	3.3297
27	6.1364	5.7975	5.4919	5.2151	4.9636	4.5243	4.1542	3.8387	3.5669	3.3305
28	6.1520	5.8099	5.5016	5.2228	4.9697	4.5281	4.1566	3.8402	3.5679	3.3312
29	6.1656	5.8204	5.5098	5.2292	4.9747	4.5312	4.1585	3.8414	3.5687	3.3317
30	6.1772	5.8294	5.5168	5.2347	4.9789	4.5338	4.1601	3.8424	3.5693	3.3321
35	6.2153	5.8582	5.5386	5.2512	4.9915	4.5411	4.1644	3.8450	3.5708	3.3330
40	6.2335	5.8713	5.5482	5.2582	4.9966	4.5439	4.1659	3.8458	3.5712	3.3332
45	6.2421	5.8773	5.5523	5.2611	4.9986	4.5449	4.1664	3.8460	3.5714	3.3333
50	6.2463	5.8801	5.5541	5.2623	4.9995	4.5452	4.1666	3.8461	3.5714	3.3333

Appendix C

Keystrokes for Solving Selected TVM Problems Using the HP-12C Calculator

Robert M. Crowe

Note: The individual keystrokes in this appendix are separated by commas.

1. Preliminary "housekeeping" and miscellaneous chores
   a. Clearing memory
      yellow f, REG or
      yellow f, FIN
   b. Setting number of decimal places displayed
      yellow f and desired number
   c. Clearing display or eliminating last keystroke
      CLX
   d. Raising a number to a power
      base number, ENTER, exponent, y^x
2. Future value of a single sum problems
   a. Finding FVSS
      amount of present value, CHS, PV, number of periods, n, interest rate, i, FV
   b. Finding approximate n
      amount of present value, CHS, PV, amount of future value, FV, interest rate, i, n
   c. Finding i
      amount of present value, CHS, PV, amount of future value, FV, number of periods, n, i
3. Present value of a single sum problems
   a. Finding PVSS
      amount of future value, FV, number of periods, n, interest rate, i, PV
   b. Finding approximate n
      see 2b above
   c. Finding i
      see 2c above
4. Future value of an annuity problems
   a. Finding FVA
      amount of one payment, CHS, PMT, interest rate, i, number of payments, n, blue g, END, FV

b. Finding approximate n
   future value of the annuity, FV, amount of one payment, CHS, PMT, blue g, END, interest rate, i, n
c. Finding i
   future value of the annuity, FV, amount of one payment, CHS, PMT, number of payments, n, blue g, END, i

5. Future value of an annuity due problems
   a. Finding FVAD
      amount of one payment, CHS, PMT, interest rate, i, number of payments, n, blue g, BEG, FV
   b. Finding approximate n
      future value of the annuity due, FV, amount of one payment, CHS, PMT, blue g, BEG, interest rate, i, n
   c. Finding i
      future value of the annuity due, FV, amount of one payment, CHS, PMT, number of payments, n, blue g, BEG, i
6. Sinking fund problems
   a. Finding sinking fund payment
      target amount of sinking fund, FV, interest rate, i, number of payments, n, blue g, BEG (or END), PMT
   b. Finding approximate n
      target amount of sinking fund, FV, interest rate, i, amount of one payment, CHS, PMT, blue g, BEG (or END), n
   c. Finding i
      target amount of sinking fund, FV, amount of one payment, CHS, PMT, number of payments, n, blue g, BEG (or END), i
7. Present value of an annuity problems
   a. Finding PVA
      amount of one payment, CHS, PMT, interest rate, i, number of payments, n, blue g, END, PV
   b. Finding approximate n
      present value of the annuity, CHS, PV, amount of one payment, PMT, blue g, END, interest rate, i, n
   c. Finding i
      present value of the annuity, CHS, PV, amount of one payment, PMT, number of payments, n, blue g, END, i
8. Present value of an annuity due problems
   a. Finding PVAD
      amount of one payment, CHS, PMT, interest rate, i, number of payments, n, blue g, BEG, PV
   b. Finding approximate n
      present value of the annuity due, CHS, PV, amount of one payment, PMT, blue g, BEG, interest rate, i, n
   c. Finding i
      present value of the annuity due, CHS, PV, amount of one

payment, PMT, number of payments, n, blue g, BEG, i

9. Debt service/capital sum liquidation problems
    a. Finding the payment
        beginning amount of loan or capital sum, CHS, PV, interest rate, i, number of payments, n, blue g, BEG (or END), PMT
    b. Finding the approximate n
        beginning amount of loan or capital sum, CHS, PV, interest rate, i, amount of one payment, PMT, blue g, BEG (or END), n
    c. Finding i
        beginning amount of loan or capital sum, CHS, PV, amount of one payment, PMT, number of payments, n, blue g, BEG (or END), i
    d. Creating an amortization schedule
        annual interest rate, i (or blue g, 12 ÷ if loan payments are to be made monthly), blue g, END (normally), beginning amount of loan, PV, amount of one loan payment, CHS, PMT, 1 (or 12 if loan payments are to be made monthly), yellow f, AMORT (to show total interest payments in first year), x $\gtrless$ y, (to show total principal payments in first year), RCL, PV (to show unpaid loan balance at end of first year); repeat 1 (or 12), yellow f, AMORT x $\gtrless$ y, RCL, PV to show the total interest payments, principal payments, and unpaid loan balance for each successive year of the loan's duration
10. Present value of uneven cash flows problems
    a. Cash flows at end of year: ungrouped data (see text for grouped data) amount of first cash flow, blue g, CFj, second cash flow, blue g, CFj, etc. through entire sequence; then interest rate, i, yellow f, NPV
    b. Cash flows at beginning of year: ungrouped data (see text for grouped data)
        amount of first cash flow, blue g, CFo, second cash flow, blue g, CFj, third cash flow, blue g, CFj, etc. through entire sequence; then interest rate, i, yellow f, NPV
    c. Cash flows that grow by a constant percentage, with first payment made immediately
        blue g, BEG, amount of first cash flow, PMT, 1 plus interest rate, ENTER, 1 plus growth rate, ÷, 1, –, 100, x, i, number of payments, n, PV
    d. Cash flows that grow by a constant percentage, with first payment made after one year
        divide answer found in 10c by (1 plus interest rate)
11. Future value of uneven cash flows problems
    a. Generally
        Compute present value as in 10a or 10b above; then ENTER, CHS PV, interest rate, i, number of years, n, FV

b. Special case: deposits growing by a constant percentage
   Compute present value as in 10c or 10d above; then STO, 1, yellow f, FIN, RCL, 1, PV, interest rate, i, number of years, n, FV

12. Net present value problems
   a. Ungrouped data
      amount of initial outflow, CHS, blue g, CFo; then amount of each succeeding inflow or outflow, including zeros, pressing blue g and CFj after each (CHS, blue g, and CFj for outflows); then interest rate, i, yellow f, NPV
   b. Grouped data
      amount of initial outflow, CHS, blue g, CFo; then amount of first inflow or outflow, including zeros, blue g, CFj (CHS, blue g, CFj for outflows); then number of times that amount occurs in succession, blue g, Nj; repeat the process for each subsequent inflow, outflow, or zero flow or group of same; then interest rate, i, yellow f, NPV
13. Internal rate of return problems
      Same as NPV problems except for last four keystrokes; instead of interest rate, i, yellow f, and NPV, press yellow f, IRR
14. Conversion of nominal interest rate to effective interest rate problems
   a. Discrete compounding or discounting
      nominal interest rate, ENTER, number of compounding periods per year, n, ÷, i, 100, CHS, ENTER, PV, FV, +
   b. Continuous compounding or discounting during 360-day year
      1, ENTER, nominal interest rate, %, blue g, e^x, Δ %

Appendix D

Keystrokes for Solving Selected TVM Problems Using the HP-17B II Calculator

Robert M. Crowe

Note: The individual keystrokes in this appendix are separated by commas. They reflect use of the Algebraic system of entry logic, rather than the Reverse Polish Notation system.

1. Preliminary "housekeeping" and miscellaneous chores
   a. Turning the machine on or off
      CLR or colored shift key, OFF
   b. Adjusting contrast on display screen
      Hold down CLR, + or –
   c. Selecting the Algebraic system of entry logic
      Shift, MODES, ALG menu key, EXIT
   d. Returning to main menu
      Shift, MAIN or EXIT one or more times
   e. Clearing a problem or data from memory
      Menu key for menu to be cleared of problem or data, shift, CLEAR DATA
   f. Setting number of decimal places to be displayed
      DSP, FIX menu key, desired number, INPUT
   g. clearing display screen
      CLR
   h. Eliminating last keystroke
      ←
   i. Setting number of payment periods/compounding periods per year to one, if both are the same
      Shift, MAIN, FIN menu key, TVM menu key, OTHER menu key, 1, P/YR menu key, shift, MAIN, CLR
   j. Setting the calculator for payments at beginning or end of each period
      Shift, MAIN, FIN menu key, TVM menu key, OTHER menu key, BEG or END menu key, shift, MAIN
   k. Raising a number to a power
      Base number, shift, y^x, exponent, =

2. Future value of a single sum problems
   a. Finding FVSS
      Shift, MAIN, FIN menu key, TVM menu key, number of periods, N menu key, periodic interest rate, I%YR menu key, amount of present value, +/–, PV menu key, FV menu key
   b. Finding n (number of periods)
      Shift, MAIN, FIN menu key, TVM menu key, periodic interest rate, I%YR menu key, amount of present value, +/–, PV menu key, amount of future value, FV menu key, N menu key
   c. Finding i (periodic interest rate)
      Shift, MAIN, FIN menu key, TVM menu key, number of periods, N menu key, amount of present value, +/–, PV menu key, amount of future value, FV menu key, I%YR menu key

3. Present value of a single sum problems
   a. Finding PVSS
      Shift, MAIN, FIN menu key, TVM menu key, number of periods, N menu key, periodic interest rate, I%YR menu key, amount of future value, FV menu key, PV menu key
   b. Finding n (number of periods)
      See 2.b. above
   c. Finding i (periodic interest rate)
      See 2.c. above

4. Future value of an annuity problems
   a. Finding FVA
      Set the calculator for end-of-period payments (see 1.j. above); set the calculator for one payment/compounding period per year, if both are the same (see, 1.i. above); shift, MAIN, FIN menu key, TVM menu key, number of payments, N menu key, periodic interest rate, I%YR menu key, amount of one payment, +/, PMT menu key, FV menu key
   b. Finding n (number of payments)
      Set the calculator for end-of-period payments (see 1.j. above); set the calculator for one payment/compounding period per year, if both are the same (see 1.i. above); shift, MAIN, FIN menu key, TVM menu key, periodic interest rate, I%YR menu key, amount of one payment, +/–, PMT menu key, future value of the annuity, FV menu key, N menu key
   c. Finding i (periodic interest rate)
      Set the calculator for end-of-period payments (see 1.j. above); set the calculator for one payment/compounding period per year, if both are the same (see 1.i. above); shift, MAIN, FIN menu key, TVM menu key, number of payments, N menu key, amount of

payment, +/–, PMT menu key, future value of the annuity, FV menu key, I% YR menu key

5. Future value of an annuity due problems
   a. Finding FVAD
      Set the calculator for beginning-of-period payments (see 1.j. above); set the calculator for one payment/compounding period per year, if both are the same (see 1.i. above); shift, MAIN, FIN menu key, TVM menu key, number of payments, N menu key, periodic interest rate, I%YR menu key, amount of one payment, +/, PMT menu key, FV menu key
   b. Finding n (number of payments)
      Set the calculator for beginning-of-period payments (see 1.j. above); set the calculator for one payment/compounding period per year, if both are the same (see 1.i. above); shift, MAIN, FIN menu key, TVM menu key, periodic interest rate, 1%YR menu key, amount of one payment, +/–, PMT menu key, future value of the annuity, FV menu key, N menu key
   c. Finding i (periodic interest rate)
      Set the calculator for beginning-of-period payments (see 1.j. above); set the calculator for one payment/compounding period per year, if both are the same (see 1.i. above); shift, MAIN, FIN menu key TVM menu key, number of payments, N menu key, amount of one payment, +/–, PMT menu key, future value of the annuity, FV menu key, I%YR menu key

6. Sinking fund problems
   a. Finding sinking fund payment
      Set the calculator for beginning-of-period or end-of-period payments, as appropriate (see 1.j. above); set the calculator for one payment/compounding period per year, if both are the same (see 1.i. above); shift, MAIN, FIN menu key, TVM menu key, target amount of sinking fund, FV menu key, periodic interest rate, I%YR menu key, number of payments, N menu key, PMT menu key
   b. Finding n (number of payments)
      Set the calculator for beginning-of-period or end-of-period payments as appropriate (see 1.j. above); set the calculator for one payment/compounding period per year, if both are the same (see 1.i. above); target amount of sinking fund, FV menu key, periodic interest rate, I%YR menu key, amount of one payment, +/–, PMT menu key, N menu key
   c. Finding i (periodic interest rate)
      Set the calculator for beginning-of-period or end-of-period payments, as appropriate (see 1.j. above); set the calculator for

one payment/compounding period per year, if both are the same (see 1.i. above); target amount of sinking fund, FV menu key, number of payments, N menu key, amount of one payment, +/–, PMT menu key, I%YR menu key

7. Present value of an annuity problems
   a. Finding PVA
      Set the calculator for end-of-period payments (see 1.j. above); set the calculator for one payment/compounding period per year, if both are the same (see 1.i. above); shift, MAIN, FIN menu key, TVM menu key, number of payments, N menu key, periodic interest rate, 1%YR menu key, amount of one payment, PMT menu key, PV menu key
   b. Finding n (number of payments)
      Set the calculator for end-of-period payments (see 1.j. above); set the calculator for one payment/compounding period per year, if both are the same (see 1.i. above); shift, MAIN, FIN menu key, TVM menu key, periodic interest rate, I%YR menu key, present value of the annuity, +/–, PV menu key, amount of one payment, PMT menu key, N menu key
   c. Finding i (periodic interest rate)
      Set the calculator for end-of-period payments (see 1.j. above); set the calculator for one payment/compounding period per year, if both are the same (see 1.i. above); shift, MAIN, FIN menu key, TVM menu key, number of payments, N menu key, present value of the annuity, +/–, PV menu key, amount of one payment, PMT menu key, I%YR menu key

8. Present value of an annuity due problems
   a. Finding PVAD
      Set the calculator for beginning-of-period payments (see 1.j. above); set the calculator for one payment/compounding period per year, if both are the same (see 1.i. above); shift, MAIN, FIN menu key, TVM menu key, number of payments, N menu key, periodic interest rate, I%YR menu key, amount of one payment, PMT menu key, PV menu key
   b. Finding n (number of payments)
      Set the calculator for beginning-of-period payments (see 1.j. above); set the calculator for one payment/compounding period per year, if both are the same (see 1.i. above); shift, MAIN, FIN menu key, TVM menu key, periodic interest rate, I%YR menu key, amount of one payment, PMT menu key, present value of the annuity, +/–, PV menu key, N menu key

c. Finding i (periodic interest rate)

Set the calculator for beginning-of-period payments (see 1.j. above); set the calculator for one payment/compounding period per year, if both are the same (see 1.i. above); shift, MAIN, FIN menu key, TVM menu key, number of payments, N menu key, amount of one payment, PMT menu key, present value of the annuity, +/–, PV menu key, I%YR menu key

9. Debt service/capital sum liquidation problems

a. Finding the payment

Set the calculator for beginning-of-period or end-of-period payments, as appropriate (see 1.j. above); set the calculator for one payment/compounding period per year, if both are the same (see 1.i. above); shift, MAIN, FIN menu key, TVM menu key, beginning amount of loan or capital sum, +/–, PV menu key, periodic interest rate, I%YR menu key, number of payments, N menu key, PMT menu key

b. Finding n (number of payments)

Set the calculator for beginning-of-period or end-of-period payments, as appropriate (see 1.j. above); set the calculator for one payment/compounding period per year, if both are the same (see 1.i. above); shift, MAIN, FIN menu key, TVM menu key, beginning amount of loan or capital sum, +/–, PV menu key, periodic interest rate, I%YR menu key, amount of one payment, PMT menu key, N menu key

c. Finding i (periodic interest rate)

Set the calculator for beginning-of-period or end-of-period payments, as appropriate (see 1.j. above); set the calculator for one payment/compounding period per year, if both are the same (see 1.i. above); shift, MAIN, FIN menu key, TVM menu key, beginning amount of loan or capital sum, +/–, PV menu key, amount of one payment, PMT menu key, number of payments, N menu key, I%YR menu key

d. Creating an amortization schedule

Set the calculator for end-of-period payments (see 1.j. above); set the calculator for one payment/compounding period per year, if both are the same (see 1.i. above); FIN menu key, TVM menu key, total number of payments, N menu key, periodic interest rate, I%YR menu key, original loan amount, +/–, PV menu key, amount of one payment, PMT menu key, OTHER menu key, AMRT menu key, 1, #P menu key, INT menu key to see total interest paid during first amortization period, PRIN menu key to show total principal repaid during first amortization period, BAL menu key to show unpaid balance at end of first amortization period, NEXT menu key to perform calculations applicable to next amortization period, INT menu key to see total interest paid during second amortization period, PRIN menu key to see total principal paid during second amortization period, BAL menu key to show unpaid balance at end of second amortization period, NEXT, etc. to end of loan period

10. Present value of uneven cash flows problems (**Editor's Note:** Each cash flow should be entered as a positive or negative amount, as appropriate.)
    a. Cash flows at end of year
       Shift, MAIN, FIN menu key, CFLO menu key, #T? menu key to ON, shift, CLEAR DATA, YES menu key, 0, INPUT, amount of first cash flow, INPUT, number of times it occurs, INPUT, amount of second cash flow, INPUT, number of times it occurs, INPUT, amount of third cash flow, INPUT, number of times it occurs, INPUT, etc. through entire sequence; then EXIT, CALC menu key, periodic interest rate, I% menu key, NPV menu key
    b. Cash flows at beginning of year
       Shift, MAIN, FIN menu key, CFLO menu key, #T? menu key to ON, shift, CLEAR DATA, YES menu key, amount of first cash flow, INPUT, amount of second cash flow (or amount of first cash flow if it is grouped data), INPUT, number of times it occurs (minus 1 if it is a continuation of the grouped data in the first cash flow), INPUT, amount of next cash flow, INPUT, number of times it occurs, INPUT, etc. through the entire sequence; then EXIT, CALC menu key, periodic interest rate, I% menu key, NPV menu key
    c. Cash flows that grow by a constant percentage, with first payment made immediately
       Set the calculator for beginning-of-period payments (see 1.j. above); set the calculator for one payment/compounding period per year, if both are the same (see 1.i. above); shift, MAIN, FIN menu key, TVM menu key, amount of first cash flow, PMT menu key, 1 plus periodic interest rate, +, 1 plus growth rate, —, 1, x, 100, =, I%YR menu key, number of payments, N menu key, PV menu key
    d. Cash flows that grow by a constant percentage, with first payment made after one period
       Divide answer found in 10.c. by (1 plus periodic interest rate)

11. Future value of uneven cash flows problems
    a. Cash flows at end of year
       Use procedure in 10.a. except for the final keystroke, which should be the NFV menu key, rather than the NPV menu key
    b. Cash flows at beginning of year
       Multiply answer found in 11.a. by (1 plus periodic interest rate)

c. Deposits growing by a constant percentage
   Compute present value as in 10.c. or d. above; then STO, 1, shift, CLEAR DATA, RCL, 1, PV menu key, periodic interest rate, I%YR menu key, number of deposits, N menu key, FV menu key

12. Net present value problems
    Use procedure in 10.a. or b. above, but press +/– key after any cash flows that are outflows

13. Internal rate of return problems
    Same as NPV except for last three keystrokes; instead of (or in addition to) periodic interest rate, I% menu key, and NPV menu key, press IRR menu key

14. Conversion of nominal interest rate to effective interest rate problems
    Shift, MAIN, ICNV menu key, PER or CONT menu key, depending on whether compounding is periodic or continuous, nominal interest rate, NOM% menu key, number of compounding periods per year, P menu key, EFF% menu key

Appendix E

Keystrokes for Solving Selected TVM Problems Using the BA-II Plus Calculator

Robert M. Crowe

Note: The individual keystrokes in this appendix are separated by commas.

1. Preliminary "housekeeping" and miscellaneous chores
   a. Clearing memory
      2nd, MEM, 2nd, CLR Work
   b. Entering and clearing the standard-calculator mode
      2nd, QUIT, 2nd, CLR TVM
   c. Entering and clearing the prompted-worksheet mode
      CF, 2nd, CLR Work (to compute NPV or IRR in uneven cash flow problems)
      OR
      2nd, Amort, 2nd, CLR Work (to solve amortization problems)
   d. Setting number of decimal places to be displayed
      2nd, Format, desired number of decimal places, ENTER
   e. Clearing display of an incorrect or unwanted number or an error message
      CE/C (one or more times)
   f. Eliminating last keystroke before entering
      →
   g. Clearing a problem from the calculator
      (1) Clearing a problem while in the standard-calculator mode
          2nd, CLR, TVM, CE/C
      (2) Clearing a problem while in the prompted-worksheet mode
          CF, 2nd, CLR Work
          or
          2nd, Amort, 2nd, CLR Work
   h. Setting number of payment periods per year and number of compounding periods per year
      2nd, P/Y, 2nd, SET, desired number of payment periods per year, ENTER, ↓, desired number of compounding periods per year, ENTER
   i. Setting the calculator for payments at beginning of period or end of period

2nd, BGN; if current setting is acceptable, 2nd, QUIT; if not, 2nd, SET, 2nd, QUIT

j. Raising a number to a power

base number, y^x, exponent, =

2. Future value of a single sum problems
   a. Finding FVSS

      amount of present value, +/–, PV, number of periods, N, interest rate, I/Y, CPT, FV
   b. Finding n

      amount of present value, +/–, PV, amount of future value, FV, interest rate, I/Y, CPT, N
   c. Finding i

      amount of present value, +/–, PV, amount of future value, FV, number of periods, N, CPT, I/Y
3. Present value of a single sum problems
   a. Finding PVSS

      amount of future value, FV, number of periods, N, interest rate, I/Y, CPT, PV
   b. Finding n

      see 2b above
   c. Finding i

      see 2c above
4. Future value of an annuity problems
   a. Finding FVA

      Set the calculator for end-of-period payments (see 1i above).
      amount of one payment, +/–, PMT, interest rate, I/Y, number of payments, N, CPT, FV
   b. Finding n

      Set the calculator for end-of-period payments (see 1i above).
      future value of the annuity, FV, amount of one payment, +/–, PMT, interest rate, I/Y, CPT, N
   c. Finding i

      Set the calculator for end-of-period payments (see 1i above).
      future value of the annuity, FV, amount of one payment, +/–, PMT, number of payments, N, CPT, I/Y
5. Future value of an annuity due problems
   a. Finding FVAD

      Set the calculator for beginning-of-period payments (see 1i above).
      amount of one payment, +/–, PMT, interest rate, I/Y, number of payments, N, CPT, FV
   b. Finding n

      Set the calculator for beginning-of-period payments (see 1i above).
      future value of the annuity due, FV, amount of one payment, +/–, PMT, interest rate, I/Y, CPT, N
   c. Finding i

Set the calculator for beginning-of-period payments (see 1i above).
future value of the annuity due, FV, amount of one payment, +/–, PMT, number of payments, N, CPT, I/Y

6. Sinking fund problems
   a. Finding sinking fund payment
      Set the calculator for beginning-of-period payments or end-of-period payments, as appropriate (see 1i above).
      target amount of sinking fund, FV, interest rate, I/Y, number of payments, N, CPT, PMT
   b. Finding n
      Set the calculator for beginning-of-period payments or end-of-period payments as appropriate (see 1i above).
      target amount of sinking fund, FV, interest rate, I/Y, amount of one payment, +/–, PMT, CPT, N
   c. Finding i
      Set the calculator for beginning-of-period payments or end-of-period payments, as appropriate (see 1i above).
      target amount of sinking fund, FV, amount of one payment, +/–, PMT, number of payments, N, CPT, I/Y
7. Present value of an annuity problems
   a. Finding PVA
      Set the calculator for end-of-period payments (see 1i above).
      amount of one payment, +/–, PMT, interest rate, I/Y, number of payments, N, CPT, PV
   b. Finding n
      Set the calculator for end-of-period payments (see 1i above).
      present value of the annuity, +/–, PV, amount of one payment, PMT, interest rate, I/Y, CPT, N
   c. Finding i
      Set the calculator for end-of-period payments (see 1i above).
      present value of the annuity, +/–, PV, amount of one payment, PMT, number of payments, N, CPT, I/Y
8. Present value of an annuity due problems
   a. Finding PVAD
      Set the calculator for beginning-of-period payments (see 1i above).
      amount of one payment, +/–, PMT, interest rate, I/Y, number of payments, N, CPT, PV
   b. Finding n
      Set the calculator for beginning-of-period payments (see 1i above).
      present value of the annuity, +/–, PV, amount of one payment, PMT, interest rate, I/Y, CPT, N
   c. Finding i
      Set the calculator for beginning-of-period payments (see 1i above).
      present value of the annuity, +/–, PV, amount of one payment, PMT, number of payments, N, CPT, I/Y

9. Debt service/capital sum liquidation problems
   a. Finding the payment

      Set the calculator for beginning-of-period payments or end-of-period payments, as appropriate (see 1i above).

      beginning amount of loan or capital sum, +/–, PV, interest rate, I/Y, number of payments, N, CPT, PMT
   b. Finding n

      Set the calculator for beginning-of-period payments or end-of-period payments, as appropriate (see 1i above).

      beginning amount of loan or capital sum, +/–, PV, interest rate, I/Y, amount of one payment, PMT, CPT, N
   c. Finding i

      Set the calculator for beginning-of-period payments or end-of-period payments, as appropriate (see 1i above).

      beginning amount of loan or capital sum, +/–, PV, amount of one payment, PMT, number of payments, N, CPT, I/Y
   d. Creating an amortization schedule

      Set the calculator for end-of-period payments (see 1i above).

      Set the calculator for the appropriate number of payments per year and number of compounding periods per year (see 1h above).

      2nd, QUIT, beginning amount of loan, +/–, PV, interest rate, I/Y, number of payments, N, CPT, PMT, 2nd, Amort, 2nd, CLR Work, 1, ENTER, ↓, 1, ENTER, ↓ (shows unpaid loan principal after first year), ↓ (shows amount paid on principal in first year), ↓ (shows amount paid as interest in first year), ↓, ↓, 2, ENTER, ↓ (shows unpaid loan principal after second year), ↓ (shows total amount paid on principal during first two years), ↓, ↓, 3, ENTER, etc. Repeat this process throughout the loan's duration to show the gradually declining loan balance at the end of each year, the total amount applied on the principal to that point, and the total amount paid as interest to that point.
10. Present value of uneven cash flows problems (Note: Each cash flow should be entered as a positive or negative amount, as appropriate.)
    a. Cash flows at end of period: ungrouped data (see text for grouped data)

       CF, 2nd, CLR Work, ENTER, ↓, amount of first cash flow, ENTER, ↓, ENTER, ↓, amount of second cash flow, ENTER, ↓, ENTER, ↓, amount of third cash flow, ENTER, ↓, ENTER, ↓, etc. through entire sequence; then NPV, interest rate, ENTER, ↓,CPT
    b. Cash flows at beginning of period: ungrouped data (see text for grouped data)

       CF, 2nd, CLR Work, amount of first cash flow, ENTER, ↓,

amount of second cash flow, ENTER, ↓, ENTER, ↓, amount of third cash flow, ENTER, ↓, ENTER, ↓, etc. through entire sequence; then NPV, interest rate, ENTER, ↓, CPT

c. Cash flows that grow by a constant percentage, with first payment made immediately

   Set the calculator for beginning-of-period payments (see 1i above). amount of first cash flow, PMT, 1 plus interest rate, ÷, 1 plus growth rate, –, 1, x, 100, =, I/Y, number of payments, N, CPT, PV

d. Cash flows that grow by a constant percentage, with first payment made after one period

   divide answer found in 10c by (1 plus interest rate)

11. Future value of uneven cash flows problems

   a. Generally

      Compute present value as in 10a or 10b above; then STO, 1, CF, 2nd, CLR Work, 2nd, QUIT, RCL, 1, +/–, PV, interest rate, I/Y, number of payments, N, CPT, FV; clear memory when completed as in 1a above.

   b. Special case: deposits growing by a constant percentage

      Compute present value as in 10c or 10d above; then STO, 1, 2nd, CLR TVM, RCL, 1, PV, interest rate, I/Y, number of payments, N, CPT, FV; clear memory when completed as in 1a above.

12. Net present value problems (Note: Typically the first cash flow is an outflow and thus is entered as a negative. In some problems one or more of the subsequent cash flows also are outflows. They too should be entered as negatives, though this is not shown in the keystroke sequences below.)

   a. Ungrouped data

      CF, 2nd, CLR Work, amount of initial outflow, +/–, ENTER, ↓, amount of second cash flow, ENTER, ↓, ENTER, ↓, amount of third cash flow, ENTER, ↓, ENTER, ↓, etc. through the entire sequence, including zeros; then NPV, interest rate, ENTER, ↓, CPT

   b. Grouped data

      CF, 2nd, CLR Work, amount of initial outflow, +/–, ENTER, ↓, amount of second cash flow, ENTER, ↓, number of times it occurs in succession, ENTER, ↓, amount of third cash flow, ENTER, ↓, number of times it occurs in succession, ENTER, ↓, etc. through the entire sequence, including zeros; then NPV, interest rate, ENTER, ↓, CPT

13. Internal rate of return problems

   Same as NPV except for (or in addition to) last five keystrokes; instead of (or after) pressing NPV, interest rate, ENTER, ↓, and CPT, press IRR, CPT

14. Conversion of nominal interest rate to effective interest rate problems
    2nd, I Conv, 2nd, CLR Work, nominal interest rate, ENTER, ↓, ↓, number of compounding periods per year, ENTER, ↑, CPT

Appendix F

Table of Effective Interest Rates

TABLE F
Effective Annual Interest Rates

	Compounding Frequency					
Nominal Rate	Semi-Annually	Quarterly	Monthly	Weekly	Daily (365 days)	Continuous
0.25%	0.2502%	0.2502%	0.2503%	0.2503%	0.2503%	0.2503%
0.50%	0.5006%	0.5009%	0.5011%	0.5012%	0.5012%	0.5013%
0.75%	0.7514%	0.7521%	0.7526%	0.7528%	0.7528%	0.7528%
1.00%	1.0025%	1.0038%	1.0046%	1.0049%	1.0050%	1.0050%
1.25%	1.2539%	1.2559%	1.2572%	1.2577%	1.2578%	1.2578%
1.50%	1.5056%	1.5085%	1.5104%	1.5111%	1.5113%	1.5113%
1.75%	1.7577%	1.7615%	1.7641%	1.7651%	1.7654%	1.7654%
2.00%	2.0100%	2.0151%	2.0184%	2.0197%	2.0201%	2.0201%
2.25%	2.2627%	2.2691%	2.2733%	2.2750%	2.2754%	2.2755%
2.50%	2.5156%	2.5235%	2.5288%	2.5309%	2.5314%	2.5315%
2.75%	2.7689%	2.7785%	2.7849%	2.7874%	2.7881%	2.7882%
3.00%	3.0225%	3.0339%	3.0416%	3.0446%	3.0453%	3.0455%
3.25%	3.2764%	3.2898%	3.2989%	3.3023%	3.3032%	3.3034%
3.50%	3.5306%	3.5462%	3.5567%	3.5608%	3.5618%	3.5620%
3.75%	3.7852%	3.8031%	3.8151%	3.8198%	3.8210%	3.8212%
4.00%	4.0400%	4.0604%	4.0742%	4.0795%	4.0808%	4.0811%
4.25%	4.2952%	4.3182%	4.3338%	4.3398%	4.3413%	4.3416%
4.50%	4.5506%	4.5765%	4.5940%	4.6008%	4.6025%	4.6028%
4.75%	4.8064%	4.8353%	4.8548%	4.8623%	4.8643%	4.8646%
5.00%	5.0625%	5.0945%	5.1162%	5.1246%	5.1267%	5.1271%
5.25%	5.3189%	5.3543%	5.3782%	5.3875%	5.3899%	5.3903%
5.50%	5.5756%	5.6145%	5.6408%	5.6510%	5.6536%	5.6541%
5.75%	5.8327%	5.8752%	5.9040%	5.9152%	5.9180%	5.9185%
6.00%	6.0900%	6.1364%	6.1678%	6.1800%	6.1831%	6.1837%
6.25%	6.3477%	6.3980%	6.4322%	6.4455%	6.4489%	6.4494%
6.50%	6.6056%	6.6602%	6.6972%	6.7116%	6.7153%	6.7159%
6.75%	6.8639%	6.9228%	6.9628%	6.9783%	6.9824%	6.9830%
7.00%	7.1225%	7.1859%	7.2290%	7.2458%	7.2501%	7.2508%
7.25%	7.3814%	7.4495%	7.4958%	7.5139%	7.5185%	7.5193%
7.50%	7.6406%	7.7136%	7.7633%	7.7826%	7.7876%	7.7884%
7.75%	7.9002%	7.9782%	8.0313%	8.0520%	8.0573%	8.0582%
8.00%	8.1600%	8.2432%	8.3000%	8.3220%	8.3278%	8.3287%
8.25%	8.4202%	8.5088%	8.5692%	8.5928%	8.5989%	8.5999%
8.50%	8.6806%	8.7748%	8.8391%	8.8642%	8.8706%	8.8717%
8.75%	8.9414%	9.0413%	9.1096%	9.1362%	9.1431%	9.1442%
9.00%	9.2025%	9.3083%	9.3807%	9.4089%	9.4162%	9.4174%
9.25%	9.4639%	9.5758%	9.6524%	9.6823%	9.6900%	9.6913%
9.50%	9.7256%	9.8438%	9.9248%	9.9564%	9.9645%	9.9659%
9.75%	9.9877%	10.1123%	10.1977%	10.2311%	10.2397%	10.2411%
10.00%	10.2500%	10.3813%	10.4713%	10.5065%	10.5156%	10.5171%

TABLE F (CONTINUED)
Effective Annual Interest Rates

	Compounding Frequency					
Nominal Rate	Semi-Annually	Quarterly	Monthly	Weekly	Daily (365 days)	Continuous
10.25%	10.5127%	10.6508%	10.7455%	10.7826%	10.7921%	10.7937%
10.50%	10.7756%	10.9207%	11.0203%	11.0593%	11.0694%	11.0711%
10.75%	11.0389%	11.1912%	11.2958%	11.3367%	11.3473%	11.3491%
11.00%	11.3025%	11.4621%	11.5719%	11.6148%	11.6260%	11.6278%
11.25%	11.5664%	11.7336%	11.8486%	11.8936%	11.9053%	11.9072%
11.50%	11.8306%	12.0055%	12.1259%	12.1731%	12.1853%	12.1873%
11.75%	12.0952%	12.2779%	12.4039%	12.4533%	12.4660%	12.4682%
12.00%	12.3600%	12.5509%	12.6825%	12.7341%	12.7475%	12.7497%
12.25%	12.6252%	12.8243%	12.9617%	13.0156%	13.0296%	13.0319%
12.50%	12.8906%	13.0982%	13.2416%	13.2978%	13.3124%	13.3148%
12.75%	13.1564%	13.3727%	13.5221%	13.5808%	13.5960%	13.5985%
13.00%	13.4225%	13.6476%	13.8032%	13.8644%	13.8802%	13.8828%
13.25%	13.6889%	13.9230%	14.0850%	14.1487%	14.1652%	14.1679%
13.50%	13.9556%	14.1989%	14.3674%	14.4337%	14.4508%	14.4537%
13.75%	14.2227%	14.4754%	14.6505%	14.7194%	14.7372%	14.7402%
14.00%	14.4900%	14.7523%	14.9342%	15.0057%	15.0243%	15.0274%
14.25%	14.7577%	15.0297%	15.2185%	15.2928%	15.3121%	15.3153%
14.50%	15.0256%	15.3077%	15.5035%	15.5806%	15.6006%	15.6040%
14.75%	15.2939%	15.5861%	15.7892%	15.8691%	15.8899%	15.8933%
15.00%	15.5625%	15.8650%	16.0755%	16.1583%	16.1798%	16.1834%
15.25%	15.8314%	16.1445%	16.3624%	16.4483%	16.4705%	16.4742%
15.50%	16.1006%	16.4244%	16.6500%	16.7389%	16.7620%	16.7658%
15.75%	16.3702%	16.7049%	16.9382%	17.0302%	17.0541%	17.0581%
16.00%	16.6400%	16.9859%	17.2271%	17.3223%	17.3470%	17.3511%
16.25%	16.9102%	17.2673%	17.5166%	17.6150%	17.6406%	17.6448%
16.50%	17.1806%	17.5493%	17.8068%	17.9085%	17.9349%	17.9393%
16.75%	17.4514%	17.8318%	18.0977%	18.2027%	18.2300%	18.2345%
17.00%	17.7225%	18.1148%	18.3892%	18.4976%	18.5258%	18.5305%
17.25%	17.9939%	18.3983%	18.6813%	18.7933%	18.8223%	18.8272%
17.50%	18.2656%	18.6823%	18.9742%	19.0896%	19.1196%	19.1246%
17.75%	18.5377%	18.9668%	19.2677%	19.3867%	19.4177%	19.4228%
18.00%	18.8100%	19.2519%	19.5618%	19.6845%	19.7164%	19.7217%
18.25%	19.0827%	19.5374%	19.8566%	19.9831%	20.0159%	20.0214%
18.50%	19.3556%	19.8235%	20.1521%	20.2823%	20.3162%	20.3218%
18.75%	19.6289%	20.1100%	20.4483%	20.5824%	20.6172%	20.6230%
19.00%	19.9025%	20.3971%	20.7451%	20.8831%	20.9190%	20.9250%
19.25%	20.1764%	20.6847%	21.0426%	21.1846%	21.2215%	21.2277%
19.50%	20.4506%	20.9728%	21.3408%	21.4868%	21.5248%	21.5311%
19.75%	20.7252%	21.2615%	21.6396%	21.7897%	21.8288%	21.8353%
20.00%	21.0000%	21.5506%	21.9391%	22.0934%	22.1336%	22.1403%

Appendix G

Job Knowledge Requirements of the Certified Financial Planner: Topics, Importance Values, and Target Cognitive Level

The following topics are effective for CFP Certification Examinations administered by the CFP Board after December 31, 1996. The importance values (the result of the 1994 Job Analysis Update) are indicated by percentages to indicate the percentage of items in an examination that should be dedicated to that content area. A single number in the parentheses is a code for one of the four cognitive levels targeted for that content area: 1=knowledge of facts/terms, 2=comprehension/application, 3=analysis/synthesis, 4=evaluation.

Financial Planning Process
Financial Planning Process

1. Establishing client-planner relationships (2.53%, 2)
   - A. Explain issues and concepts related to the overall financial planning process, as appropriate to the client
   - B. Explain services provided, the process of planning, documentation required
   - C. Clarify client's and CFP licensee's responsibilities

2. Gathering client data and determining goals and expectations (5.98%, 2)
   - A. Obtain information from client through interview/questionnaire about financial resources and obligations
   - B. Determine client's personal and financial goals, needs and priorities
   - C. Assess client's values, attitudes, and expectations
   - D. Determine client's time horizons
   - E. Determine client's risk tolerance level
   - F. Collect applicable client records and documents

3. Determining the client's financial status by analyzing and evaluating (23.02%, 4)
   - A. General
     1) Current financial status (e.g., assets, liabilities, cash flow, debt management)
     2) Capital needs
     3) Attitudes and expectations
     4) Risk tolerance
     5) Risk management
     6) Risk exposure
   - B. Special needs
     1) Divorce/remarriage considerations
     2) Charitable planning
     3) Adult dependent needs
     4) Disabled child needs

5) Education needs
6) Terminal illness planning
7) Closely-held business planning

C. Risk management
1) Life insurance needs and current coverage
2) Disability insurance needs and current coverage
3) Health insurance needs and current coverage
4) Long-term care insurance needs and current coverage
5) Homeowners insurance needs and current coverage
6) Auto insurance needs and current coverage
7) Other liability insurance needs and current coverage (e.g., umbrella, professional, errors and omissions, directors, and officers)
8) Commercial insurance needs and current coverage

D. Investments
1) Current investments
2) Current investment strategies and policies

E. Taxation
1) Tax returns
2) Current tax strategies
3) Tax compliance status (e.g., estimated tax)
4) Current tax liabilities

F. Retirement
1) Current retirement plan tax exposures (e.g., excise tax, premature distribution tax)
2) Current retirement plans
3) Social Security benefits
4) Retirement strategies

G. Employee benefits
1) Available employee benefits
2) Current participation in employee benefits

H. Estate planning
1) Estate planning documents
2) Estate planning strategies
3) Estate tax exposures

4. Developing and presenting the financial plan (23.1%, 4)

A. Developing and preparing a client-specific financial plan tailored to meet the goals and objectives of the client, commensurate with client's values, temperament, and risk tolerance, covering:

1) Financial position
   a) Current statement
   b) Projected statement
   c) Projected statement with recommendations
2) Cash flow
   a) Projection
   b) Recommendations
   c) Projection with recommendations
3) Estate tax
   a) Projections
   b) Recommendations
   c) Projections with recommendations
4) Capital needs at retirement
   a) Projections
   b) Recommendations
   c) Projections with recommendations
5) Capital needs projections at death
   a) Recommendations
   b) Projections with recommendations
6) Capital needs: disability
   a) Recommendations
   b) Projections with recommendations
7) Capital needs: special needs
   a) Recommendations

b) Projections with recommendations
8) Income tax
a) Projections
b) Recommendations
c) Projections with strategy recommendations
9) Employee benefits
a) Projections
10) Asset allocation
a) Statement
b) Strategy recommendations
c) Statement with recommendations
11) Investment
a) Recommendations
b) Policy statement
c) Policy recommendations
d) Policy statement with recommendations
12) Risk
a) Assessment
b) Recommendations
13) List of prioritized action items

B. Presenting and reviewing the plan with the client
C. Collaborating with the client to ensure that plan meets the goals and objectives of the client, and revising as appropriate

5. Implementing the financial plan (1.62%, 4)
A. Assist the client in implementing the recommendations
B. Coordinate as necessary with other professionals, such as accountants, attorneys, real estate agents, investment advisers, stock brokers, and insurance agents

6. Monitoring the financial plan (3.76%, 4)
A. Monitor and evaluate soundness of recommendations
B. Review the progress of the plan with the client
C. Discuss and evaluate changes in client's personal circumstances, (e.g., birth/death, age, illness, divorce, retirement)
D. Review and evaluate changing tax laws and economic circumstances
E. Make recommendations to accommodate new or changing circumstances

Job Knowledge Requirements

General Principles (11.62%)

7. Regulatory requirements for CFP licensees (4)
A. Registration and licensing
B. Sources of information

8. Ethical and professional considerations in financial planning (4)

9. Assessment of risk and client behavior (4)
A. Client attitudes
B. Client knowledge
C. Client behavior

10. Financial planning for special needs (4)
A. Options for funding education
B. Other special needs and options (e.g., divorce, disability)

11. Economic environment and indicators (4)
A. Inflation/deflation
B. Interest rates/yield curves
C. Life-cycle hypothesis
D. Monetary and fiscal policy

- E. The business cycle
- F. Financial institutions
  - 1) Characteristics
  - 2) Safety and regulation

12. Calculate and interpret time value of money (4)
    - A. Future value using single sums
    - B. Present value using single sums
    - C. Number of compounding periods using single sums
    - D. Interest rate using single sums
    - E. Inflation-adjusted interest rates
    - F. Annuities

13. Asset valuation for financial planning functions (4)

14. Forms of business ownership/entity relationships (4)
    - A. Sole proprietorships
    - B. General partnerships
    - C. Limited partnerships (including family limited partnerships)
    - D. Limited liability companies
    - E. C corporations
    - F. S corporations
    - G. Trusts
    - H. Foundations/exempt organizations
    - I. Professional associations/corporations
    - J. Other

15. Ways of taking title to property (sole, joint, community, etc.) (4)
    - A. Characteristics
    - B. Implications

16. Legal aspects of financial planning (4)
    - A. Contracts
    - B. Negotiable instruments
    - C. Torts
    - D. Professional liability
    - E. Fiduciary responsibility
    - F. Agency law

17. Budgeting (4)
    - A. Cash management
    - B. Emergency fund planning
    - C. Debt management/uses of debt
    - D. Liquidity

18. Personal use-asset management (4)
    - A. Home equity
    - B. Types of mortgages
    - C. Buy vs. lease
    - D. Refinancing

Insurance Policies and Strategies (3.39%)

19. Principles of insurance (4)
    - A. Concept of insurable risk
    - B. Elements of insurance
    - C. Methods to avoid, reduce, and eliminate loss

20. Identification of life, health, homeowners, auto and other property and liability risk exposures (4)
    - A. Analysis of present coverage
    - B. Loss of income to family
    - C. Final expenses

21. Legal aspects of insurance (4)
    - A. The law of agency as applied to insurance
    - B. Tort liability as applied to insurance
    - C. Basic components of an insurance contract
    - D. Loss adjustment for various types of insurance

22. Insurance industry regulation (4)
    - A. State regulation
    - B. Federal regulation

23. Property and liability policy analysis (4)
    - A. Homeowners insurance
    - B. Personal auto insurance

C. Other liability insurance
   1) Umbrella
   2) Professional liability

24. Policy analysis (4)
   A. Pricing fundamentals
      1) Yield on assets
      2) Mortality/morbidity
      3) Lapses
      4) Expenses
   B. Factors affecting suitability of policy to client needs
   C. Contractual provisions vs. illustrations
   D. Insurance company crediting methods (i.e., new premium, interest, net investment yield crediting methods)

25. Life insurance policy analysis (4)
   A. Types of life insurance policies
   B. Life insurance policy provisions
   C. Life insurance policy riders
   D. Types, benefits, and risks of life insurance (including use of policy provisions and riders)
   E. Life insurance needs analysis
      1) Needs approach
      2) Capital needs approach
   F. Life insurance policy selection and replacement
      1) Cost and cost comparison methods
      2) Duration of coverage
      3) Guarantees
      4) Dividend histories
      5) Industry analysis reports and surveys
      6) Treatment of old policyholders
   G. Life insurance policy replacement
      1) Replacement forms
      2) Anti-churning legislation
      3) Disclosure requirements
      4) Insurability and non-contestability
   H. Methods of analyzing life insurance policy illustrations

26. Annuity policy analysis (4)
   A. Types of annuities
      1) Immediate
      2) Deferred
   B. Structured settlements

27. Health insurance policy analysis (4)
   A. Medical expense
      1) Types of coverage
      2) Determination of appropriate coverage
   B. Long-term care
      1) Long-term care policies
      2) Special life insurance benefits (i.e. viatical settlements)
   C. Disability income
      1) Characteristics
      2) Policy riders and provisions
      3) Determination of appropriate coverage

28. Taxation of insurance products (4)
   A. Income taxation of life insurance
      1) IRS definition
      2) Modified endowment contracts
         a) Material changes
         b) Pre-TEFRA contracts
         c) Excise tax and exceptions
      3) Dividends
      4) Withdrawals and loans
      5) § 1035 exchange
      6) Transfer for value and exemptions
   B. Estate taxation of life insurance
      1) Inclusion in the estate
      2) Effects of ownership and beneficiary designations

C. Taxation of annuities
   1) Exclusion ratios
   2) Taxation of withdrawals
   3) Excise tax
   4) Taxation at death
   5) Current taxation in corporations
D. Tax implications of owning individual medical and disability insurance
   1) Deductibility of premiums
   2) Taxation of benefits

29. Selecting insurance companies and agencies (4)
   A. Financial strength
      1) Rating agencies
      2) Other considerations (i.e., risk-based capital, ratios, etc.)
   B. Use by insurance company of sub-accounts and general accounts

Risk Management (1.69%)

30. Client assessment (4)
   A. Financial goals: time, dollars, priorities
   B. Risk tolerance and risk exposures
   C. Client tax situation
   D. Liquidity/marketability needs
   E. Analysis and evaluation of client financial statements
   F. Client preferences and investment understanding and experience

31. Marketability/liquidity (4)

32. Types of investment risk (4)
   A. Business
   B. Market
   C. Reinvestment
   D. Interest rate
   E. Purchasing power
   F. Regulation (tax audit, tax assessment, legislation)

33. Measurement of risk (4)
   A. Volatility
   B. Standard deviation
   C. Beta

34. Influence of time on investment risk (4)
   A. Effects of time
   B. Duration

Investment Vehicles (2.41%)

35. Government regulation of securities and markets (4)

36. Investment vehicles (4)
   A. Corporate bonds
   B. U.S. government and agency securities
   C. Mortgage-backed securities
   D. Municipal bonds
   E. Derivatives
      1) Options
      2) Futures
      3) Other
   F. Insurance-based investments
   G. Investment companies
      1) Unit investment trusts
      2) Open-end mutual funds
      3) Closed-end investment companies
   H. Certificates of deposit and cash equivalents
   I. Common stock
   J. Real estate, investor-managed
   K. Real estate, indirect ownership
   L. International investments
   M. Preferred stock
   N. Tangible assets (collectibles)
   O. Natural resources

37. Types and measures of investment returns (4)
   A. Annualized return
   B. Real (inflation-adjusted) return
   C. Total return

D. Risk-adjusted return
E. After-tax return
F. Holding period return
G. Internal rate of return
H. Yield-to-maturity
I. Yield-to-call
J. After-tax yield
K. Realized compound yield

38. Bond and stock valuation methods (4)
    A. Capitalized earnings
    B. Dividend growth
    C. Price/earnings
    D. Intrinsic value

Investment Theory and Strategies (4.41%)

39. Portfolio performance measurement (4)
    A. Benchmark portfolios
    B. Risk-adjusted returns
    C. Modern portfolio theory
    D. Time- vs. dollar-weighted return

40. Formula investing (4)
    A. Dollar cost averaging
    B. Dividend reinvestment
    C. Other

41. "Active" and "passive" strategies (4)
    A. Market timing
    B. Securities selection
    C. Bond swaps
    D. Indexed portfolios
    E. Maturity selection
    F. Buy-hold
    G. Immunization

42. Leverage and use of borrowed funds for investing (4)

43. Hedging and option strategies (4)
    A. Options
    B. Covered calls and puts
    C. Portfolio insurance
    D. Short sales

44. Asset allocation: active and passive (4)
    A. Among classes: market timing and fixed mix
    B. Within classes: security selection and index funds

45. Pricing models (4)
    A. Capital asset pricing model (CAPM)
    B. Arbitrage pricing model (APM)
    C. Option pricing model (OPM)
    D. Other

46. Efficient market hypothesis (4)
    A. Strong form
    B. Semi-strong form
    C. Weak form
    D. Anomalies

47. Investment vehicles match to client needs (4)

48. Tax impact on time value analysis of investments (4)
    A. Net present value concepts
    B. Internal rate of return
    C. Risk

Tax Planning Considerations (1.95%)

49. Ethical considerations in tax planning (4)
    A. Privileged communications
    B. Tax evasion

50. Income tax fundamentals (4)
    A. Steps in conducting tax law research
    B. Sources of tax law authority

51. Tax compliance matters (4)
    A. Filing tax returns
    B. The audit process
    C. Judicial review

52. Taxation terminology (4)
    A. Inclusions
    B. Exclusions

Tax Computations (1.38%)

53. Tax calculations and special rules (4)
    A. Gross income
    B. Adjusted gross income
    C. Itemized deductions
    D. Taxable income
    E. Tax liability

54. Tax accounting (4)
    A. Cash method
    B. Accrual method
    C. "Hybrid" method
    D. Long-term contracts
    E. Installment sales
    F. Accounting periods

55. Tax characteristics of business forms (4)
    A. Sole proprietorship
    B. Limited and general partnerships
    C. Family limited partnerships
    D. Limited liability partnerships
    E. Limited liability companies
    F. Regular or C corporations
    G. S corporations
    H. Trusts
    I. Foundations/exempt organizations
    J. Professional associations/corporations
    K. Other

56. Basis and cost recovery concepts (4)
    A. Original basis rules (purchases, gifts, estates, etc.)
    B. Carryover basis
    C. Adjustments to basis

57. Concepts of property dispositions (4)
    A. Determination of gain or loss
    B. Characterization of gain or loss
    C. Netting rules
    D. Capital loss limitations

58. Interest expense deduction (4)
    A. Qualified residence interest
    B. Trade or business interest
    C. Investment interest
    D. Personal interest
    E. In connection with a passive activity
    F. In connection with an unpaid tax liability

Tax Planning Strategies (1.90%)

59. Tax management techniques (4)
    A. Deferral and acceleration
    B. Maximization of exclusions and credits
    C. Managing loss limitations
    D. Minimization of rates
    E. Capital asset transactions
    F. Minimizing (or re-characterizing) non-deductible expenditures
    G. Installment sales

60. Non-taxable transactions (4)
    A. Like-kind exchanges
    B. Disposition of personal residence (§ 1034)

61. Passive activity loss and credit rules (4)
    A. Taxpayers subject to § 469
    B. Definition of passive activity
    C. Computation of passive activity losses and credits
    D. Treatment of disallowed losses and credits

62. Tax implications of marriage dissolution (4)
    A. Alimony
    B. Child support
    C. Personal exemption
    D. Property settlement

63. Interest and penalty taxes and other charges (4)
    A. Failure to file tax return or to pay tax
    B. Preparer penalties
    C. Accuracy related penalties
    D. Fraud penalties

64. Tax pitfalls (4)
    A. Statutory
    B. Judicial
    C. Tax penalties

65. Miscellaneous (4)
    A. Alternative minimum tax
    B. Social Security self-employment tax
    C. Home office and vacation home rules

Government Plans (1.40%)

66. Social Security, Medicare, and Medicaid (4)
    A. Basic provisions of OASDHI
    B. Eligibility
    C. Level of benefits

Retirement Plans and Strategies (4.32%)

67. Ethical considerations in retirement planning and employee benefits (4)
    A. ERISA fiduciary obligations
    B. Prohibited transactions, parties-in-interest, disqualified parties

68. Types of retirement plans (4)
    A. Definitions
    B. Factors affecting suitability (for individuals or types of business)

69. Qualified plan characteristics (4)
    A. Feasibility of installation of a qualified plan
        1) Objectives
        2) Factors
        3) Recommendations: problem-solving, tax benefits, meeting objectives
    B. Qualified plan coverage and eligibility requirements
        1) Age/service
        2) Coverage requirement
        3) Minimum participation
    C. Qualified plan vesting schedule
        1) Types
        2) Top-heavy plans
        3) Recommendations: vesting schedule selection
    D. Integration with Social Security/disparity limits
        1) Defined-benefit plans
        2) Defined-contribution plans
    E. Factors affecting qualified plan contributions or benefits
        1) Tax considerations
        2) Nature of defined contribution
        3) Nature of defined benefit
        4) Comparison of defined contribution and defined benefit
        5) Definition of compensation
        6) Multiple plans
    F. Top-heavy plans
        1) Definitions
        2) Vesting
        3) Effects on contributions or benefits

70. Distributions and distribution options (4)
    A. Retirement plan distribution options
    B. Tax treatment of plan distributions
    C. Tax on excess distributions

71. Retirement needs analysis (4)
    A. Determination of financial objectives at retirement
    B. Calculation of retirement funds available to meet objectives
    C. Calculation of additional funds needed to meet objectives

72. Recommendation of the most appropriate type of retirement plan (4)
    A. Analysis of key factors affecting plan selection

73. Suitability of an investment portfolio for a qualified plan situation (4)
    A. Investment risk
    B. Investment constraints (unrelated business taxable income)
    C. Investment portfolio evaluation

Employee Benefits (1.55%)

74. Life, medical, and disability plans in employee benefit programs (4)
    A. Basic provisions
    B. Income tax implications
    C. Deductibility
    D. Imputed income
    E. Employee benefit analysis and application

75. Other employee benefits (4)
    A. Death benefits
    B. Fringe benefits
    C. Cafeteria plan
    D. Flexible spending accounts
    E. Voluntary Employees' Beneficiary Association
    F. COBRA

76. Business applications of individual life and disability insurance (4)
    A. Business continuation (buy/sell plans)
    B. Business overhead disability plan
    C. Executive/owner benefits
    D. Split dollar
    E. Key employee insurance
    F. Salary continuation plans
    G. Non-qualified deferred compensation
       1) Recognition: requirements necessary to defer recognition
       2) Types of plans and applications
       3) Tax implications
       4) Funding methods

Estate Planning Benefits and Strategies (3.61%)

77. Estate planning overview (4)
    A. The meaning of "estate planning"
    B. Situations in which individuals need estate planning and consequences of integrated planning
    C. Steps in estate planning process
    D. The financial planner's role on the estate planning team

78. Estate planning pitfalls and weaknesses (4)
    A. Weaknesses in a client's existing estate plan
    B. Common pitfalls to avoid during estate planning

79. Methods for property transfer at death (4)
    A. The probate process (wills and intestate succession)
    B. Title (operation of law)
    C. Trusts
    D. Contracts (insurance/pensions)

80. Estate planning documents (4)
    A. Wills
    B. Trusts
    C. Personal care documents

D. Marital agreements
E. Durable power of attorney for property
F. Business agreements

81. Overview of the federal unified tax system (4)
    A. Unified transfer tax system
    B. Generation-skipping transfer tax

82. Federal gift taxation (4)
    A. Basic concepts
    B. Techniques for managing gift tax liability
    C. Analysis and calculation of federal gift tax liability

83. Federal gross estate (4)
    A. Inclusions in a decedent's gross estate
    B. Exclusions from a decedent's gross estate

84. Valuation techniques and the federal gross estate (4)
    A. Valuation of specific property interests
    B. Valuation techniques

85. Federal estate tax deductions (4)
    A. Defining the gross estate
    B. Deductions (debts and expenses)
    C. Adjusted gross estate
    D. Deductions (marital/charitable)
    E. Taxable estate
    F. Adjusted taxable gifts
    G. Tax base

86. Calculation of federal estate tax liability (4)
    A. Steps to calculate the estate tax
    B. Various credits affecting the estate tax calculation (unified credit, state death tax, prior transfer, etc.)

87. Characteristics and tax aspects of property interests (4)
    A. Title forms
    B. Other interests
    C. Advantages and disadvantages of forms of property interests
    D. Taxation aspects
    E. Recommendation and justification of the most appropriate form of property interests

88. Probate (4)
    A. Probate process
    B. Advantages and disadvantages of probate
    C. Techniques of avoiding probate
    D. Recommendation and justification of the most appropriate probate avoidance techniques

89. Liquidity planning (4)
    A. Sale of assets
    B. Life insurance
    C. Special techniques for closely-held business owners (e.g., § 6166, 303, 2032A and buy-sell agreements)

90. Powers of appointment (4)
    A. Use and purpose in estate planning
    B. General and special (limited)
    C. "5 & 5" power (§ 2041(b)(2))
    D. Federal gift and estate tax implications

91. Features of trusts (4)
    A. Classification of trusts
    B. Characteristics of selected trust provisions
    C. Rule against perpetuities

92. Taxation of trusts and estates (4)
    A. Income tax implications of trusts
        1) Exemptions
        2) Simple and complex trusts
        3) Distributable net income
    B. Federal gift tax implications of trusts
    C. Federal estate tax implications of trusts
    D. Income tax implications of estates
    E. Recommendation and justification of the most appropriate trust
    F. Excise tax on retirement plans at death

93. Estate freeze issues
    A. Limitations on corporate and partnership freezes (§ 2701)
    B. Trust freezes (§ 2702 including qualified personal residence trusts)

94. Life insurance for estate planning (4)
    A. Advantages and disadvantages of specific life insurance techniques in estate planning
    B. Life insurance trusts
    C. Ownership, beneficiary designation and settlement options
    D. Gift and estate taxation of life insurance
    E. Recommendation and justification of the most appropriate life insurance technique

95. Gifts (4)
    A. Suitability of gifts for client and recipient
    B. Techniques for gift-giving

96. Taxation of gifts (4)
    A. Income taxation of lifetime transfers
    B. Federal gift taxation of lifetime transfers
    C. Circumstances causing inclusion of gifts in gross estate
    D. Calculation and analysis of the effect of a lifetime gift program

97. Recommendation and justification of the most appropriate property to give as a gift (4)
    A. Selection of the most appropriate property to give as a gift
    B. The most appropriate lifetime gift-giving techniques
    C. Justification of the lifetime gift-giving techniques selected for the client's situation

98. Marital deduction and bypass planning (4)
    A. Characteristics of the marital deduction
    B. Recommendation and justification of property interests that qualify for the marital deduction
    C. QTIP planning and the prior transfer credit
    D. Special planning for non-U.S. spouse

99. Federal estate tax implications of the marital deduction and bypass planning (4)
    A. Federal estate tax implications of using the marital deduction
    B. Calculation of increased wealth transfer generated from modifying a client's estate plan

100. Recommendation of the most appropriate marital or non-marital transfer (4)

A. Factors to consider in selecting the optimum mix of marital and non-marital transfers
B. Selection of the most appropriate single or combination of marital and/or non-marital transfers for a client's situation
C. Justification of the marital and non-marital transfer techniques selected for the client's situation

101. Estate planning for nontraditional relationships (4)
   A. Children of another relationship
   B. Cohabitation
   C. Adoptions
   D. Same sex relationships
   E. Communal relationships

102. Charitable contributions and transfers (4)
   A. Considerations for contributions and transfers
   B. Requirements for a gift to qualify for a charitable deduction
      1) Charitable remainder trusts
      2) Charitable lead trusts
   C. Tax and non-tax characteristics of specific forms of charitable transfers including alternative minimum tax considerations
   D. Charitable income tax deduction limitations
   E. Calculation of the maximum total and/or maximum current year income tax deduction for a client's situation
   F. Recommendation and justification of the most appropriate property and form of charitable transfer

103. Intra-family business and property transfers (4)
   A. Characteristics of intra-family transfers
   B. Federal income, gift and estate tax implications of intra-family transfers
   C. Recommendation and justification of the most appropriate intra-family business and property transfer technique

104. Postmortem planning techniques (4)
   A. Characteristics of postmortem estate planning techniques
   B. Determination of whether a client qualifies for special tax treatment
   C. Recommendation and justification of the most appropriate postmortem planning technique

105. Planning for incapacity (4)
   A. Definition of incapacity
   B. Care of client's dependents
   C. Personal care of incapacitated client
   D. Care of incapacitated client's property

106. Special topics in estate planning (4)
   A. Divorce/remarriage
   B. Selection of fiduciaries and guardians

Version: 6/97

About the Authors

Ken Cooper, PhD, is professor of management and finance at Ohio Northern University and former holder of the Charles Lamont Post Chair of Ethics and the Professions at The American College.

Robert M. Crowe, PhD, CLU, ChFC, CFP, is a financial consultant and a former faculty member at The American College. He has been a dean at Memphis State University and the University of Tulsa, and served as an economic affairs officer of the United Nations.

Robbin Derry, PhD, is a senior lecturer at the University of Pennsylvania's Wharton School and former holder of the Charles Lamont Post Chair of Ethics and the Professions at The American College.

Ronald F. Duska, PhD, is professor of ethics and chairholder of the Charles Lamont Post Chair of Ethics and Professions at The American College. Duska received his PhD in philosophy from Northwestern University. He was formerly professor of philosophy at Rosemont College and has taught at Villanova University, St. Joseph's University, Pennsylvania State University, and the University of Pennsylvania's Wharton School.

Jeffrey B. Kelvin, JD, LLM, CLU, ChFC, is an attorney specializing in securities registration. He is a former associate professor of taxation at The American College.

Stephan R. Leimberg, JD, CLU, is professor of taxation and estate planning at The American College and is adjunct professor of the Masters of Taxation Program of Temple University School of Law. He is author of more than 40 books in estate planning, financial planning, and employee benefits.

Lewis B. Morgan, PhD, is professor of counseling and human relations at Villanova University.

Michael J. Roszkowski, PhD, is associate professor of psychology and director of marketing research at The American College. Dr. Roszkowski earned his BS at St. Joseph's University and his MEd and PhD at Temple University.

Index

Editor's note: A lowercase *n.* following a page number refers the reader to a note on said page. Thus "218 n. 17" refers to note 17 on page 218.